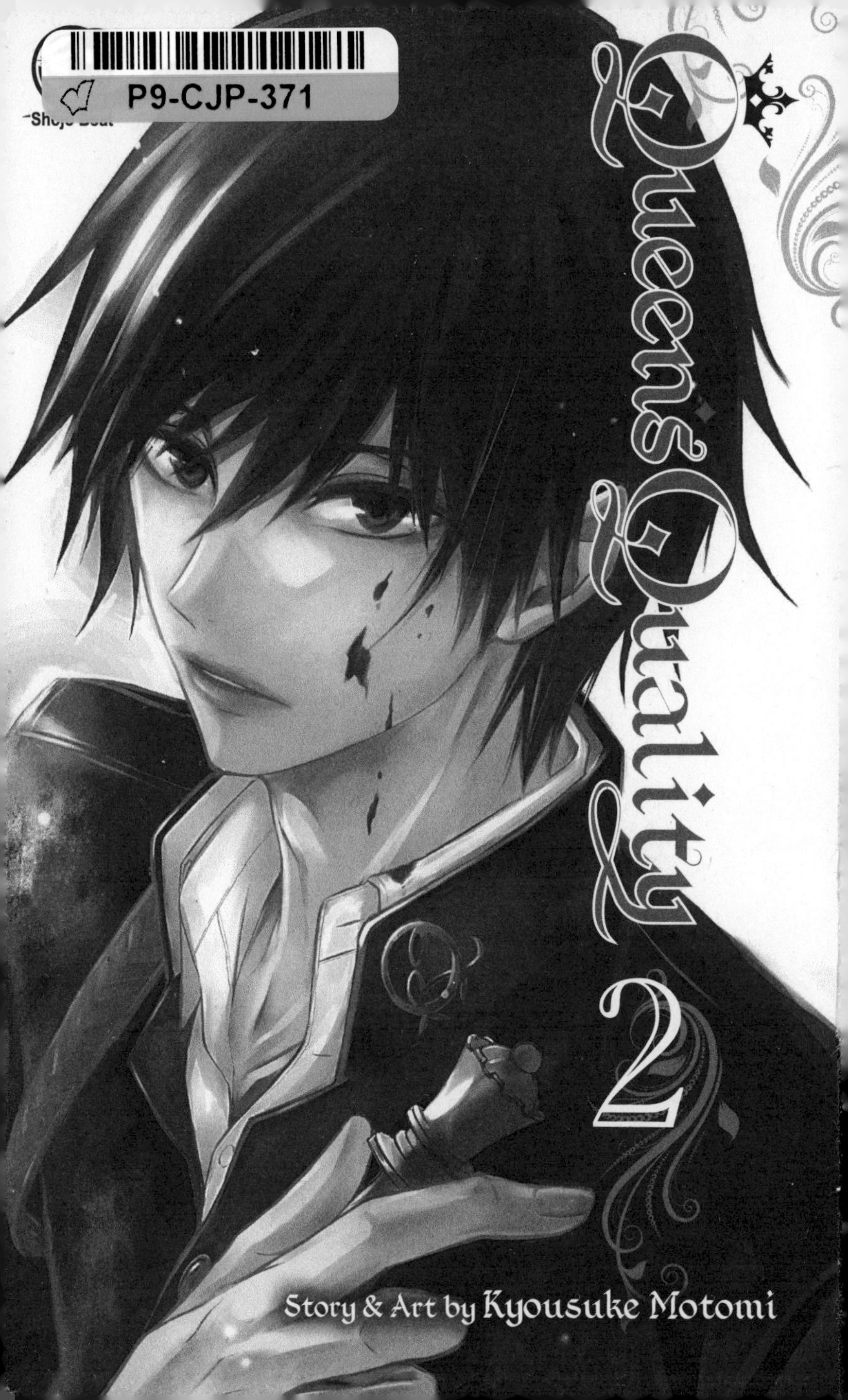
Shojo Beat
Queen's Quality
2
Story & Art by Kyousuke Motomi

Queen's Quality

CONTENTS

2

This is the Last Page!

It's true: In keeping with the original Japanese comic format, this book reads from right to left—so action, sound effects and word balloons are completely reversed. This preserves the orientation of the original artwork—plus, it's fun! Check out the diagram shown here to get the hang of things, and then turn to the other side of the book to get started!

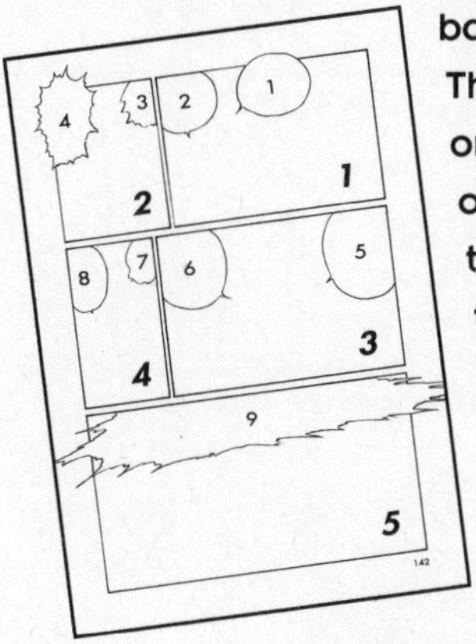

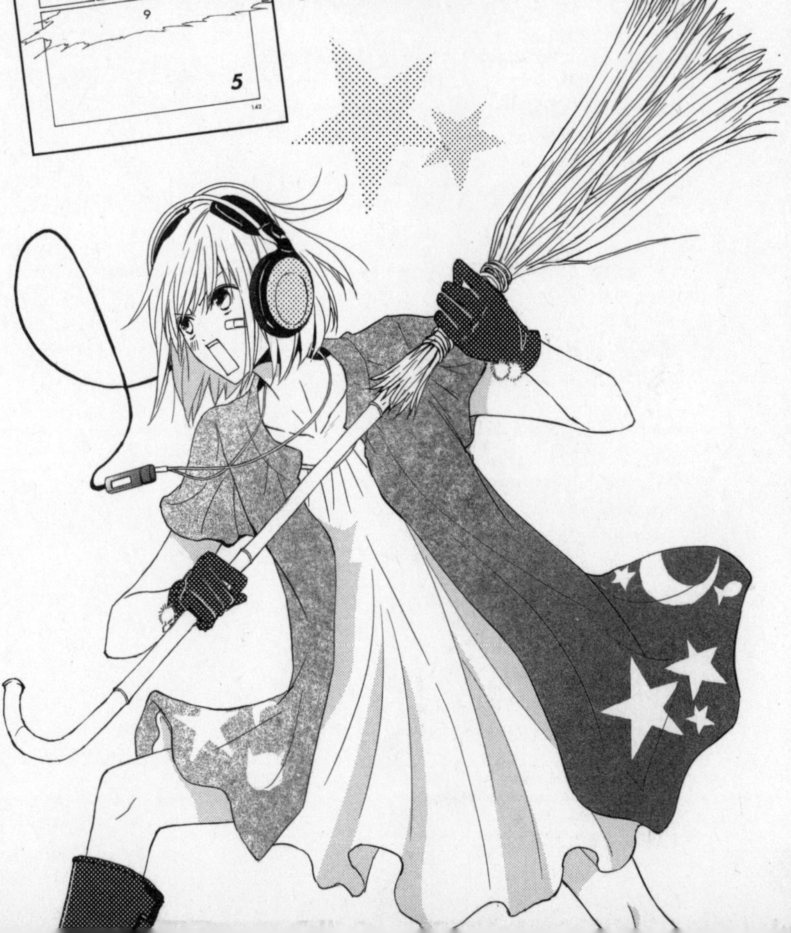

Queen's Quality

Vol. 2
Shojo Beat Edition

STORY AND ART BY
KYOUSUKE MOTOMI

QUEEN'S QUALITY Vol. 2
by Kyousuke MOTOMI
© 2016 Kyousuke MOTOMI
All rights reserved.
Original Japanese edition published by SHOGAKUKAN.
English translation rights in the United States of America, Canada, the United
Kingdom, Ireland, Australia and New Zealand arranged with SHOGAKUKAN.

ORIGINAL DESIGN/Chie SATO+Bay Bridge Studio

English Adaptation/Ysabet Reinhardt MacFarlane
Translation/JN Productions
Touch-Up Art & Lettering/Rina Mapa
Design/Julian [JR] Robinson
Editor/Amy Yu

Printed in the U.S.A.

Published by VIZ Media, LLC
P.O. Box 77010
San Francisco, CA 94107

10 9 8 7 6 5 4 3 2 1
First printing, December 2017

www.viz.com   www.shojobeat.com

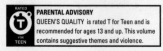

Chapter 6

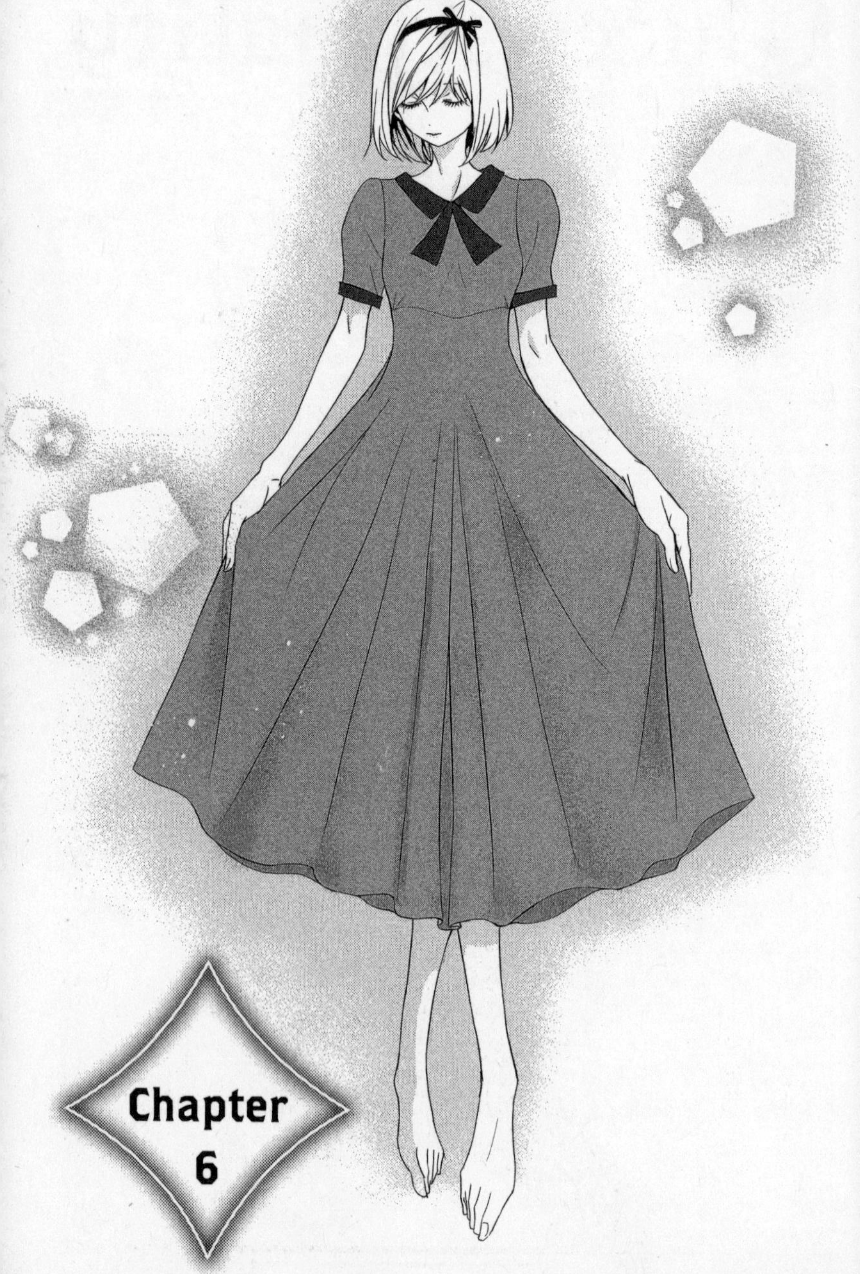

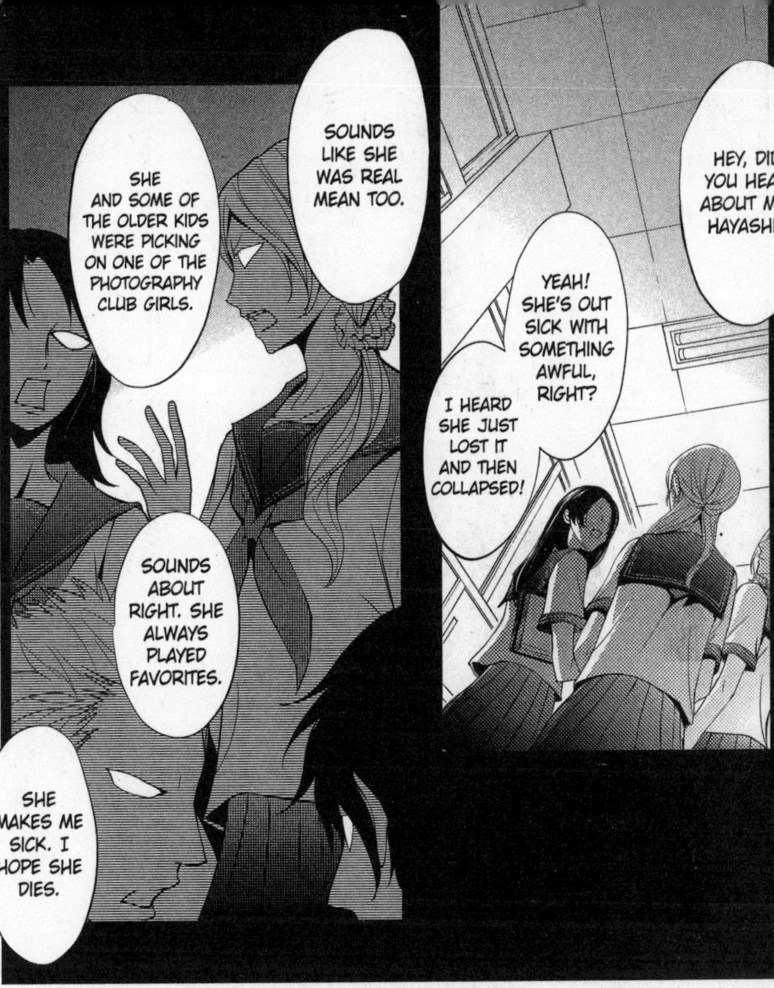
HEY, DID YOU HEAR ABOUT MS. HAYASHI?
YEAH! SHE'S OUT SICK WITH SOMETHING AWFUL, RIGHT?
I HEARD SHE JUST LOST IT AND THEN COLLAPSED!
SOUNDS LIKE SHE WAS REAL MEAN TOO.
SHE AND SOME OF THE OLDER KIDS WERE PICKING ON ONE OF THE PHOTOGRAPHY CLUB GIRLS.
SOUNDS ABOUT RIGHT. SHE ALWAYS PLAYED FAVORITES.
SHE MAKES ME SICK. I HOPE SHE DIES.

Hi, everyone, this is Kyousuke Motomi! Thanks so much for picking up volume 2 of *Queen's Quality*. I've started nicknaming this series "Queequa." It kinda reminds me of the cry of some powerful bird.

I hope you enjoy volume 2 of Queequa!

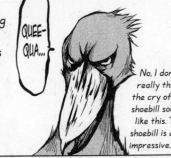

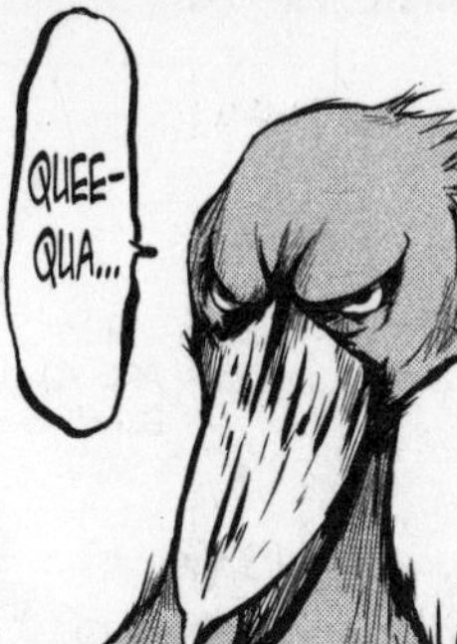
QUEE-QUA...

No, I don't really think the cry of the shoebill sounds like this. The shoebill is quite impressive, huh?

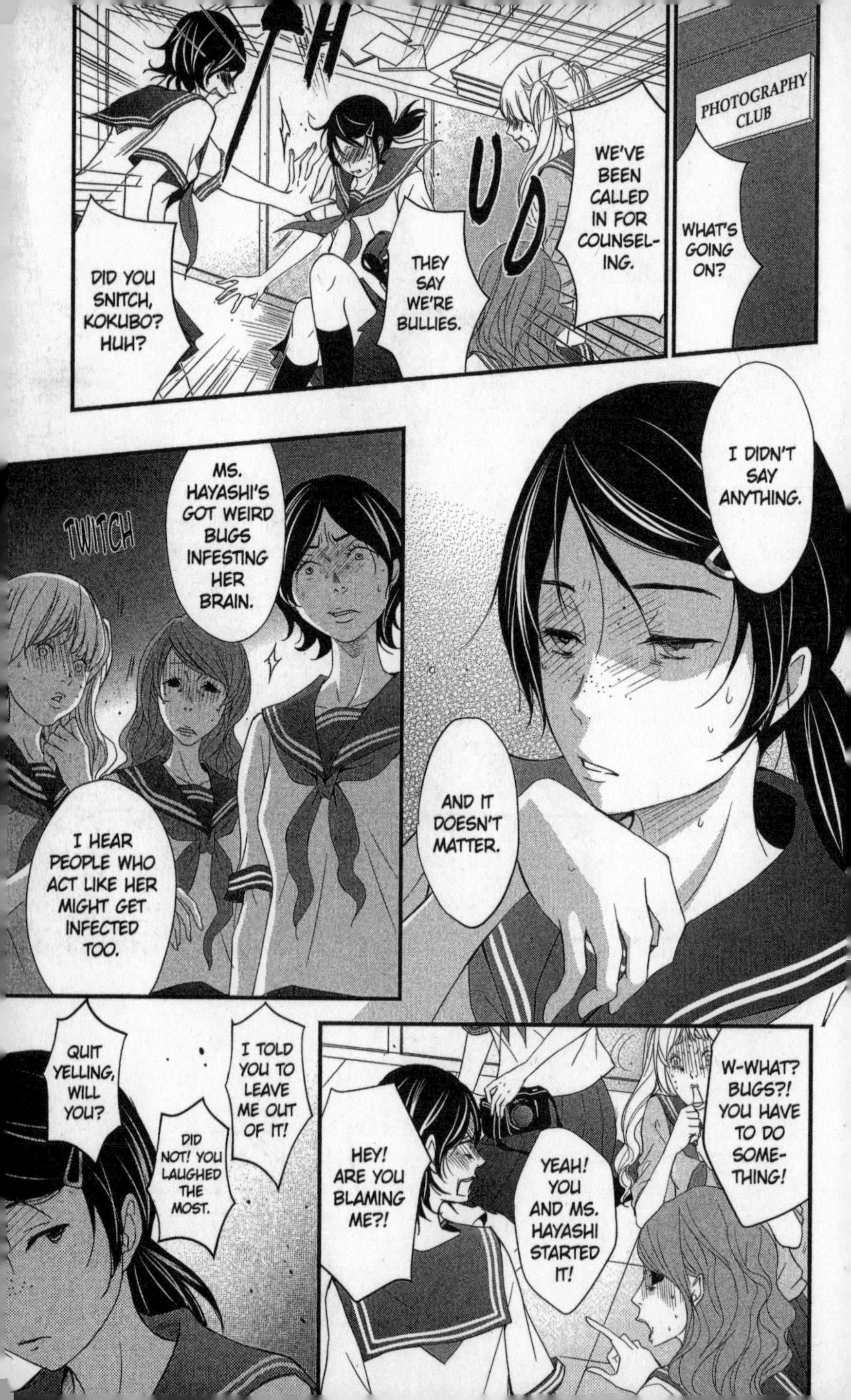
PHOTOGRAPHY CLUB
WHAT'S GOING ON?
WE'VE BEEN CALLED IN FOR COUNSEL-ING.
THEY SAY WE'RE BULLIES.
DID YOU SNITCH, KOKUBO? HUH?
I DIDN'T SAY ANYTHING.
AND IT DOESN'T MATTER.
MS. HAYASHI'S GOT WEIRD BUGS INFESTING HER BRAIN.
TWITCH
I HEAR PEOPLE WHO ACT LIKE HER MIGHT GET INFECTED TOO.
W-WHAT? BUGS?! YOU HAVE TO DO SOME-THING!
YEAH! YOU AND MS. HAYASHI STARTED IT!
HEY! ARE YOU BLAMING ME?!
I TOLD YOU TO LEAVE ME OUT OF IT!
DID NOT! YOU LAUGHED THE MOST.
QUIT YELLING, WILL YOU?

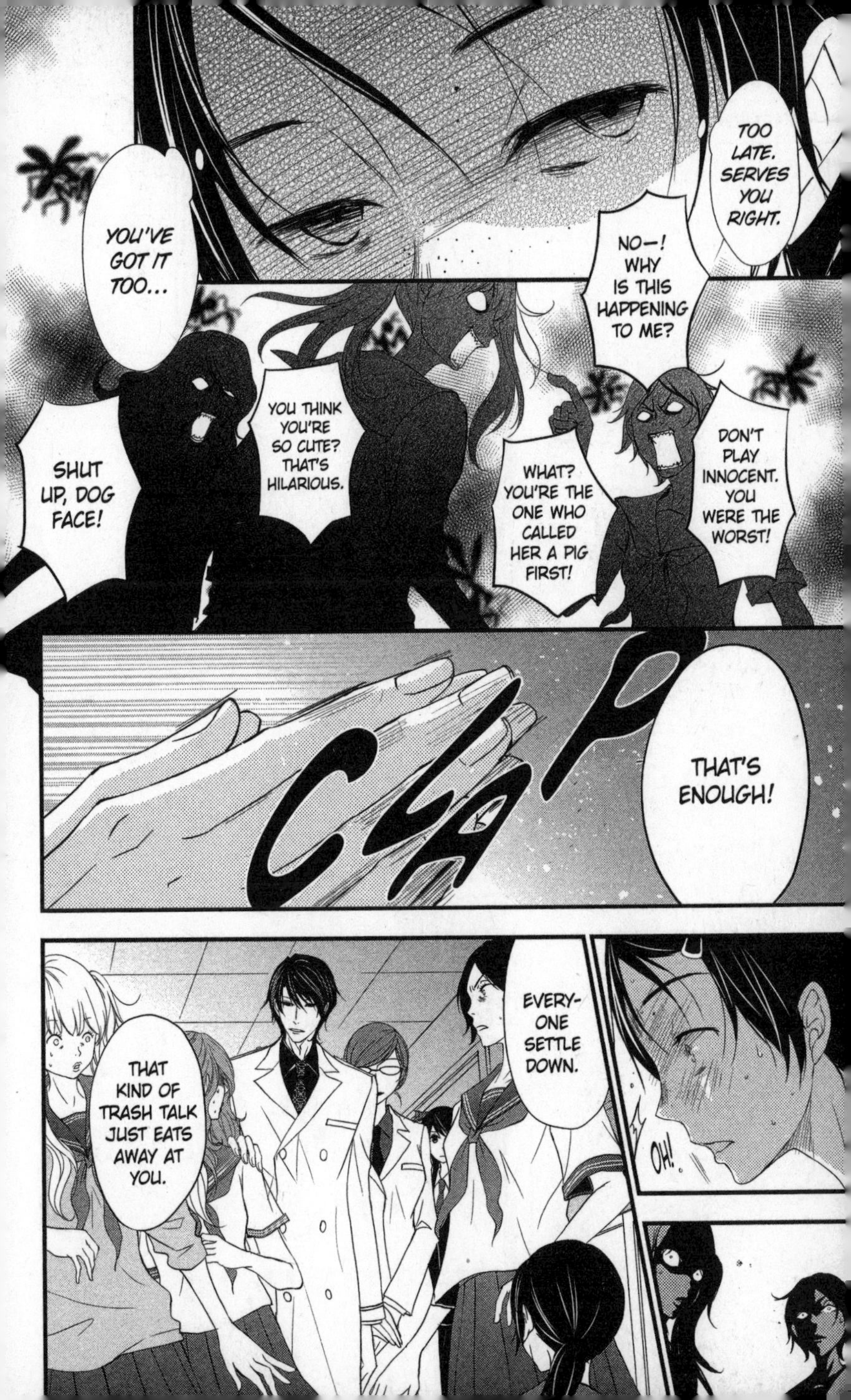
TOO LATE. SERVES YOU RIGHT.
YOU'VE GOT IT TOO...
NO—! WHY IS THIS HAPPENING TO ME?
DON'T PLAY INNOCENT. YOU WERE THE WORST!
WHAT? YOU'RE THE ONE WHO CALLED HER A PIG FIRST!
YOU THINK YOU'RE SO CUTE? THAT'S HILARIOUS.
SHUT UP, DOG FACE!
THAT'S ENOUGH!
CLAP
OH!
EVERY-ONE SETTLE DOWN.
THAT KIND OF TRASH TALK JUST EATS AWAY AT YOU.

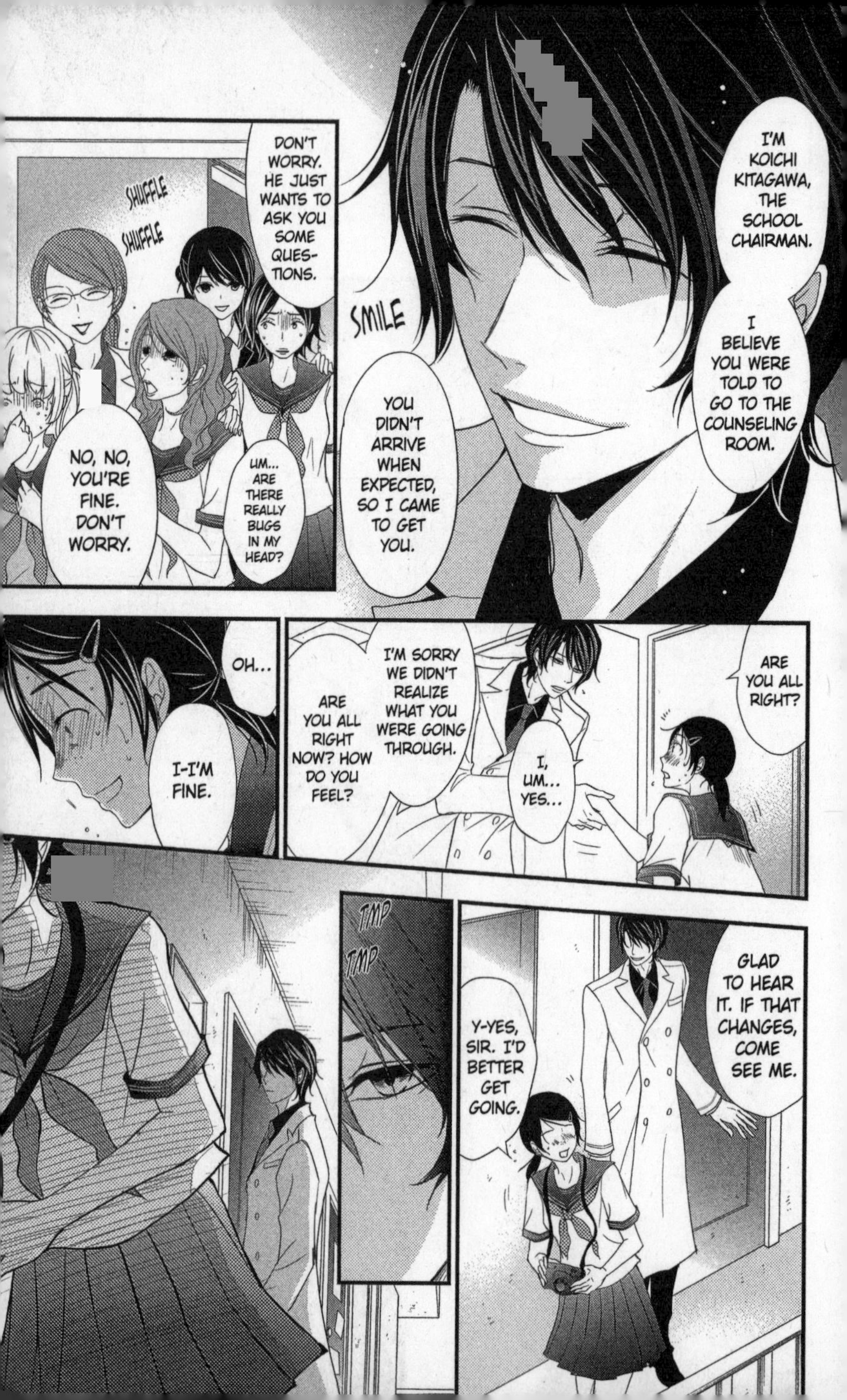
I'M KOICHI KITAGAWA, THE SCHOOL CHAIRMAN.
I BELIEVE YOU WERE TOLD TO GO TO THE COUNSELING ROOM.
SMILE
YOU DIDN'T ARRIVE WHEN EXPECTED, SO I CAME TO GET YOU.
DON'T WORRY. HE JUST WANTS TO ASK YOU SOME QUES-TIONS.
SHUFFLE
SHUFFLE
UM... ARE THERE REALLY BUGS IN MY HEAD?
NO, NO, YOU'RE FINE. DON'T WORRY.
ARE YOU ALL RIGHT?
I, UM... YES...
I'M SORRY WE DIDN'T REALIZE WHAT YOU WERE GOING THROUGH.
ARE YOU ALL RIGHT NOW? HOW DO YOU FEEL?
OH...
I-I'M FINE.
GLAD TO HEAR IT. IF THAT CHANGES, COME SEE ME.
Y-YES, SIR. I'D BETTER GET GOING.
TMP
TMP

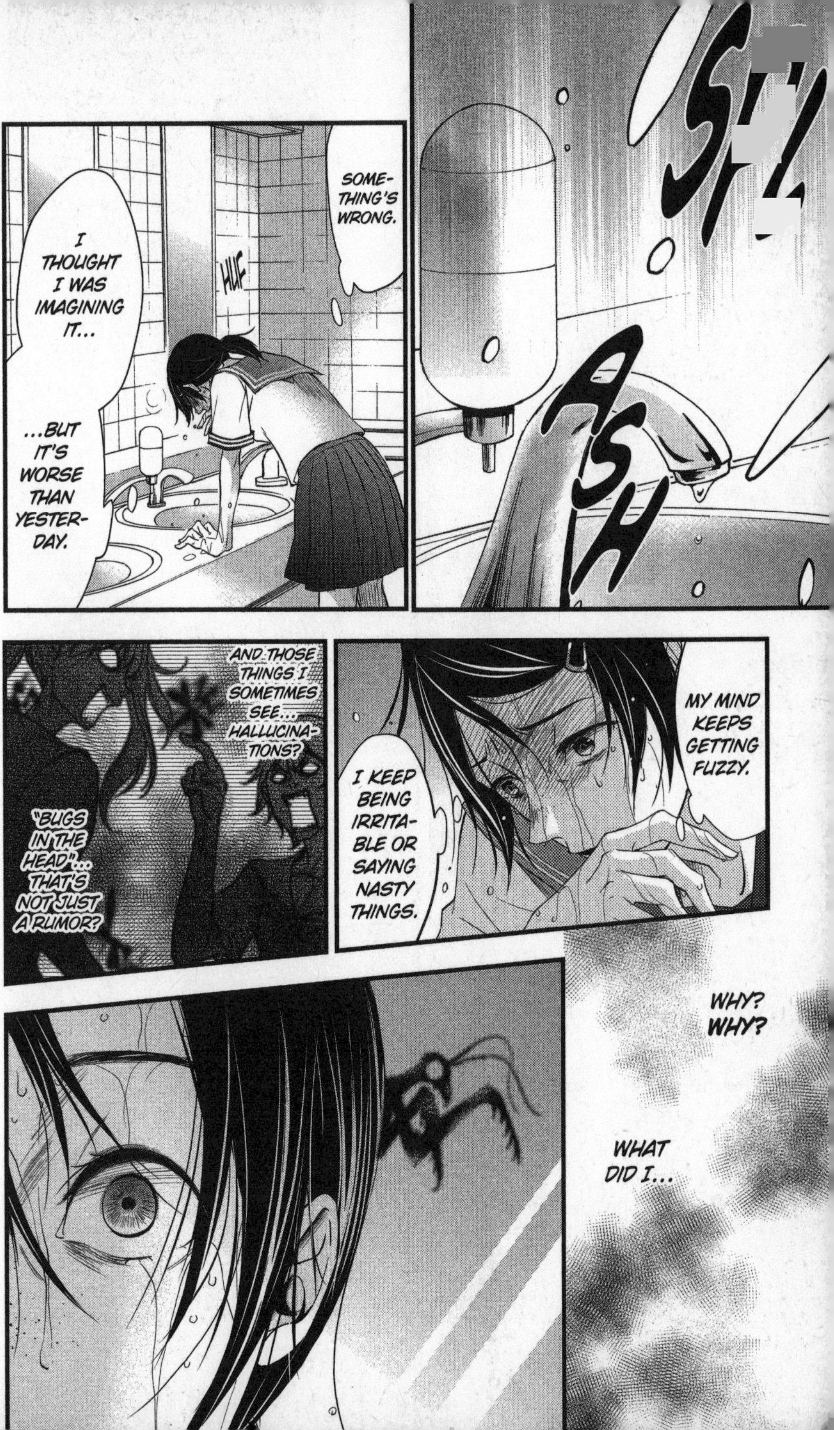
ASH
SOME-THING'S WRONG.
I THOUGHT I WAS IMAGINING IT...
HUF
...BUT IT'S WORSE THAN YESTER-DAY.
MY MIND KEEPS GETTING FUZZY.
I KEEP BEING IRRITA-BLE OR SAYING NASTY THINGS.
AND THOSE THINGS I SOMETIMES SEE... HALLUCINA-TIONS?
"BUGS IN THE HEAD"... THAT'S NOT JUST A RUMOR?
WHY? WHY?
WHAT DID I...

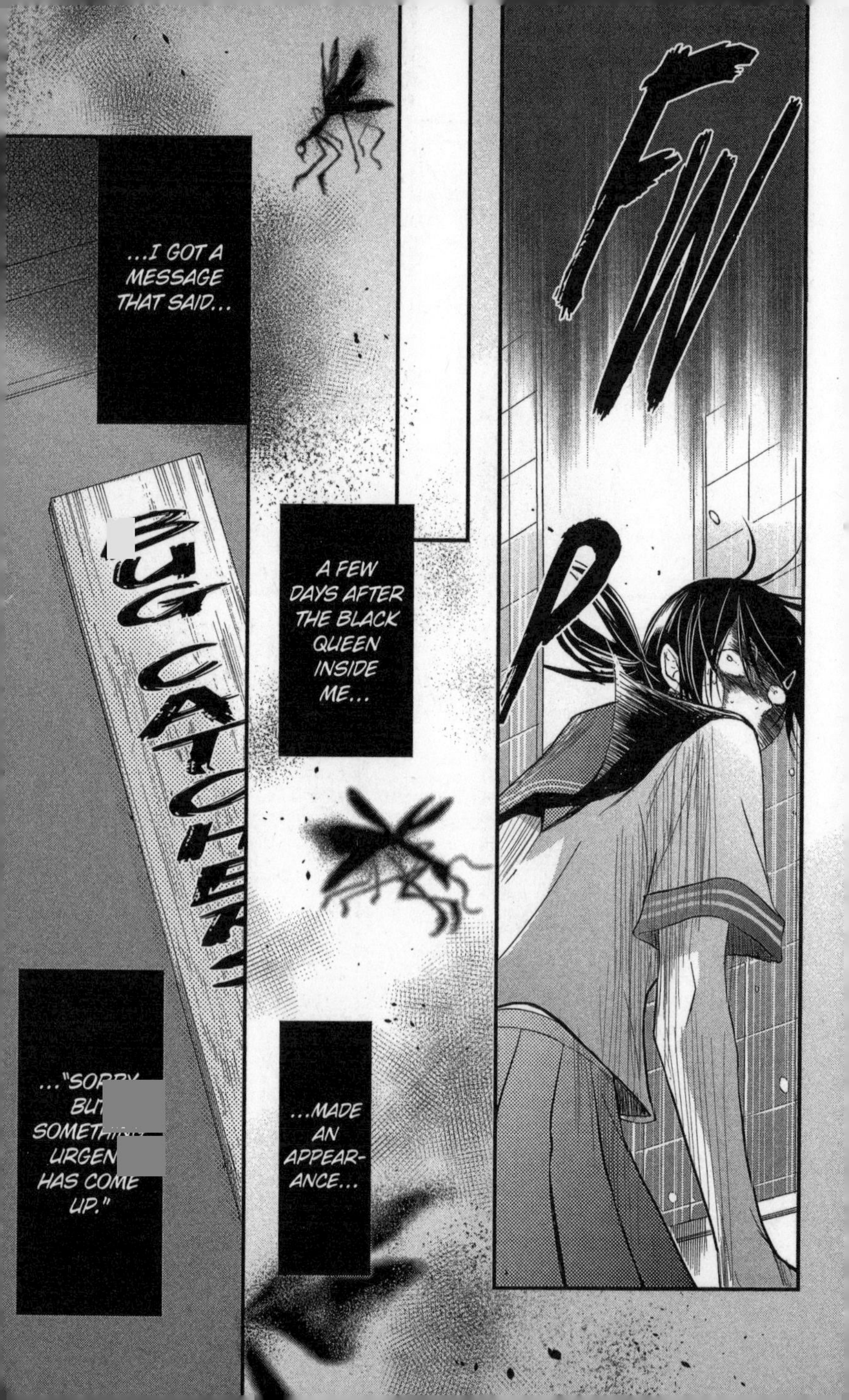
A FEW DAYS AFTER THE BLACK QUEEN INSIDE ME...
...MADE AN APPEARANCE...
...I GOT A MESSAGE THAT SAID...
..."SORR
BUT
SOMETHIN
URGEN
HAS COME UP."

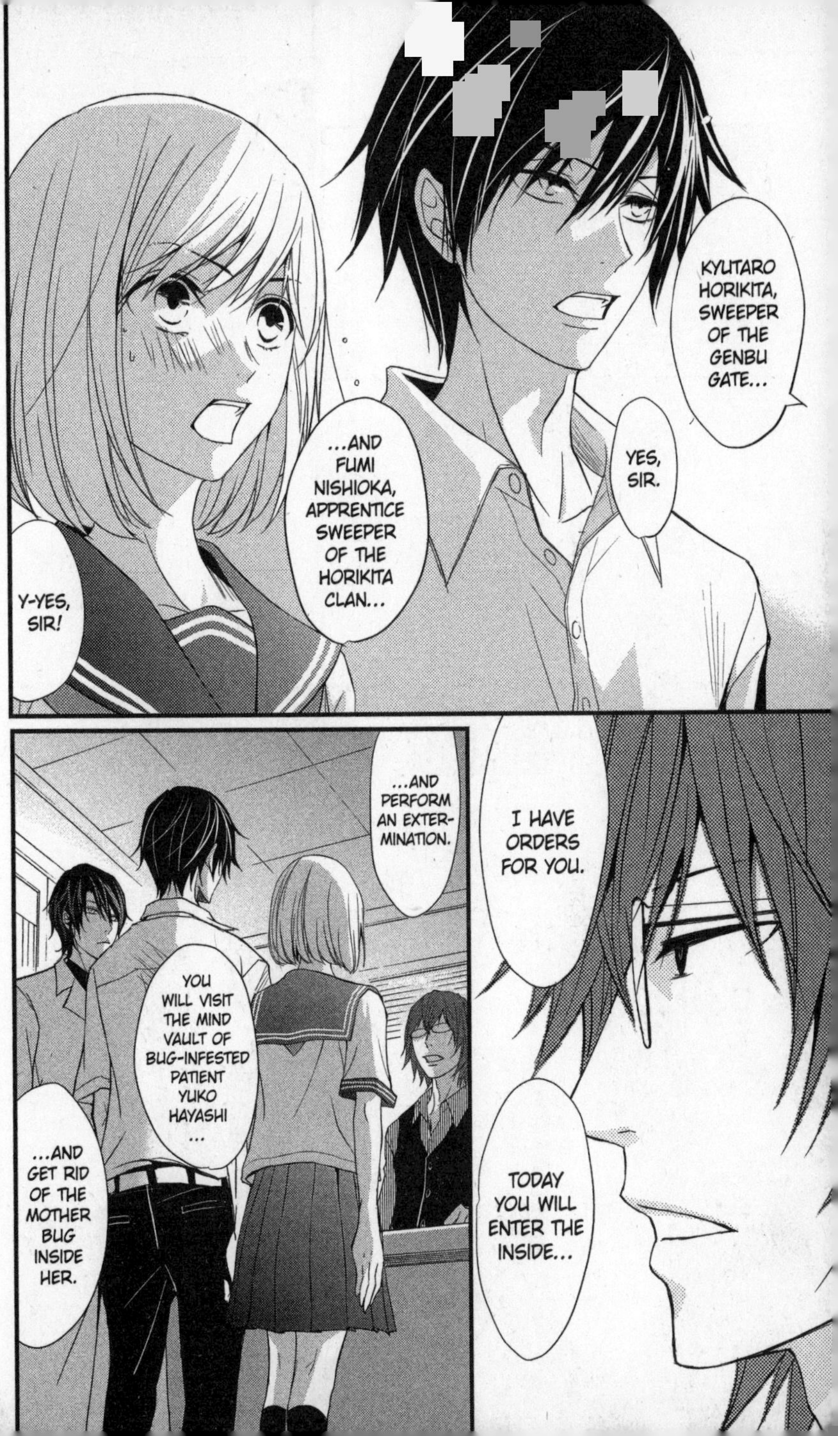
KYUTARO HORIKITA, SWEEPER OF THE GENBU GATE...
YES, SIR.
...AND FUMI NISHIOKA, APPRENTICE SWEEPER OF THE HORIKITA CLAN...
Y-YES, SIR!
I HAVE ORDERS FOR YOU.
TODAY YOU WILL ENTER THE INSIDE...
...AND PERFORM AN EXTERMINATION.
YOU WILL VISIT THE MIND VAULT OF BUG-INFESTED PATIENT YUKO HAYASHI...
...AND GET RID OF THE MOTHER BUG INSIDE HER.

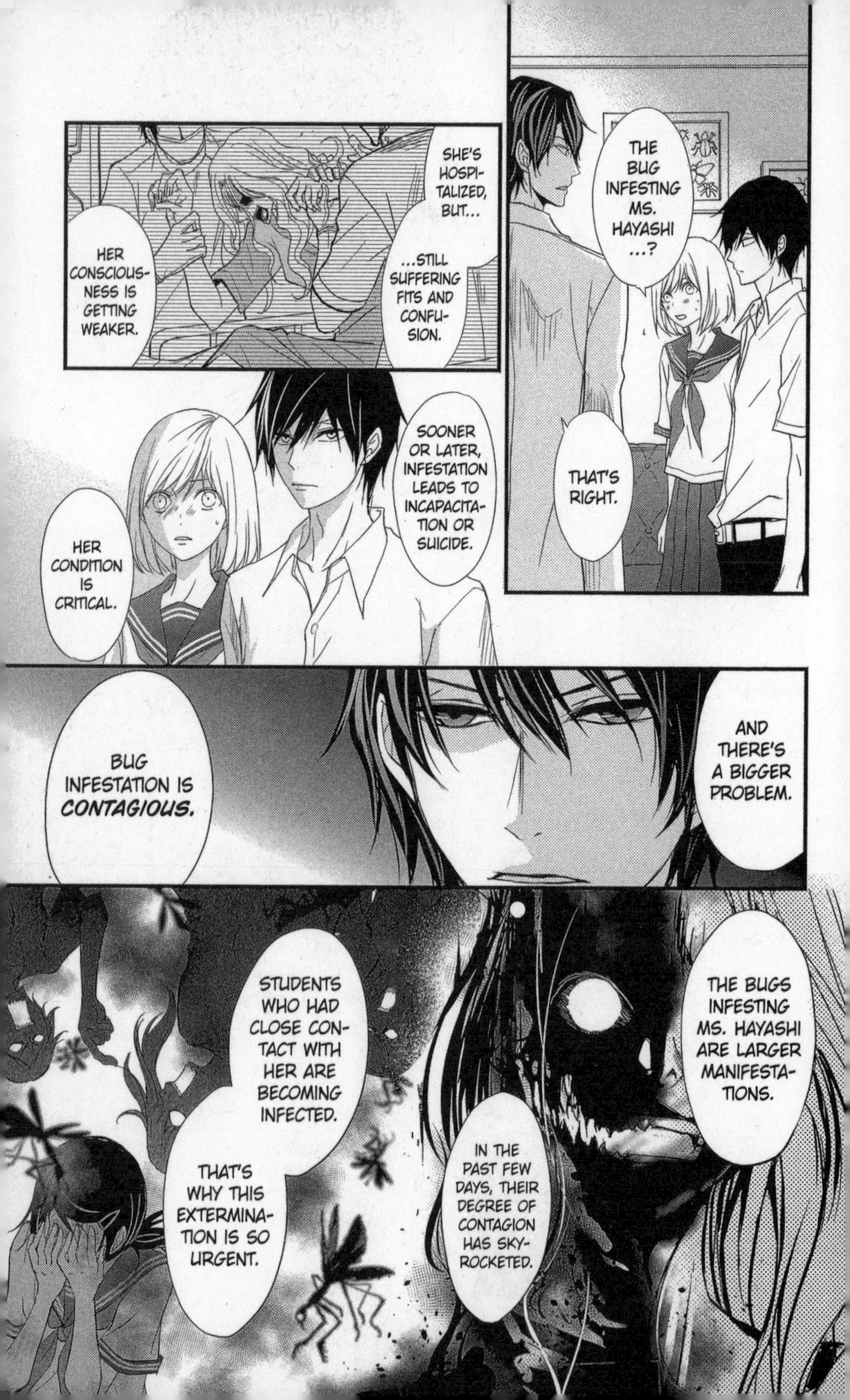
THE BUG INFESTING MS. HAYASHI ...?
THAT'S RIGHT.
SHE'S HOSPITALIZED, BUT...
...STILL SUFFERING FITS AND CONFUSION.
HER CONSCIOUSNESS IS GETTING WEAKER.
SOONER OR LATER, INFESTATION LEADS TO INCAPACITATION OR SUICIDE.
HER CONDITION IS CRITICAL.
AND THERE'S A BIGGER PROBLEM.
BUG INFESTATION IS *CONTAGIOUS.*
THE BUGS INFESTING MS. HAYASHI ARE LARGER MANIFESTATIONS.
IN THE PAST FEW DAYS, THEIR DEGREE OF CONTAGION HAS SKYROCKETED.
STUDENTS WHO HAD CLOSE CONTACT WITH HER ARE BECOMING INFECTED.
THAT'S WHY THIS EXTERMINATION IS SO URGENT.

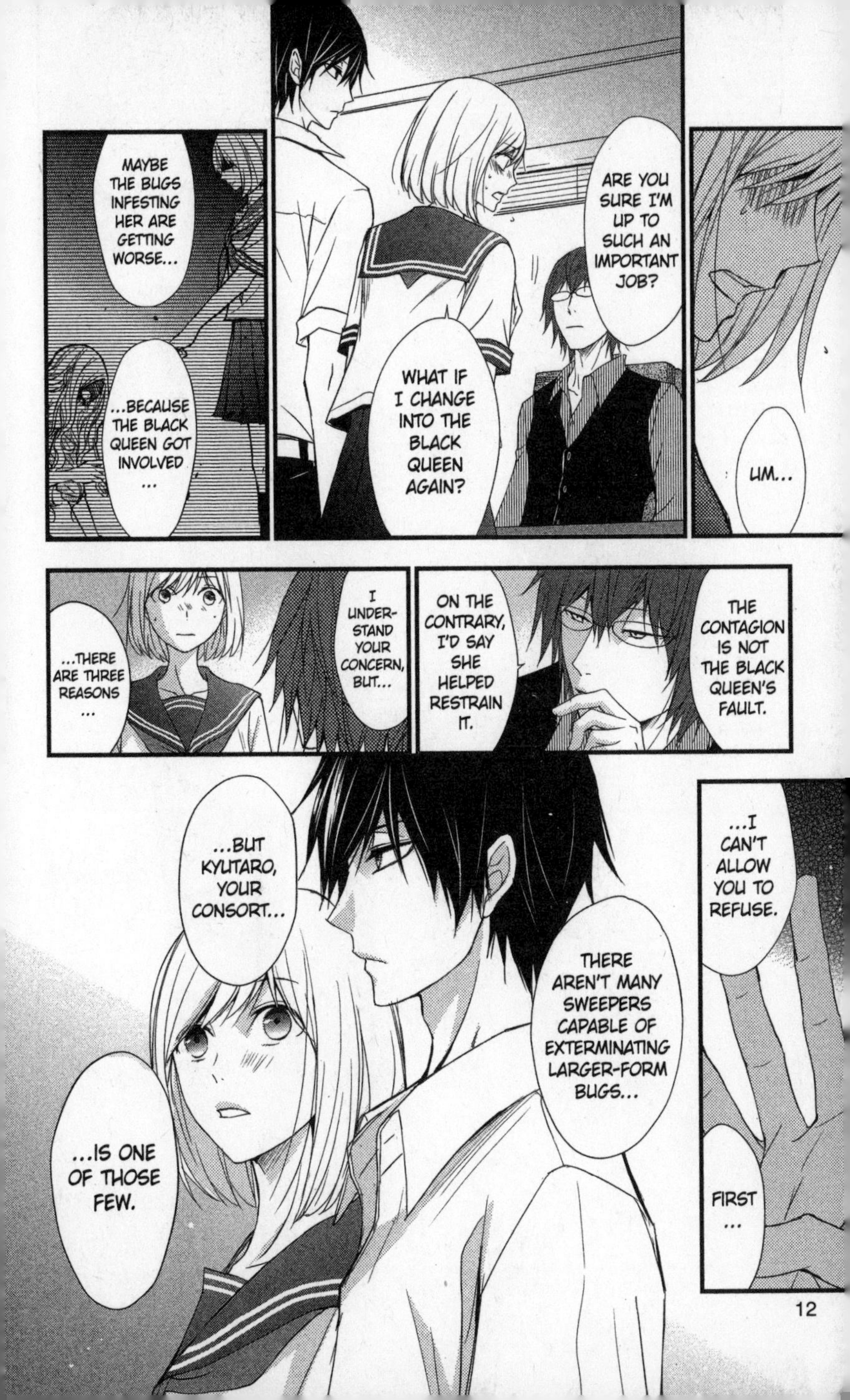
UM...
ARE YOU SURE I'M UP TO SUCH AN IMPORTANT JOB?
WHAT IF I CHANGE INTO THE BLACK QUEEN AGAIN?
MAYBE THE BUGS INFESTING HER ARE GETTING WORSE...
...BECAUSE THE BLACK QUEEN GOT INVOLVED...
THE CONTAGION IS NOT THE BLACK QUEEN'S FAULT.
ON THE CONTRARY, I'D SAY SHE HELPED RESTRAIN IT.
I UNDER-STAND YOUR CONCERN, BUT...
...THERE ARE THREE REASONS...
...I CAN'T ALLOW YOU TO REFUSE.
FIRST...
THERE AREN'T MANY SWEEPERS CAPABLE OF EXTERMINATING LARGER-FORM BUGS...
...BUT KYUTARO, YOUR CONSORT...
...IS ONE OF THOSE FEW.

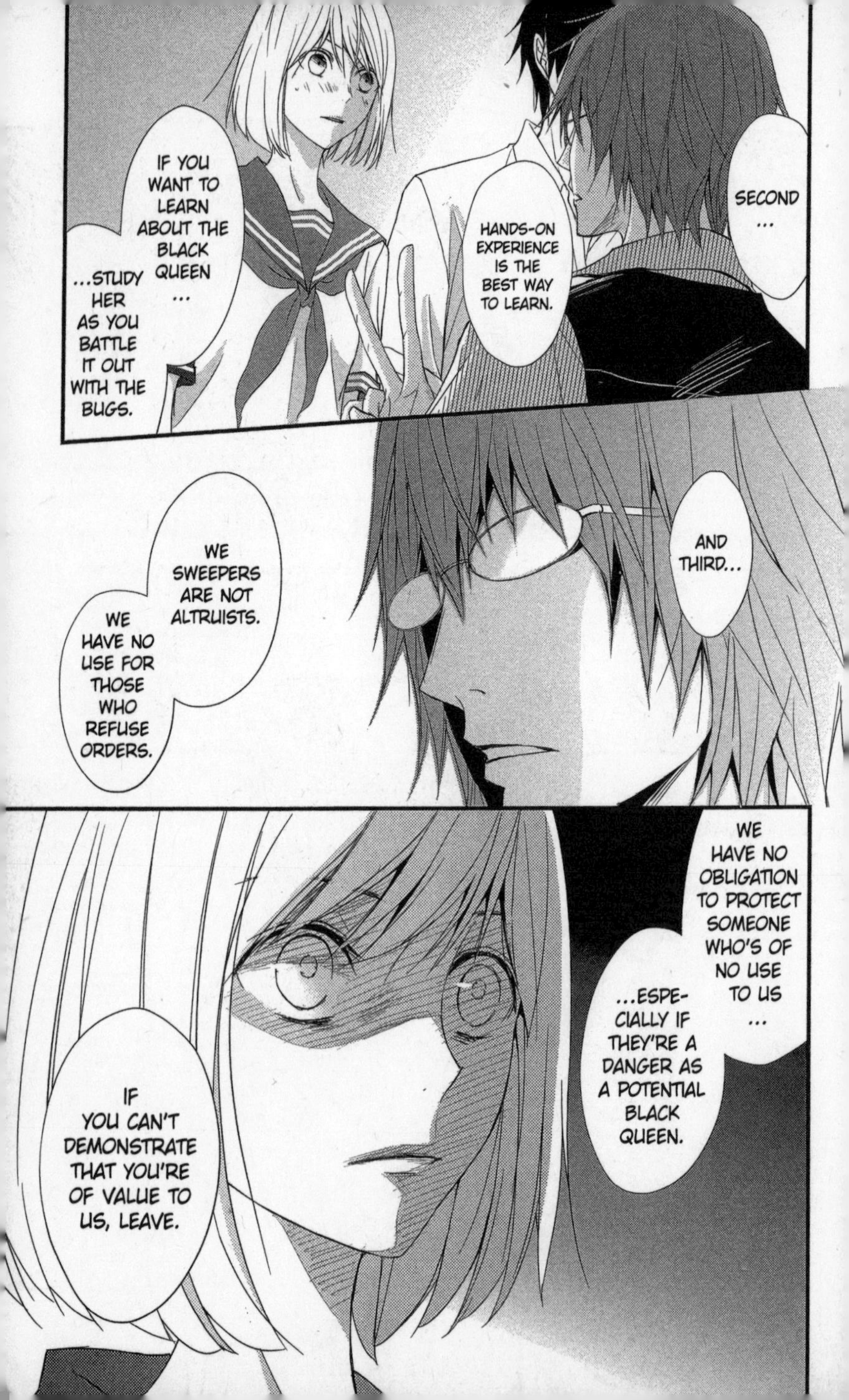
SECOND...
HANDS-ON EXPERIENCE IS THE BEST WAY TO LEARN.
IF YOU WANT TO LEARN ABOUT THE BLACK QUEEN...
...STUDY HER AS YOU BATTLE IT OUT WITH THE BUGS.
AND THIRD...
WE SWEEPERS ARE NOT ALTRUISTS.
WE HAVE NO USE FOR THOSE WHO REFUSE ORDERS.
WE HAVE NO OBLIGATION TO PROTECT SOMEONE WHO'S OF NO USE TO US...
...ESPECIALLY IF THEY'RE A DANGER AS A POTENTIAL BLACK QUEEN.
IF YOU CAN'T DEMONSTRATE THAT YOU'RE OF VALUE TO US, LEAVE.

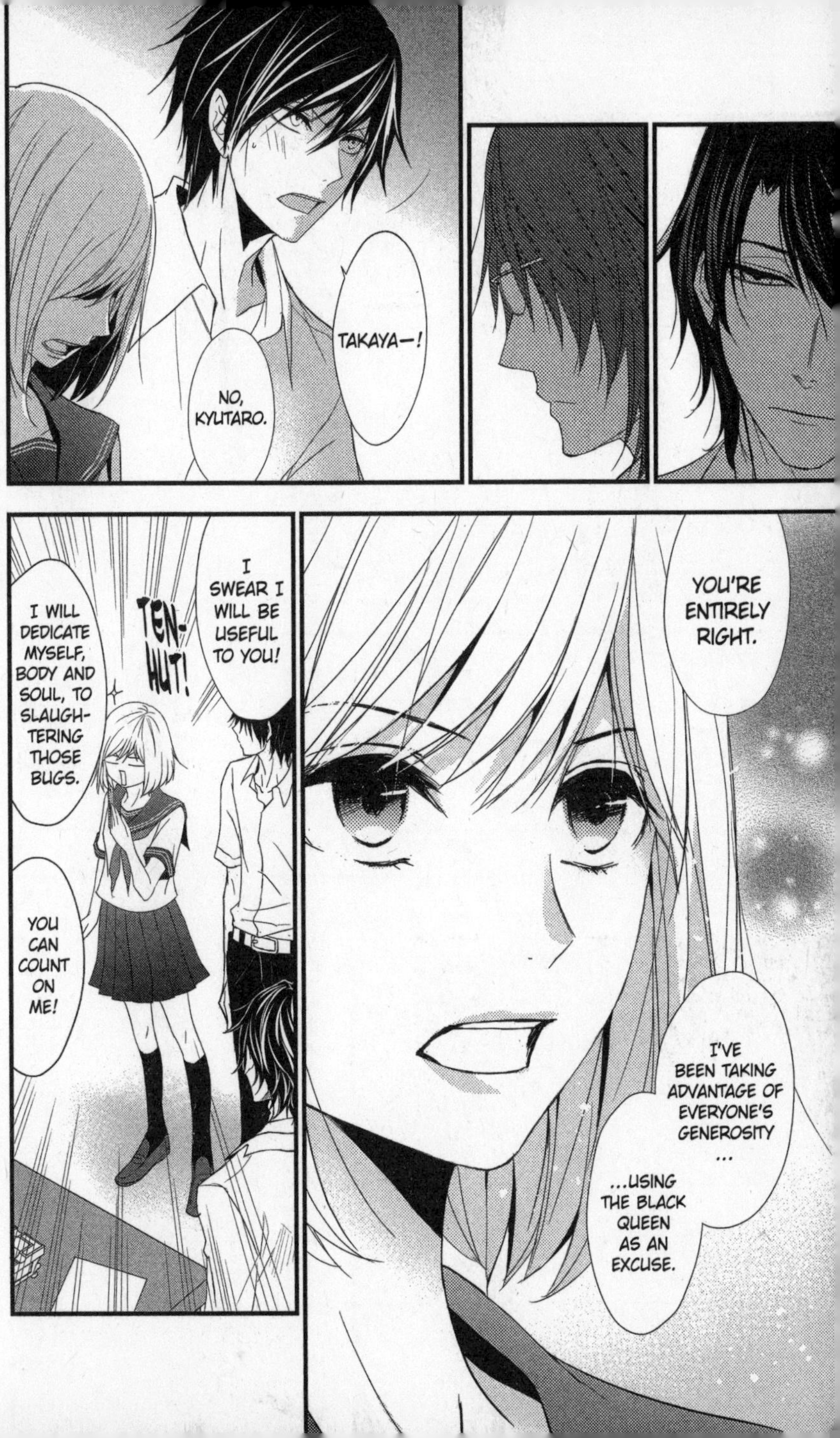
TAKAYA—!
NO, KYUTARO.
YOU'RE ENTIRELY RIGHT.
I'VE BEEN TAKING ADVANTAGE OF EVERYONE'S GENEROSITY ...
...USING THE BLACK QUEEN AS AN EXCUSE.
I SWEAR I WILL BE USEFUL TO YOU!
TEN-HUT!
I WILL DEDICATE MYSELF, BODY AND SOUL, TO SLAUGHTERING THOSE BUGS.
YOU CAN COUNT ON ME!

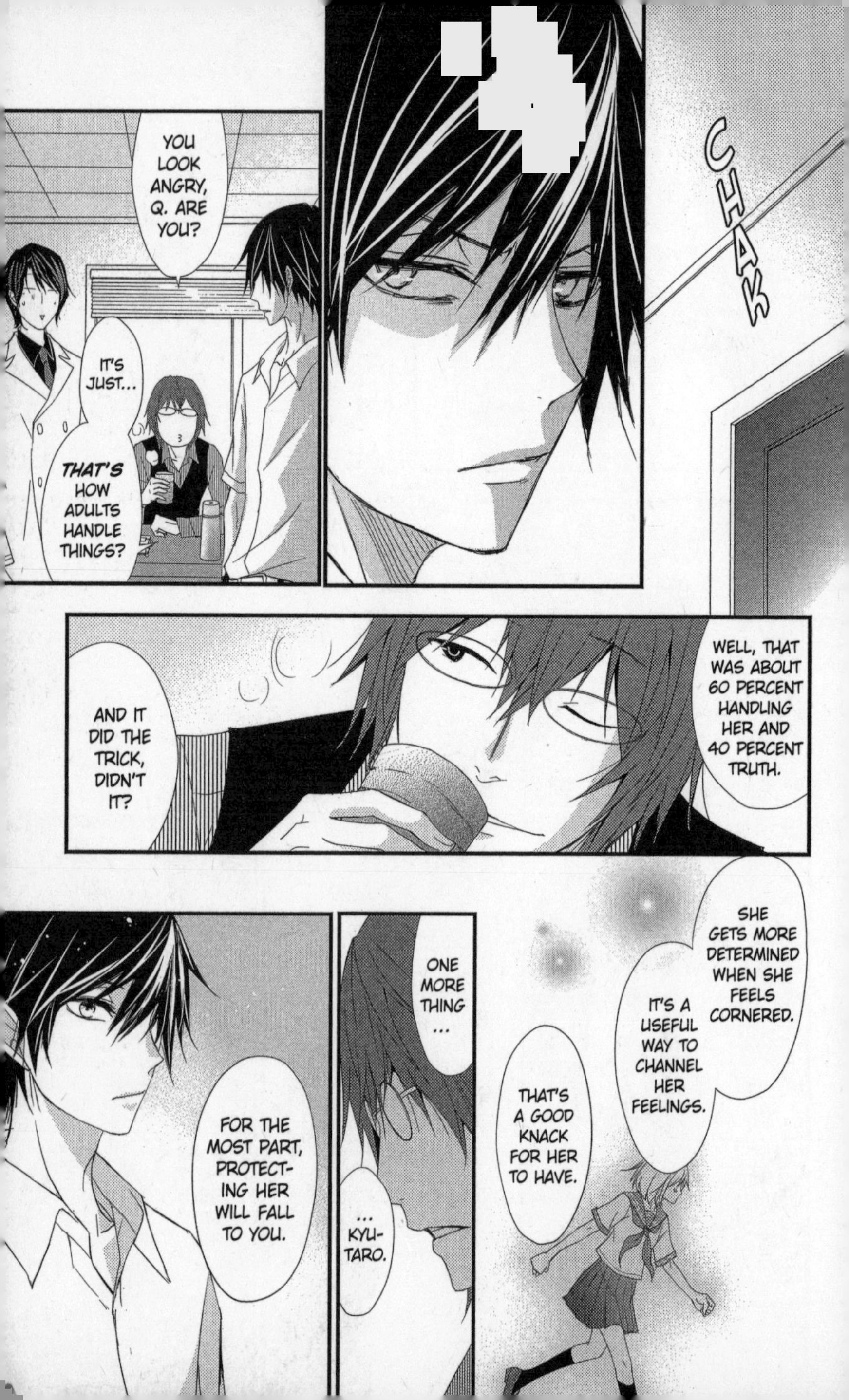
CHAK
YOU LOOK ANGRY, Q. ARE YOU?
IT'S JUST...
THAT'S HOW ADULTS HANDLE THINGS?
WELL, THAT WAS ABOUT 60 PERCENT HANDLING HER AND 40 PERCENT TRUTH.
AND IT DID THE TRICK, DIDN'T IT?
SHE GETS MORE DETERMINED WHEN SHE FEELS CORNERED.
IT'S A USEFUL WAY TO CHANNEL HER FEELINGS.
THAT'S A GOOD KNACK FOR HER TO HAVE.
ONE MORE THING...
...KYU-TARO.
FOR THE MOST PART, PROTECT-ING HER WILL FALL TO YOU.

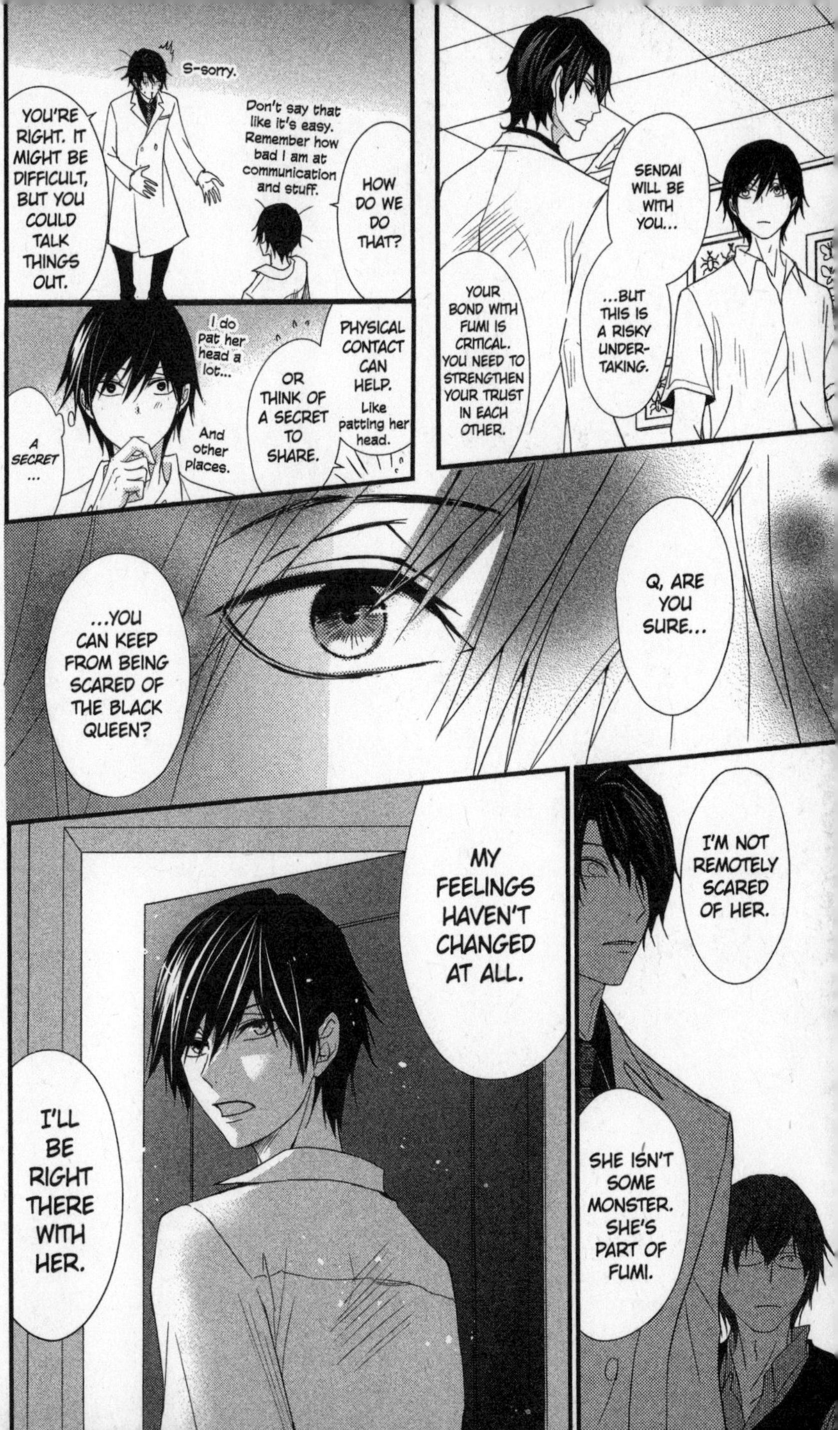
SENDAI WILL BE WITH YOU...
...BUT THIS IS A RISKY UNDERTAKING.
YOUR BOND WITH FUMI IS CRITICAL. YOU NEED TO STRENGTHEN YOUR TRUST IN EACH OTHER.
HOW DO WE DO THAT?
YOU'RE RIGHT. IT MIGHT BE DIFFICULT, BUT YOU COULD TALK THINGS OUT.
Don't say that like it's easy. Remember how bad I am at communication and stuff.
S-sorry.
PHYSICAL CONTACT CAN HELP.
Like patting her head.
OR THINK OF A SECRET TO SHARE.
I do pat her head a lot...
And other places.
A SECRET...
Q, ARE YOU SURE...
...YOU CAN KEEP FROM BEING SCARED OF THE BLACK QUEEN?
I'M NOT REMOTELY SCARED OF HER.
SHE ISN'T SOME MONSTER. SHE'S PART OF FUMI.
MY FEELINGS HAVEN'T CHANGED AT ALL.
I'LL BE RIGHT THERE WITH HER.

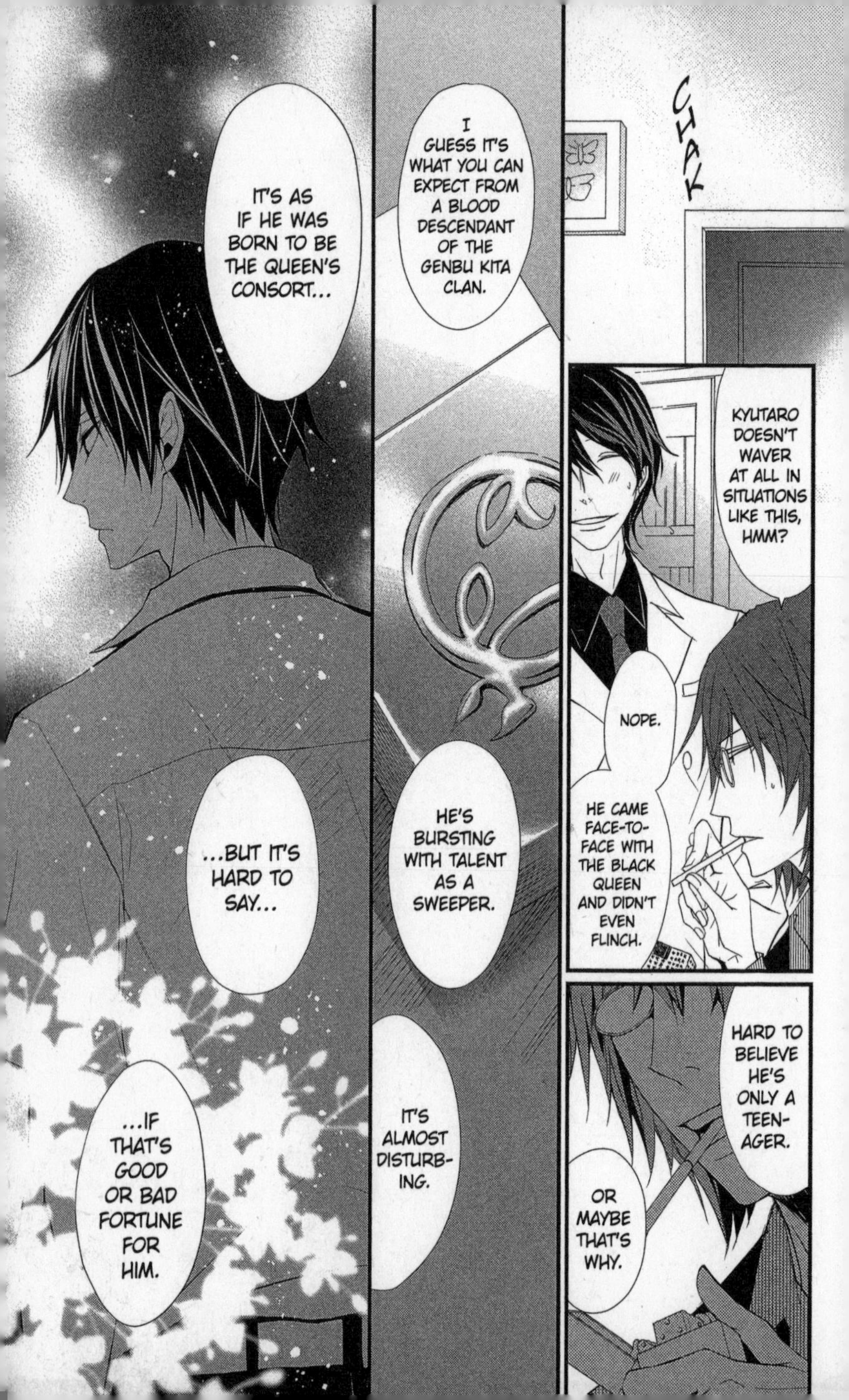
CHAK
KYUTARO DOESN'T WAVER AT ALL IN SITUATIONS LIKE THIS, HMM?
NOPE.
HE CAME FACE-TO-FACE WITH THE BLACK QUEEN AND DIDN'T EVEN FLINCH.
HARD TO BELIEVE HE'S ONLY A TEEN-AGER.
OR MAYBE THAT'S WHY.
I GUESS IT'S WHAT YOU CAN EXPECT FROM A BLOOD DESCENDANT OF THE GENBU KITA CLAN.
HE'S BURSTING WITH TALENT AS A SWEEPER.
IT'S ALMOST DISTURB-ING.
IT'S AS IF HE WAS BORN TO BE THE QUEEN'S CONSORT...
...BUT IT'S HARD TO SAY...
...IF THAT'S GOOD OR BAD FORTUNE FOR HIM.

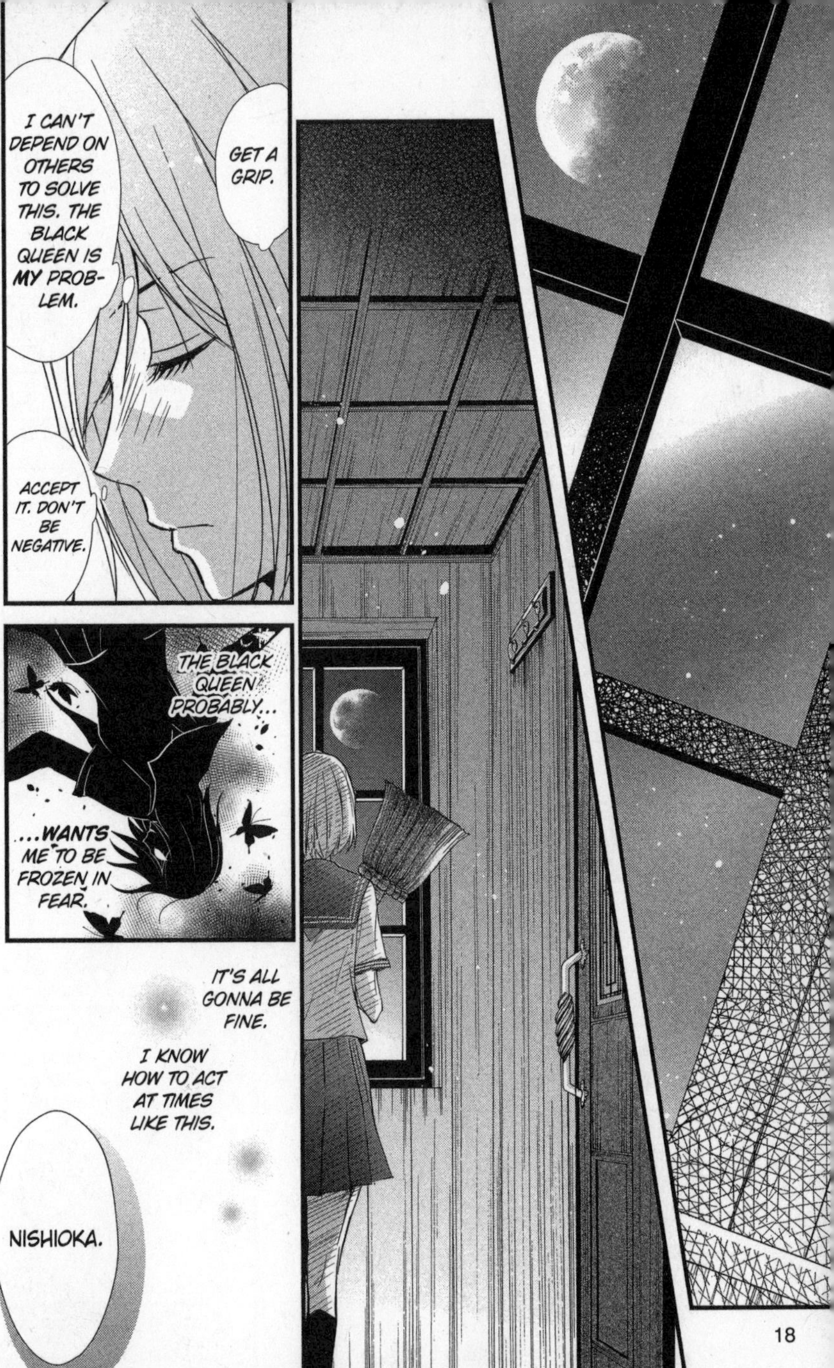
GET A GRIP.
I CAN'T DEPEND ON OTHERS TO SOLVE THIS. THE BLACK QUEEN IS MY PROB-LEM.
ACCEPT IT. DON'T BE NEGATIVE.
THE BLACK QUEEN PROBABLY...
...WANTS ME TO BE FROZEN IN FEAR.
IT'S ALL GONNA BE FINE.
I KNOW HOW TO ACT AT TIMES LIKE THIS.
NISHIOKA.

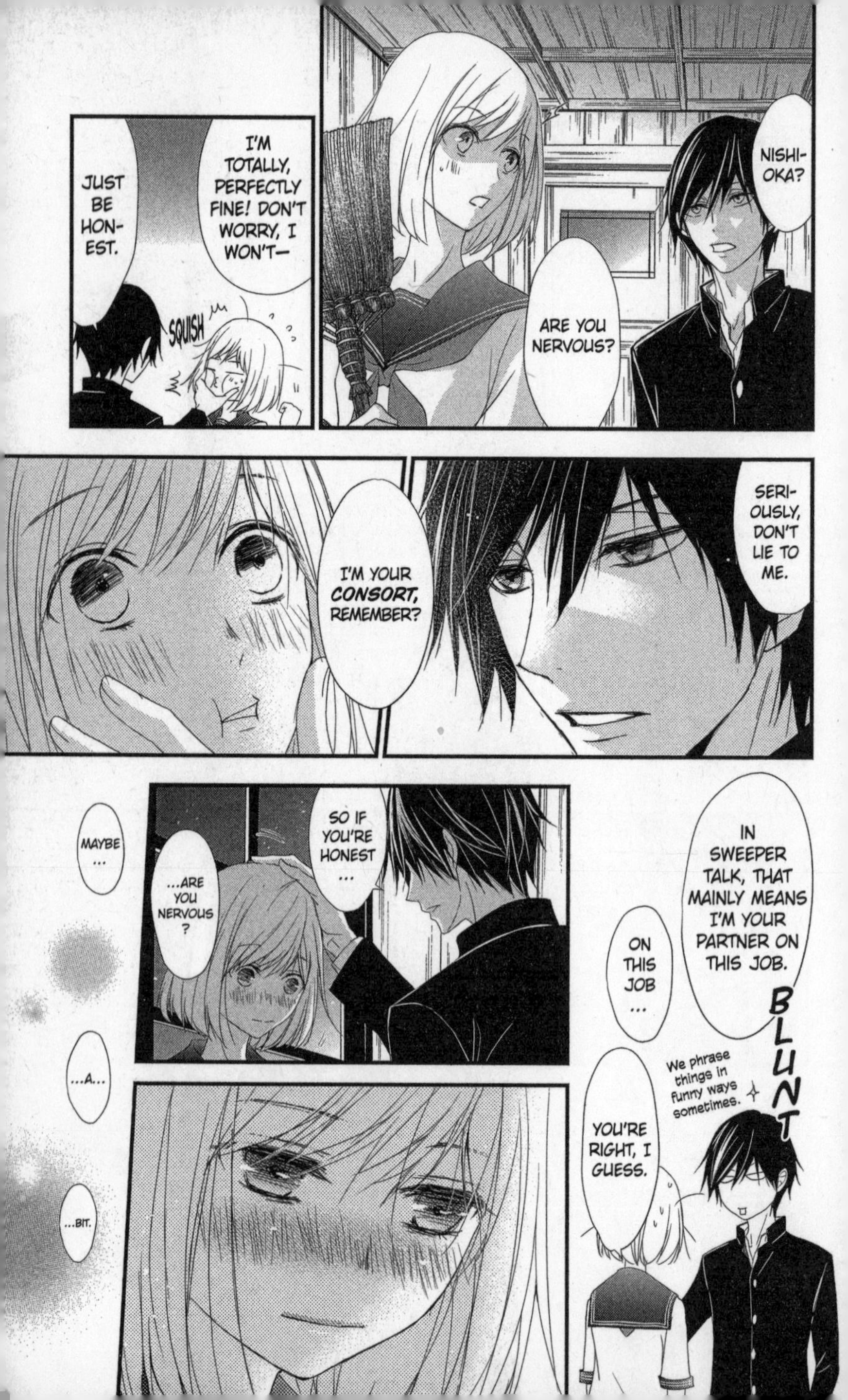
NISHI-OKA?
ARE YOU NERVOUS?
I'M TOTALLY, PERFECTLY FINE! DON'T WORRY, I WON'T—
SQUISH
JUST BE HON-EST.
SERI-OUSLY, DON'T LIE TO ME.
I'M YOUR CONSORT, REMEMBER?
IN SWEEPER TALK, THAT MAINLY MEANS I'M YOUR PARTNER ON THIS JOB.
ON THIS JOB ...
BLUNT
We phrase things in funny ways sometimes.
YOU'RE RIGHT, I GUESS.
SO IF YOU'RE HONEST ...
...ARE YOU NERVOUS ?
MAYBE ...
...A...
...BIT.

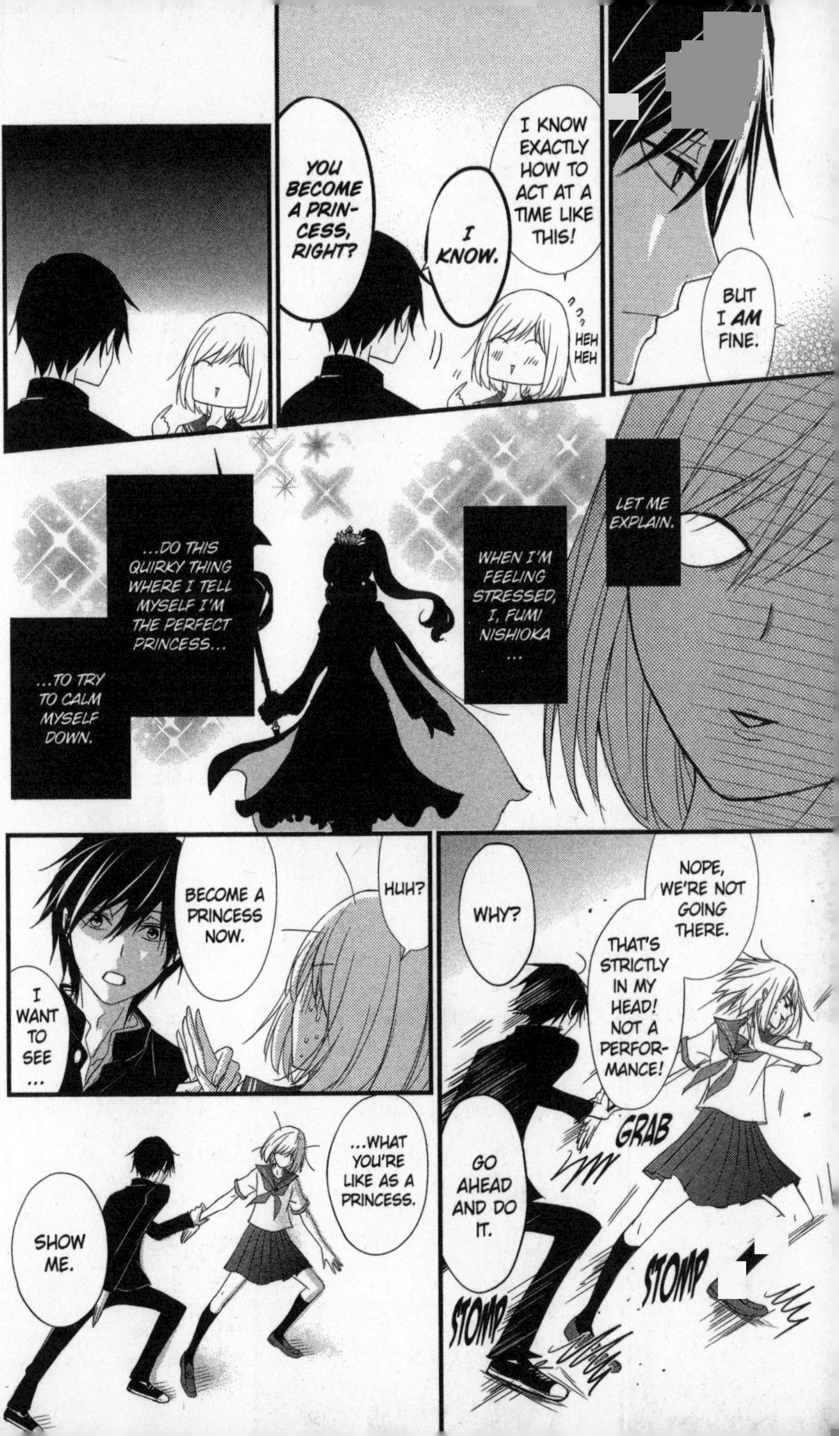
BUT I *AM* FINE.
I KNOW EXACTLY HOW TO ACT AT A TIME LIKE THIS!
HEH HEH
I KNOW.
YOU BECOME A PRINCESS, RIGHT?
LET ME EXPLAIN.
WHEN I'M FEELING STRESSED, I, FUMI NISHIOKA...
...DO THIS QUIRKY THING WHERE I TELL MYSELF I'M THE PERFECT PRINCESS...
...TO TRY TO CALM MYSELF DOWN.
NOPE, WE'RE NOT GOING THERE.
WHY?
THAT'S STRICTLY IN MY HEAD! NOT A PERFORMANCE!
GRAB
GO AHEAD AND DO IT.
STOMP
STOMP
HUH?
BECOME A PRINCESS NOW.
I WANT TO SEE...
...WHAT YOU'RE LIKE AS A PRINCESS.
SHOW ME.

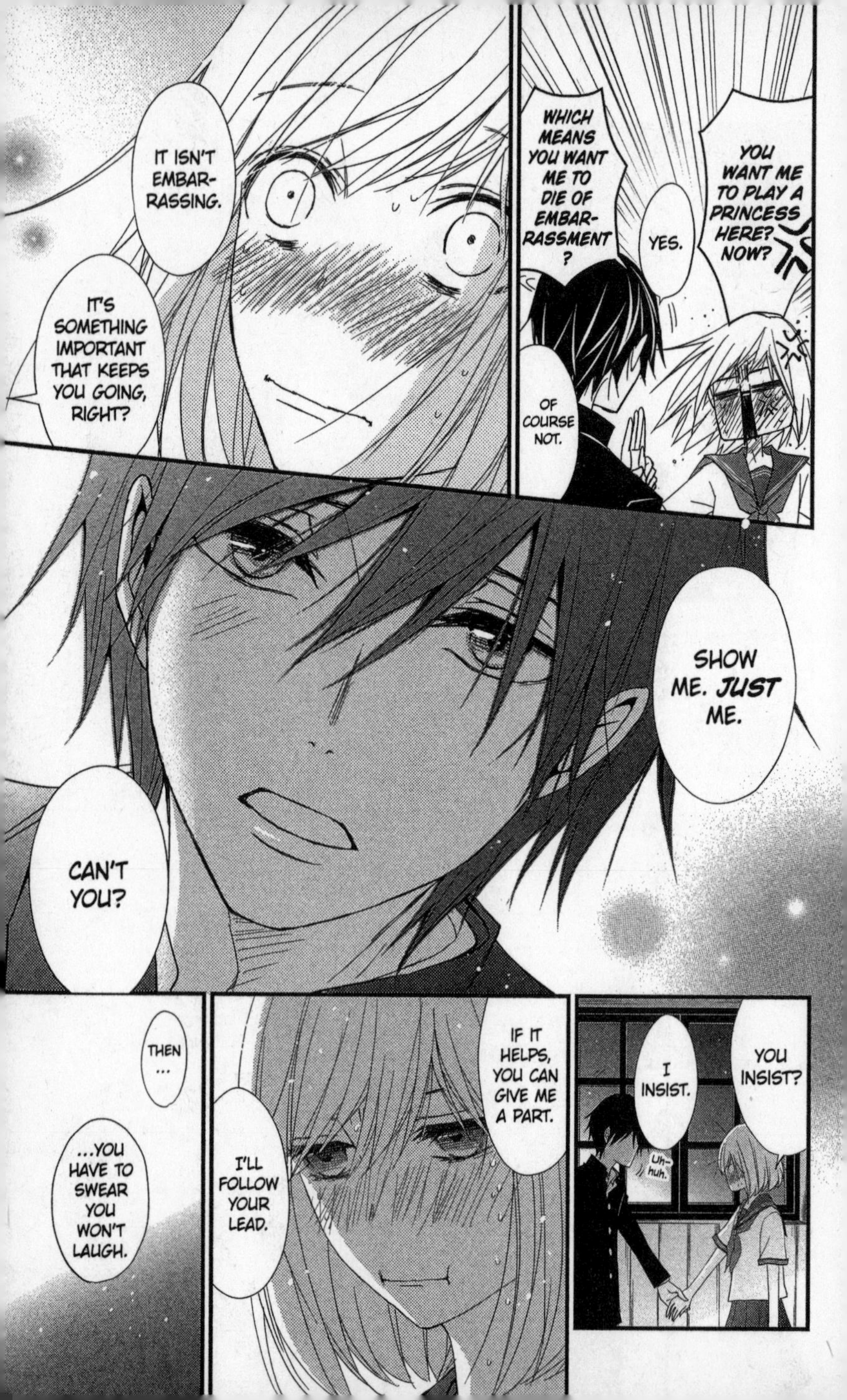
YOU WANT ME TO PLAY A PRINCESS HERE? NOW?
YES.
WHICH MEANS YOU WANT ME TO DIE OF EMBARRASSMENT?
OF COURSE NOT.
IT ISN'T EMBARRASSING.
IT'S SOMETHING IMPORTANT THAT KEEPS YOU GOING, RIGHT?
SHOW ME. JUST ME.
CAN'T YOU?
YOU INSIST?
I INSIST.
Uh-huh.
IF IT HELPS, YOU CAN GIVE ME A PART.
I'LL FOLLOW YOUR LEAD.
THEN...
...YOU HAVE TO SWEAR YOU WON'T LAUGH.

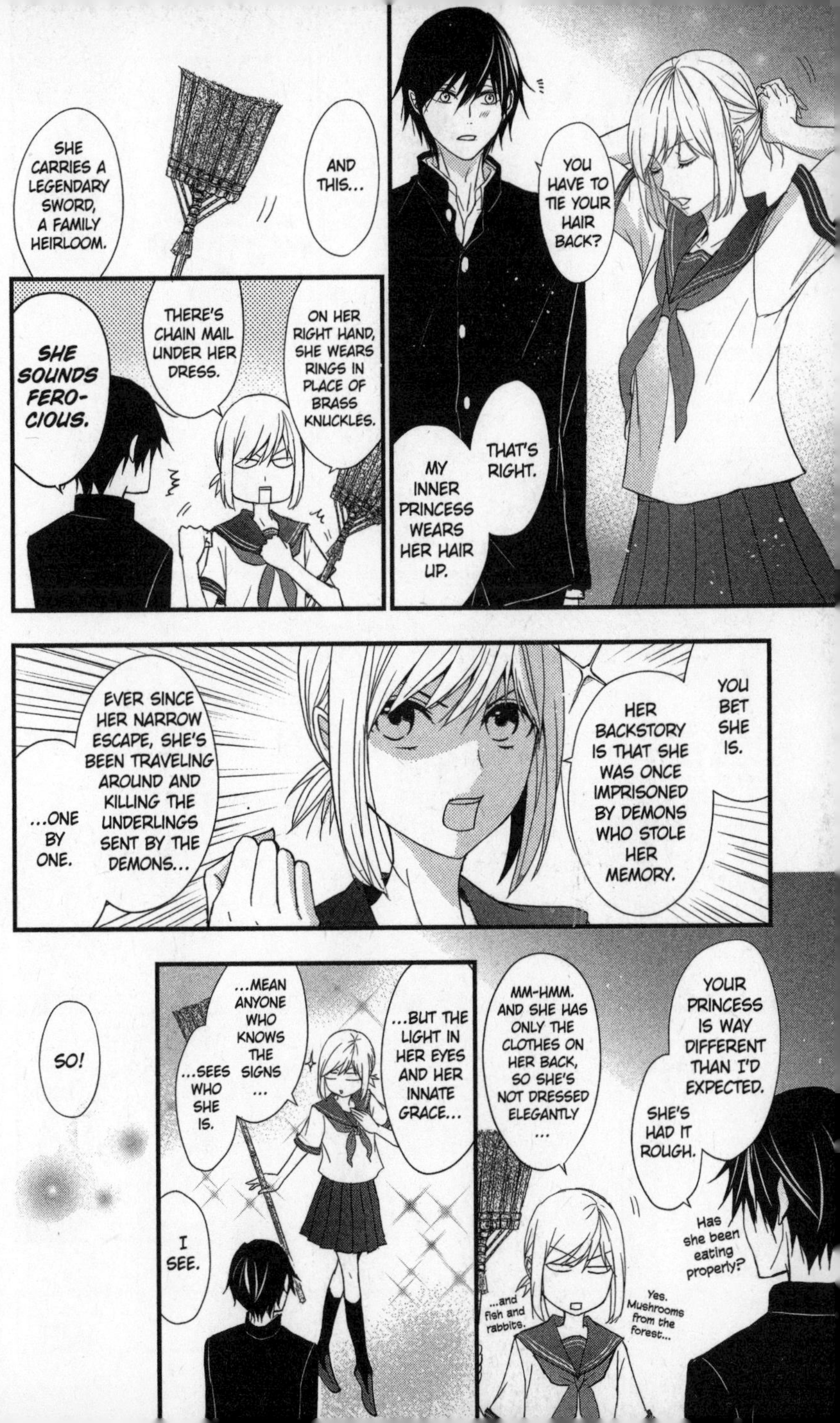
YOU HAVE TO TIE YOUR HAIR BACK?
THAT'S RIGHT.
MY INNER PRINCESS WEARS HER HAIR UP.
AND THIS...
SHE CARRIES A LEGENDARY SWORD, A FAMILY HEIRLOOM.
ON HER RIGHT HAND, SHE WEARS RINGS IN PLACE OF BRASS KNUCKLES.
THERE'S CHAIN MAIL UNDER HER DRESS.
SHE SOUNDS FERO-CIOUS.
YOU BET SHE IS.
HER BACKSTORY IS THAT SHE WAS ONCE IMPRISONED BY DEMONS WHO STOLE HER MEMORY.
EVER SINCE HER NARROW ESCAPE, SHE'S BEEN TRAVELING AROUND AND KILLING THE UNDERLINGS SENT BY THE DEMONS...
...ONE BY ONE.
YOUR PRINCESS IS WAY DIFFERENT THAN I'D EXPECTED.
SHE'S HAD IT ROUGH.
MM-HMM. AND SHE HAS ONLY THE CLOTHES ON HER BACK, SO SHE'S NOT DRESSED ELEGANTLY...
Has she been eating properly?
Yes. Mushrooms from the forest...
...and fish and rabbits.
...BUT THE LIGHT IN HER EYES AND HER INNATE GRACE...
...MEAN ANYONE WHO KNOWS THE SIGNS...
...SEES WHO SHE IS.
I SEE.
SO!

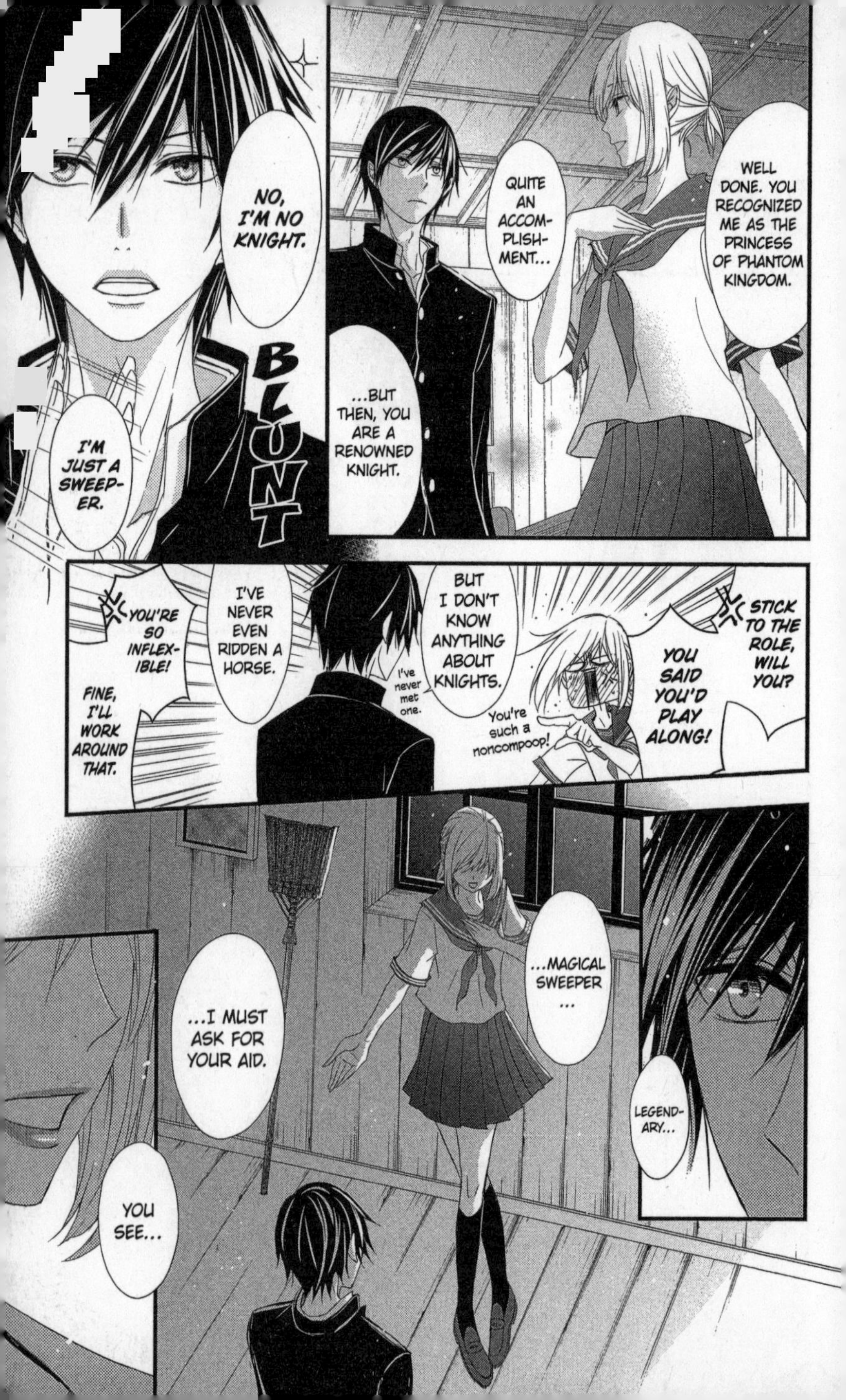
WELL DONE. YOU RECOGNIZED ME AS THE PRINCESS OF PHANTOM KINGDOM.
QUITE AN ACCOM-PLISH-MENT...
...BUT THEN, YOU ARE A RENOWNED KNIGHT.
NO, I'M NO KNIGHT.
BLUNT
I'M JUST A SWEEP-ER.
STICK TO THE ROLE, WILL YOU?
YOU SAID YOU'D PLAY ALONG!
You're such a noncompoop!
BUT I DON'T KNOW ANYTHING ABOUT KNIGHTS.
I've never met one.
I'VE NEVER EVEN RIDDEN A HORSE.
YOU'RE SO INFLEX-IBLE!
FINE, I'LL WORK AROUND THAT.
LEGEND-ARY...
...MAGICAL SWEEPER ...
...I MUST ASK FOR YOUR AID.
YOU SEE...

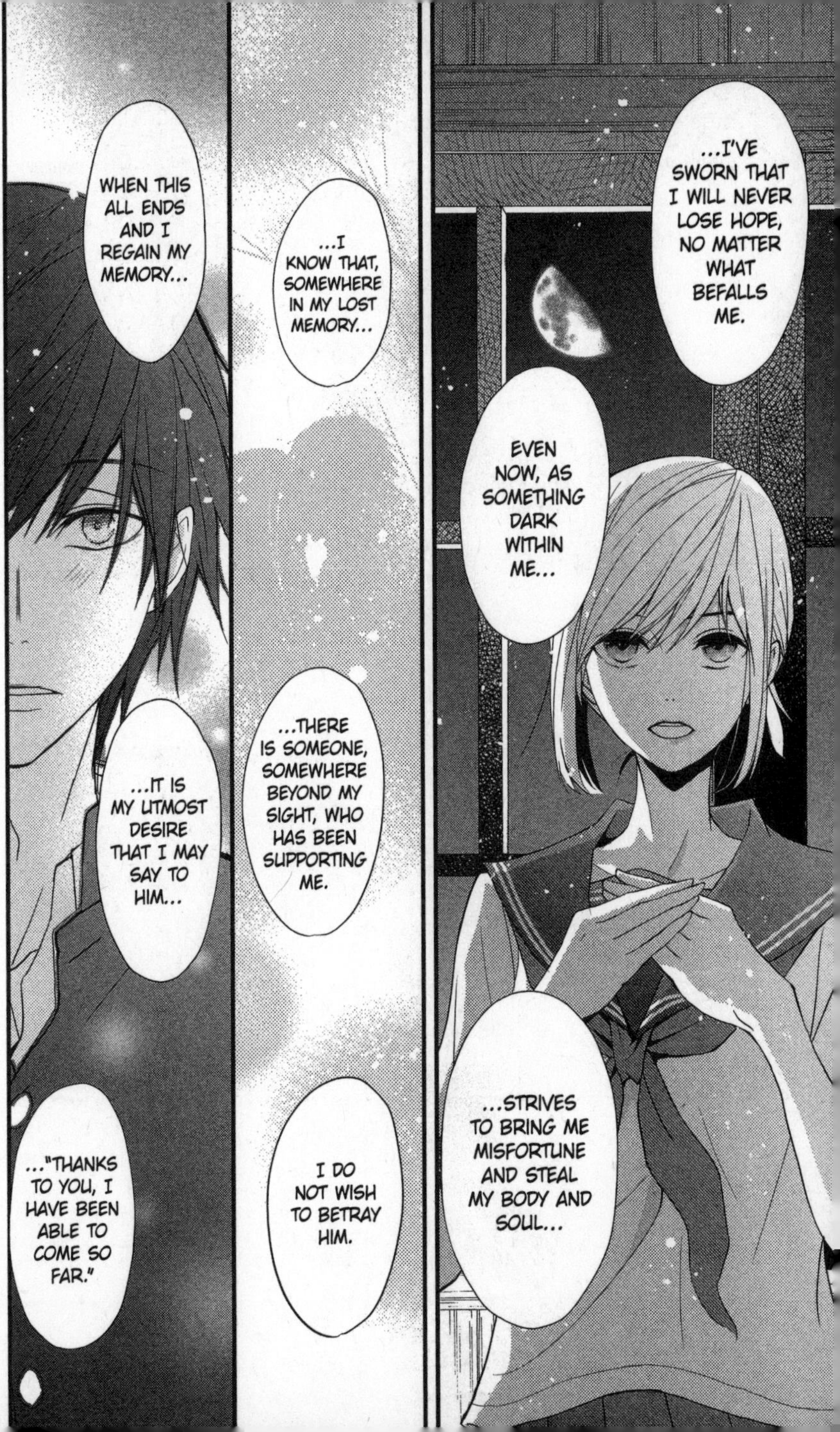
...I'VE SWORN THAT I WILL NEVER LOSE HOPE, NO MATTER WHAT BEFALLS ME.
EVEN NOW, AS SOMETHING DARK WITHIN ME...
...STRIVES TO BRING ME MISFORTUNE AND STEAL MY BODY AND SOUL...
...I KNOW THAT, SOMEWHERE IN MY LOST MEMORY...
...THERE IS SOMEONE, SOMEWHERE BEYOND MY SIGHT, WHO HAS BEEN SUPPORTING ME.
I DO NOT WISH TO BETRAY HIM.
WHEN THIS ALL ENDS AND I REGAIN MY MEMORY...
...IT IS MY UTMOST DESIRE THAT I MAY SAY TO HIM...
..."THANKS TO YOU, I HAVE BEEN ABLE TO COME SO FAR."

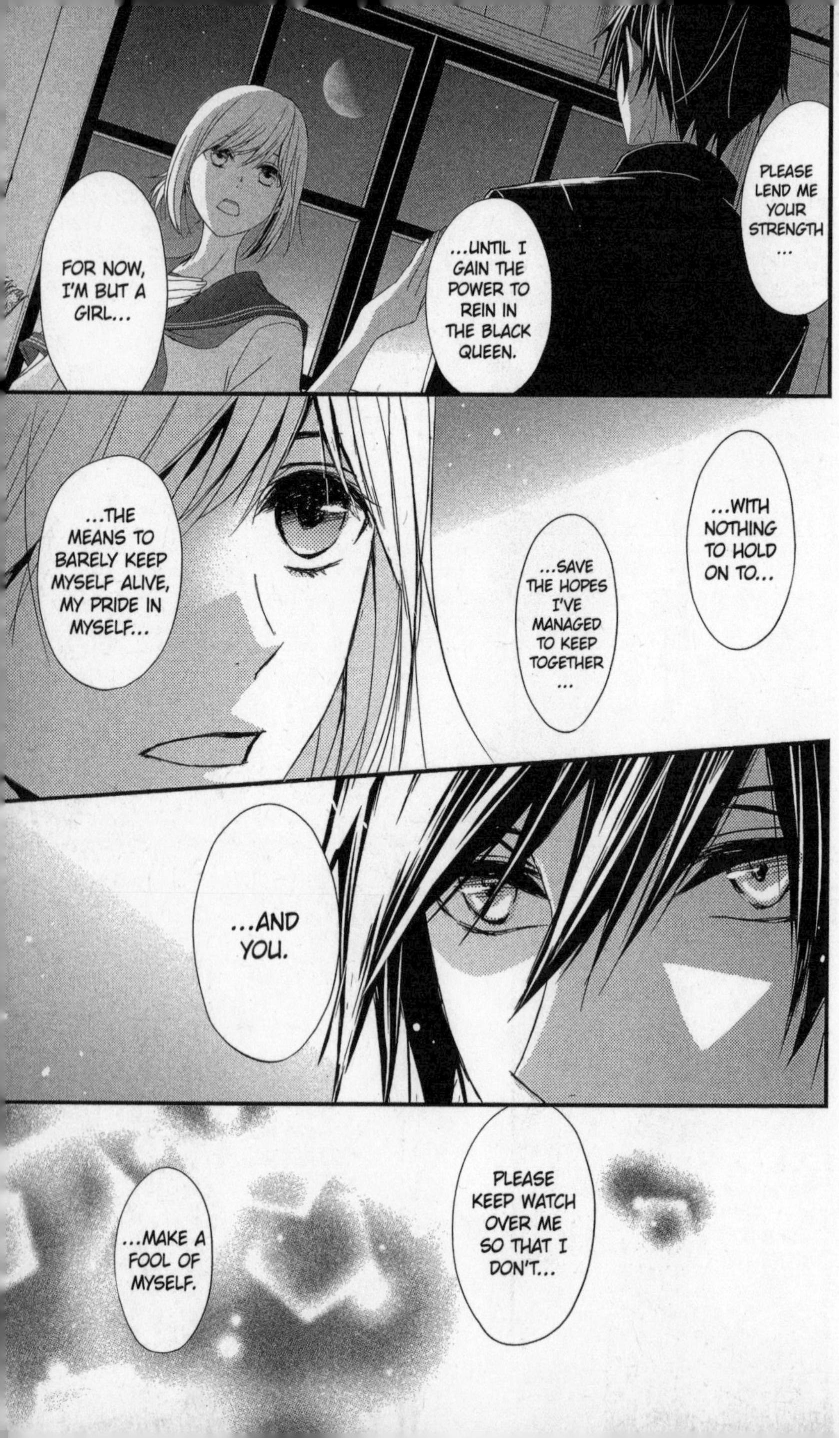
PLEASE LEND ME YOUR STRENGTH...
...UNTIL I GAIN THE POWER TO REIN IN THE BLACK QUEEN.
FOR NOW, I'M BUT A GIRL...
...WITH NOTHING TO HOLD ON TO...
...SAVE THE HOPES I'VE MANAGED TO KEEP TOGETHER...
...THE MEANS TO BARELY KEEP MYSELF ALIVE, MY PRIDE IN MYSELF...
...AND YOU.
PLEASE KEEP WATCH OVER ME SO THAT I DON'T...
...MAKE A FOOL OF MYSELF.

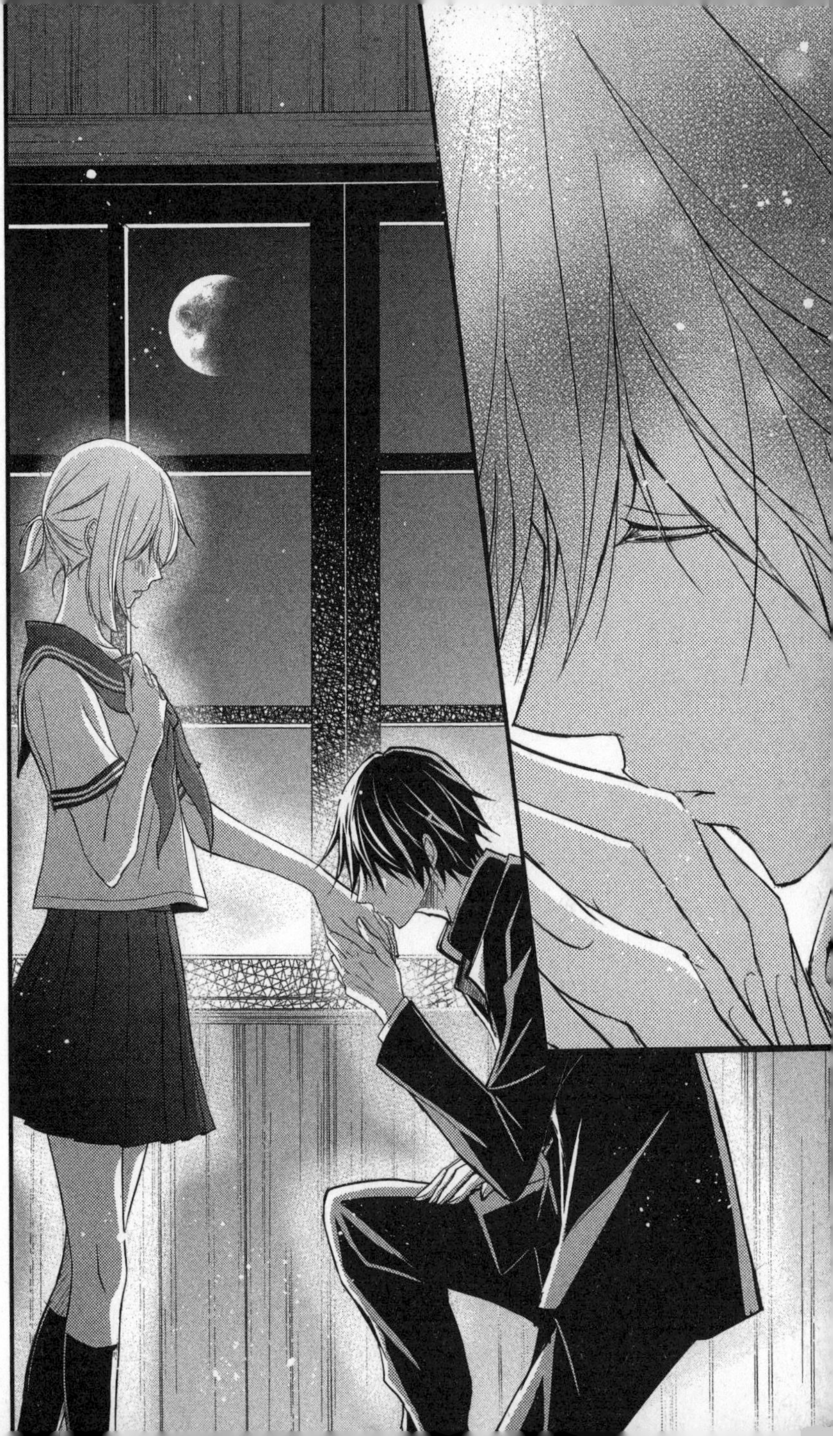

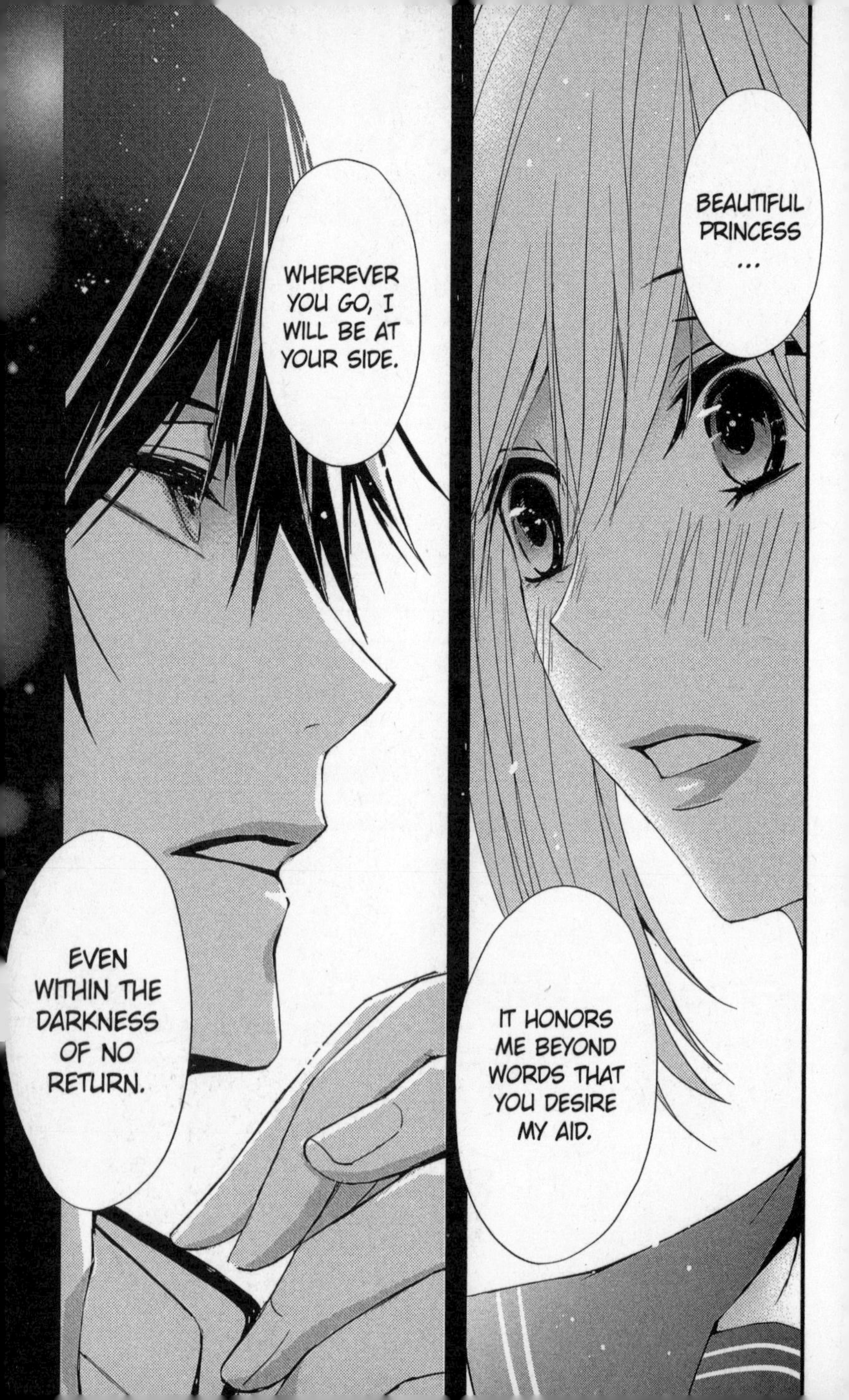
BEAUTIFUL PRINCESS...
IT HONORS ME BEYOND WORDS THAT YOU DESIRE MY AID.
WHEREVER YOU GO, I WILL BE AT YOUR SIDE.
EVEN WITHIN THE DARKNESS OF NO RETURN.

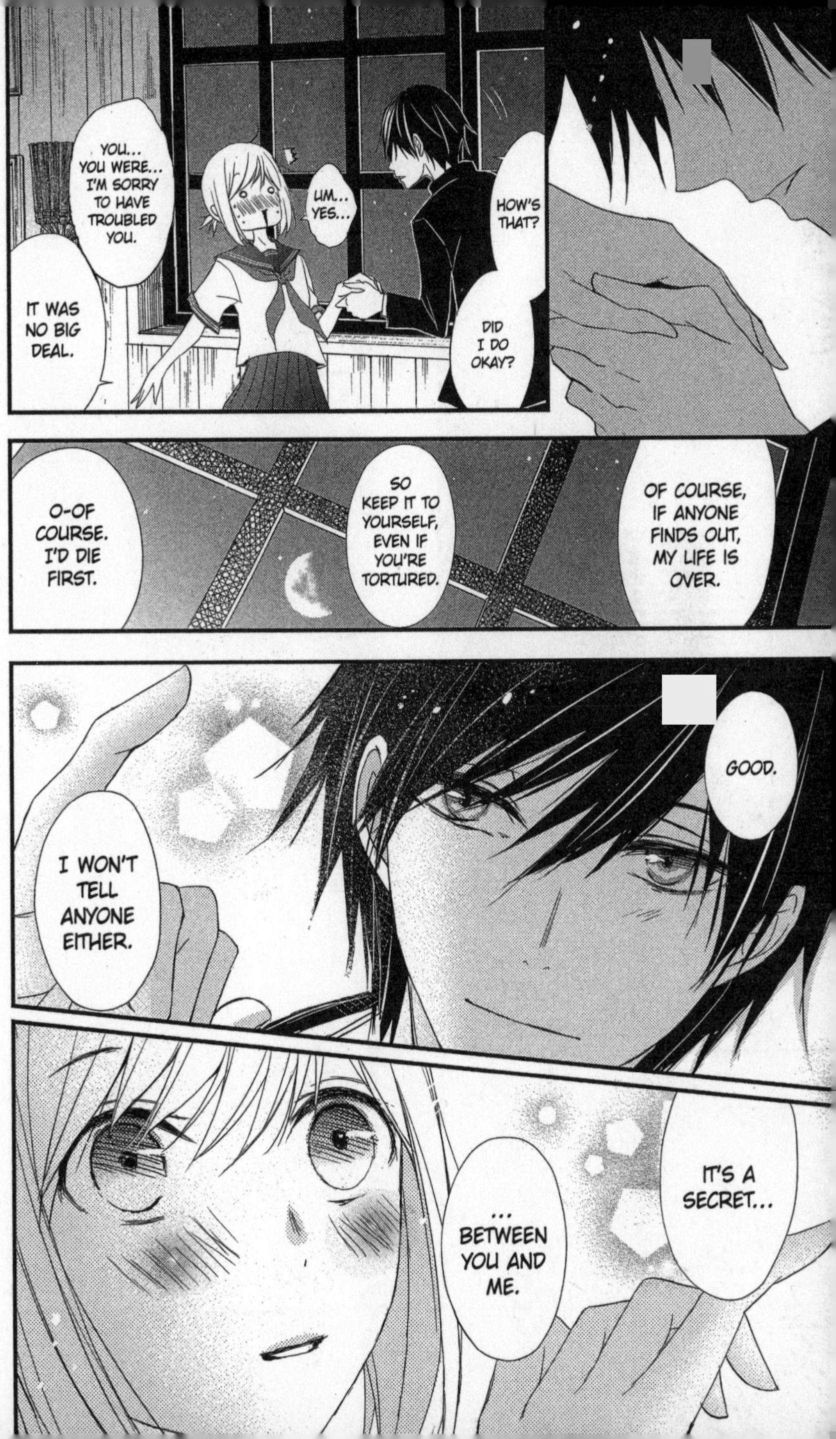
HOW'S THAT?
DID I DO OKAY?
UM... YES...
YOU... YOU WERE... I'M SORRY TO HAVE TROUBLED YOU.
IT WAS NO BIG DEAL.
OF COURSE, IF ANYONE FINDS OUT, MY LIFE IS OVER.
SO KEEP IT TO YOURSELF, EVEN IF YOU'RE TORTURED.
O-OF COURSE. I'D DIE FIRST.
GOOD.
I WON'T TELL ANYONE EITHER.
IT'S A SECRET...
...BETWEEN YOU AND ME.

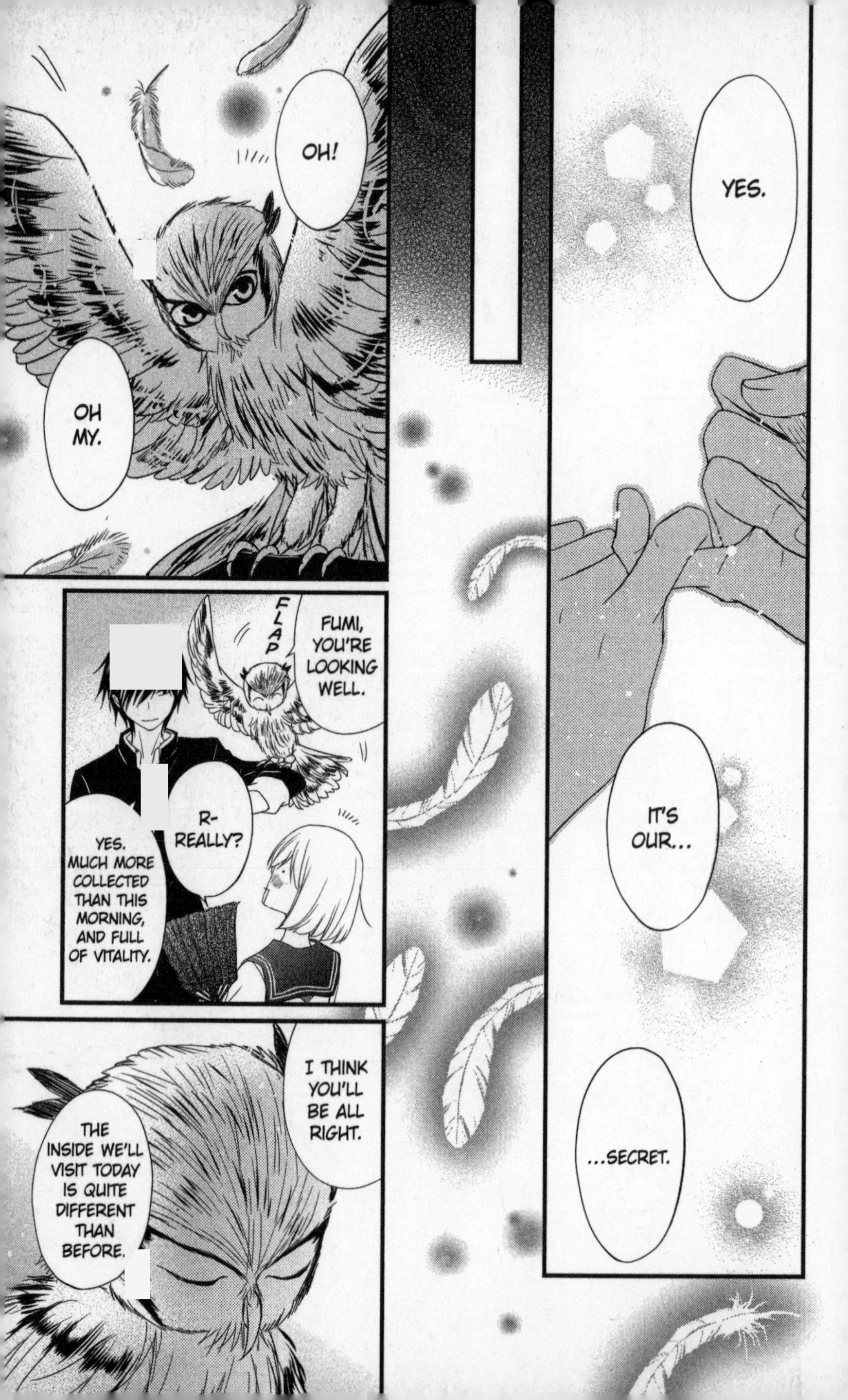
YES.
IT'S OUR...
...SECRET.
OH!
OH MY.
FUMI, YOU'RE LOOKING WELL.
FLAP
R-REALLY?
YES. MUCH MORE COLLECTED THAN THIS MORNING, AND FULL OF VITALITY.
I THINK YOU'LL BE ALL RIGHT.
THE INSIDE WE'LL VISIT TODAY IS QUITE DIFFERENT THAN BEFORE.

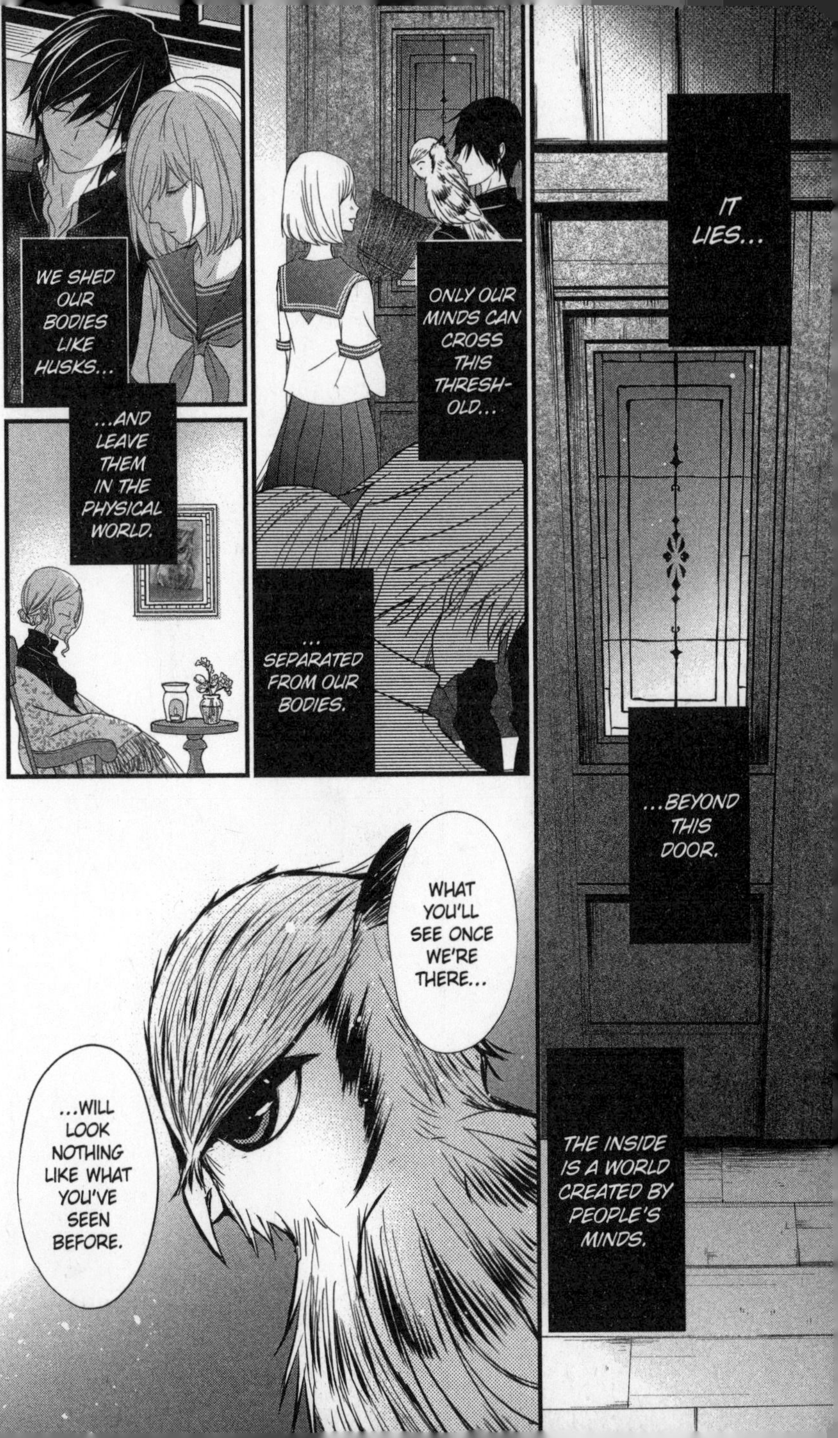
IT LIES...
...BEYOND THIS DOOR.
THE INSIDE IS A WORLD CREATED BY PEOPLE'S MINDS.
ONLY OUR MINDS CAN CROSS THIS THRESH-OLD...
... SEPARATED FROM OUR BODIES.
WE SHED OUR BODIES LIKE HUSKS...
...AND LEAVE THEM IN THE PHYSICAL WORLD.
WHAT YOU'LL SEE ONCE WE'RE THERE...
...WILL LOOK NOTHING LIKE WHAT YOU'VE SEEN BEFORE.

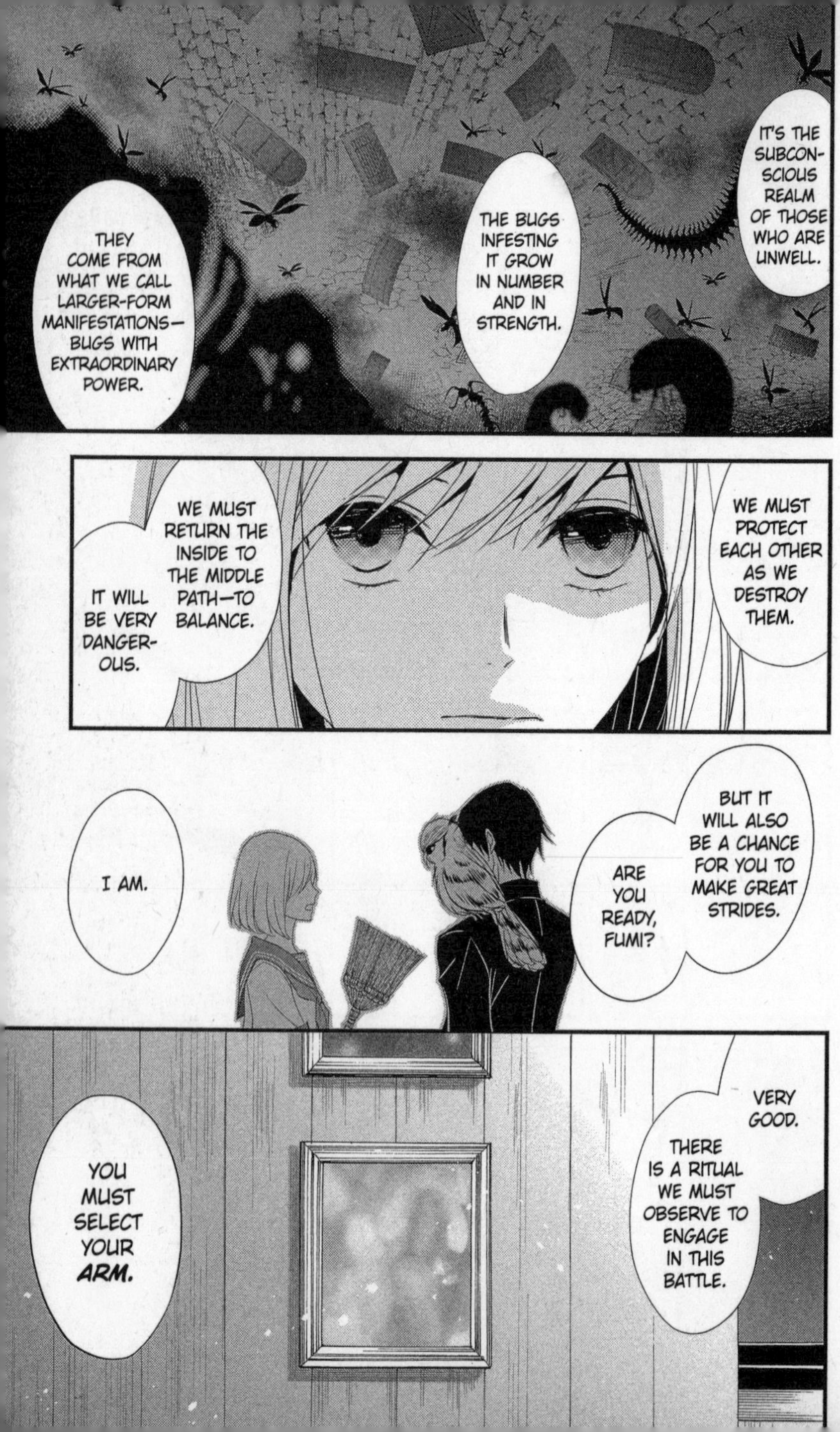
IT'S THE SUBCON-SCIOUS REALM OF THOSE WHO ARE UNWELL.
THE BUGS INFESTING IT GROW IN NUMBER AND IN STRENGTH.
THEY COME FROM WHAT WE CALL LARGER-FORM MANIFESTATIONS—BUGS WITH EXTRAORDINARY POWER.
WE MUST PROTECT EACH OTHER AS WE DESTROY THEM.
WE MUST RETURN THE INSIDE TO THE MIDDLE PATH—TO BALANCE.
IT WILL BE VERY DANGER-OUS.
BUT IT WILL ALSO BE A CHANCE FOR YOU TO MAKE GREAT STRIDES.
ARE YOU READY, FUMI?
I AM.
VERY GOOD.
THERE IS A RITUAL WE MUST OBSERVE TO ENGAGE IN THIS BATTLE.
YOU MUST SELECT YOUR **ARM.**

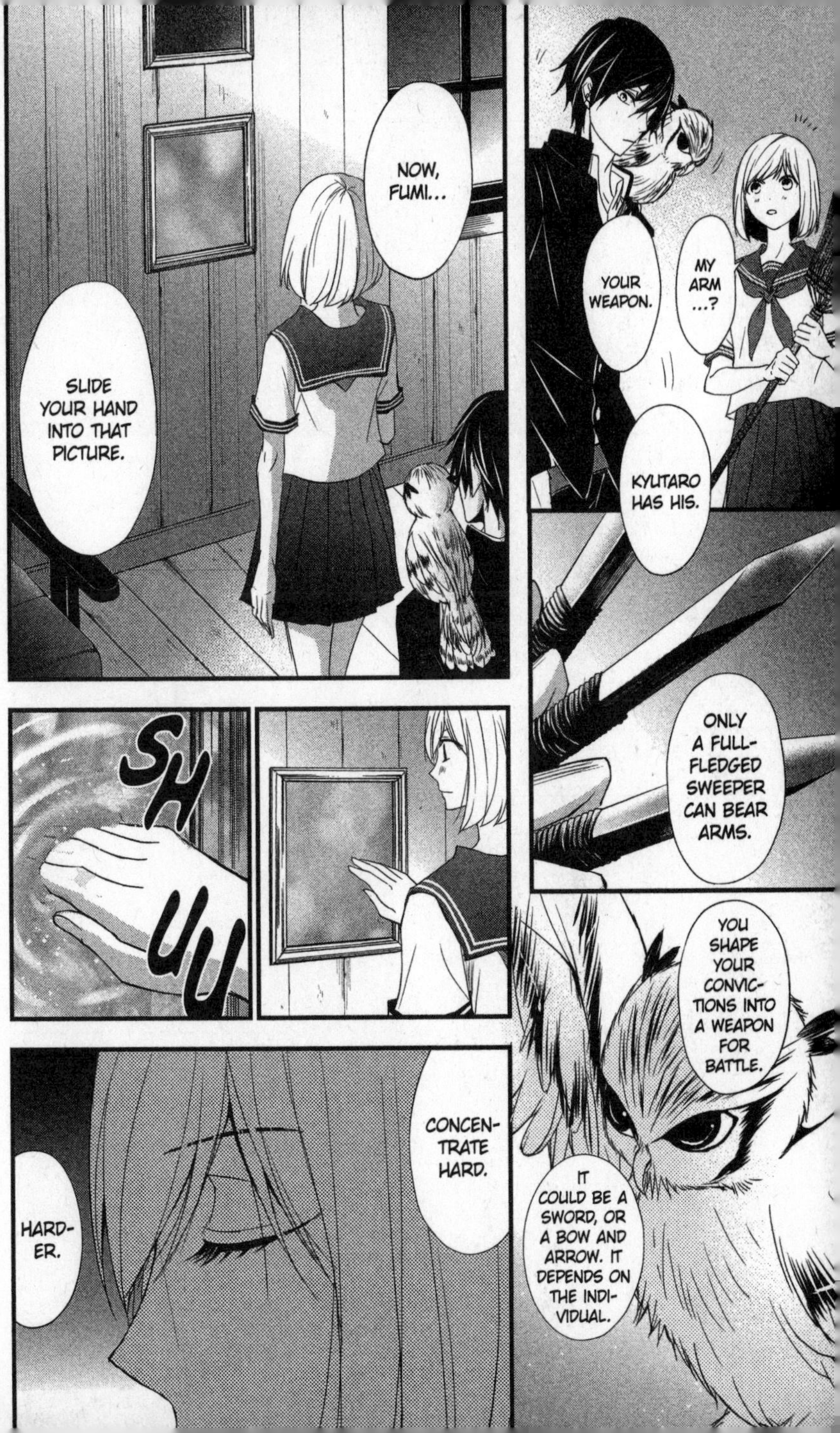
MY ARM ...?
YOUR WEAPON.
KYUTARO HAS HIS.
ONLY A FULL-FLEDGED SWEEPER CAN BEAR ARMS.
YOU SHAPE YOUR CONVICTIONS INTO A WEAPON FOR BATTLE.
IT COULD BE A SWORD, OR A BOW AND ARROW. IT DEPENDS ON THE INDIVIDUAL.
NOW, FUMI...
SLIDE YOUR HAND INTO THAT PICTURE.
SHUU
CONCENTRATE HARD.
HARDER.

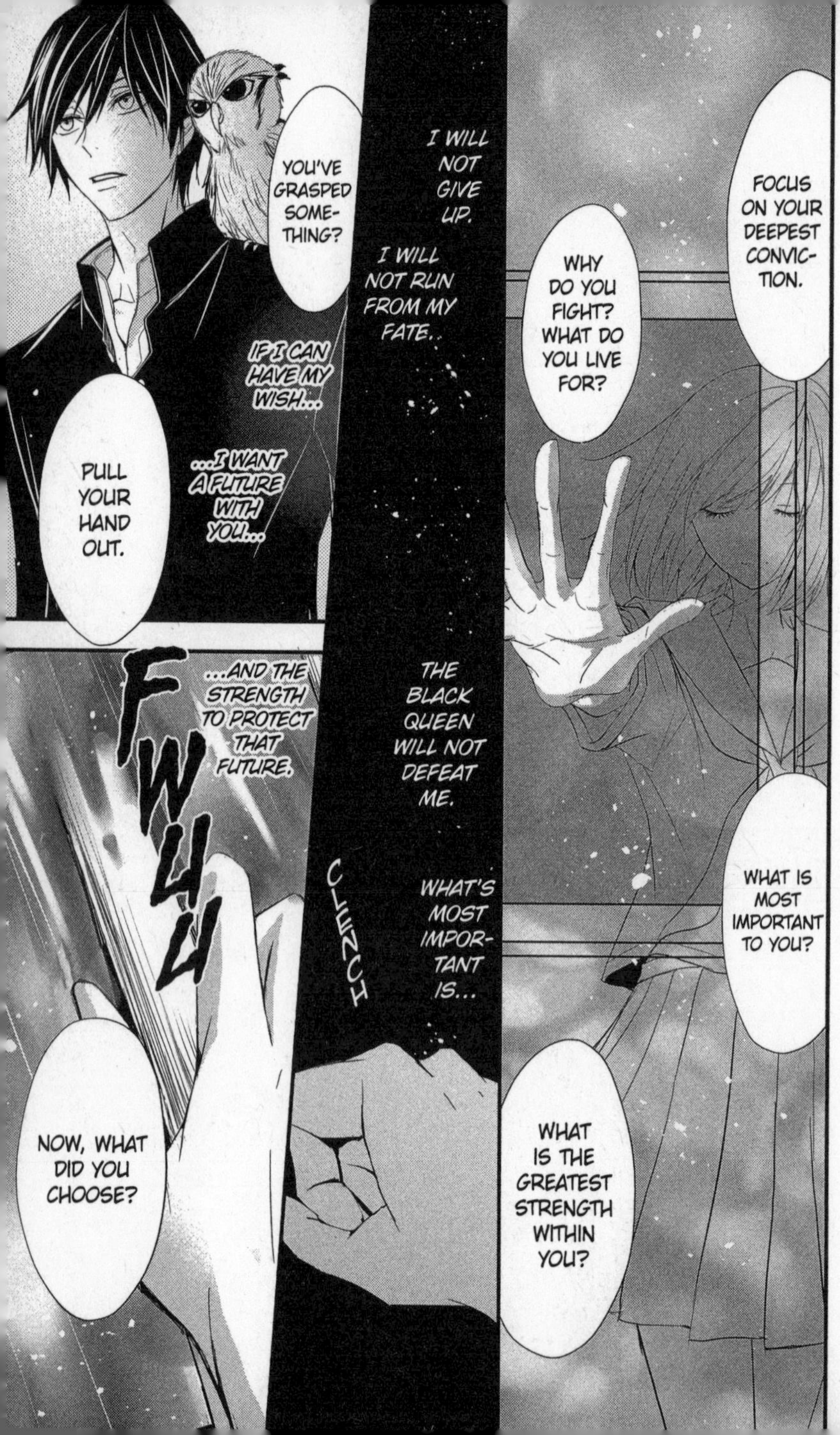
FOCUS ON YOUR DEEPEST CONVICTION.
WHY DO YOU FIGHT? WHAT DO YOU LIVE FOR?
WHAT IS MOST IMPORTANT TO YOU?
WHAT IS THE GREATEST STRENGTH WITHIN YOU?
I WILL NOT GIVE UP.
I WILL NOT RUN FROM MY FATE..
THE BLACK QUEEN WILL NOT DEFEAT ME.
WHAT'S MOST IMPORTANT IS...
CLENCH
YOU'VE GRASPED SOMETHING?
IF I CAN HAVE MY WISH...
...I WANT A FUTURE WITH YOU...
PULL YOUR HAND OUT.
...AND THE STRENGTH TO PROTECT THAT FUTURE.
FWUU
NOW, WHAT DID YOU CHOOSE?

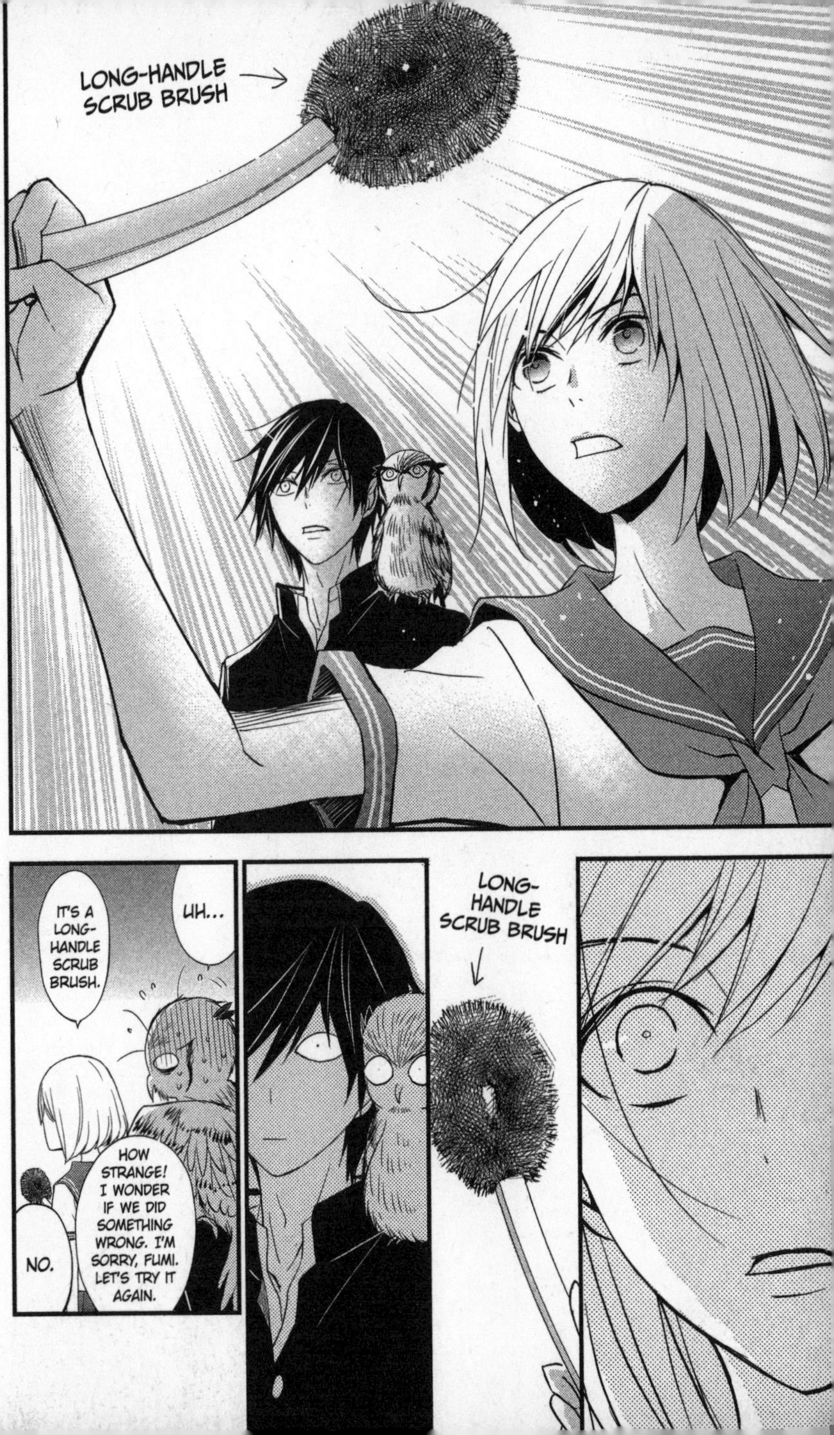
LONG-HANDLE SCRUB BRUSH
LONG-HANDLE SCRUB BRUSH
UH...
IT'S A LONG-HANDLE SCRUB BRUSH.
HOW STRANGE! I WONDER IF WE DID SOMETHING WRONG. I'M SORRY, FUMI. LET'S TRY IT AGAIN.
NO.

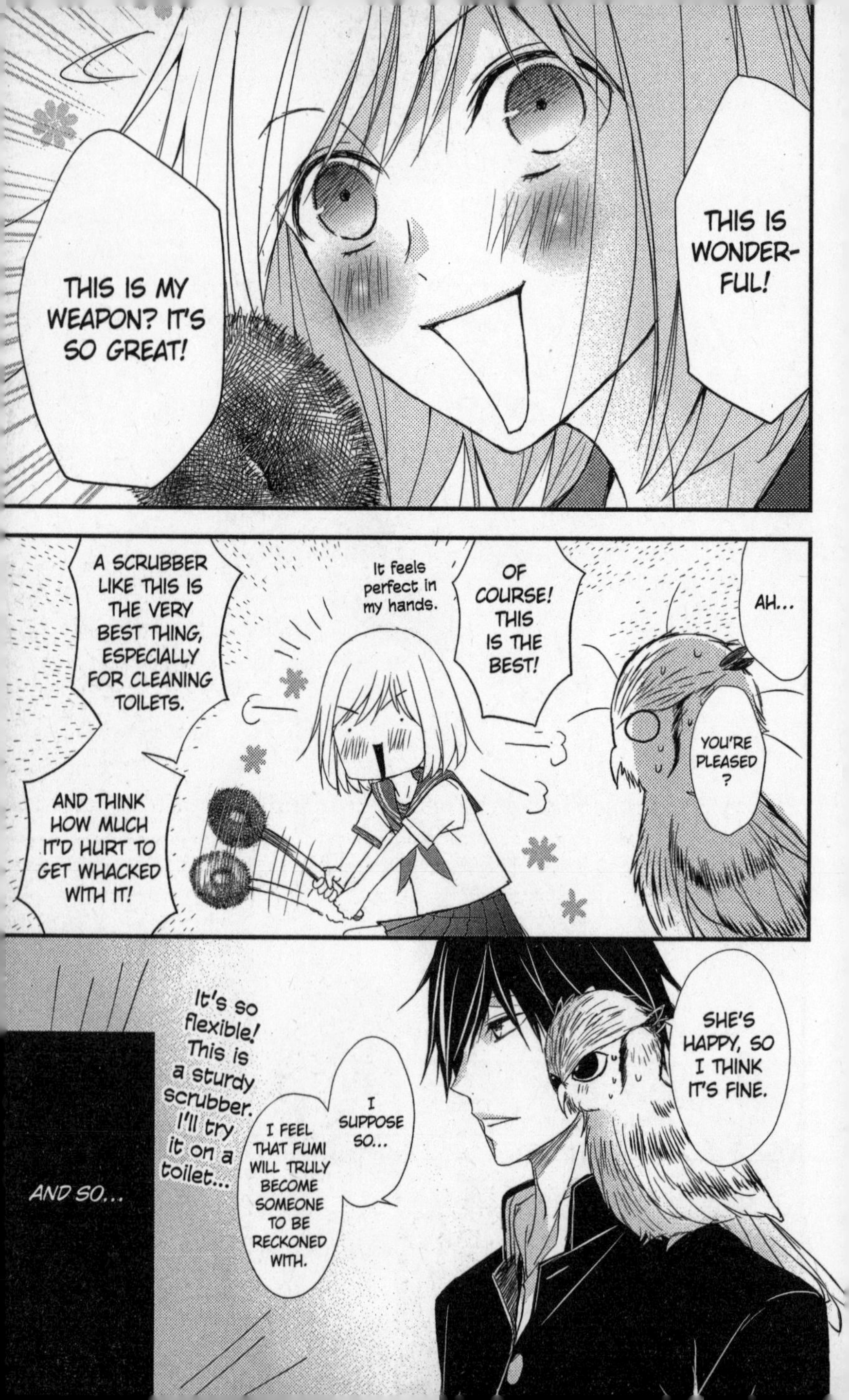
THIS IS WONDERFUL!
THIS IS MY WEAPON? IT'S SO GREAT!
AH...
YOU'RE PLEASED?
OF COURSE! THIS IS THE BEST!
It feels perfect in my hands.
A SCRUBBER LIKE THIS IS THE VERY BEST THING, ESPECIALLY FOR CLEANING TOILETS.
AND THINK HOW MUCH IT'D HURT TO GET WHACKED WITH IT!
SHE'S HAPPY, SO I THINK IT'S FINE.
I SUPPOSE SO...
I FEEL THAT FUMI WILL TRULY BECOME SOMEONE TO BE RECKONED WITH.
It's so flexible! This is a sturdy scrubber. I'll try it on a toilet...
AND SO...

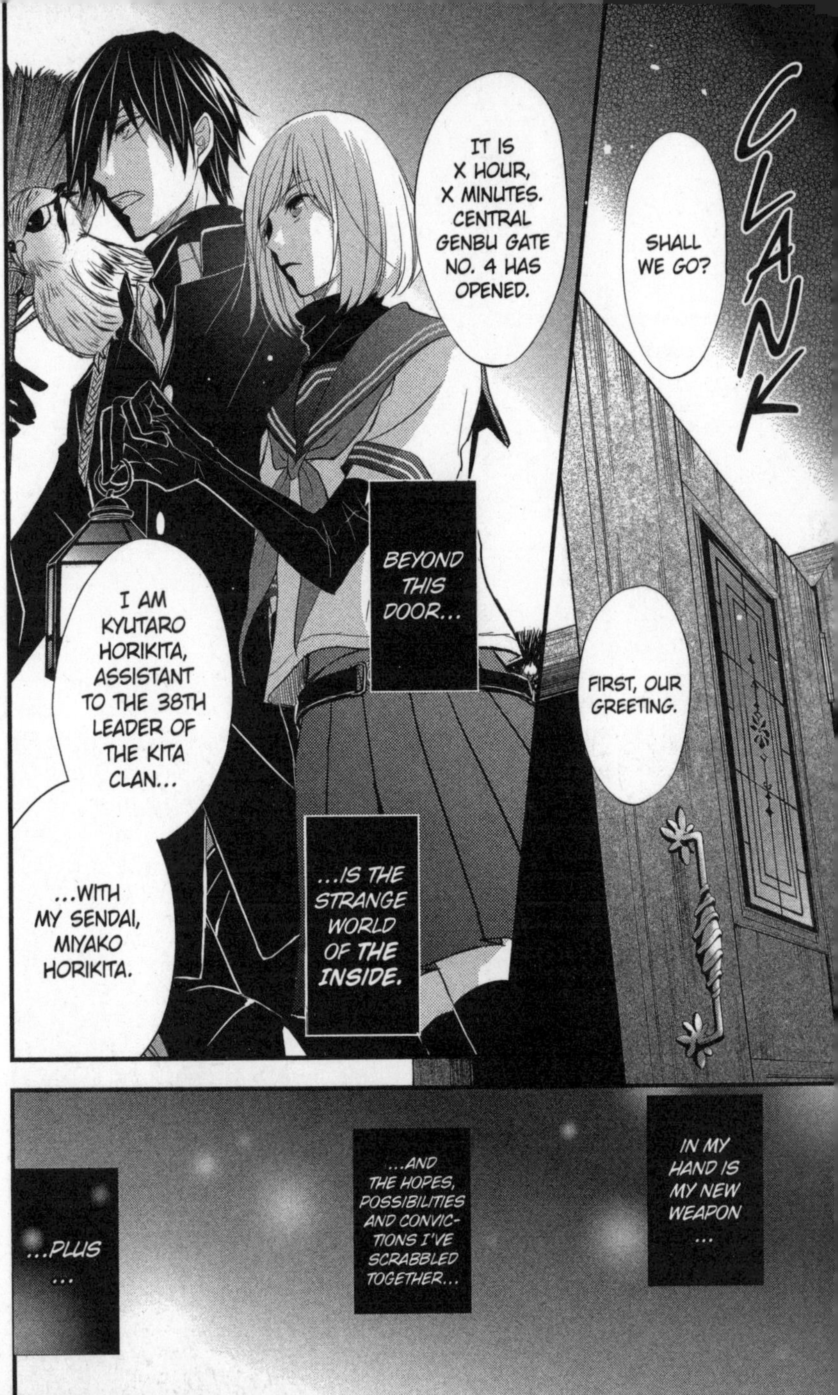
CLANK
SHALL WE GO?
IT IS X HOUR, X MINUTES. CENTRAL GENBU GATE NO. 4 HAS OPENED.
FIRST, OUR GREETING.
BEYOND THIS DOOR...
I AM KYUTARO HORIKITA, ASSISTANT TO THE 38TH LEADER OF THE KITA CLAN...
...IS THE STRANGE WORLD OF THE INSIDE.
...WITH MY SENDAI, MIYAKO HORIKITA.
IN MY HAND IS MY NEW WEAPON...
...AND THE HOPES, POSSIBILITIES AND CONVIC-TIONS I'VE SCRABBLED TOGETHER...
...PLUS...

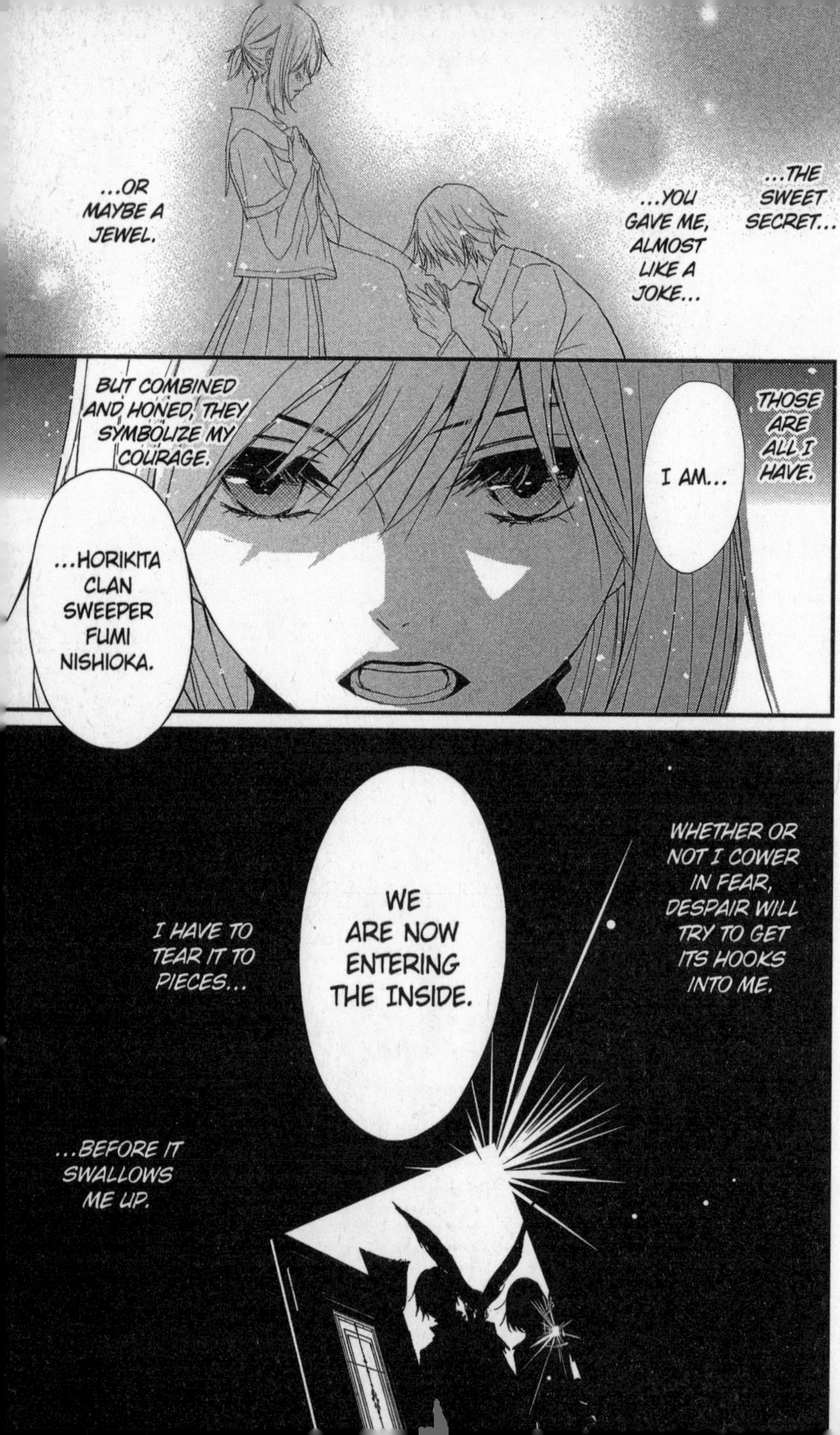
...THE SWEET SECRET...
...YOU GAVE ME, ALMOST LIKE A JOKE...
...OR MAYBE A JEWEL.
THOSE ARE ALL I HAVE.
I AM...
BUT COMBINED AND HONED, THEY SYMBOLIZE MY COURAGE.
...HORIKITA CLAN SWEEPER FUMI NISHIOKA.
WHETHER OR NOT I COWER IN FEAR, DESPAIR WILL TRY TO GET ITS HOOKS INTO ME.
WE ARE NOW ENTERING THE INSIDE.
I HAVE TO TEAR IT TO PIECES...
...BEFORE IT SWALLOWS ME UP.

MONTHLY BETSUCOMI SALE DATE NOTICE ON TWITTER

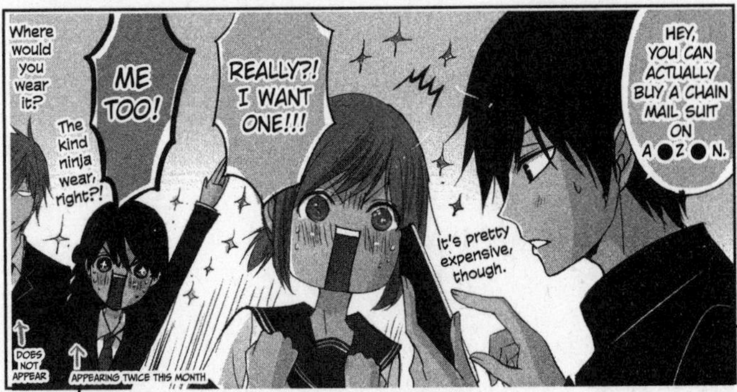
HEY, YOU CAN ACTUALLY BUY A CHAIN MAIL SUIT ON A●Z●N.
It's pretty expensive, though.
REALLY?! I WANT ONE!!!
ME TOO!
Where would you wear it?
The kind ninja wear, right?!
DOES NOT APPEAR
APPEARING TWICE THIS MONTH

CHAPTER 6

Teru and Kurosaki from my previous series *Dengeki Daisy*

WHAT'S UP IN *QUEEN'S QUALITY* THIS MONTH?

(1) THEY AREN'T GERMS... I DIDN'T HAVE MUCH MATERIAL ON FLYING PRAYING MANTISES TO GO BY.
(2) WHAT DO YOU MEAN BY "AND OTHER PLACES" (BESIDES HER HEAD)?
(3) I WANTED A CHAIN MAIL SUIT TOO, WHEN I WAS IN MIDDLE SCHOOL.

IN CHAPTER 6, FUMI FINALLY ATTAINS THAT MOST POWERFUL THING!

WHAT'S UP IN *QUEEN'S QUALITY* THIS MONTH?

(1) SUDDENLY SHE'S IN KNEE-HIGHS!
(2) LISTEN, KYUTARO. IF YOU HUG HER FROM BEHIND LIKE THAT, YOU'LL GET THAT SCRUB BRUSH!
(3) HUH? IS THAT A NEW CHARACTER?

IN CHAPTER 7, SOMETHING IS GOING ON THAT KYUTARO KNOWS NOTHING ABOUT!

This is also Kurosaki.

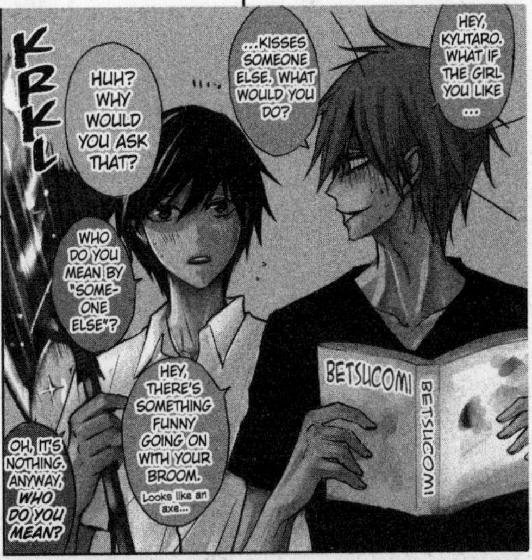
HEY, KYUTARO. WHAT IF THE GIRL YOU LIKE ...
...KISSES SOMEONE ELSE. WHAT WOULD YOU DO?
HUH? WHY WOULD YOU ASK THAT?
KRKL
WHO DO YOU MEAN BY "SOMEONE ELSE"?
HEY, THERE'S SOMETHING FUNNY GOING ON WITH YOUR BROOM.
Looks like an axe...
OH, IT'S NOTHING. ANYWAY, WHO DO YOU MEAN?
BETSUCOMI
BETSUCOMI

CHAPTER 7

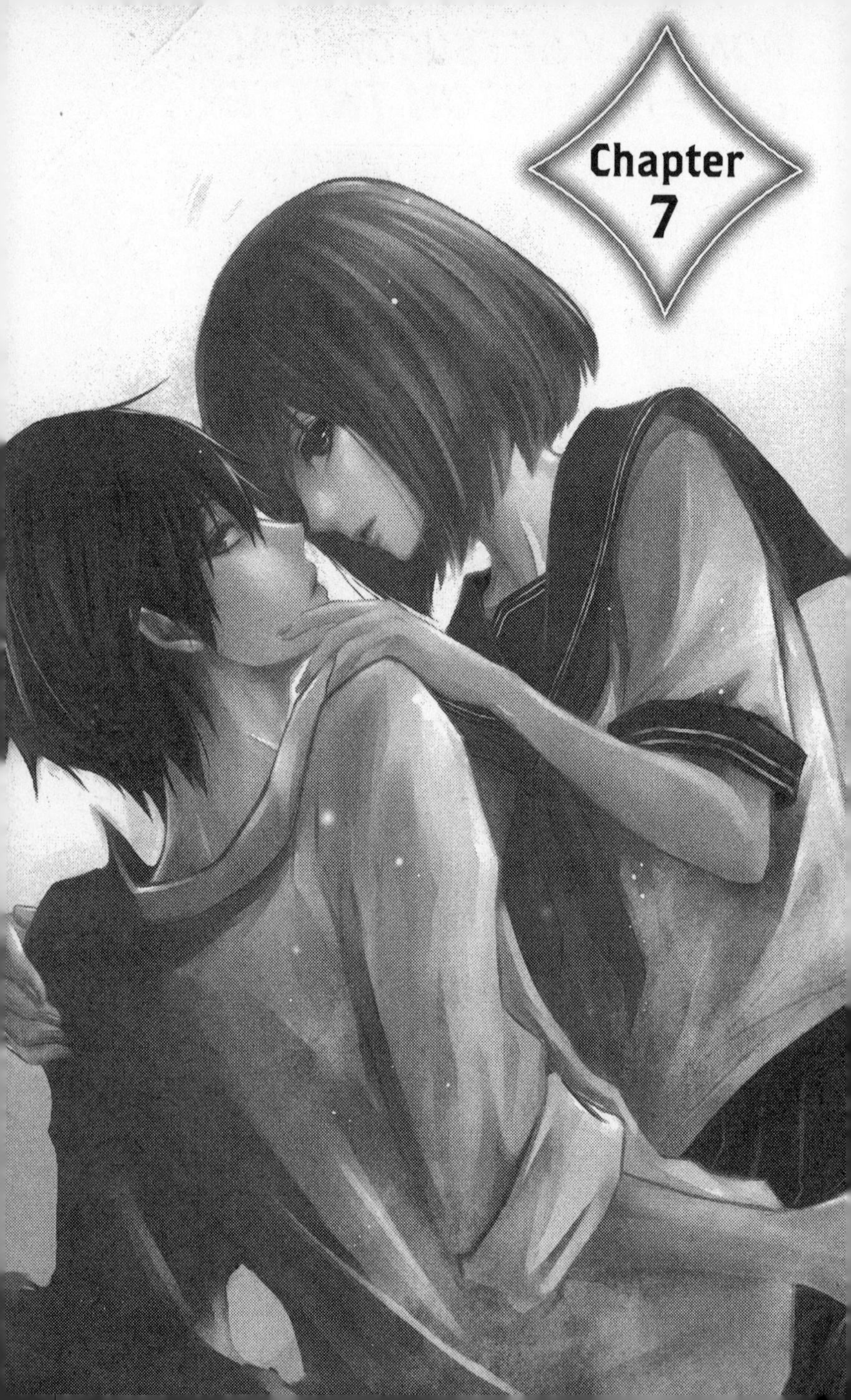
Chapter
7

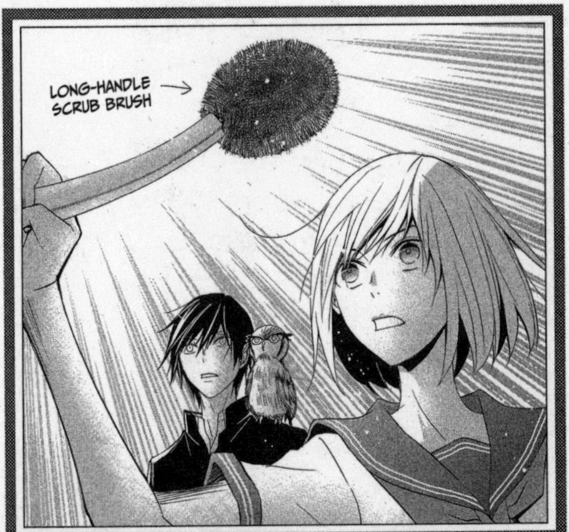
LONG-HANDLE
SCRUB BRUSH

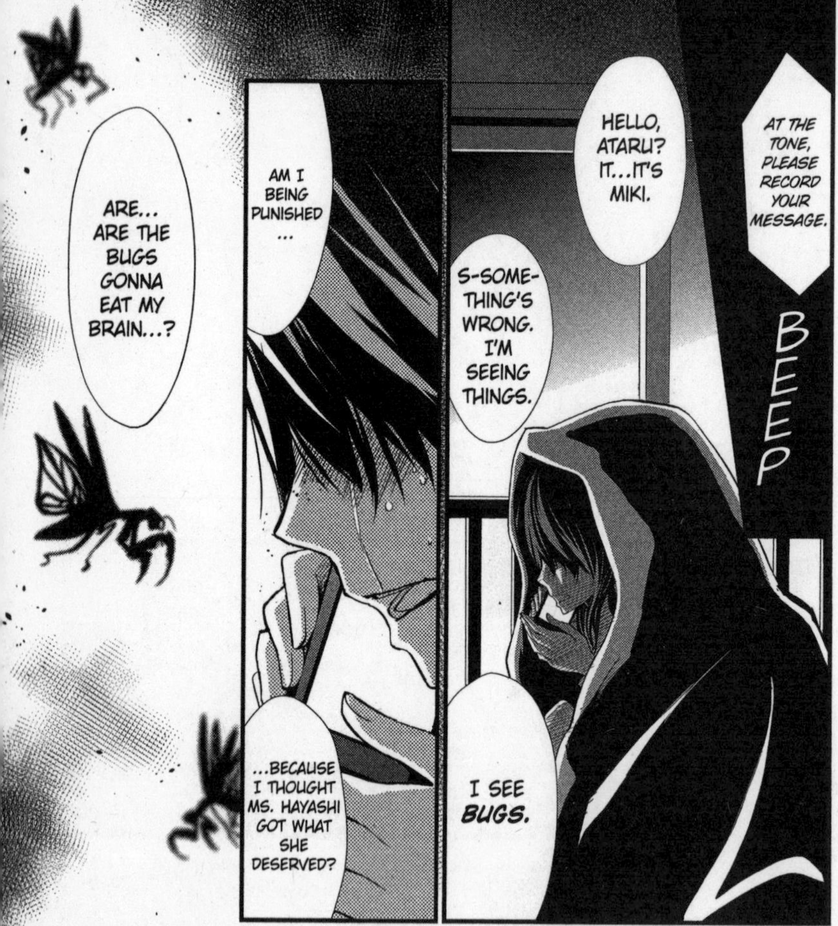
AT THE TONE, PLEASE RECORD YOUR MESSAGE.
BEEP
HELLO, ATARU? IT...IT'S MIKI.
S-SOMETHING'S WRONG. I'M SEEING THINGS.
I SEE *BUGS.*
AM I BEING PUNISHED...
...BECAUSE I THOUGHT MS. HAYASHI GOT WHAT SHE DESERVED?
ARE... ARE THE BUGS GONNA EAT MY BRAIN...?

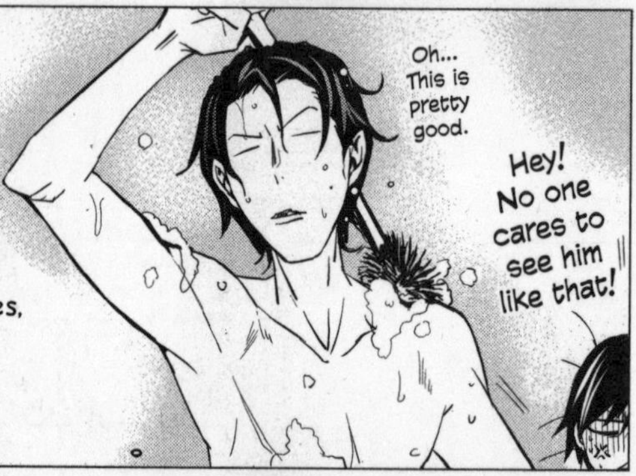
Oh... This is pretty good.
Hey! No one cares to see him like that!

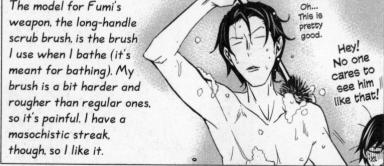

The model for Fumi's weapon, the long-handle scrub brush, is the brush I use when I bathe (it's meant for bathing). My brush is a bit harder and rougher than regular ones, so it's painful. I have a masochistic streak, though, so I like it.

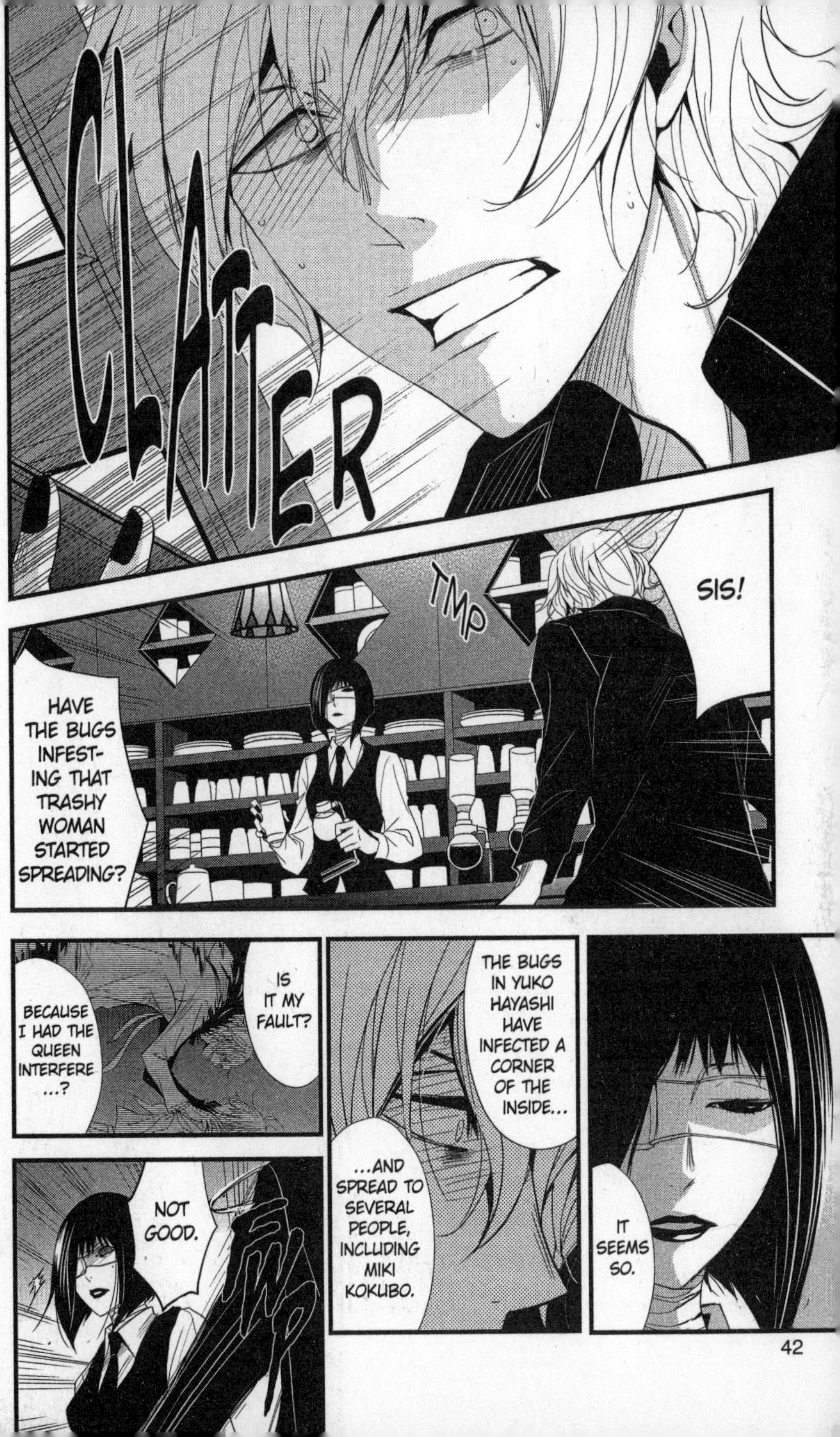
CLATTER
SIS!
TMP
HAVE THE BUGS INFESTING THAT TRASHY WOMAN STARTED SPREADING?
IT SEEMS SO.
THE BUGS IN YUKO HAYASHI HAVE INFECTED A CORNER OF THE INSIDE...
...AND SPREAD TO SEVERAL PEOPLE, INCLUDING MIKI KOKUBO.
IS IT MY FAULT?
BECAUSE I HAD THE QUEEN INTERFERE...?
NOT GOOD.

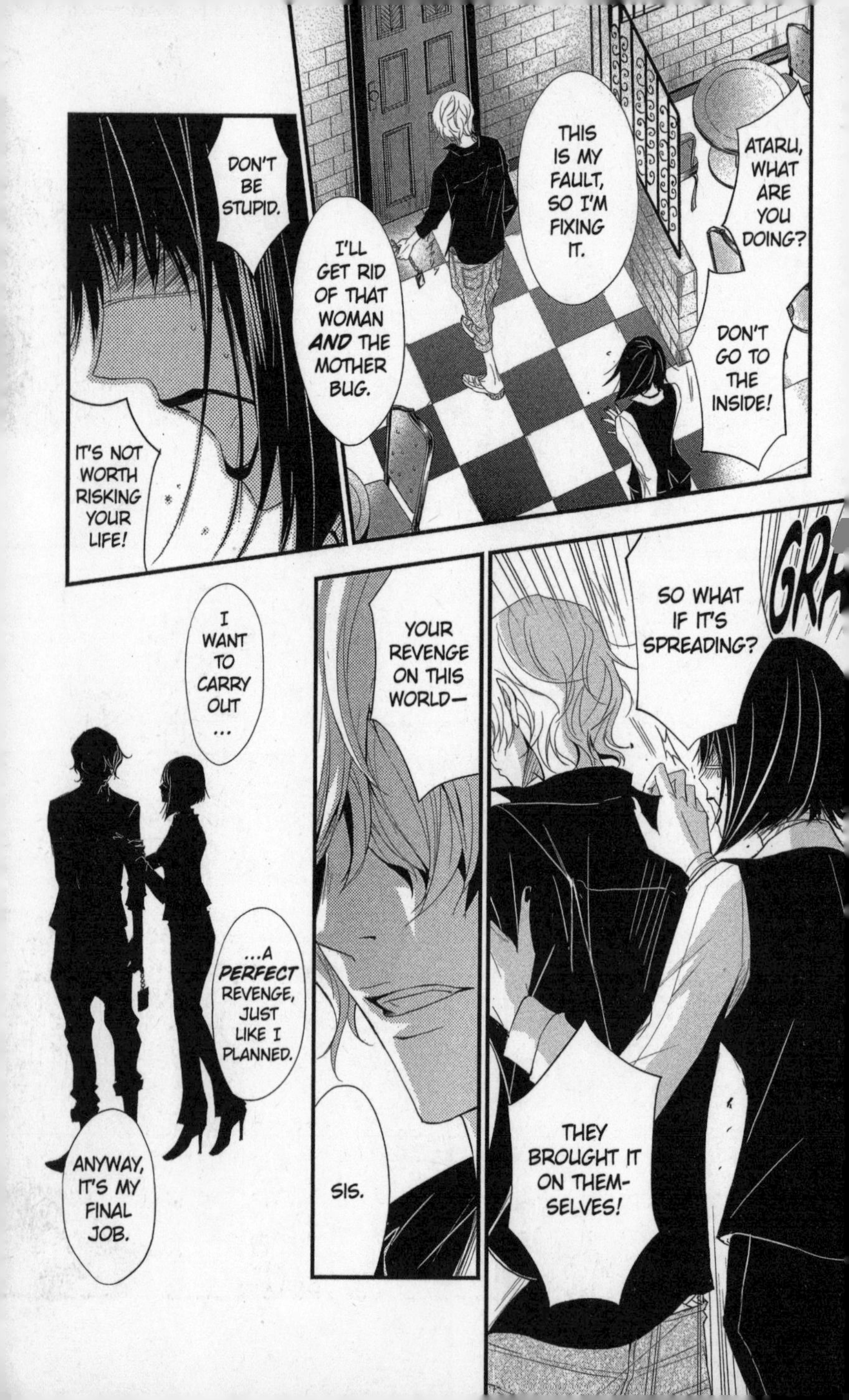
ATARU, WHAT ARE YOU DOING?
THIS IS MY FAULT, SO I'M FIXING IT.
DON'T GO TO THE INSIDE!
I'LL GET RID OF THAT WOMAN **AND** THE MOTHER BUG.
DON'T BE STUPID.
IT'S NOT WORTH RISKING YOUR LIFE!
GR
SO WHAT IF IT'S SPREADING?
THEY BROUGHT IT ON THEM-SELVES!
YOUR REVENGE ON THIS WORLD—
SIS.
I WANT TO CARRY OUT ...
...A ***PERFECT*** REVENGE, JUST LIKE I PLANNED.
ANYWAY, IT'S MY FINAL JOB.

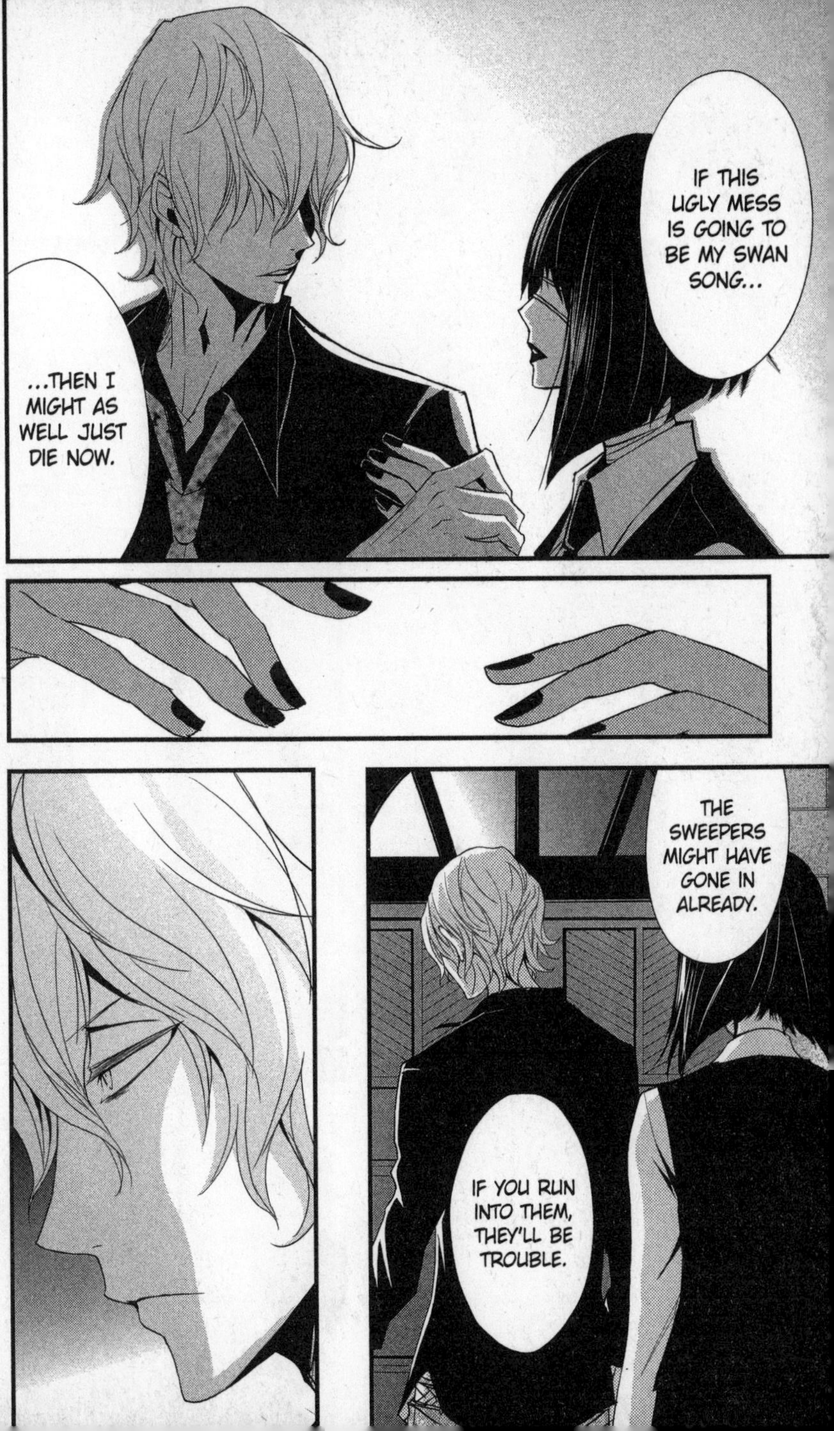
IF THIS UGLY MESS IS GOING TO BE MY SWAN SONG...
...THEN I MIGHT AS WELL JUST DIE NOW.
THE SWEEPERS MIGHT HAVE GONE IN ALREADY.
IF YOU RUN INTO THEM, THEY'LL BE TROUBLE.

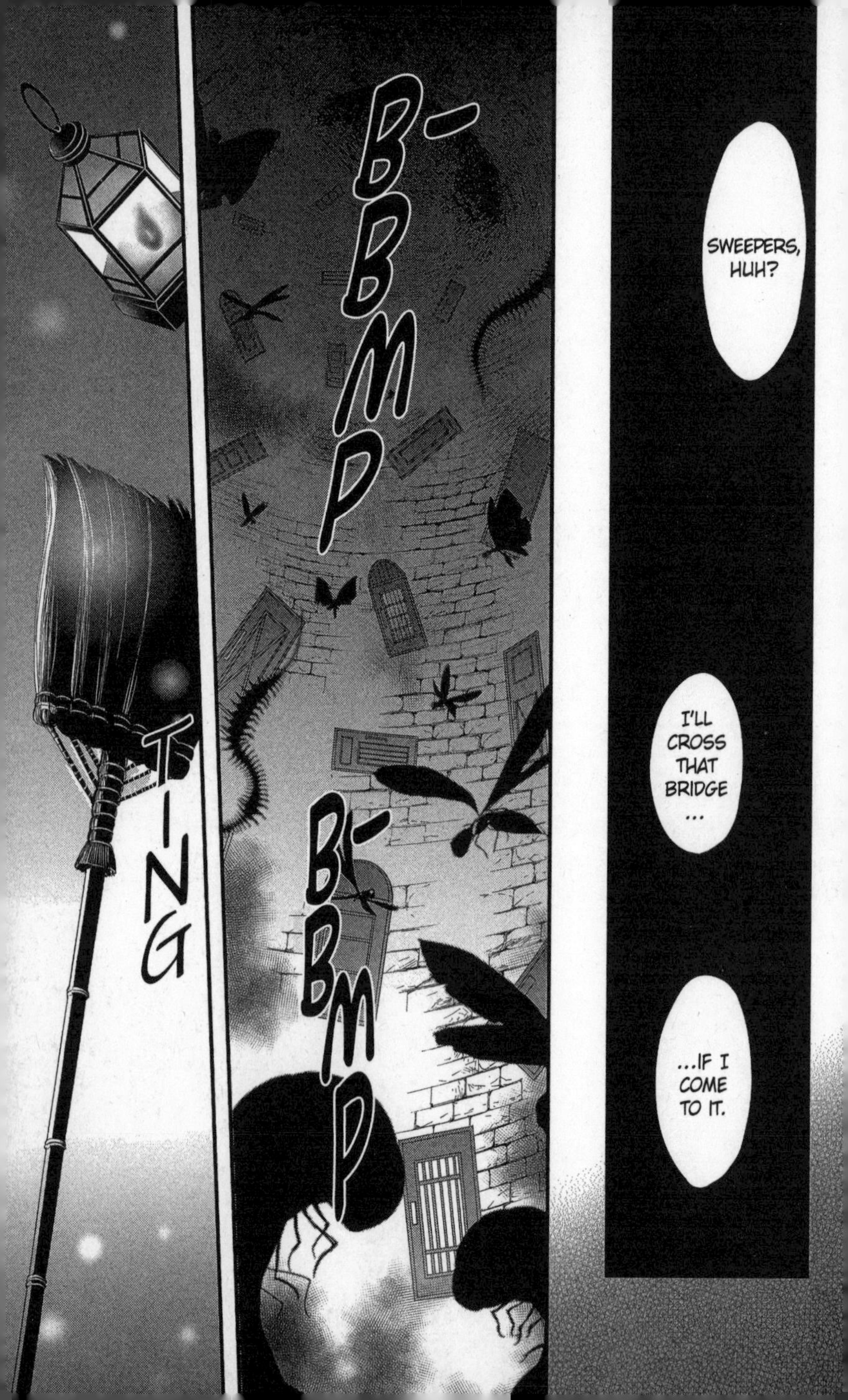
SWEEPERS, HUH?
I'LL CROSS THAT BRIDGE ...
...IF I COME TO IT.
B-BBMP
B-BBMP
TING

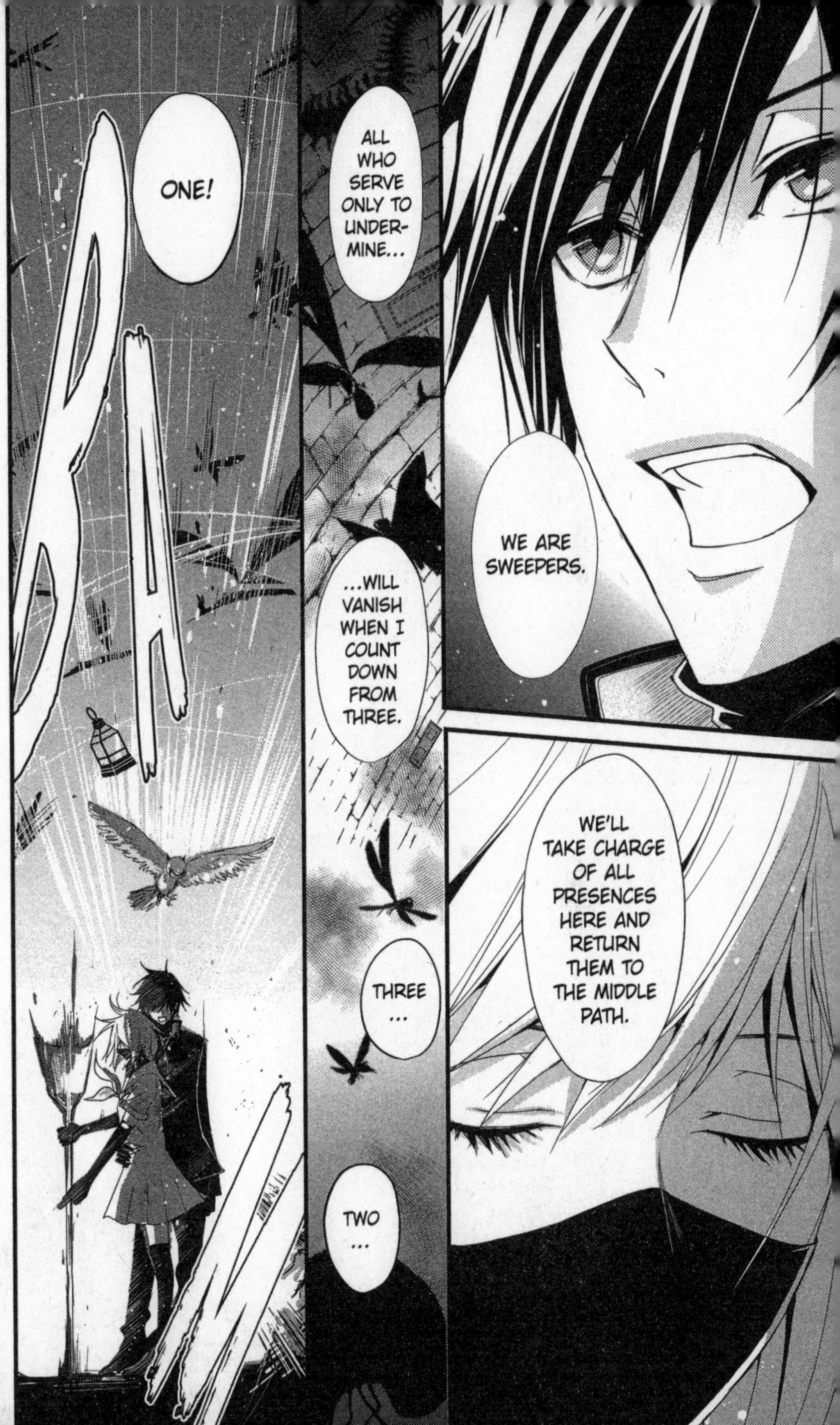
WE ARE SWEEPERS.
WE'LL TAKE CHARGE OF ALL PRESENCES HERE AND RETURN THEM TO THE MIDDLE PATH.
ALL WHO SERVE ONLY TO UNDERMINE...
...WILL VANISH WHEN I COUNT DOWN FROM THREE.
THREE ...
TWO ...
ONE!

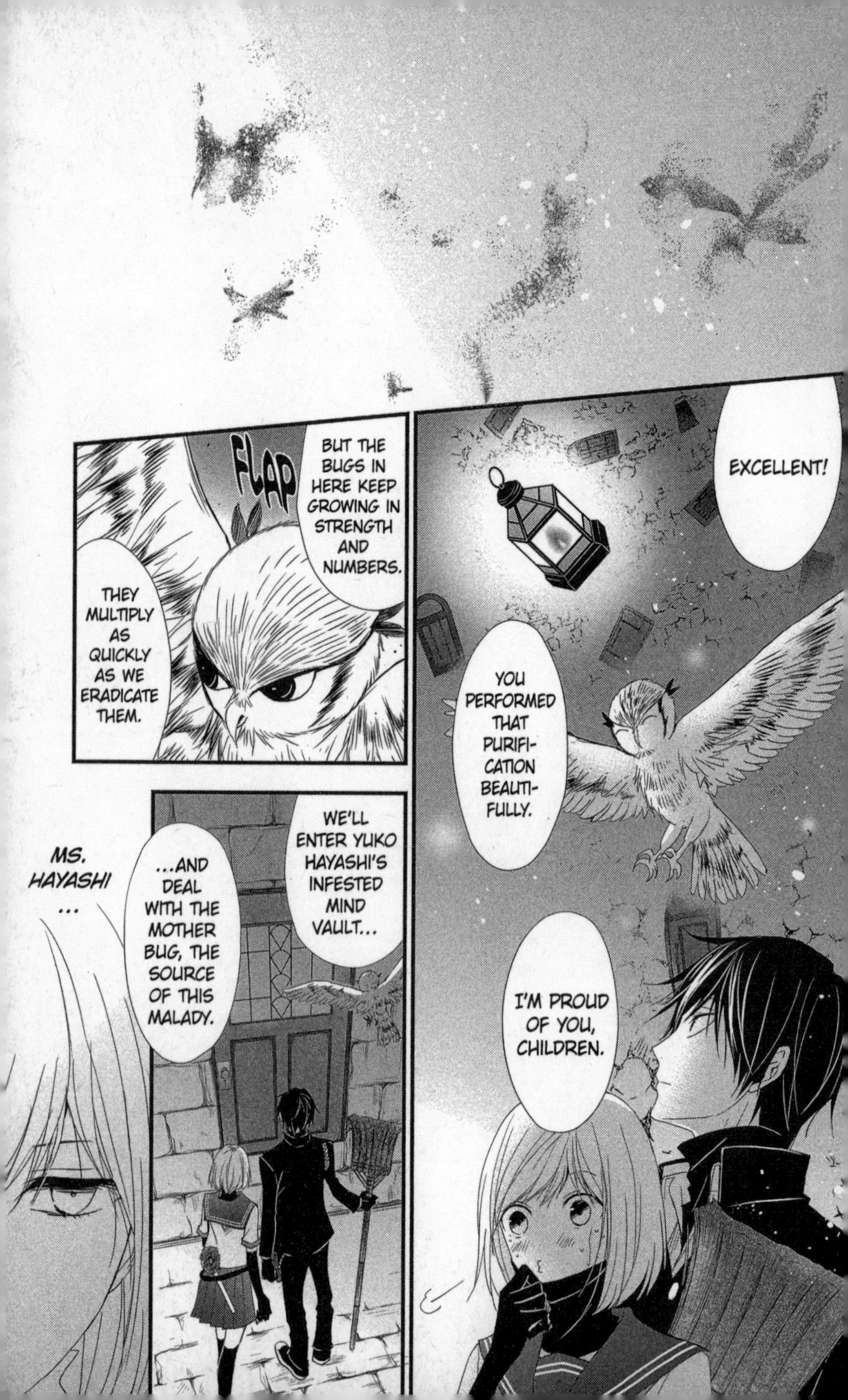
EXCELLENT!
YOU PERFORMED THAT PURIFICATION BEAUTIFULLY.
I'M PROUD OF YOU, CHILDREN.
FLAP
BUT THE BUGS IN HERE KEEP GROWING IN STRENGTH AND NUMBERS.
THEY MULTIPLY AS QUICKLY AS WE ERADICATE THEM.
WE'LL ENTER YUKO HAYASHI'S INFESTED MIND VAULT...
...AND DEAL WITH THE MOTHER BUG, THE SOURCE OF THIS MALADY.
MS. HAYASHI...

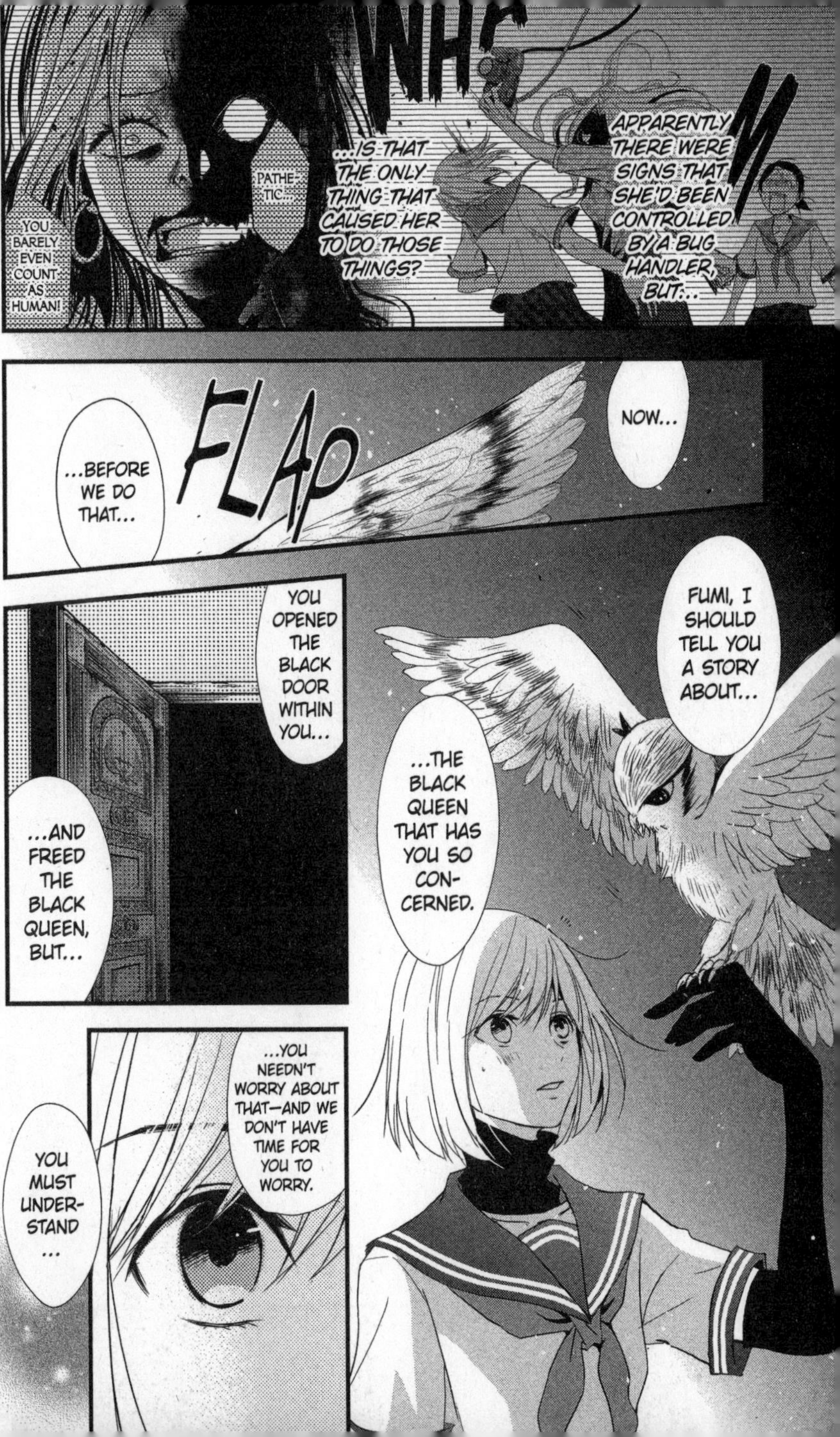
APPARENTLY THERE WERE SIGNS THAT SHE'D BEEN CONTROLLED BY A BUG HANDLER, BUT...
...IS THAT THE ONLY THING THAT CAUSED HER TO DO THOSE THINGS?
PATHETIC...
YOU BARELY EVEN COUNT AS HUMAN!
NOW...
FLAP
...BEFORE WE DO THAT...
FUMI, I SHOULD TELL YOU A STORY ABOUT...
...THE BLACK QUEEN THAT HAS YOU SO CONCERNED.
YOU OPENED THE BLACK DOOR WITHIN YOU...
...AND FREED THE BLACK QUEEN, BUT...
...YOU NEEDN'T WORRY ABOUT THAT—AND WE DON'T HAVE TIME FOR YOU TO WORRY.
YOU MUST UNDERSTAND...

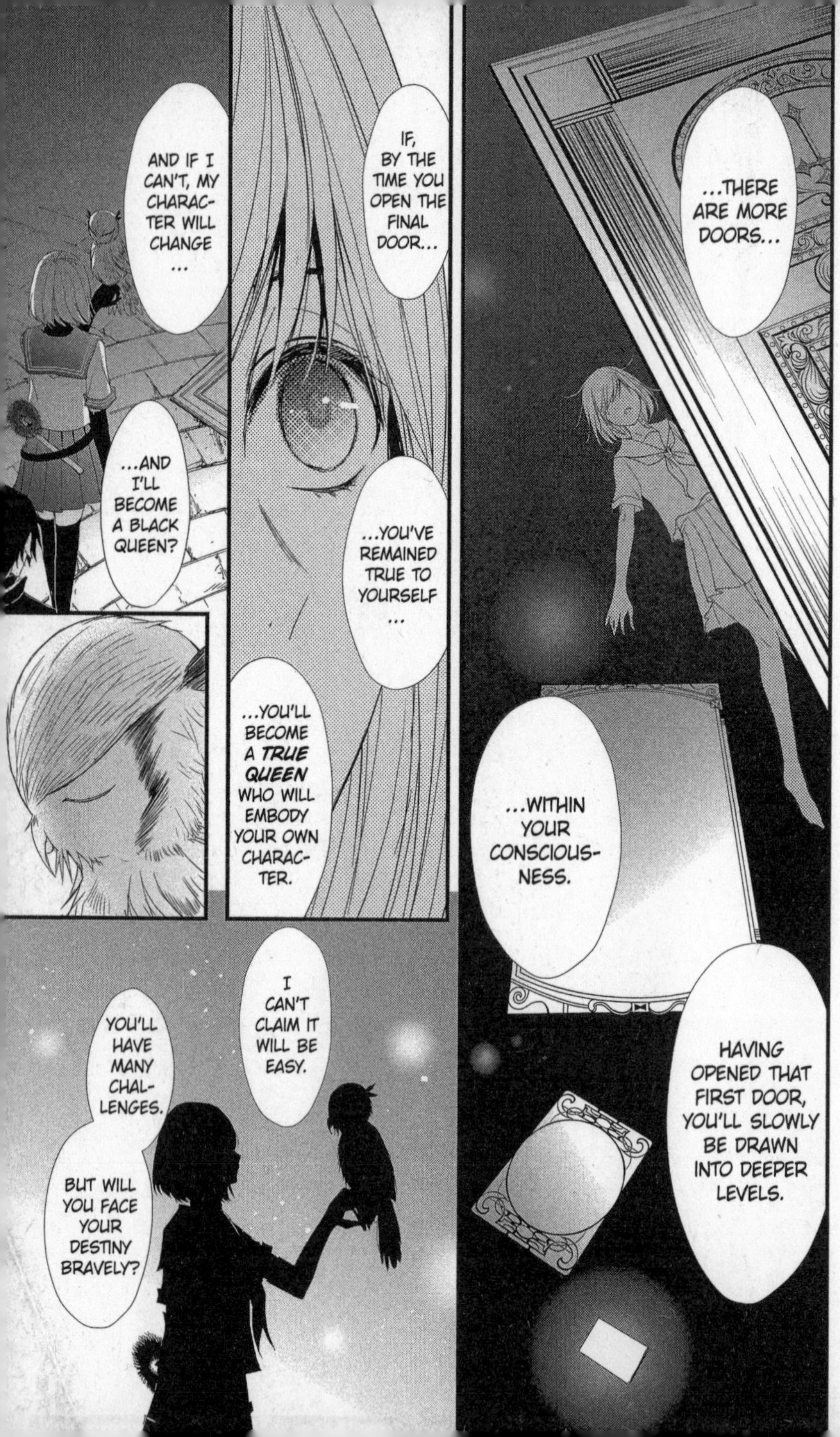
...THERE ARE MORE DOORS...
...WITHIN YOUR CONSCIOUSNESS.
HAVING OPENED THAT FIRST DOOR, YOU'LL SLOWLY BE DRAWN INTO DEEPER LEVELS.
IF, BY THE TIME YOU OPEN THE FINAL DOOR...
...YOU'VE REMAINED TRUE TO YOURSELF...
...YOU'LL BECOME A ***TRUE QUEEN*** WHO WILL EMBODY YOUR OWN CHARACTER.
AND IF I CAN'T, MY CHARACTER WILL CHANGE...
...AND I'LL BECOME A BLACK QUEEN?
I CAN'T CLAIM IT WILL BE EASY.
YOU'LL HAVE MANY CHALLENGES.
BUT WILL YOU FACE YOUR DESTINY BRAVELY?

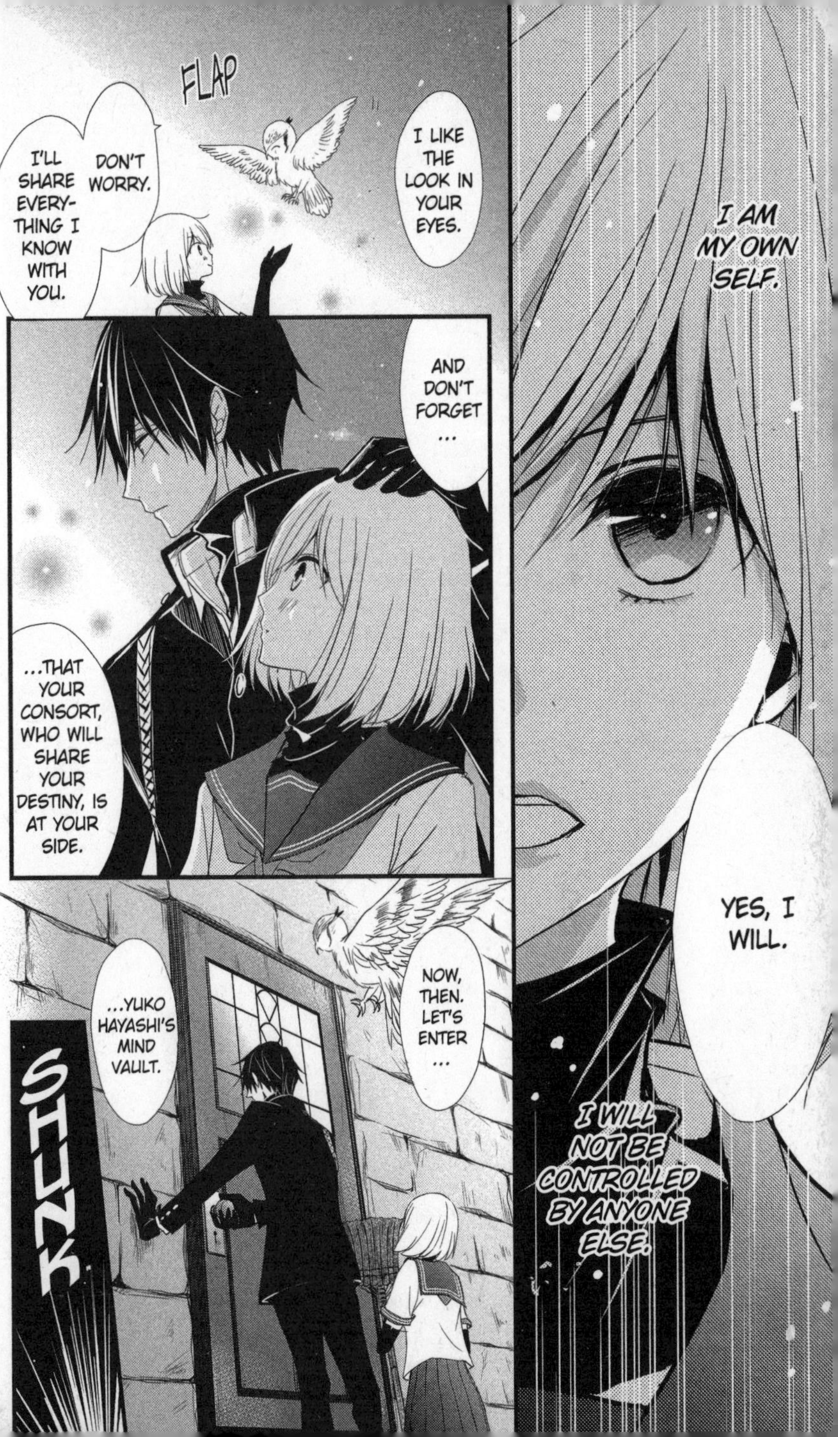
I AM MY OWN SELF.
YES, I WILL.
I WILL NOT BE CONTROLLED BY ANYONE ELSE.
I LIKE THE LOOK IN YOUR EYES.
FLAP
DON'T WORRY.
I'LL SHARE EVERY-THING I KNOW WITH YOU.
AND DON'T FORGET...
...THAT YOUR CONSORT, WHO WILL SHARE YOUR DESTINY, IS AT YOUR SIDE.
NOW, THEN. LET'S ENTER...
...YUKO HAYASHI'S MIND VAULT.
SHUNK

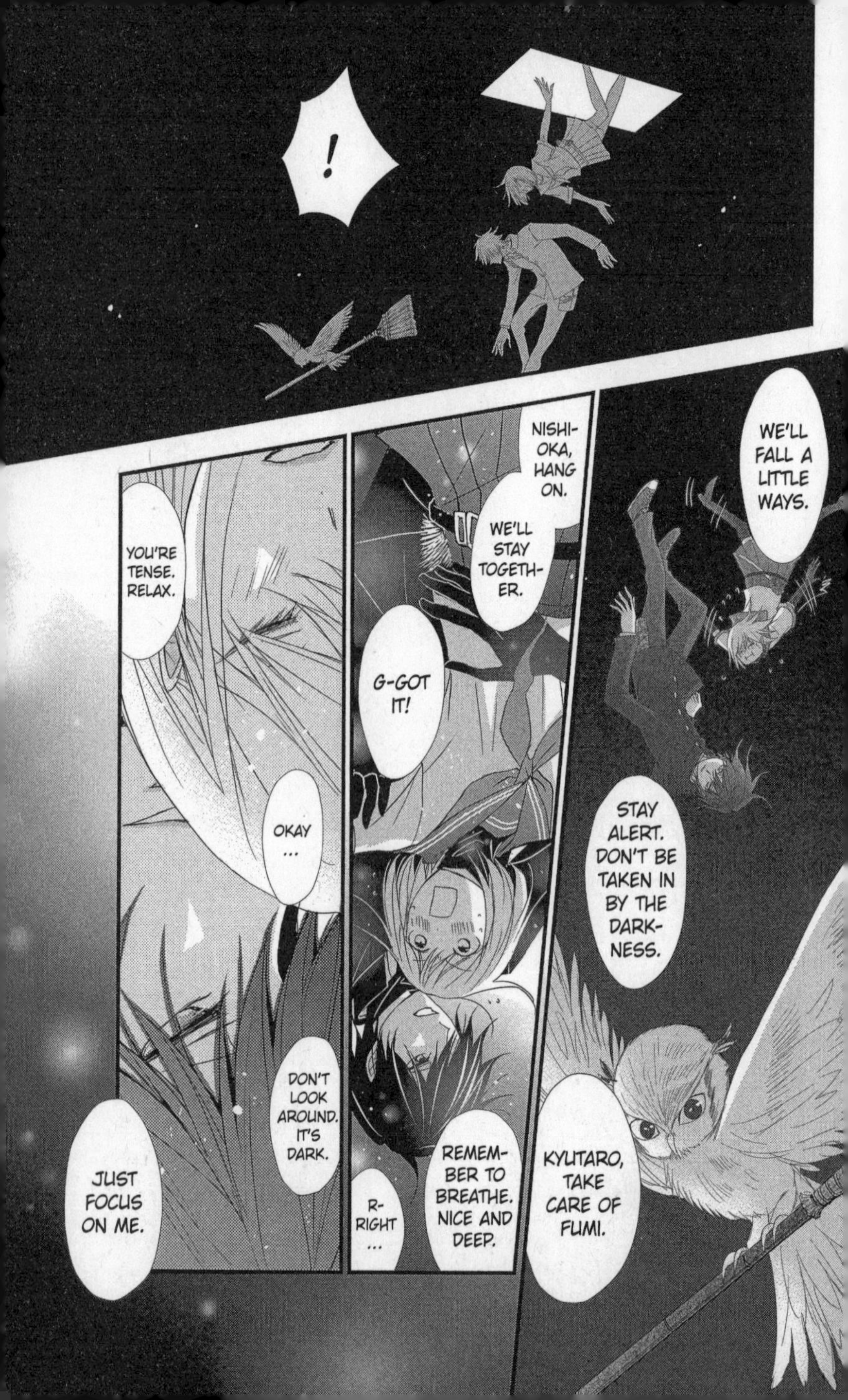
!
WE'LL FALL A LITTLE WAYS.
STAY ALERT. DON'T BE TAKEN IN BY THE DARKNESS.
KYUTARO, TAKE CARE OF FUMI.
NISHIOKA, HANG ON.
WE'LL STAY TOGETHER.
G-GOT IT!
REMEMBER TO BREATHE. NICE AND DEEP.
R-RIGHT...
YOU'RE TENSE. RELAX.
OKAY...
DON'T LOOK AROUND. IT'S DARK.
JUST FOCUS ON ME.

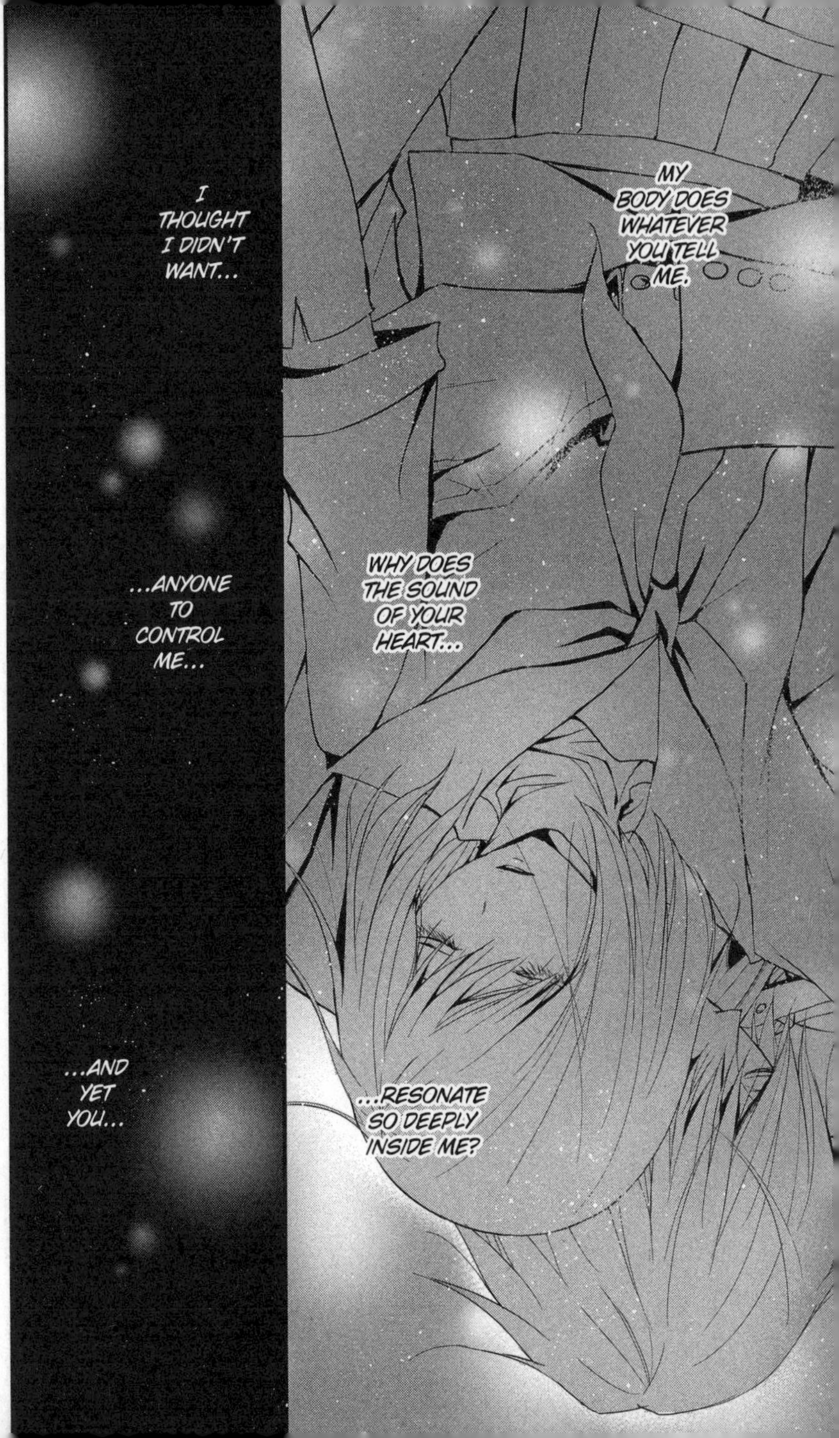
MY BODY DOES WHATEVER YOU TELL ME.
WHY DOES THE SOUND OF YOUR HEART...
...RESONATE SO DEEPLY INSIDE ME?
I THOUGHT I DIDN'T WANT...
...ANYONE TO CONTROL ME...
...AND YET YOU...

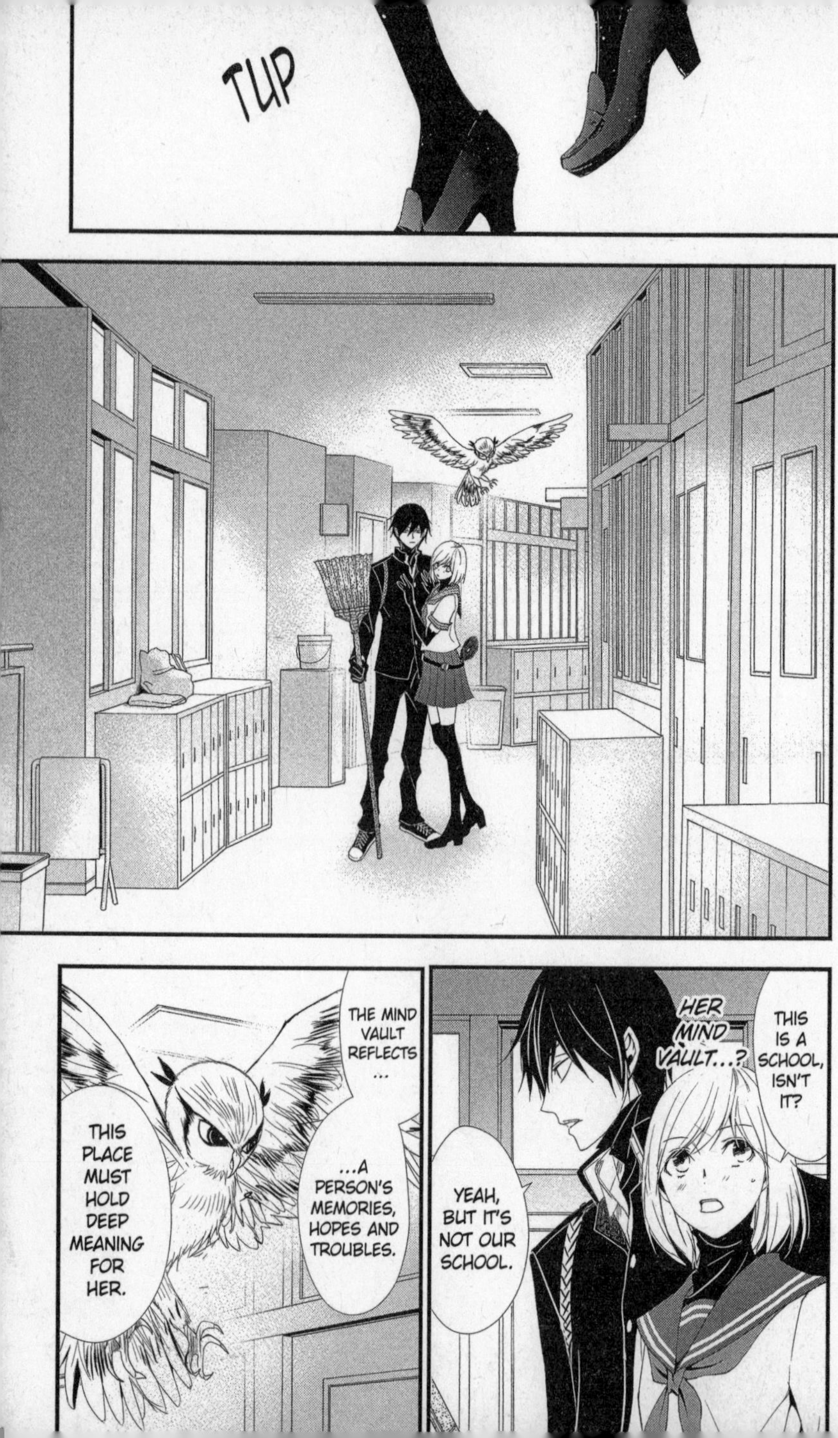
TUP
THIS IS A SCHOOL, ISN'T IT?
HER MIND VAULT...?
YEAH, BUT IT'S NOT OUR SCHOOL.
THE MIND VAULT REFLECTS...
...A PERSON'S MEMORIES, HOPES AND TROUBLES.
THIS PLACE MUST HOLD DEEP MEANING FOR HER.

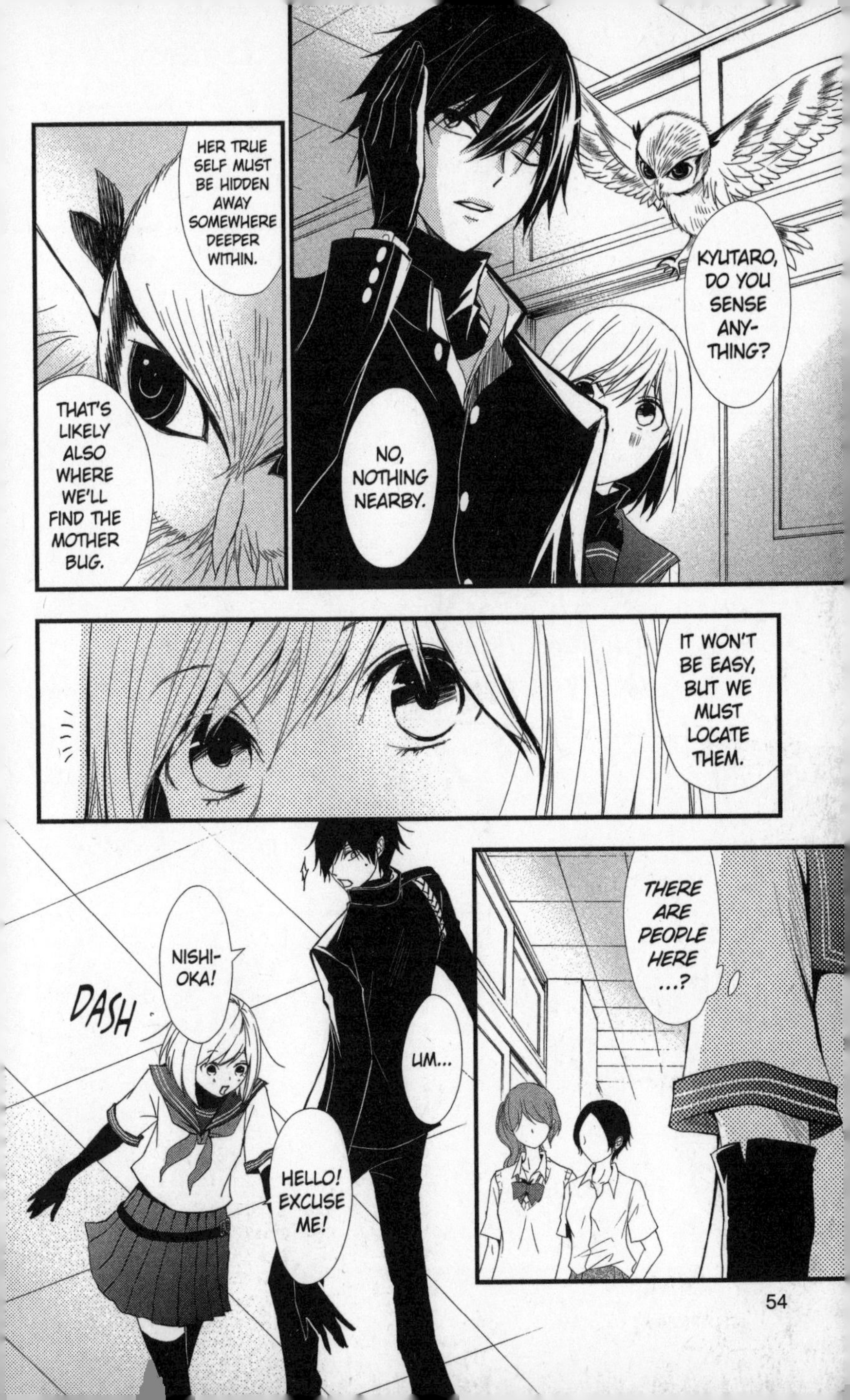
KYUTARO, DO YOU SENSE ANY-THING?
NO, NOTHING NEARBY.
HER TRUE SELF MUST BE HIDDEN AWAY SOMEWHERE DEEPER WITHIN.
THAT'S LIKELY ALSO WHERE WE'LL FIND THE MOTHER BUG.
IT WON'T BE EASY, BUT WE MUST LOCATE THEM.
THERE ARE PEOPLE HERE ...?
NISHI-OKA!
DASH
UM...
HELLO! EXCUSE ME!

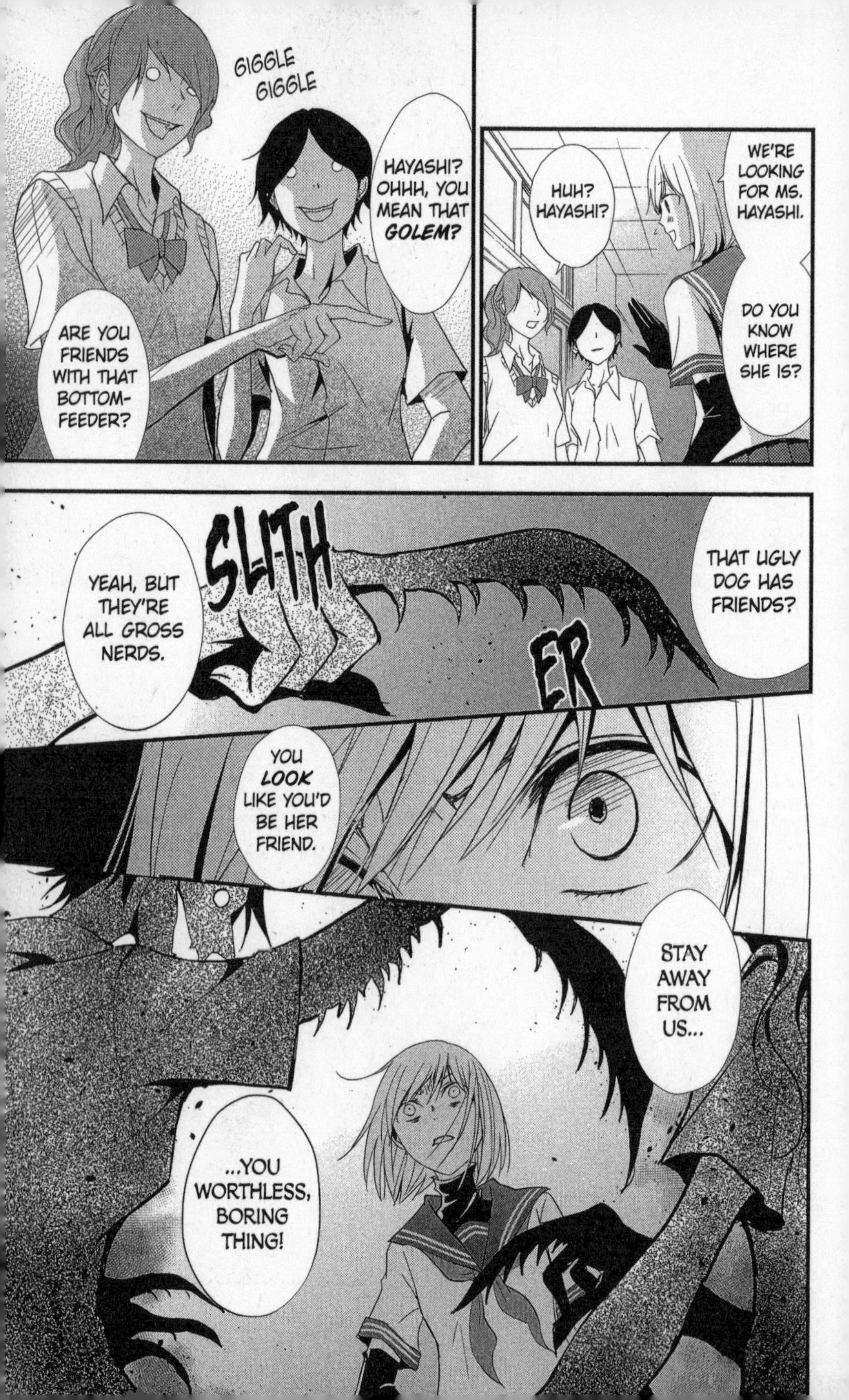
WE'RE LOOKING FOR MS. HAYASHI.
DO YOU KNOW WHERE SHE IS?
HUH? HAYASHI?
GIGGLE GIGGLE
HAYASHI? OHHH, YOU MEAN THAT GOLEM?
ARE YOU FRIENDS WITH THAT BOTTOM-FEEDER?
THAT UGLY DOG HAS FRIENDS?
SLITH
ER
YEAH, BUT THEY'RE ALL GROSS NERDS.
YOU LOOK LIKE YOU'D BE HER FRIEND.
STAY AWAY FROM US...
...YOU WORTHLESS, BORING THING!

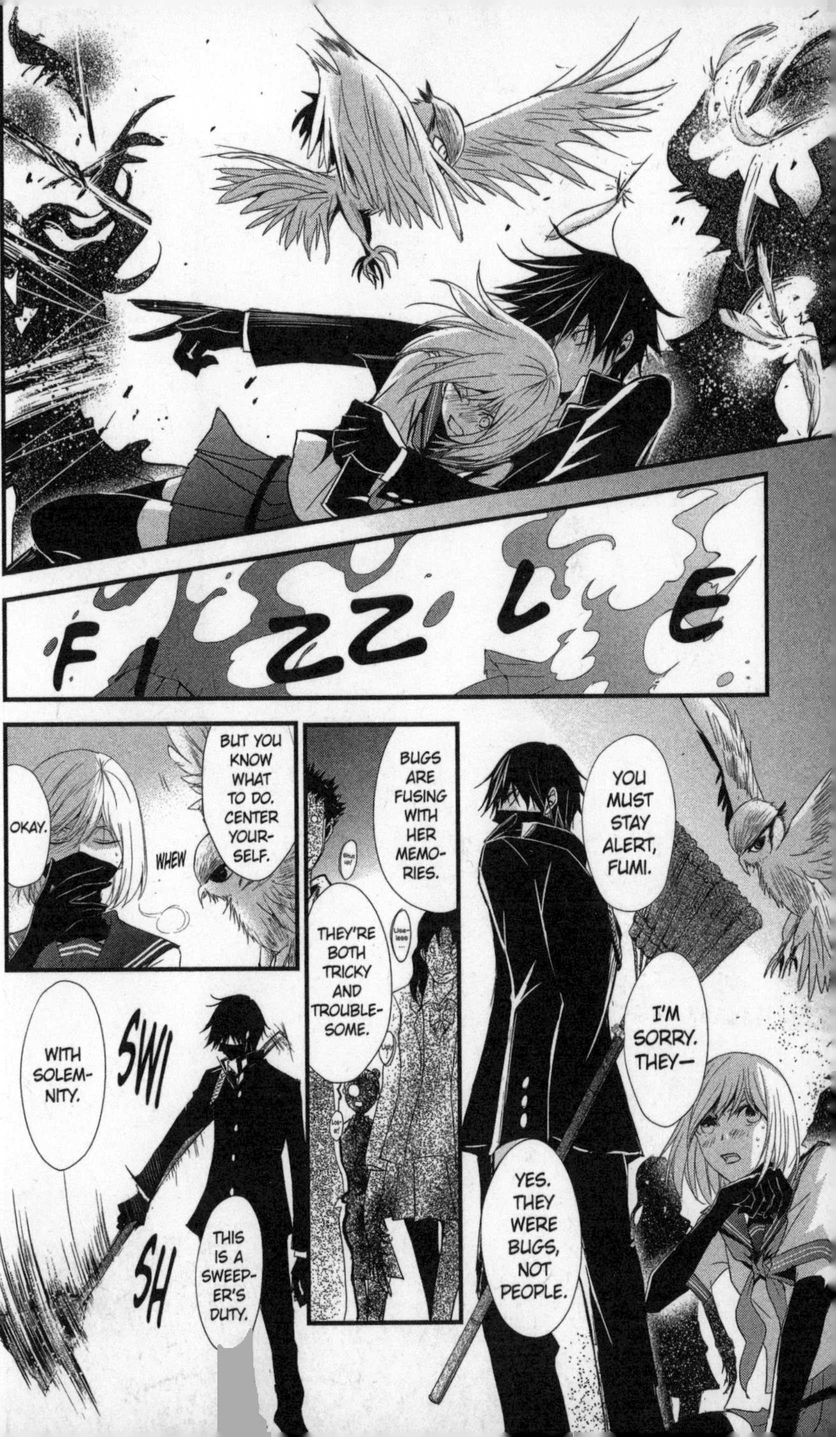
FIZZLE
YOU MUST STAY ALERT, FUMI.
I'M SORRY. THEY—
YES. THEY WERE BUGS, NOT PEOPLE.
BUGS ARE FUSING WITH HER MEMORIES.
THEY'RE BOTH TRICKY AND TROUBLE-SOME.
BUT YOU KNOW WHAT TO DO. CENTER YOUR-SELF.
WHEW
OKAY.
WITH SOLEM-NITY.
SWISH
THIS IS A SWEEP-ER'S DUTY.

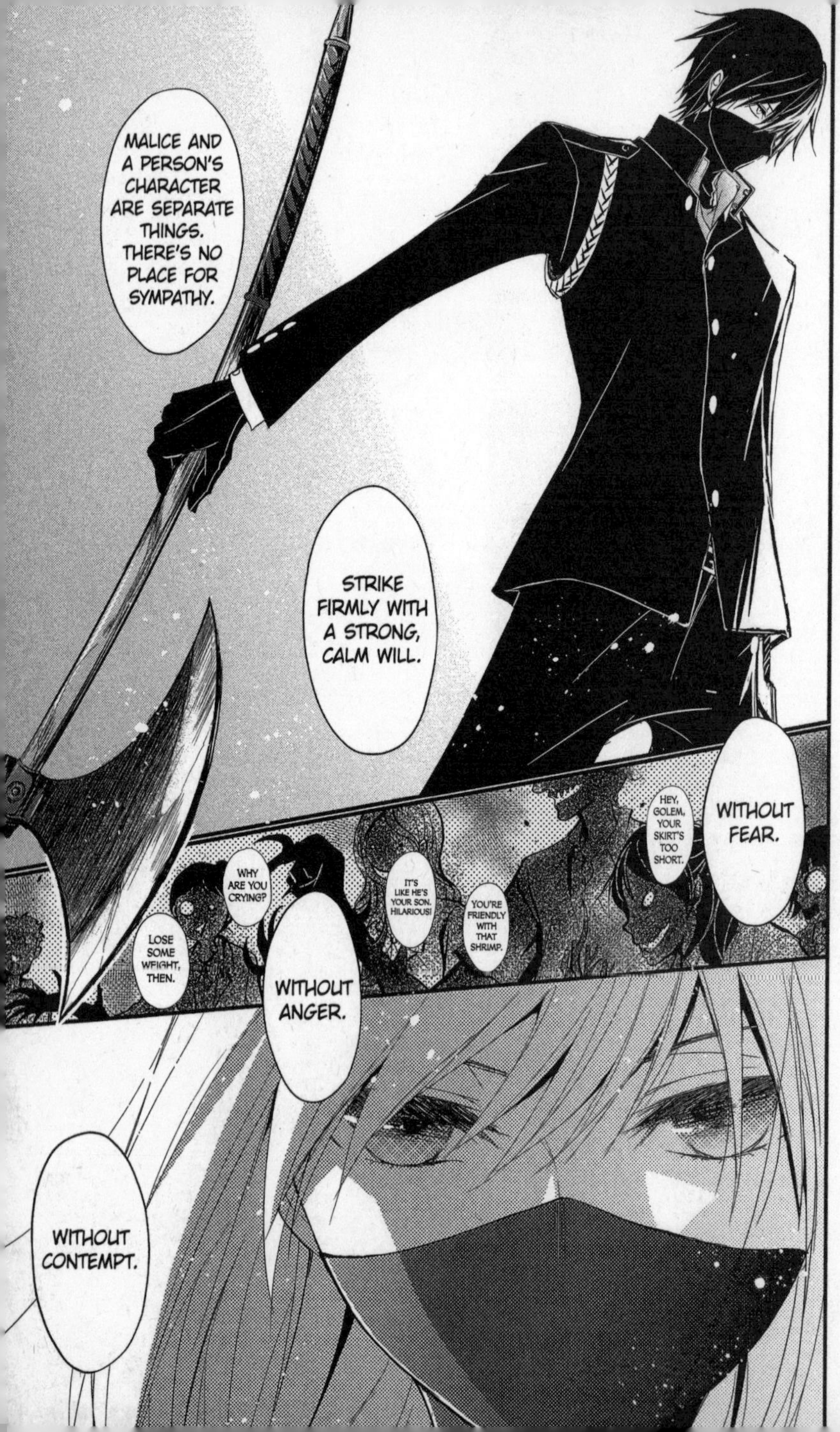
MALICE AND A PERSON'S CHARACTER ARE SEPARATE THINGS. THERE'S NO PLACE FOR SYMPATHY.
STRIKE FIRMLY WITH A STRONG, CALM WILL.
WITHOUT FEAR.
HEY, GOLEM, YOUR SKIRT'S TOO SHORT.
YOU'RE FRIENDLY WITH THAT SHRIMP.
IT'S LIKE HE'S YOUR SON. HILARIOUS!
WHY ARE YOU CRYING?
LOSE SOME WEIGHT, THEN.
WITHOUT ANGER.
WITHOUT CONTEMPT.

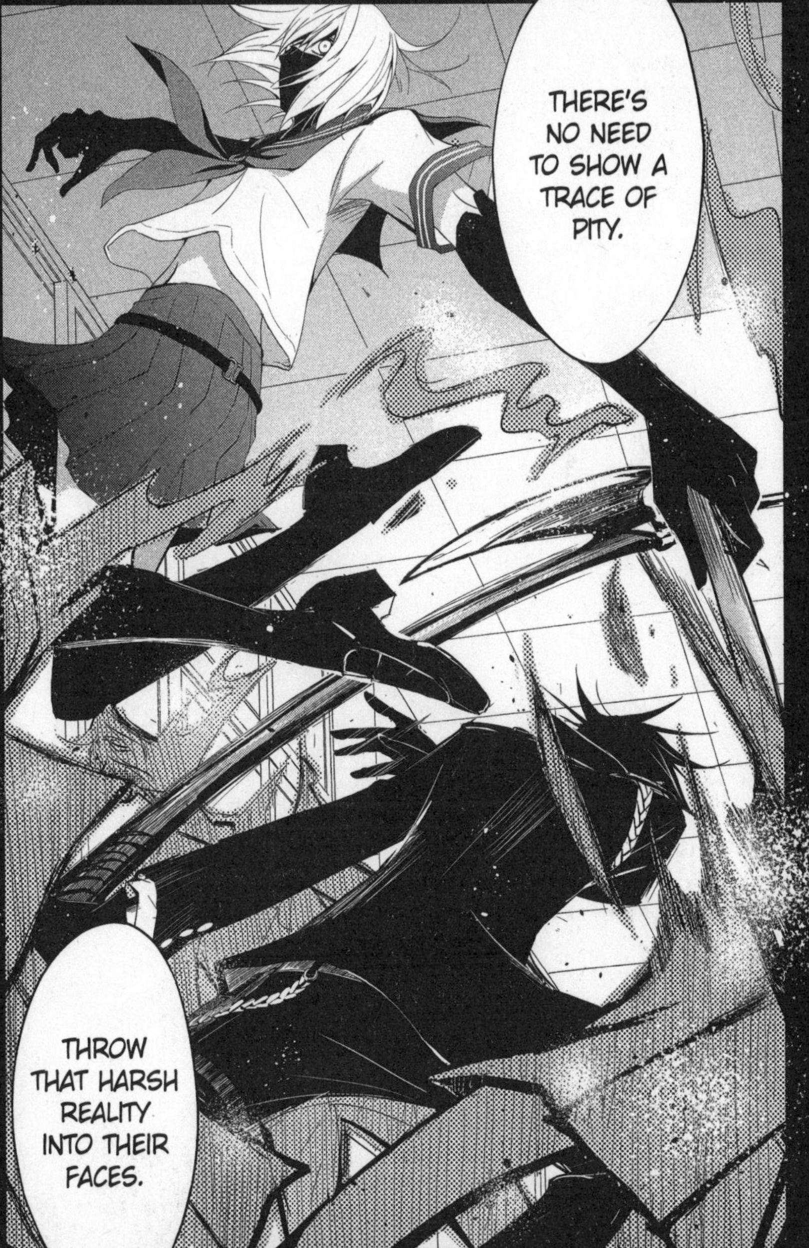
THERE'S NO NEED TO SHOW A TRACE OF PITY.
THROW THAT HARSH REALITY INTO THEIR FACES.

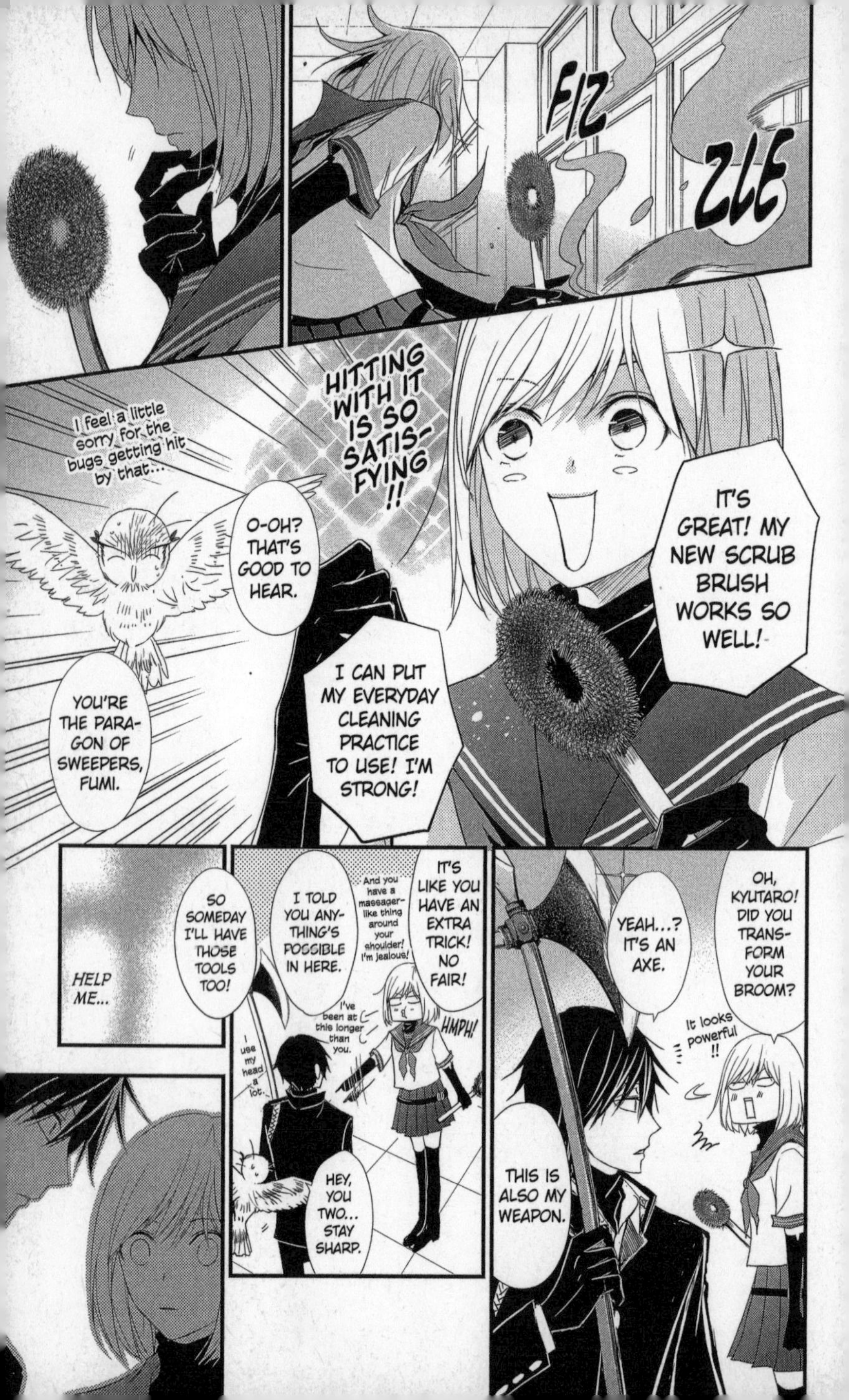
FIZZLE
IT'S GREAT! MY NEW SCRUB BRUSH WORKS SO WELL!
HITTING WITH IT IS SO SATISFYING!!
O-OH? THAT'S GOOD TO HEAR.
I CAN PUT MY EVERYDAY CLEANING PRACTICE TO USE! I'M STRONG!
I feel a little sorry for the bugs getting hit by that...
YOU'RE THE PARAGON OF SWEEPERS, FUMI.
OH, KYUTARO! DID YOU TRANSFORM YOUR BROOM?
It looks powerful!!
YEAH...? IT'S AN AXE.
THIS IS ALSO MY WEAPON.
IT'S LIKE YOU HAVE AN EXTRA TRICK! NO FAIR!
And you have a massager-like thing around your shoulder! I'm jealous!
HMPH!
I TOLD YOU ANYTHING'S POSSIBLE IN HERE.
I've been at this longer than you.
I use my head a lot.
SO SOMEDAY I'LL HAVE THOSE TOOLS TOO!
HEY, YOU TWO... STAY SHARP.
HELP ME...

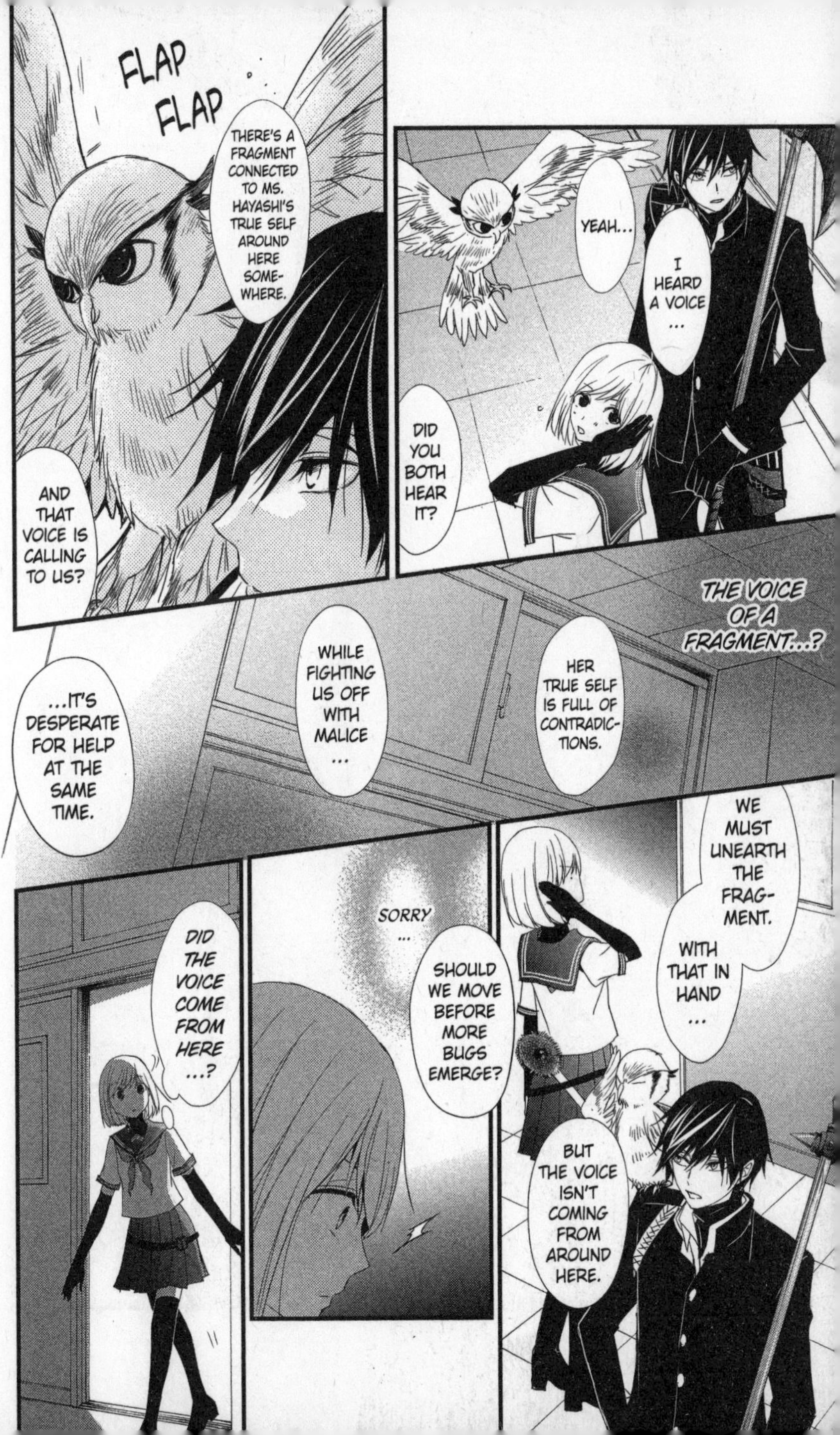
I HEARD A VOICE...
YEAH...
DID YOU BOTH HEAR IT?
FLAP FLAP
THERE'S A FRAGMENT CONNECTED TO MS. HAYASHI'S TRUE SELF AROUND HERE SOME-WHERE.
AND THAT VOICE IS CALLING TO US?
THE VOICE OF A FRAGMENT...?
HER TRUE SELF IS FULL OF CONTRADIC-TIONS.
WHILE FIGHTING US OFF WITH MALICE...
...IT'S DESPERATE FOR HELP AT THE SAME TIME.
WE MUST UNEARTH THE FRAG-MENT.
WITH THAT IN HAND...
BUT THE VOICE ISN'T COMING FROM AROUND HERE.
SORRY...
SHOULD WE MOVE BEFORE MORE BUGS EMERGE?
DID THE VOICE COME FROM HERE...?

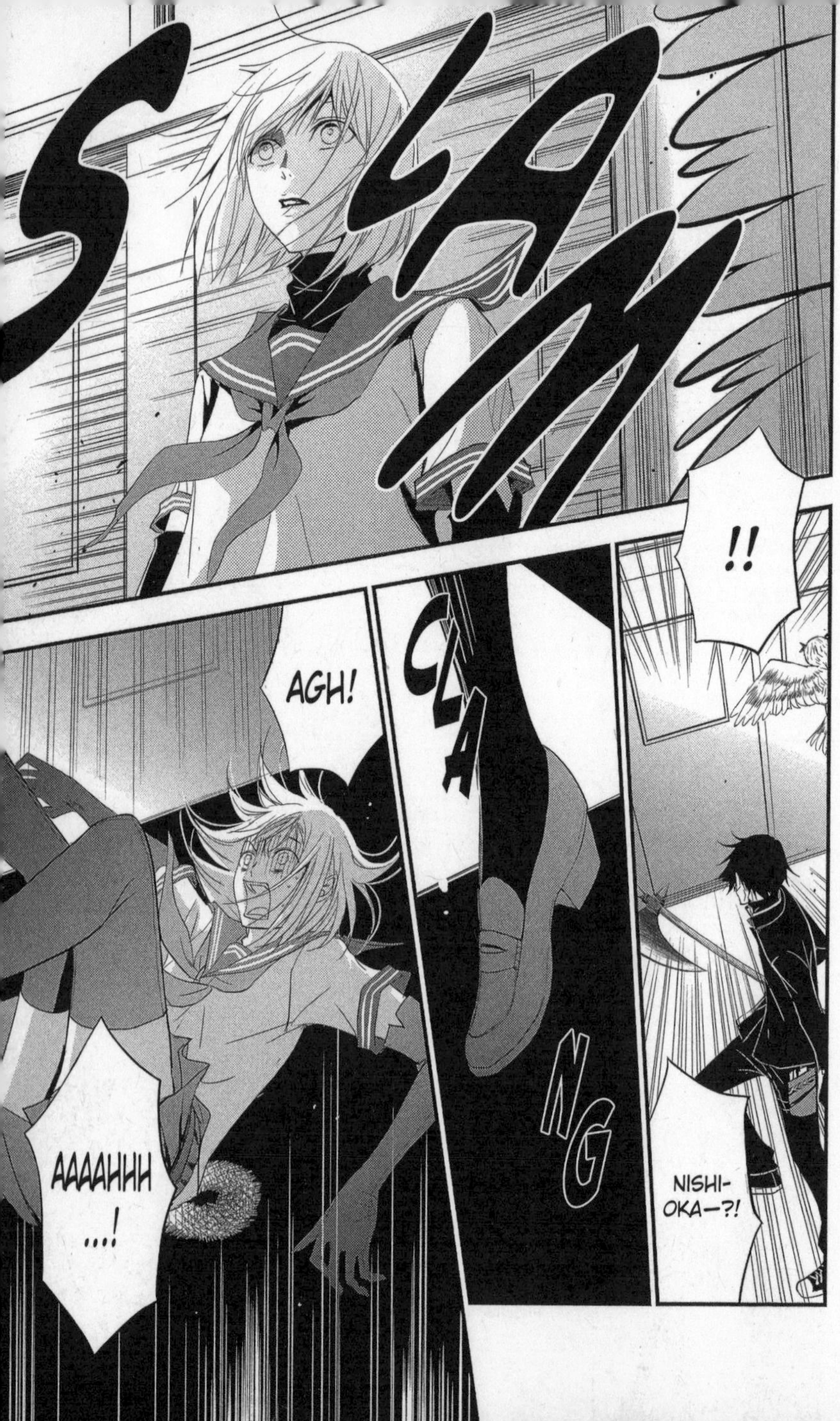
SLAM
!!
NISHI-OKA—?!
CLANG
AGH!
AAAAHHH ...!

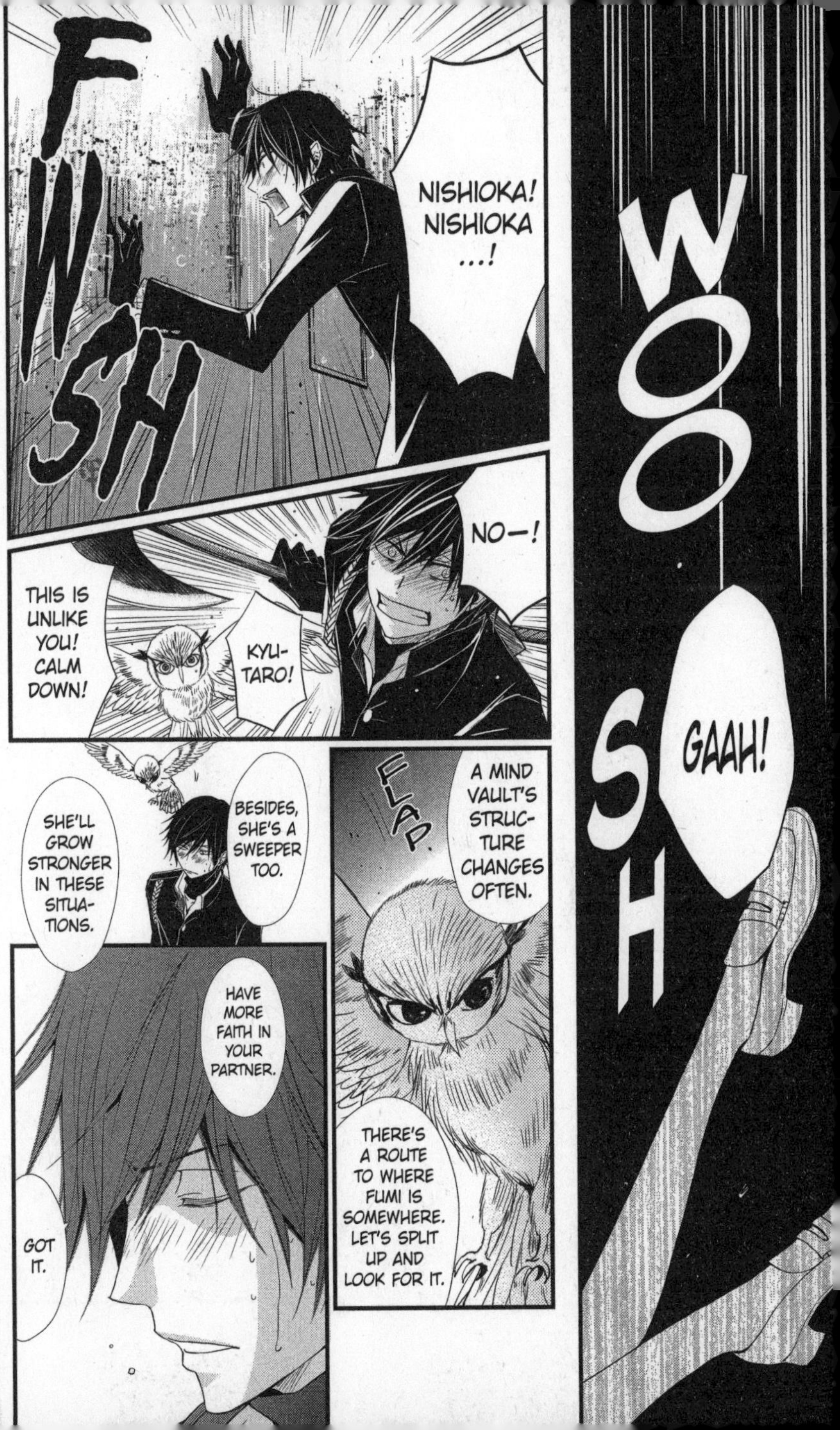
WOOOSH
GAAH!
FWISH
NISHIOKA! NISHIOKA ...!
NO—!
KYU-TARO!
THIS IS UNLIKE YOU! CALM DOWN!
FLAP
A MIND VAULT'S STRUC-TURE CHANGES OFTEN.
THERE'S A ROUTE TO WHERE FUMI IS SOMEWHERE. LET'S SPLIT UP AND LOOK FOR IT.
BESIDES, SHE'S A SWEEPER TOO.
SHE'LL GROW STRONGER IN THESE SITUA-TIONS.
HAVE MORE FAITH IN YOUR PARTNER.
GOT IT.

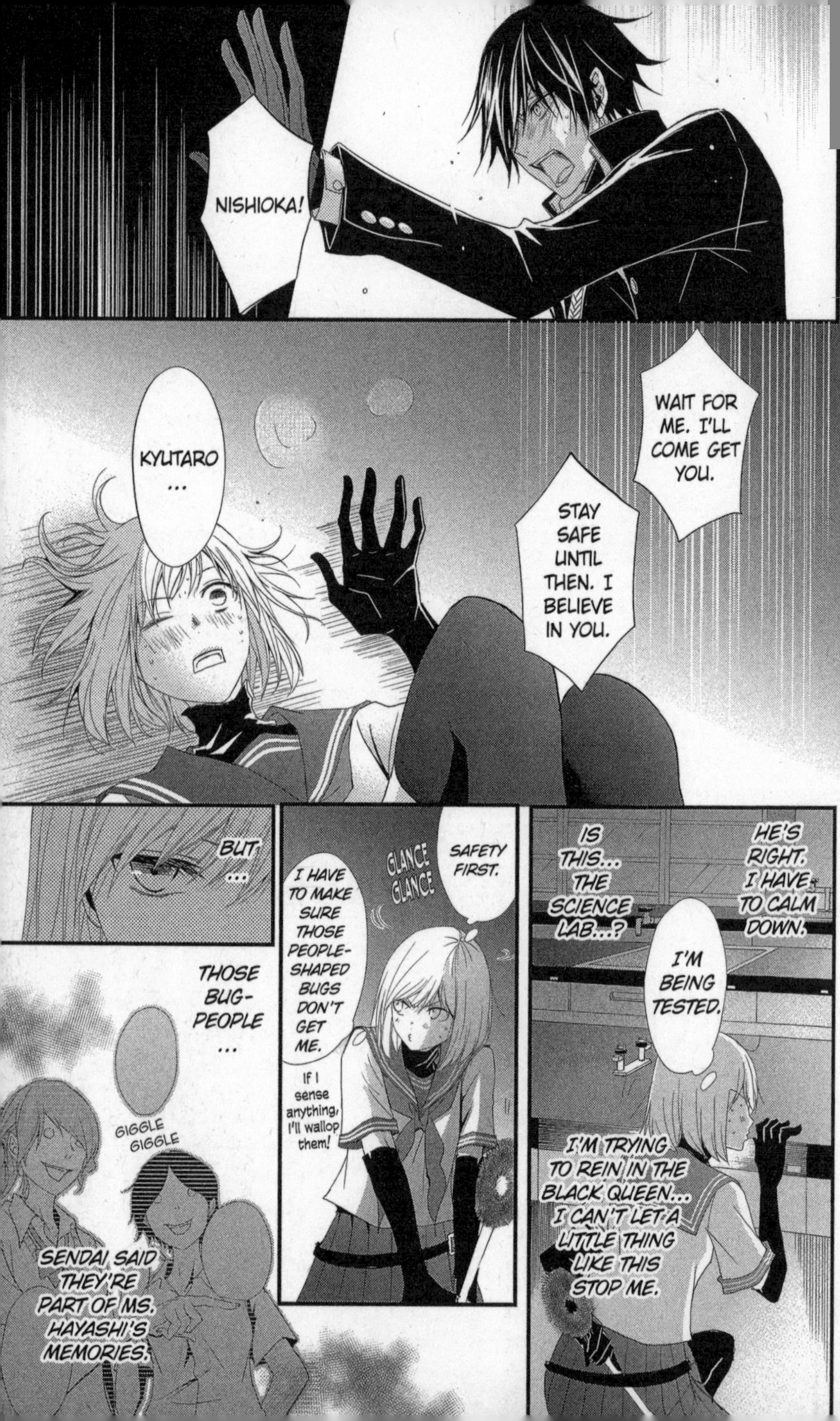
NISHIOKA!
WAIT FOR ME. I'LL COME GET YOU.
STAY SAFE UNTIL THEN. I BELIEVE IN YOU.
KYUTARO ...
HE'S RIGHT. I HAVE TO CALM DOWN.
IS THIS... THE SCIENCE LAB...?
I'M BEING TESTED.
I'M TRYING TO REIN IN THE BLACK QUEEN... I CAN'T LET A LITTLE THING LIKE THIS STOP ME.
SAFETY FIRST.
GLANCE GLANCE
I HAVE TO MAKE SURE THOSE PEOPLE-SHAPED BUGS DON'T GET ME.
If I sense anything, I'll wallop them!
BUT ...
THOSE BUG-PEOPLE ...
GIGGLE GIGGLE
SENDAI SAID THEY'RE PART OF MS. HAYASHI'S MEMORIES.

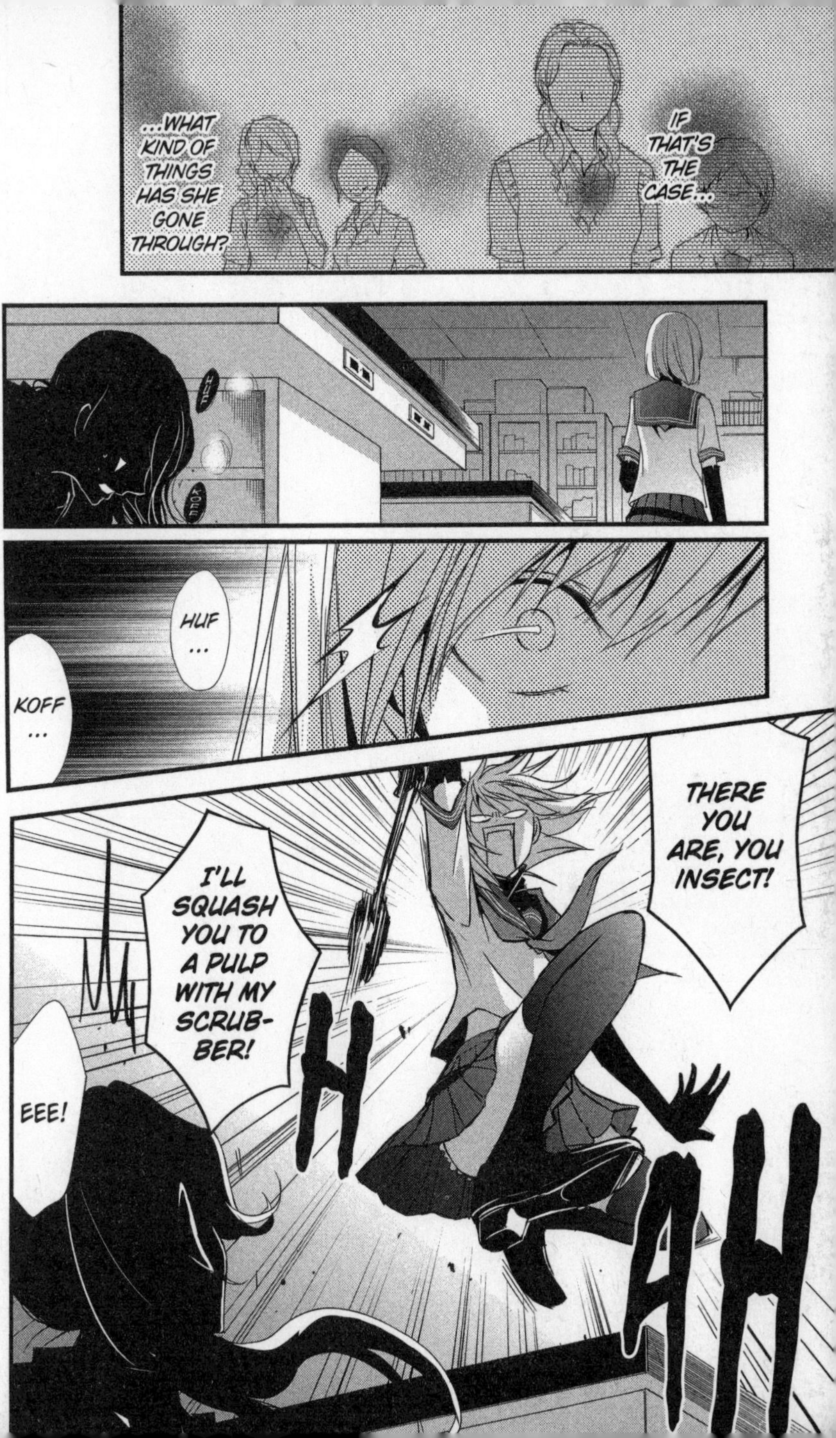
IF THAT'S THE CASE...
...WHAT KIND OF THINGS HAS SHE GONE THROUGH?
HUF
KOFF
HUF...
KOFF...
THERE YOU ARE, YOU INSECT!
I'LL SQUASH YOU TO A PULP WITH MY SCRUB-BER!
HAH
EEE!

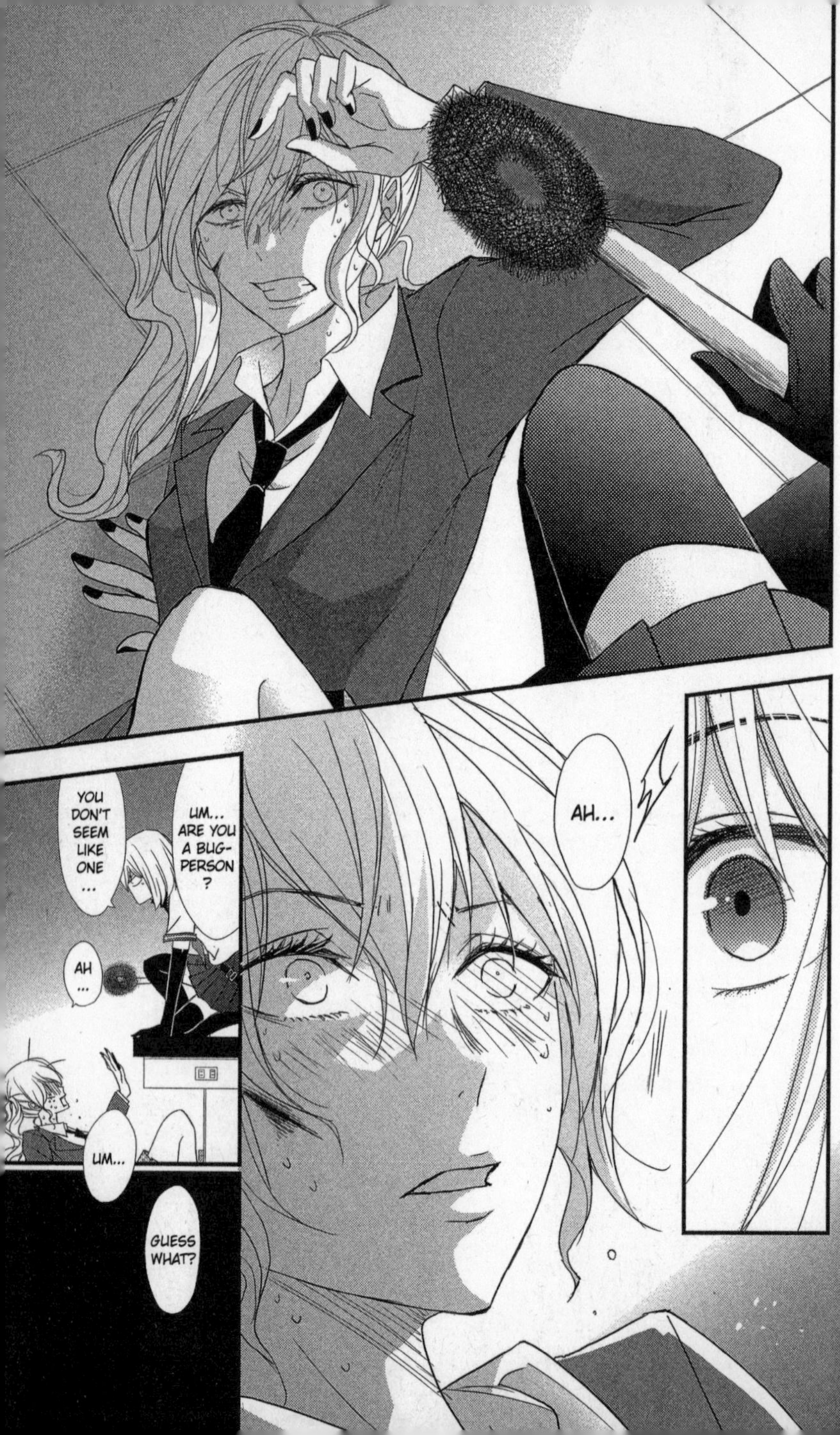
AH...
UM... ARE YOU A BUG-PERSON?
YOU DON'T SEEM LIKE ONE ...
AH ...
UM...
GUESS WHAT?

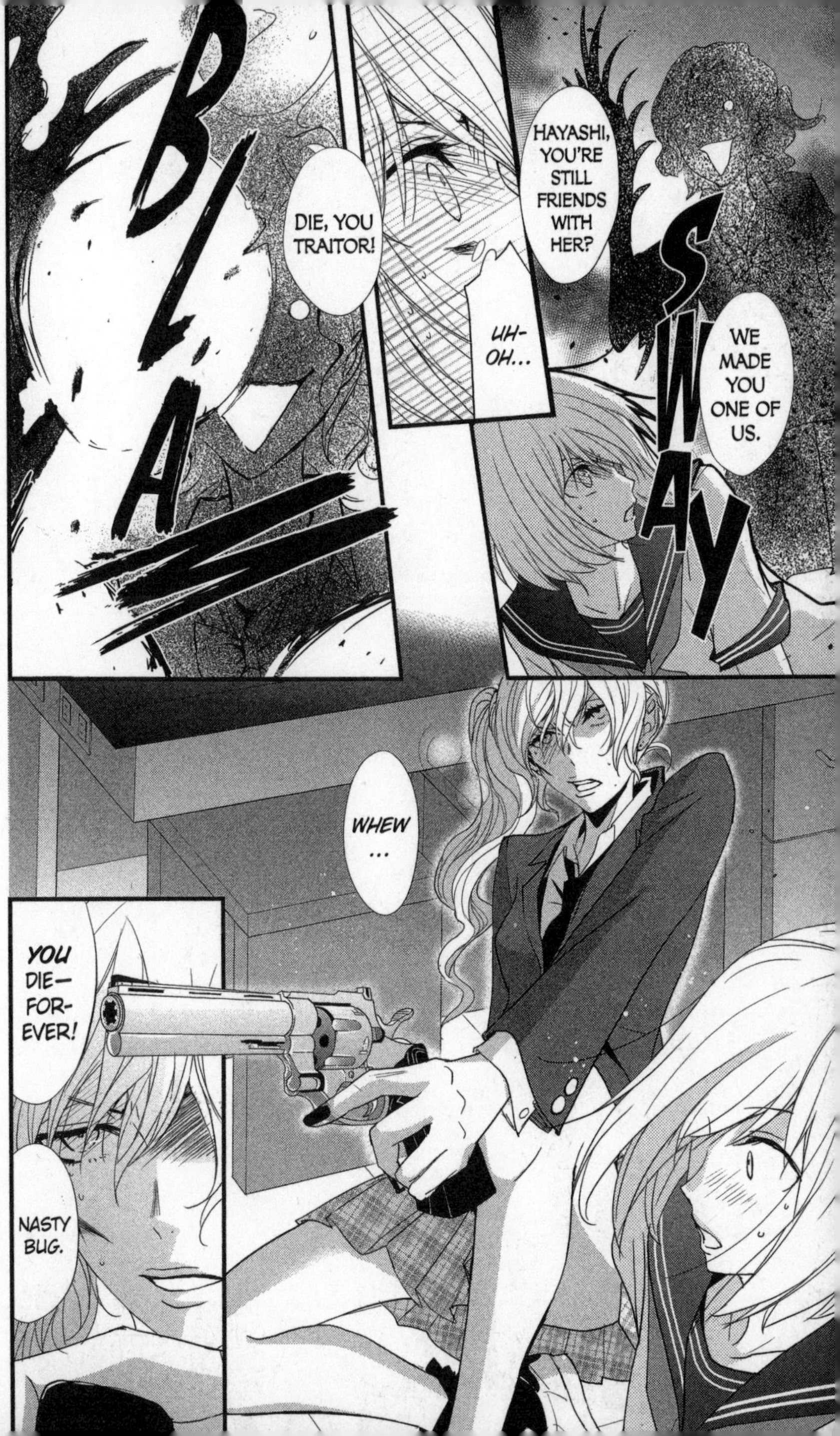
HAYASHI, YOU'RE STILL FRIENDS WITH HER?
WE MADE YOU ONE OF US.
SWAY
UH-OH...
DIE, YOU TRAITOR!
BLA
WHEW...
YOU DIE— FOREVER!
NASTY BUG.

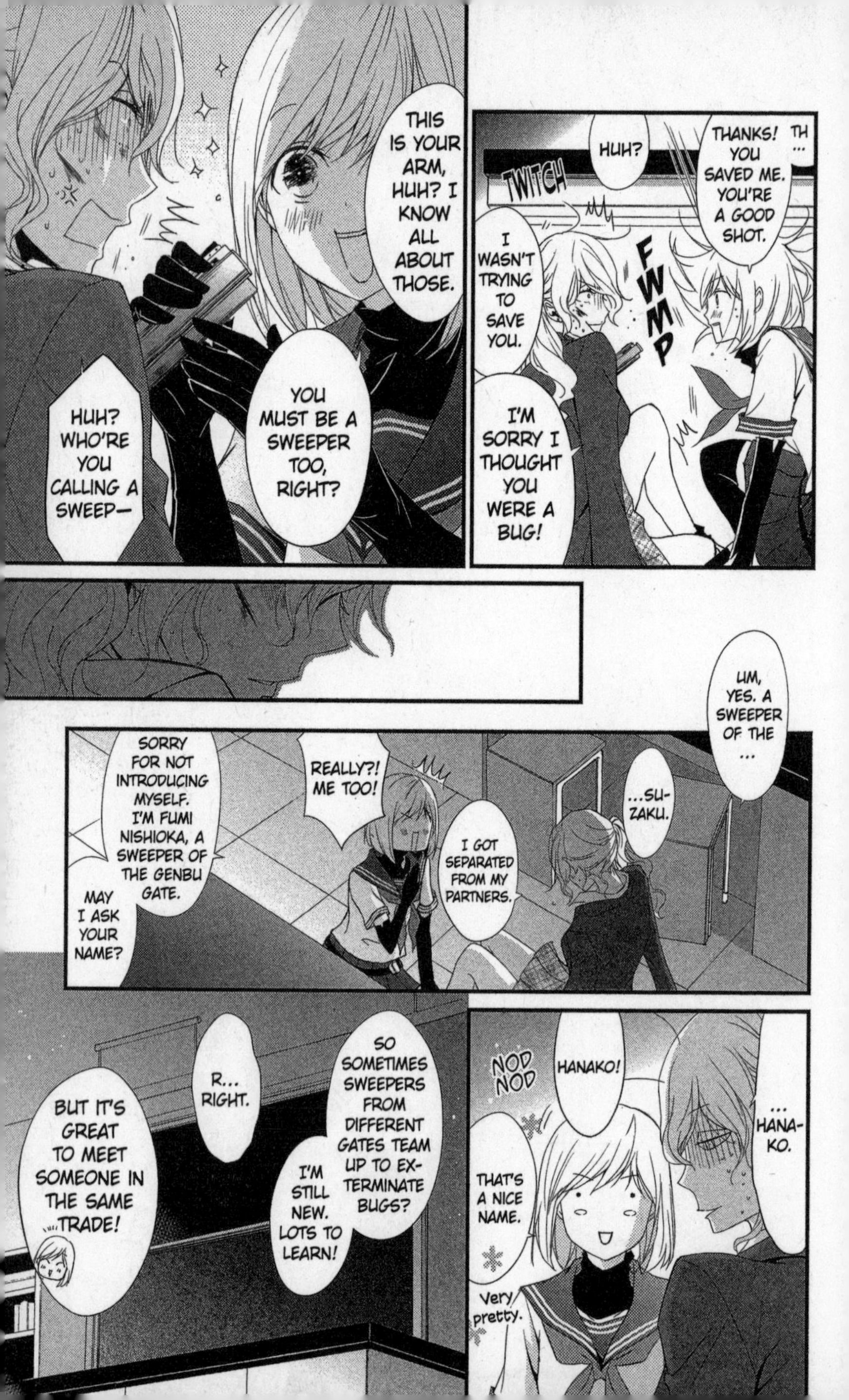
TH ...
THANKS! YOU SAVED ME. YOU'RE A GOOD SHOT.
HUH?
TWITCH
FWMP
I WASN'T TRYING TO SAVE YOU.
I'M SORRY I THOUGHT YOU WERE A BUG!
THIS IS YOUR ARM, HUH? I KNOW ALL ABOUT THOSE.
YOU MUST BE A SWEEPER TOO, RIGHT?
HUH? WHO'RE YOU CALLING A SWEEP—
UM, YES. A SWEEPER OF THE ...
...SU-ZAKU.
I GOT SEPARATED FROM MY PARTNERS.
REALLY?! ME TOO!
SORRY FOR NOT INTRODUCING MYSELF. I'M FUMI NISHIOKA, A SWEEPER OF THE GENBU GATE.
MAY I ASK YOUR NAME?
... HANA-KO.
HANAKO!
NOD NOD
THAT'S A NICE NAME.
Very pretty.
SO SOMETIMES SWEEPERS FROM DIFFERENT GATES TEAM UP TO EX-TERMINATE BUGS?
R... RIGHT.
I'M STILL NEW. LOTS TO LEARN!
BUT IT'S GREAT TO MEET SOMEONE IN THE SAME TRADE!

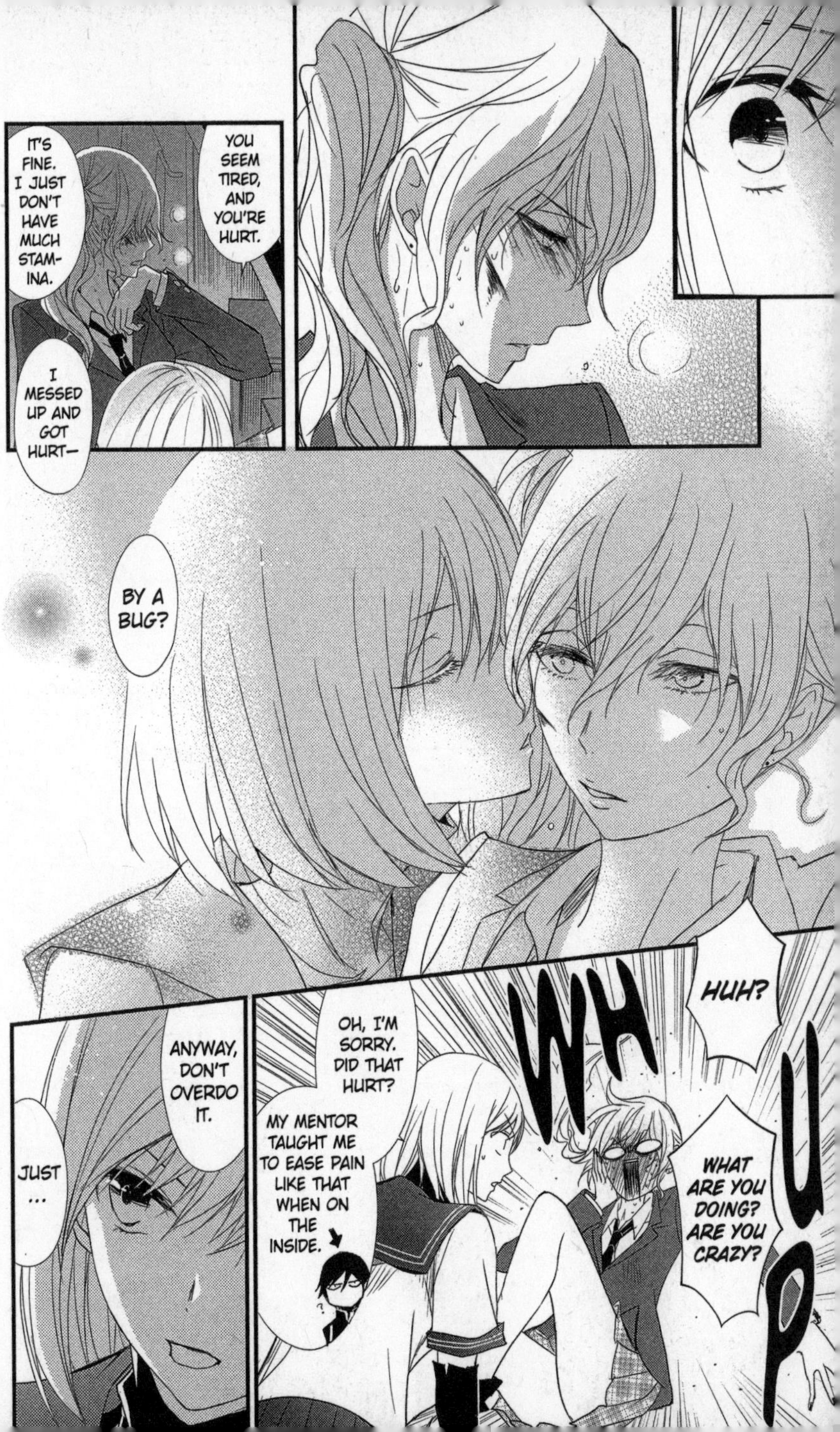
YOU SEEM TIRED, AND YOU'RE HURT.
IT'S FINE. I JUST DON'T HAVE MUCH STAMINA.
I MESSED UP AND GOT HURT—
BY A BUG?
HUH?
WHUP
WHAT ARE YOU DOING? ARE YOU CRAZY?
OH, I'M SORRY. DID THAT HURT?
MY MENTOR TAUGHT ME TO EASE PAIN LIKE THAT WHEN ON THE INSIDE.
ANYWAY, DON'T OVERDO IT.
JUST ...

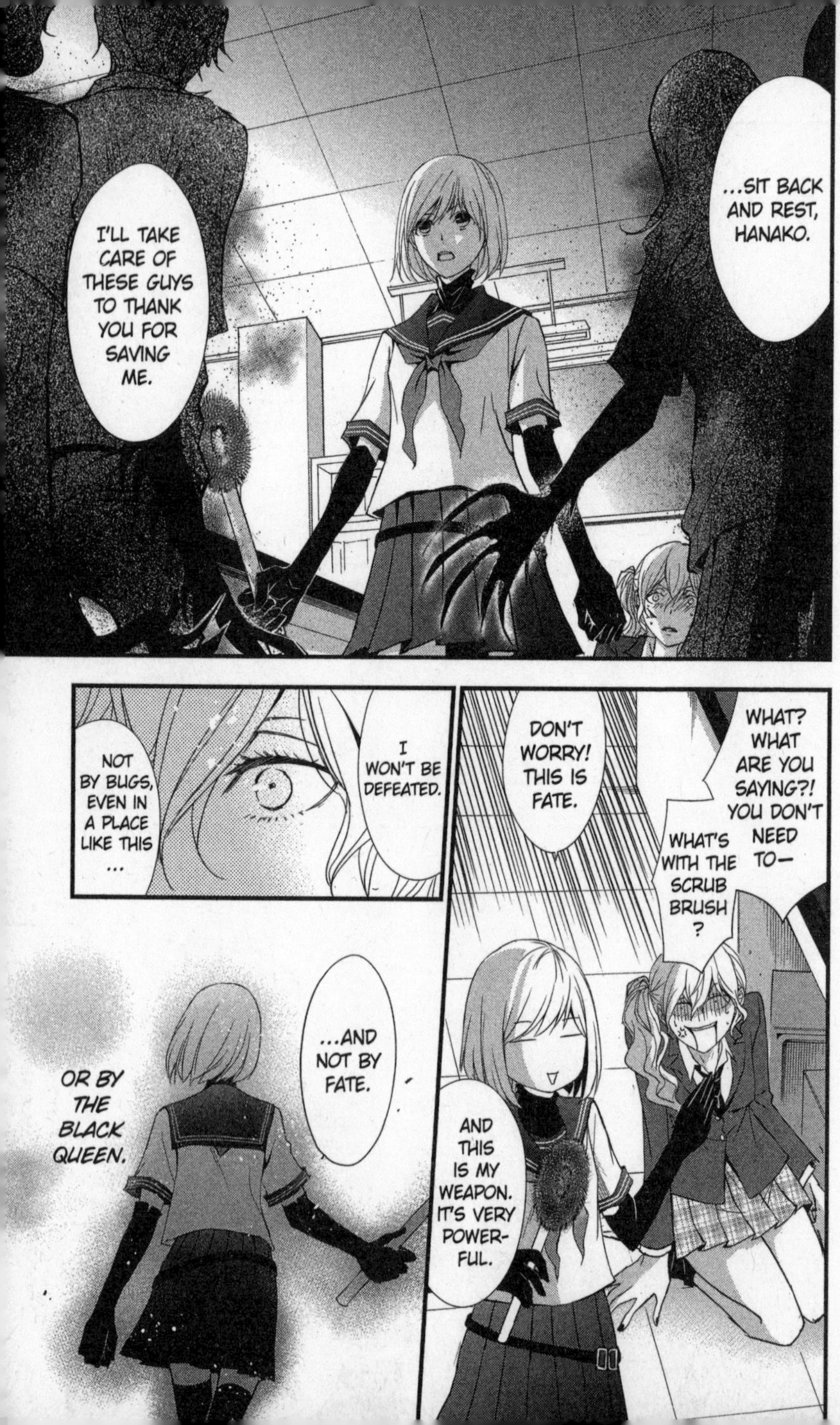
...SIT BACK AND REST, HANAKO.
I'LL TAKE CARE OF THESE GUYS TO THANK YOU FOR SAVING ME.
WHAT? WHAT ARE YOU SAYING?! YOU DON'T NEED TO—
WHAT'S WITH THE SCRUB BRUSH?
DON'T WORRY! THIS IS FATE.
AND THIS IS MY WEAPON. IT'S VERY POWER-FUL.
I WON'T BE DEFEATED.
NOT BY BUGS, EVEN IN A PLACE LIKE THIS...
...AND NOT BY FATE.
OR BY THE BLACK QUEEN.

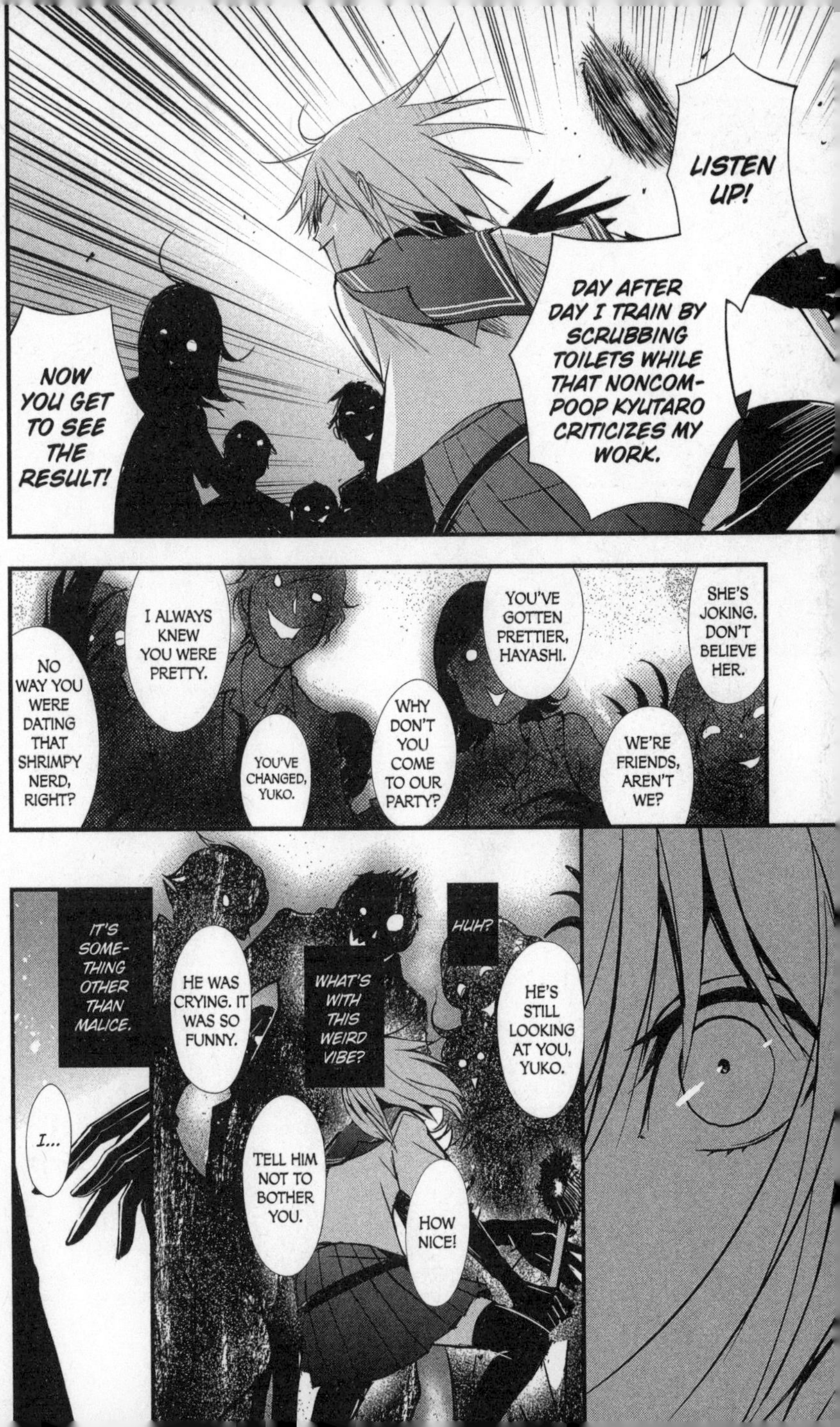

LISTEN UP!
DAY AFTER DAY I TRAIN BY SCRUBBING TOILETS WHILE THAT NONCOMPOOP KYUTARO CRITICIZES MY WORK.
NOW YOU GET TO SEE THE RESULT!
SHE'S JOKING. DON'T BELIEVE HER.
WE'RE FRIENDS, AREN'T WE?
YOU'VE GOTTEN PRETTIER, HAYASHI.
WHY DON'T YOU COME TO OUR PARTY?
I ALWAYS KNEW YOU WERE PRETTY.
YOU'VE CHANGED, YUKO.
NO WAY YOU WERE DATING THAT SHRIMPY NERD, RIGHT?
HUH?
HE'S STILL LOOKING AT YOU, YUKO.
WHAT'S WITH THIS WEIRD VIBE?
HE WAS CRYING. IT WAS SO FUNNY.
IT'S SOMETHING OTHER THAN MALICE.
HOW NICE!
TELL HIM NOT TO BOTHER YOU.
I...

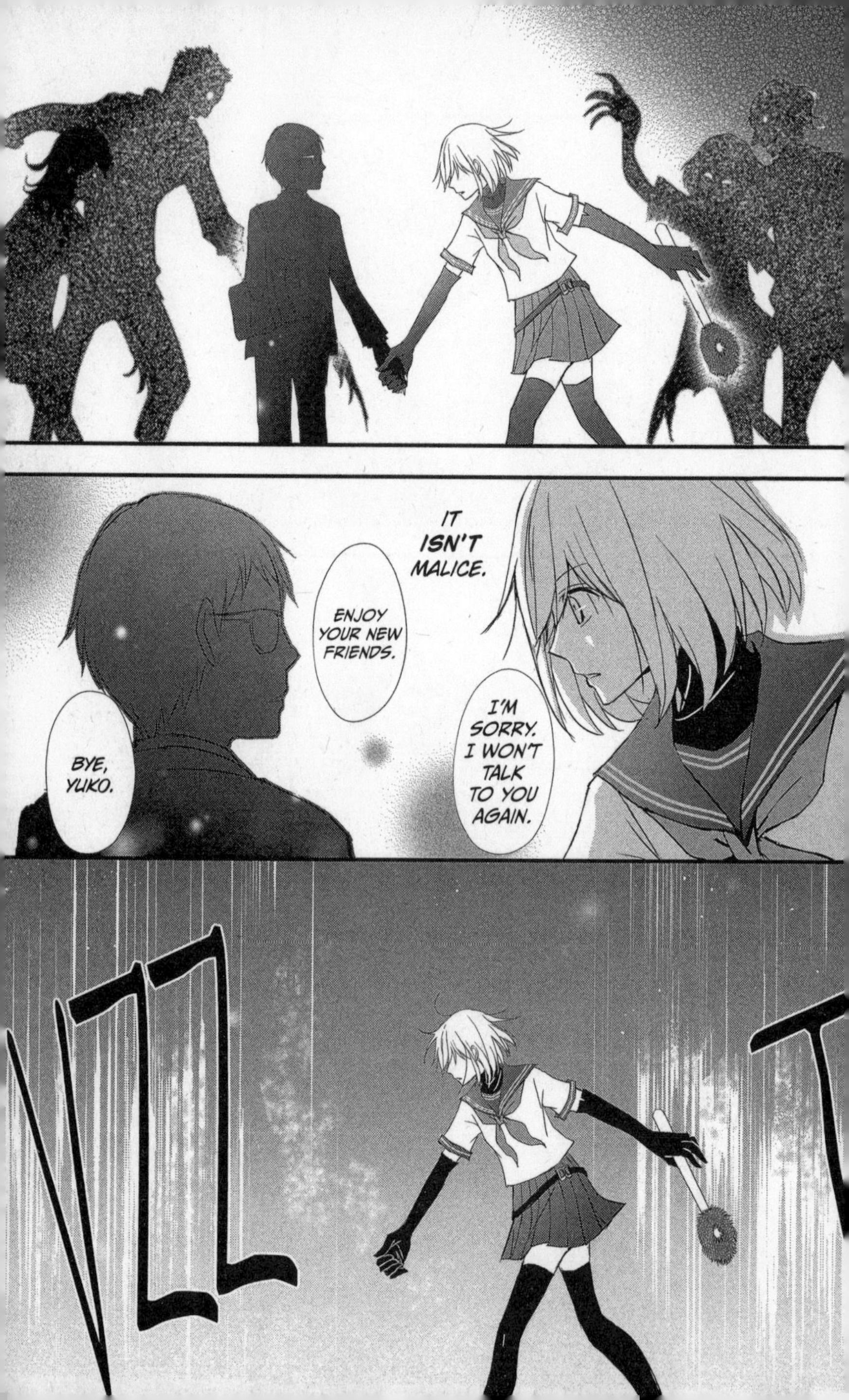
IT ISN'T MALICE.
I'M SORRY. I WON'T TALK TO YOU AGAIN.
ENJOY YOUR NEW FRIENDS.
BYE, YUKO.

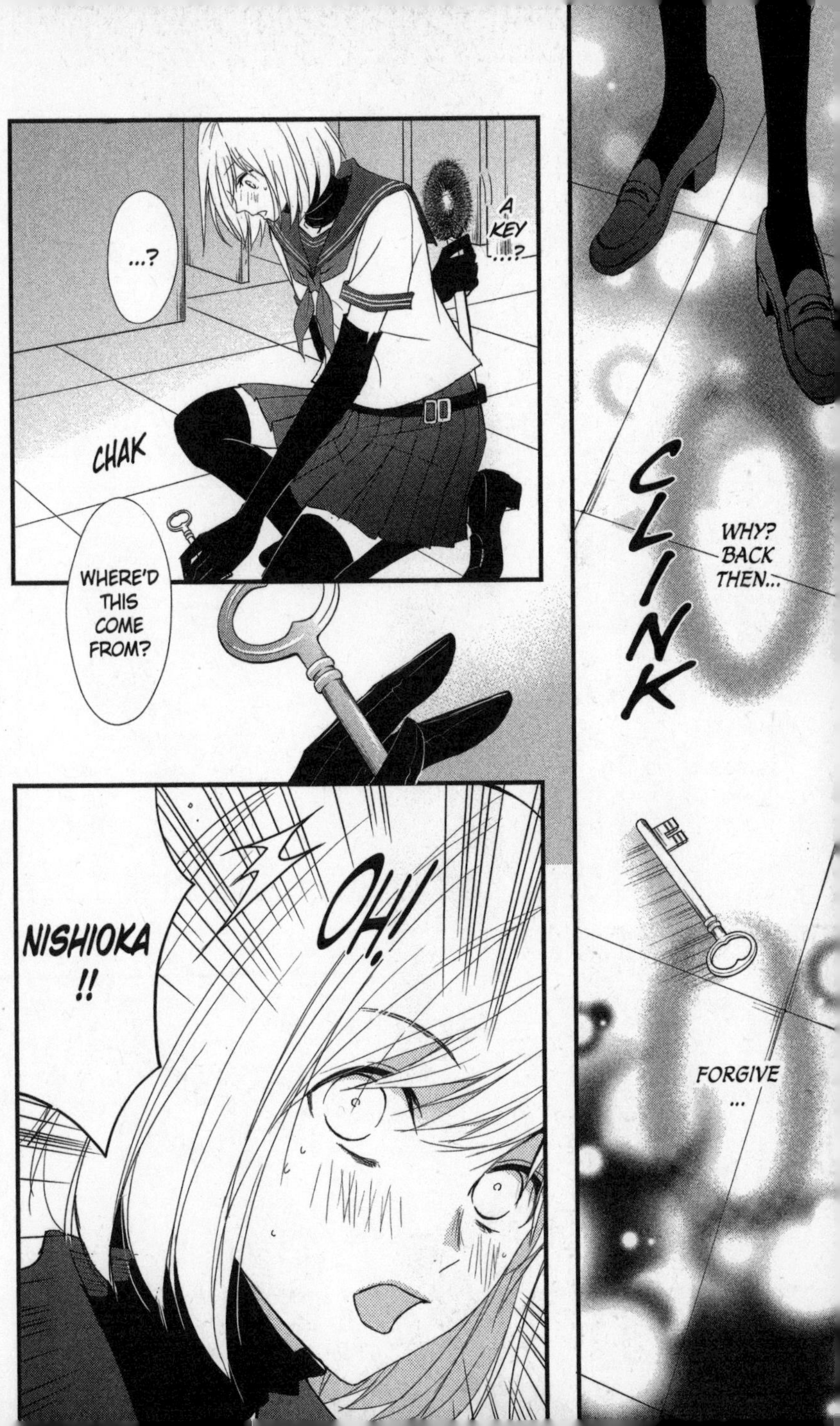
CLINK
WHY? BACK THEN...
FORGIVE ...
A KEY ...?
...?
CHAK
WHERE'D THIS COME FROM?
OH!
NISHIOKA !!

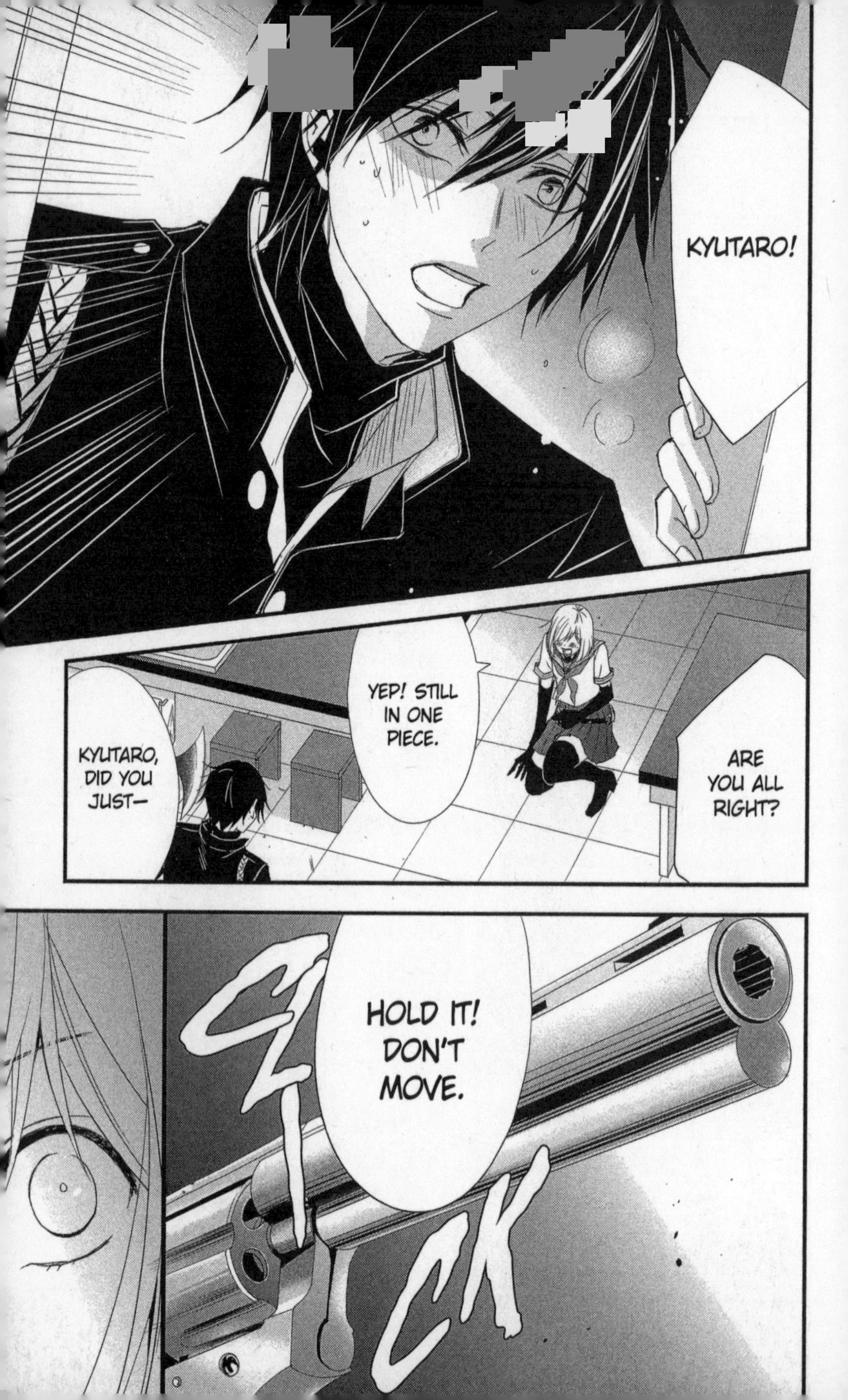
KYUTARO!
ARE YOU ALL RIGHT?
YEP! STILL IN ONE PIECE.
KYUTARO, DID YOU JUST—
HOLD IT! DON'T MOVE.

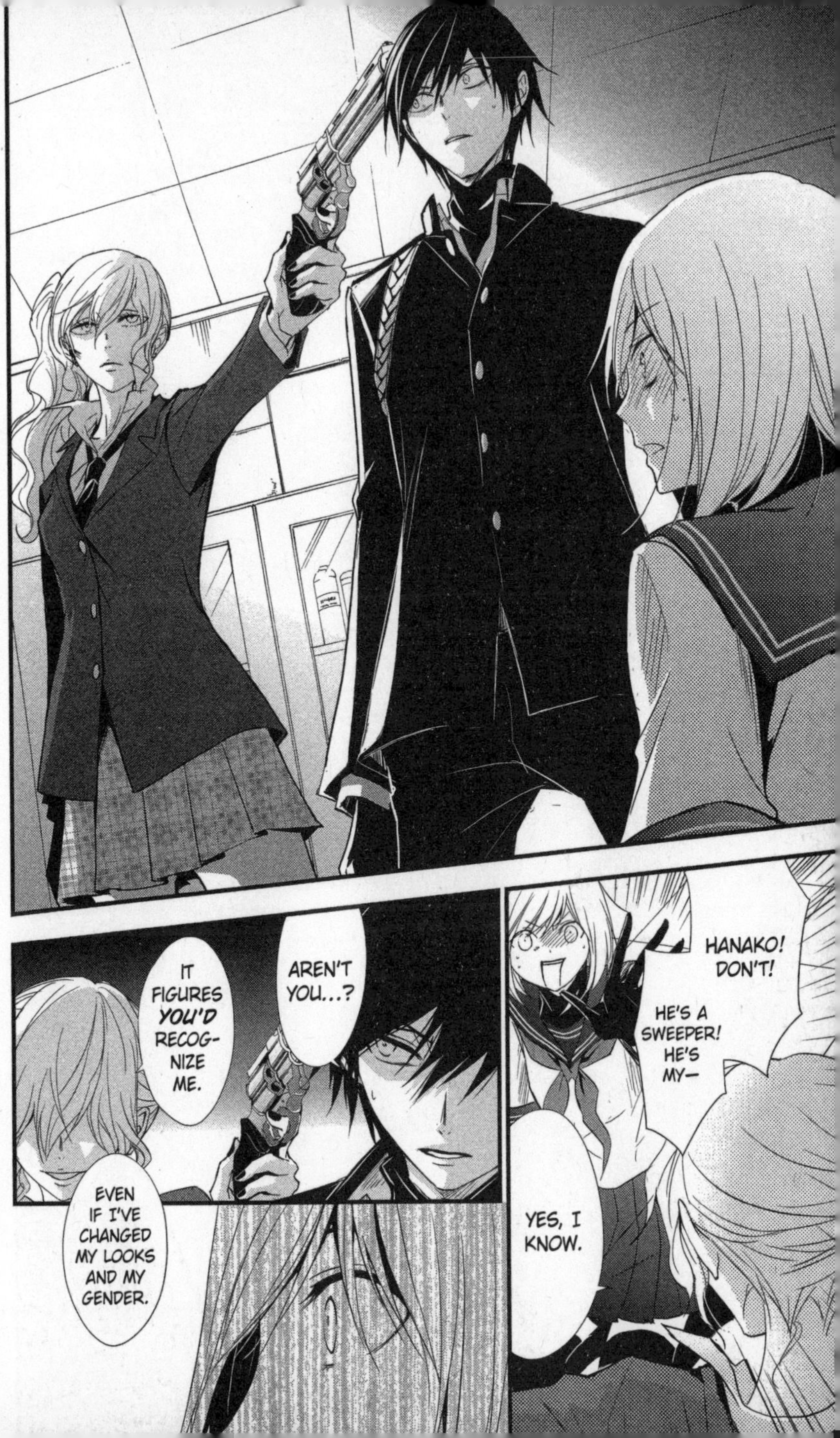
HANAKO! DON'T!
HE'S A SWEEPER! HE'S MY—
YES, I KNOW.
AREN'T YOU...?
IT FIGURES *YOU'D* RECOG-NIZE ME.
EVEN IF I'VE CHANGED MY LOOKS AND MY GENDER.

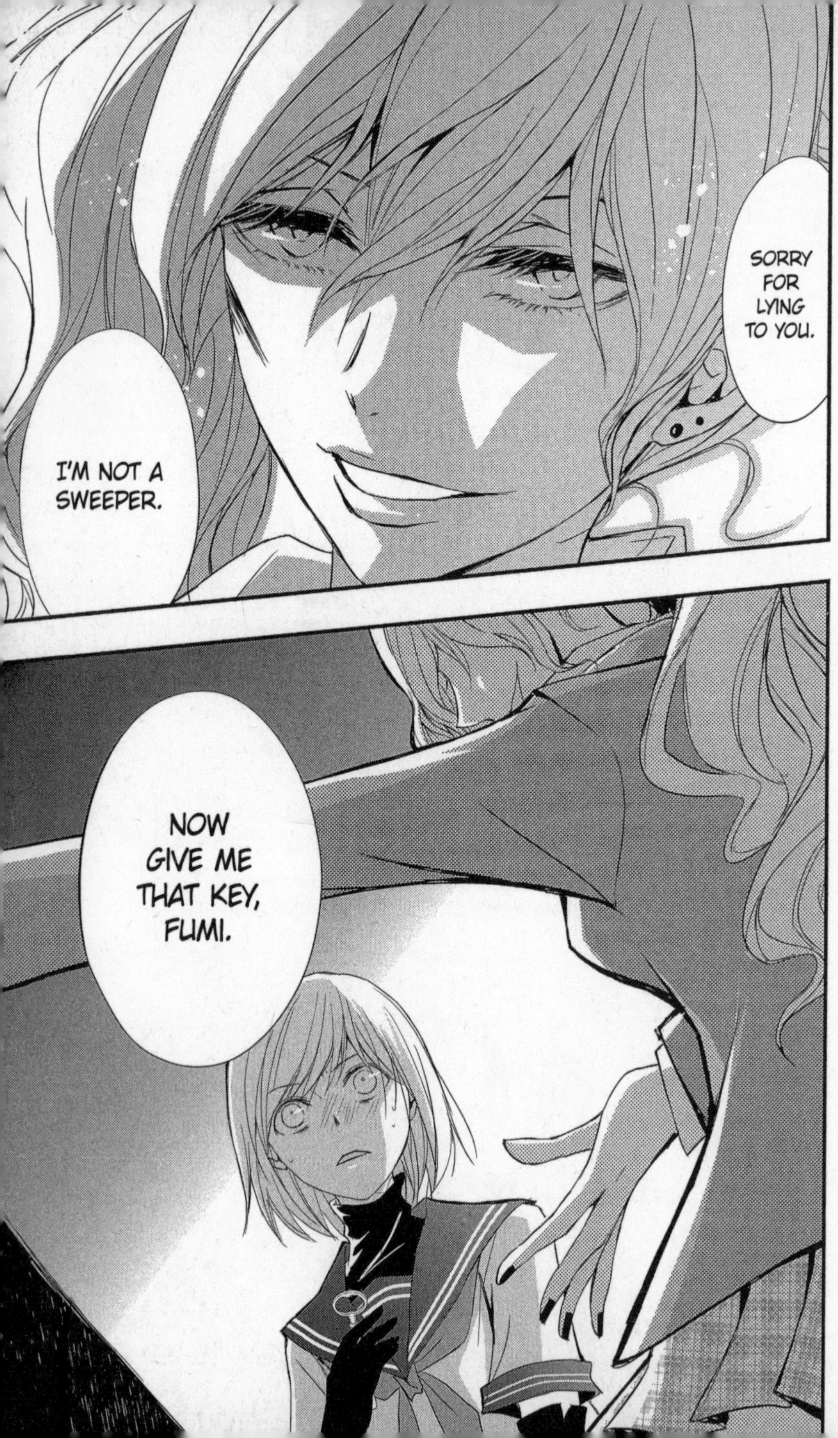
SORRY FOR LYING TO YOU.
I'M NOT A SWEEPER.
NOW GIVE ME THAT KEY, FUMI.

MONTHLY BETSUCOMI SALE DATE NOTICE ON TWITTER

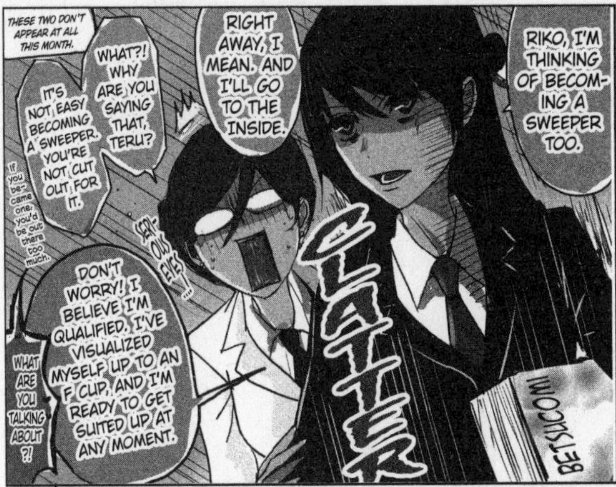
RIKO, I'M THINKING OF BECOMING A SWEEPER TOO.
RIGHT AWAY, I MEAN. AND I'LL GO TO THE INSIDE.
WHAT?! WHY ARE YOU SAYING THAT, TERU?
IT'S NOT EASY BECOMING A SWEEPER. YOU'RE NOT CUT OUT FOR IT.
If you became one, you'd be out there too much.
THESE TWO DON'T APPEAR AT ALL THIS MONTH.
SERIOUS EYES!!
CLATTER
BETSUCOMI
DON'T WORRY! I BELIEVE I'M QUALIFIED. I'VE VISUALIZED MYSELF UP TO AN F CUP, AND I'M READY TO GET SUITED UP AT ANY MOMENT.
WHAT ARE YOU TALKING ABOUT?!

CHAPTER 8

← THESE TWO ARE FROM *DENGEKI DAISY*: TERU (A CUP) AND RIKO (D CUP). THEY ALSO APPEAR BRIEFLY IN *QUEEN'S QUALITY*.

WHAT'S UP IN *QUEEN'S QUALITY* THIS MONTH?
(1) SENDAI REALLY LET DOWN HER GUARD.
(2) MALE ARTISTS SEEM TO DRAW FEMALE BREASTS BETTER THAN I DO.
(3) CALL THE NEW CHARACTER YUKO.
IN CHAPTER 8, YUKO JUST HAS TOO MUCH FUN, SO FUMI AND THIS AUTHOR ARE REALLY MAD!

WHAT'S UP IN *QUEEN'S QUALITY* THIS MONTH?
(1) MY EDITOR'S THE ONE WHO TOLD ME TO DRAW MORE TENTACLES.
(2) ATARU'S SISTER'S STEPPING ON HIS FOOT.
(3) SO, KYUTARO, WHY ARE YOU LOOKING AT HER THIGH?
EVEN WITH SO MANY CHARACTERS DRESSED ALL IN WHITE, CHAPTER 9 STILL LOOKS DARK!

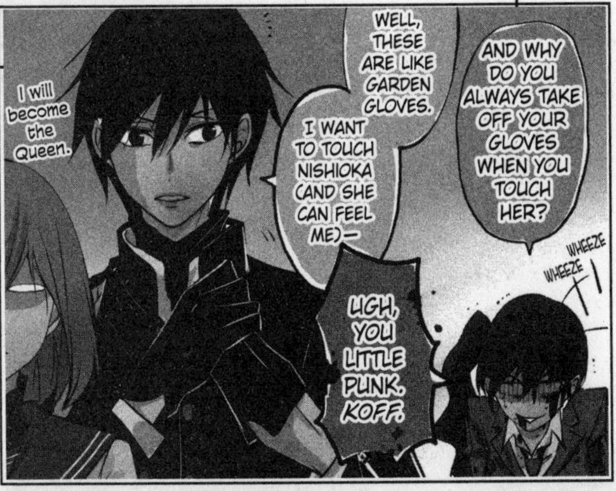
AND WHY DO YOU ALWAYS TAKE OFF YOUR GLOVES WHEN YOU TOUCH HER?
WELL, THESE ARE LIKE GARDEN GLOVES.
I WANT TO TOUCH NISHIOKA (AND SHE CAN FEEL ME)—
I will become the Queen.
WHEEZE
WHEEZE
UGH, YOU LITTLE PUNK. KOFF.

CHAPTER 9

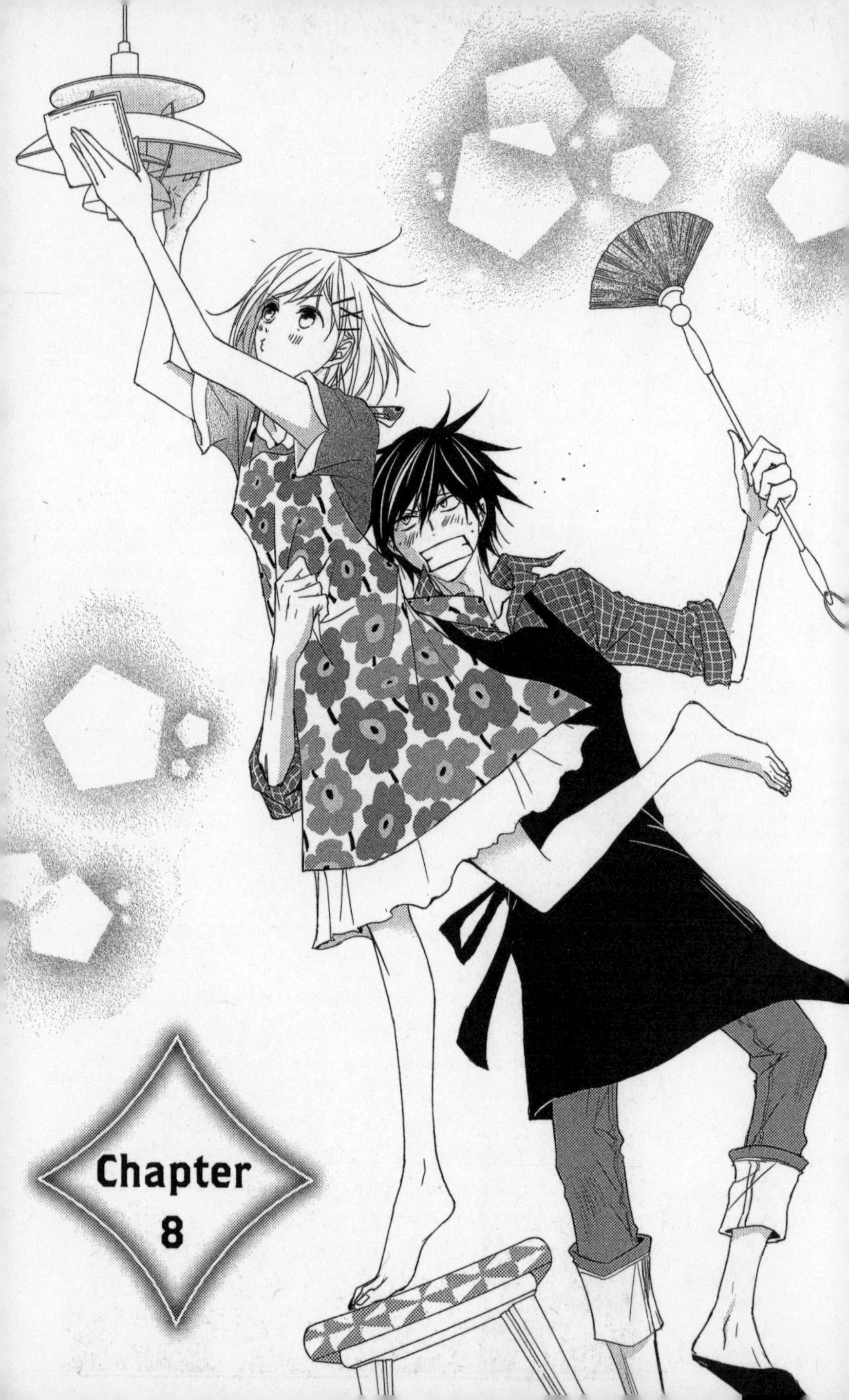
Chapter
8

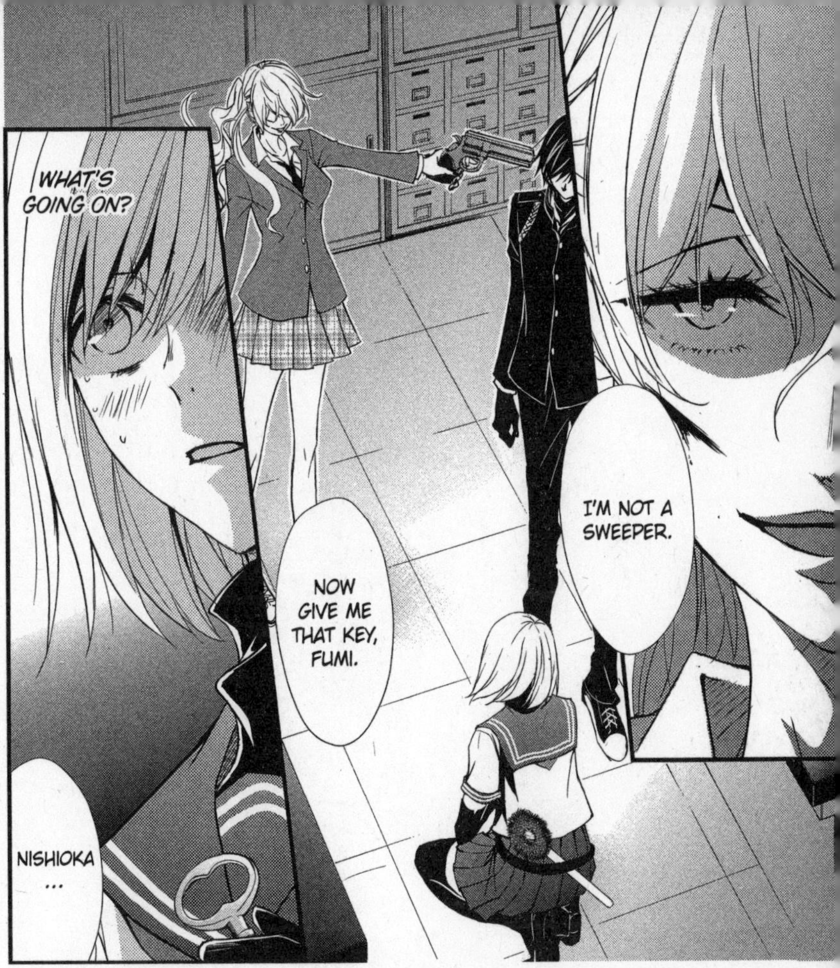
I'M NOT A SWEEPER.
NOW GIVE ME THAT KEY, FUMI.
WHAT'S GOING ON?
NISHIOKA ...

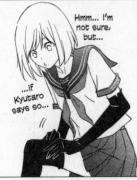

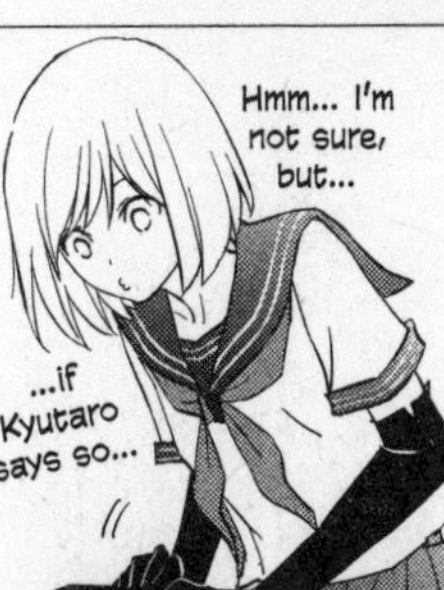
Hmm... I'm not sure, but...
...if Kyutaro says so...

About the outfits our two leads wear when entering The Inside: the braid on Kyutaro's shoulder seems to show his rank as a sweeper, but Fumi's stockings presumably reflect someone's taste. I suppose Sendai might have said something to the effect of "showing too much skin could attract bugs," or that it wasn't good for her to get cold, but I think Kyutaro might have stressed that "wearing tights just wouldn't be right."

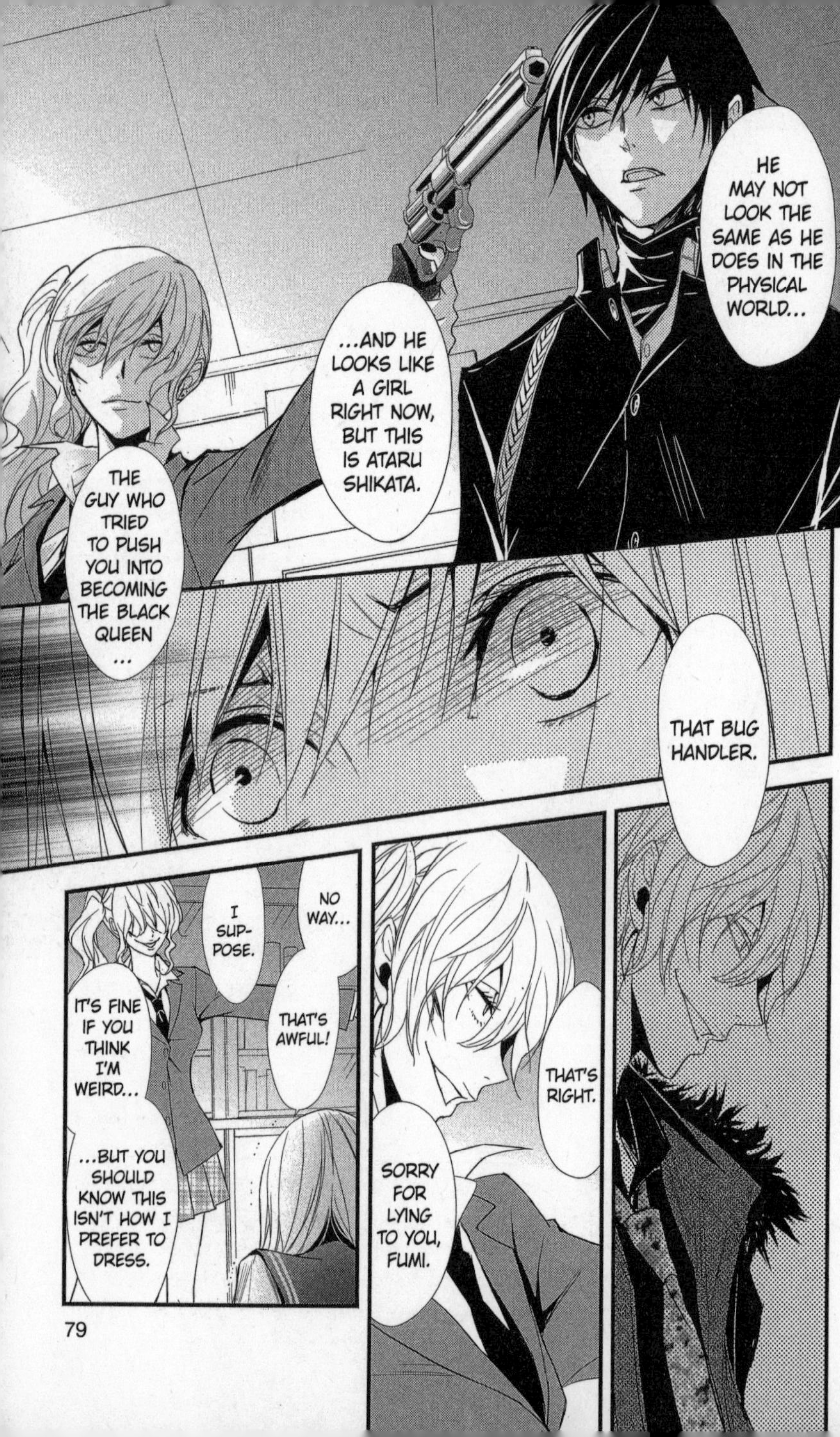
HE MAY NOT LOOK THE SAME AS HE DOES IN THE PHYSICAL WORLD...
...AND HE LOOKS LIKE A GIRL RIGHT NOW, BUT THIS IS ATARU SHIKATA.
THE GUY WHO TRIED TO PUSH YOU INTO BECOMING THE BLACK QUEEN ...
THAT BUG HANDLER.
THAT'S RIGHT.
SORRY FOR LYING TO YOU, FUMI.
NO WAY...
I SUP-POSE.
THAT'S AWFUL!
IT'S FINE IF YOU THINK I'M WEIRD...
...BUT YOU SHOULD KNOW THIS ISN'T HOW I PREFER TO DRESS.

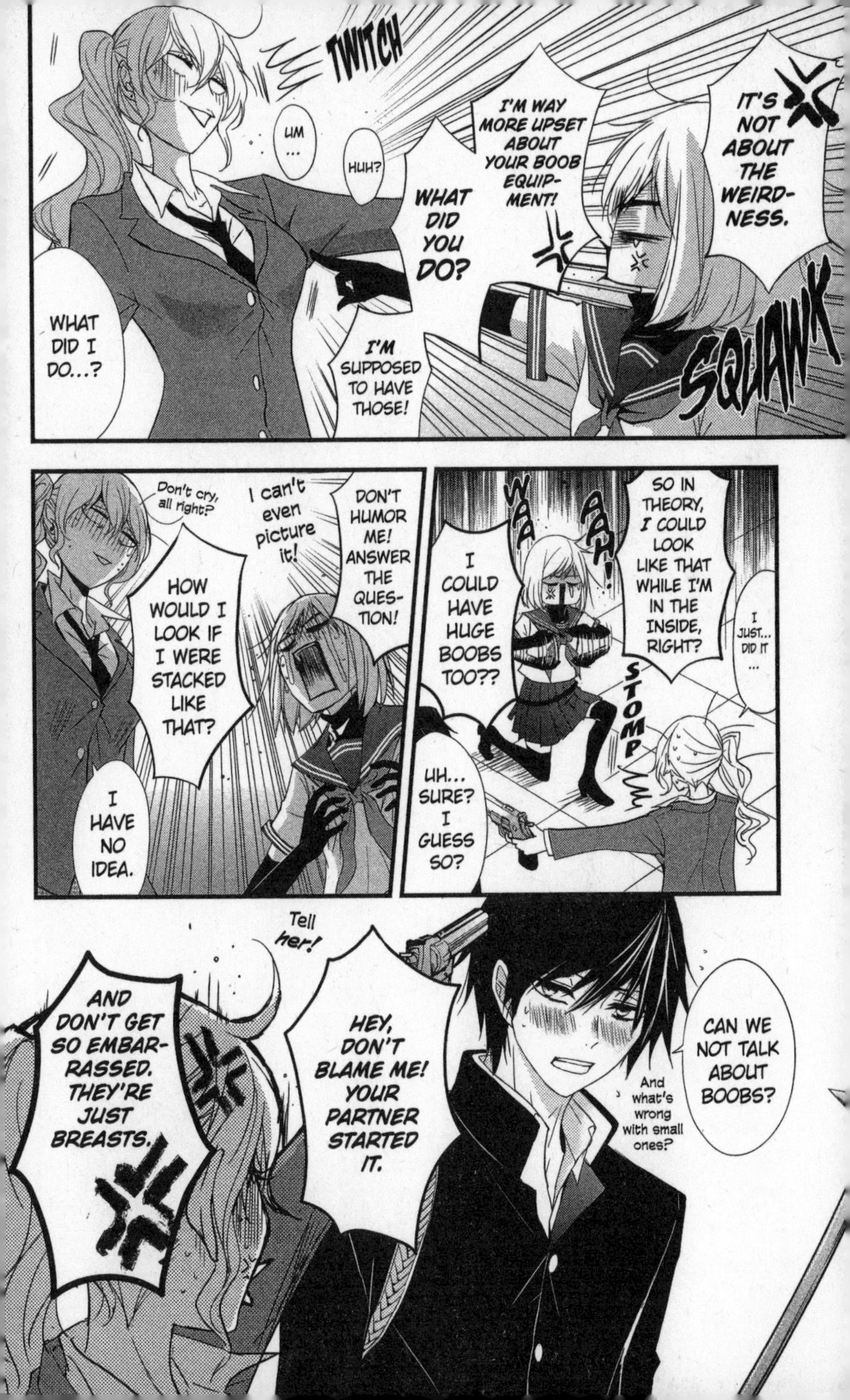
TWITCH
IT'S NOT ABOUT THE WEIRDNESS.
I'M WAY MORE UPSET ABOUT YOUR BOOB EQUIPMENT!
WHAT DID YOU DO?
HUH?
UM ...
SQUAWK
I'M SUPPOSED TO HAVE THOSE!
WHAT DID I DO...?
SO IN THEORY, I COULD LOOK LIKE THAT WHILE I'M IN THE INSIDE, RIGHT?
I JUST... DID IT ...
WAA AAH!
I COULD HAVE HUGE BOOBS TOO??
STOMP
UH... SURE? I GUESS SO?
DON'T HUMOR ME! ANSWER THE QUESTION!
I can't even picture it!
Don't cry, all right?
HOW WOULD I LOOK IF I WERE STACKED LIKE THAT?
I HAVE NO IDEA.
CAN WE NOT TALK ABOUT BOOBS?
And what's wrong with small ones?
Tell her!
HEY, DON'T BLAME ME! YOUR PARTNER STARTED IT.
AND DON'T GET SO EMBARRASSED. THEY'RE JUST BREASTS.

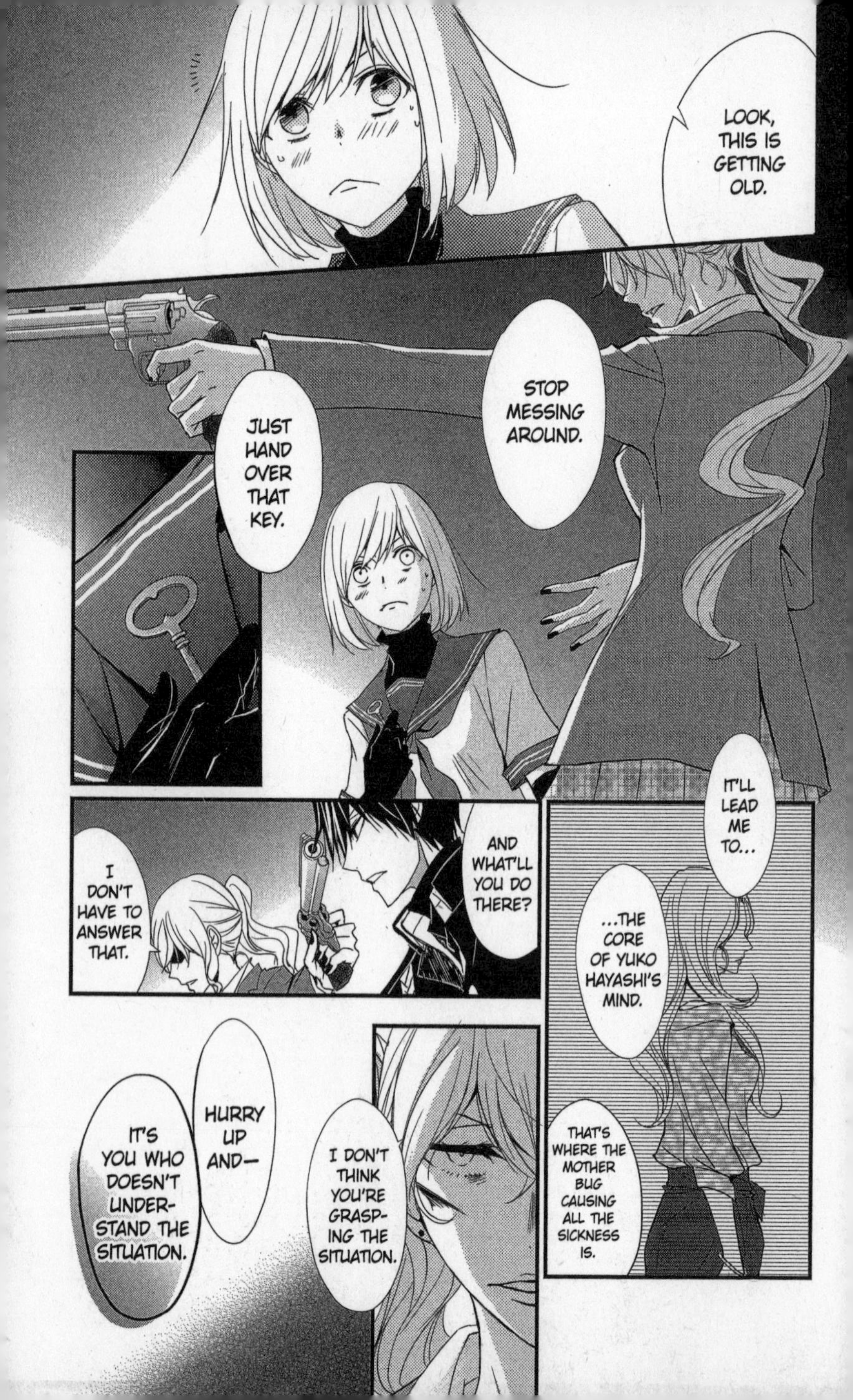
LOOK, THIS IS GETTING OLD.
STOP MESSING AROUND.
JUST HAND OVER THAT KEY.
IT'LL LEAD ME TO...
...THE CORE OF YUKO HAYASHI'S MIND.
THAT'S WHERE THE MOTHER BUG CAUSING ALL THE SICKNESS IS.
AND WHAT'LL YOU DO THERE?
I DON'T HAVE TO ANSWER THAT.
I DON'T THINK YOU'RE GRASP-ING THE SITUATION.
HURRY UP AND—
IT'S YOU WHO DOESN'T UNDER-STAND THE SITUATION.

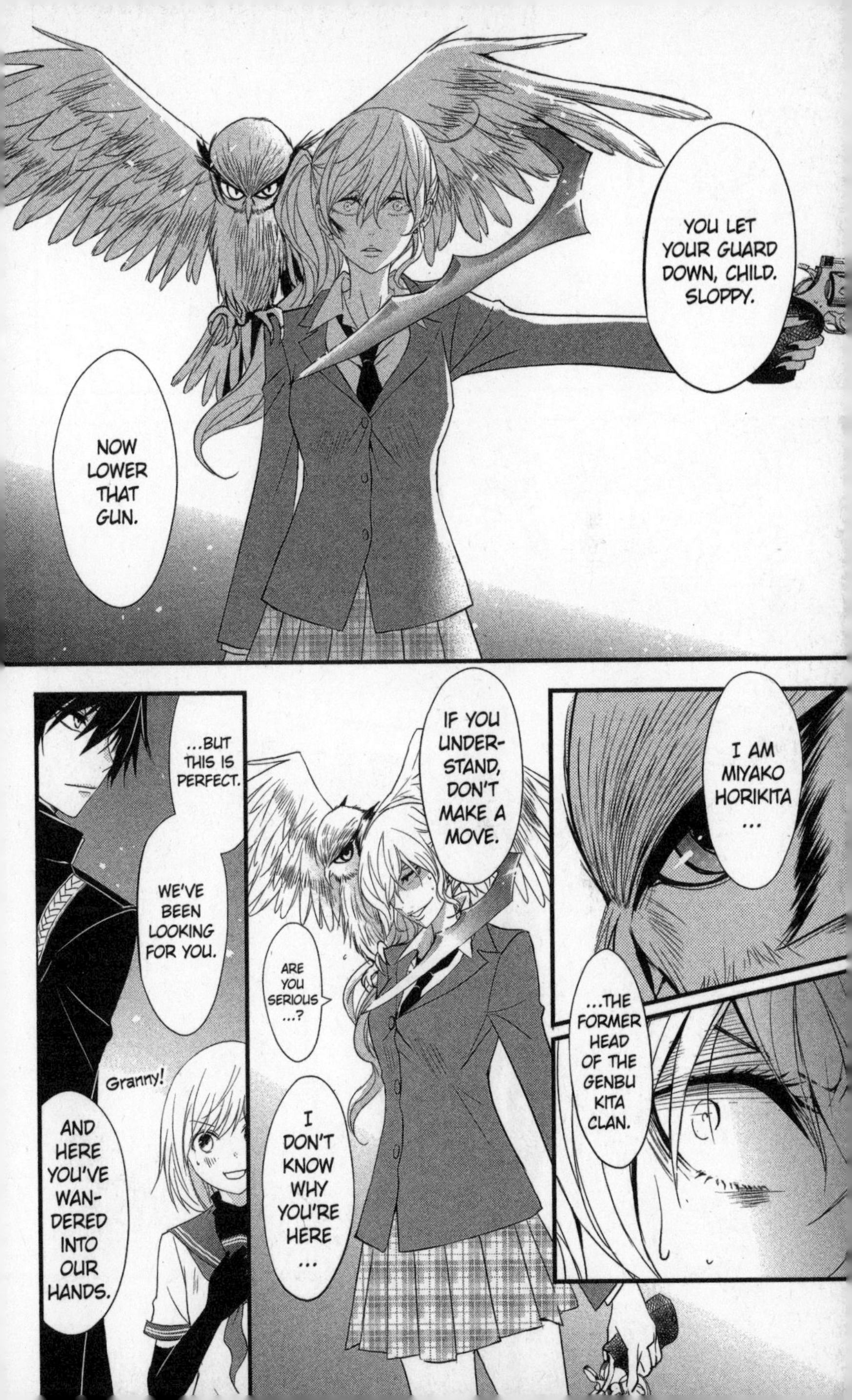
YOU LET YOUR GUARD DOWN, CHILD. SLOPPY.
NOW LOWER THAT GUN.
I AM MIYAKO HORIKITA...
...THE FORMER HEAD OF THE GENBU KITA CLAN.
IF YOU UNDERSTAND, DON'T MAKE A MOVE.
ARE YOU SERIOUS...?
I DON'T KNOW WHY YOU'RE HERE...
...BUT THIS IS PERFECT.
WE'VE BEEN LOOKING FOR YOU.
Granny!
AND HERE YOU'VE WANDERED INTO OUR HANDS.

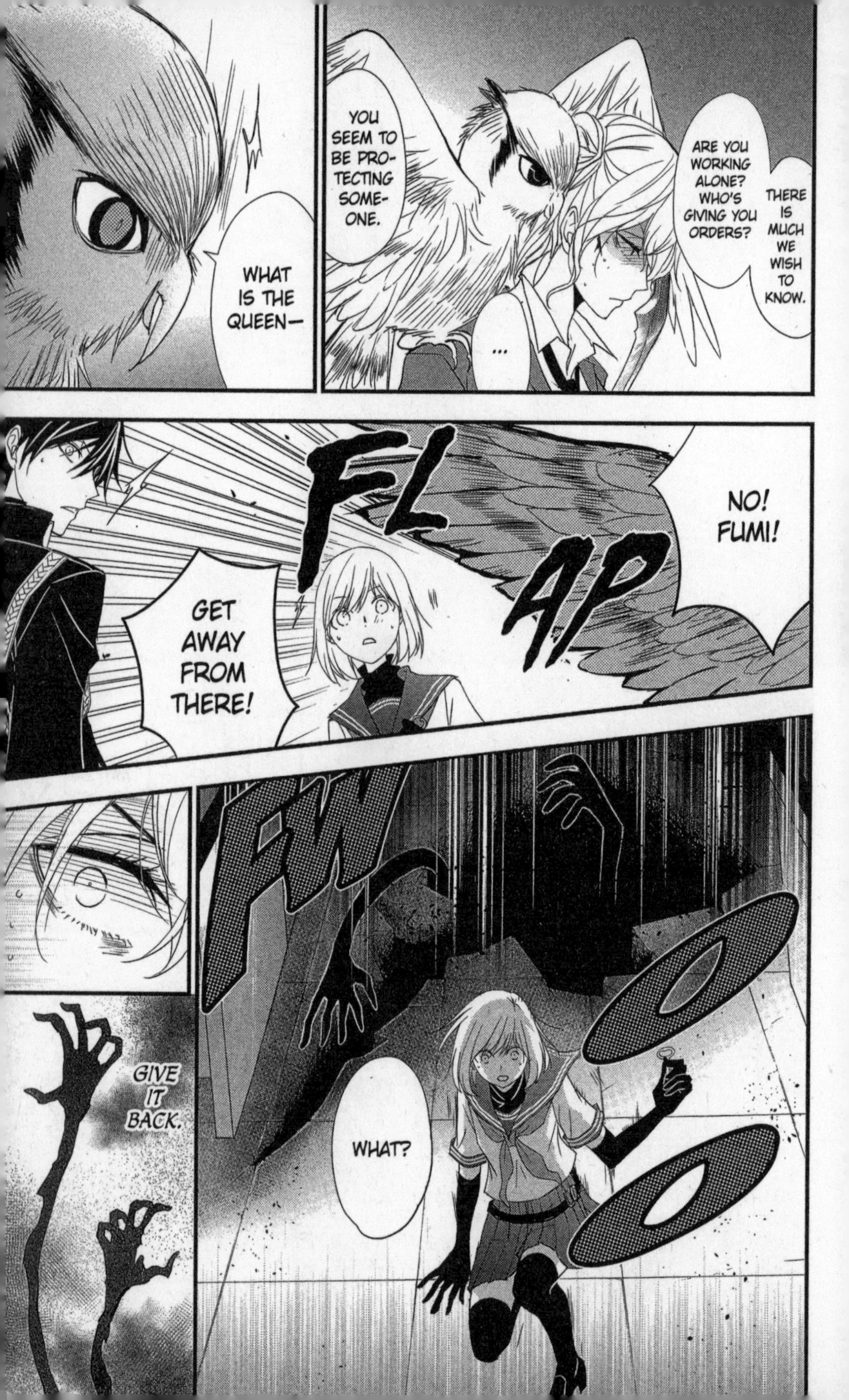
THERE IS MUCH WE WISH TO KNOW.
ARE YOU WORKING ALONE? WHO'S GIVING YOU ORDERS?
YOU SEEM TO BE PRO-TECTING SOME-ONE.
...
WHAT IS THE QUEEN—
NO! FUMI!
FLAP
GET AWAY FROM THERE!
FWOO
WHAT?
GIVE IT BACK.

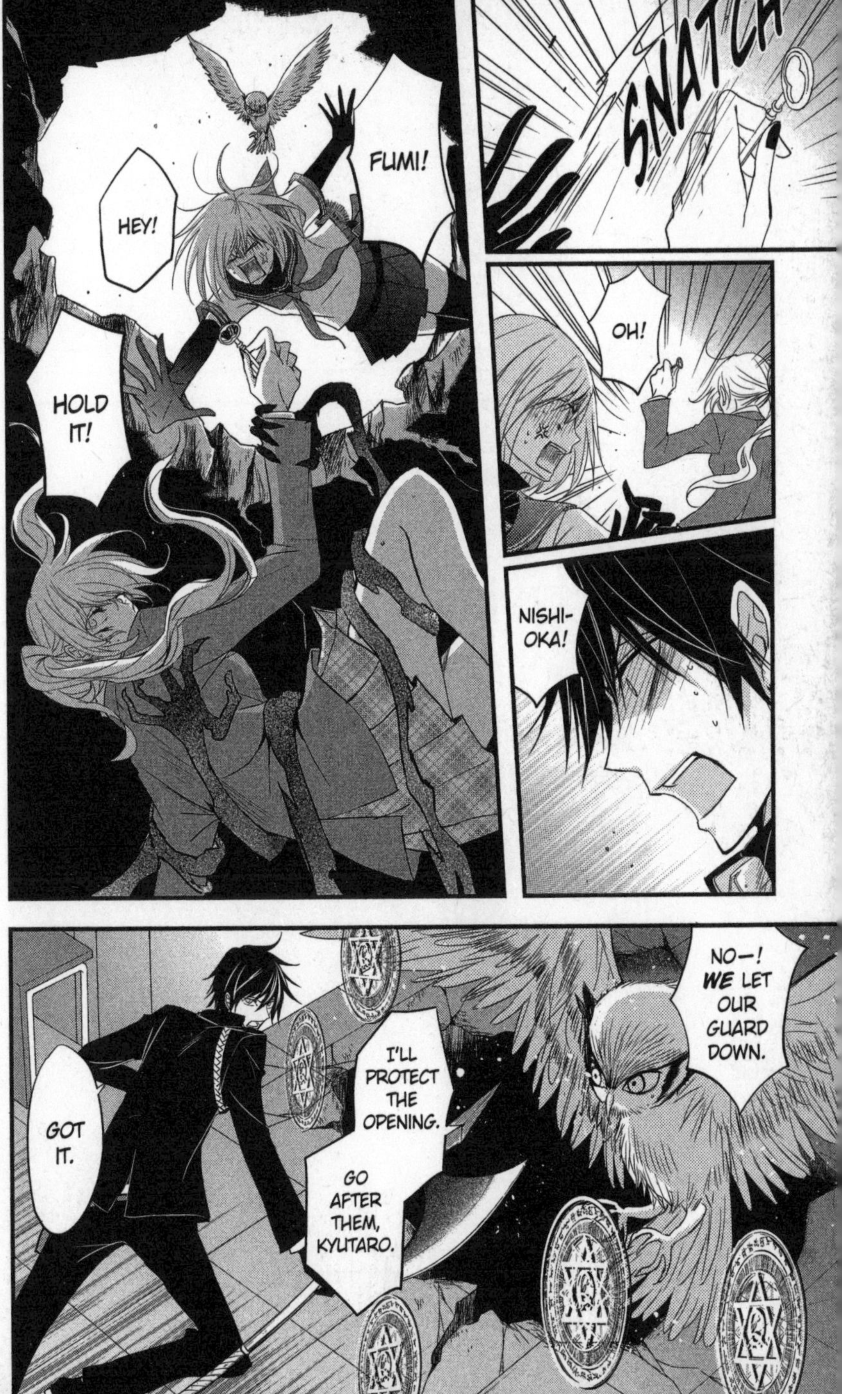
SNATCH
OH!
NISHI-OKA!
FUMI!
HEY!
HOLD IT!
NO—! **WE** LET OUR GUARD DOWN.
I'LL PROTECT THE OPENING.
GO AFTER THEM, KYUTARO.
GOT IT.

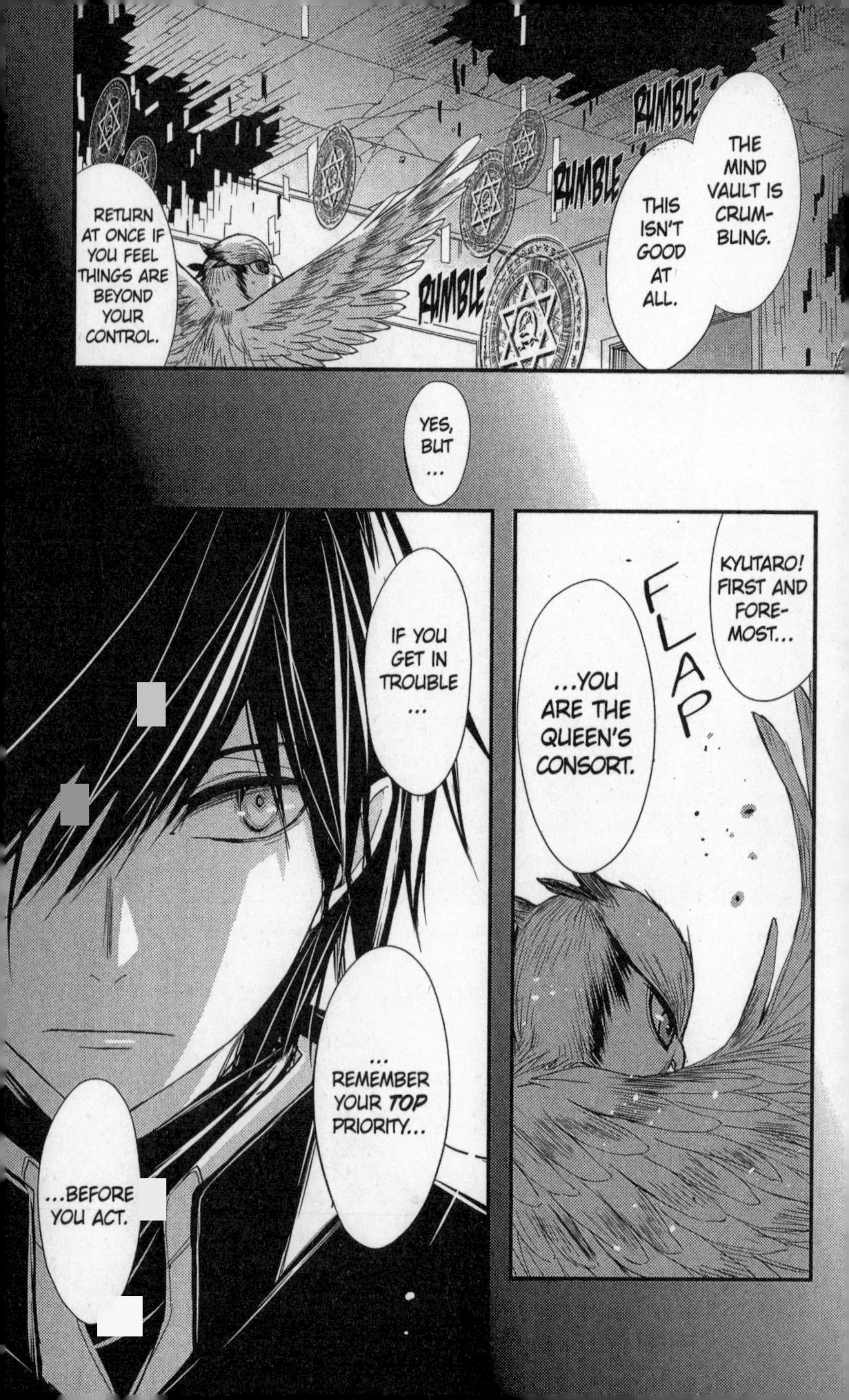

THE MIND VAULT IS CRUM-BLING.
THIS ISN'T GOOD AT ALL.
RUMBLE
RUMBLE
RUMBLE
RETURN AT ONCE IF YOU FEEL THINGS ARE BEYOND YOUR CONTROL.
YES, BUT ...
KYUTARO! FIRST AND FORE-MOST...
FLAP
...YOU ARE THE QUEEN'S CONSORT.
IF YOU GET IN TROUBLE ...
... REMEMBER YOUR *TOP* PRIORITY...
...BEFORE YOU ACT.

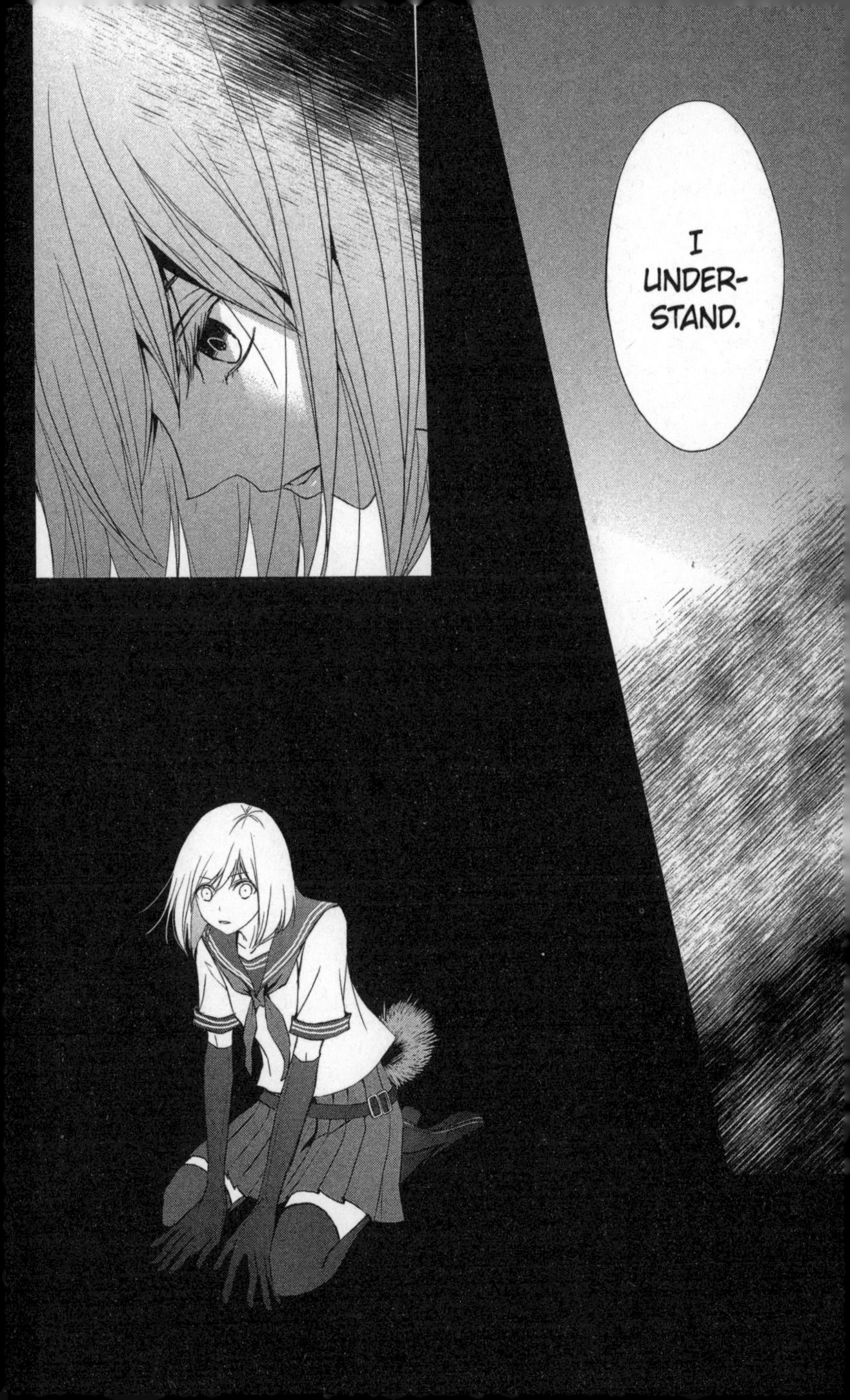
I UNDER-STAND.

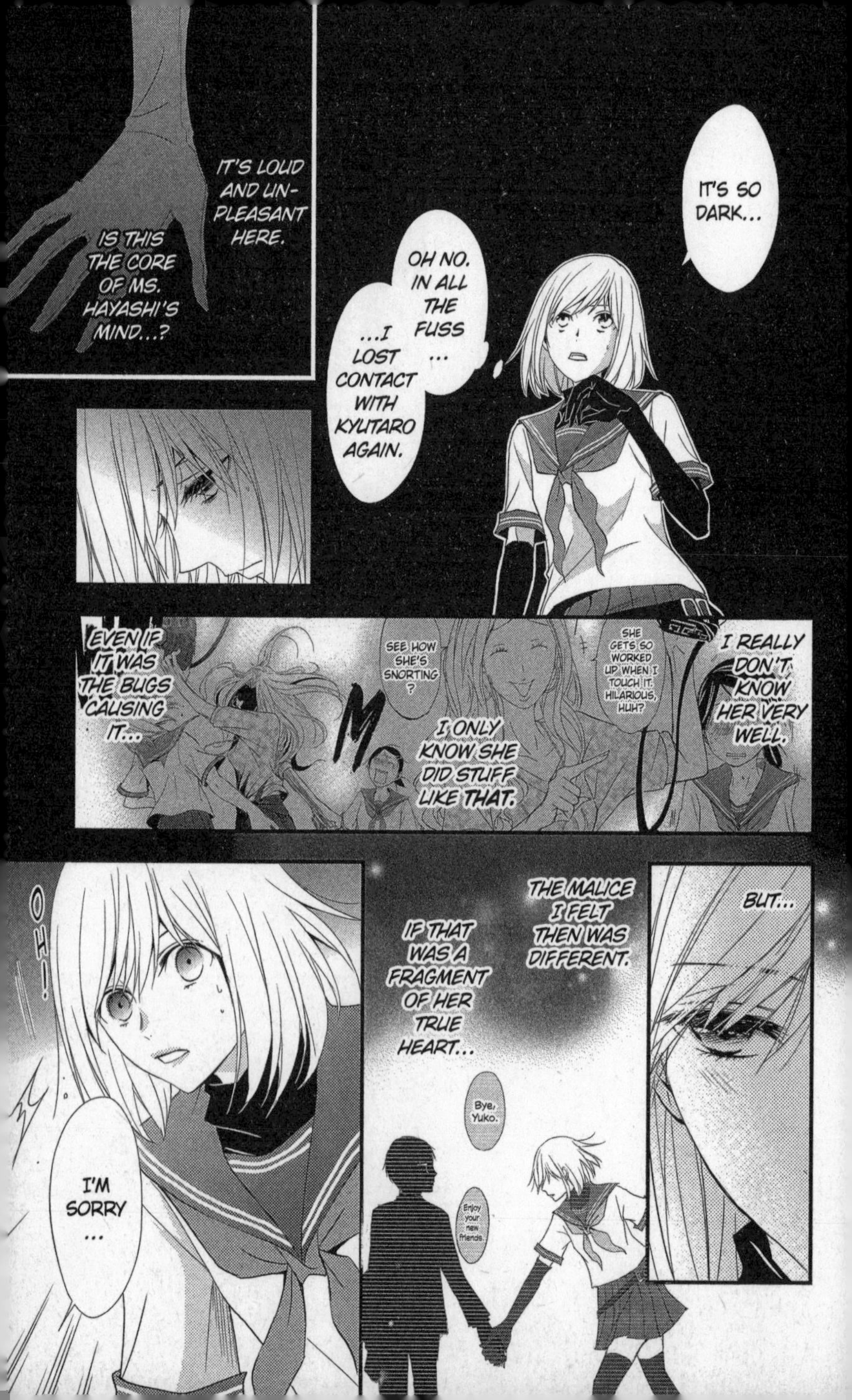
IT'S SO DARK...
OH NO. IN ALL THE FUSS...
...I LOST CONTACT WITH KYUTARO AGAIN.
IT'S LOUD AND UN-PLEASANT HERE.
IS THIS THE CORE OF MS. HAYASHI'S MIND...?
I REALLY DON'T KNOW HER VERY WELL.
SHE GETS SO WORKED UP WHEN I TOUCH IT. HILARIOUS, HUH?
I ONLY KNOW SHE DID STUFF LIKE THAT.
SEE HOW SHE'S SNORTING?
M
EVEN IF IT WAS THE BUGS CAUSING IT...
BUT...
THE MALICE I FELT THEN WAS DIFFERENT.
IF THAT WAS A FRAGMENT OF HER TRUE HEART...
Bye, Yuko.
Enjoy your new friends.
OH!
I'M SORRY...

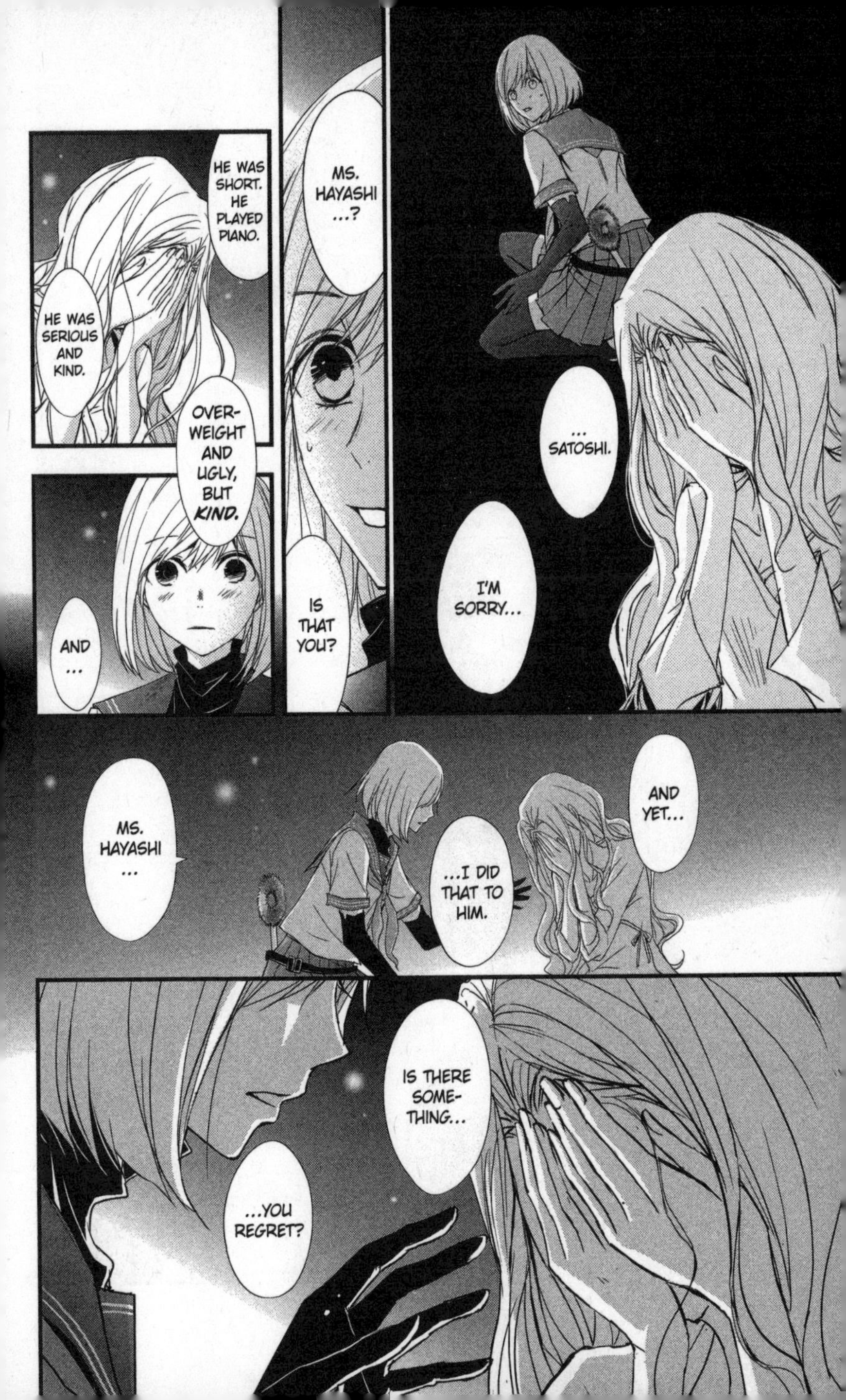
...SATOSHI.
I'M SORRY...
MS. HAYASHI...?
IS THAT YOU?
HE WAS SHORT. HE PLAYED PIANO.
HE WAS SERIOUS AND KIND.
OVER-WEIGHT AND UGLY, BUT *KIND.*
AND...
AND YET...
...I DID THAT TO HIM.
MS. HAYASHI...
IS THERE SOME-THING...
...YOU REGRET?

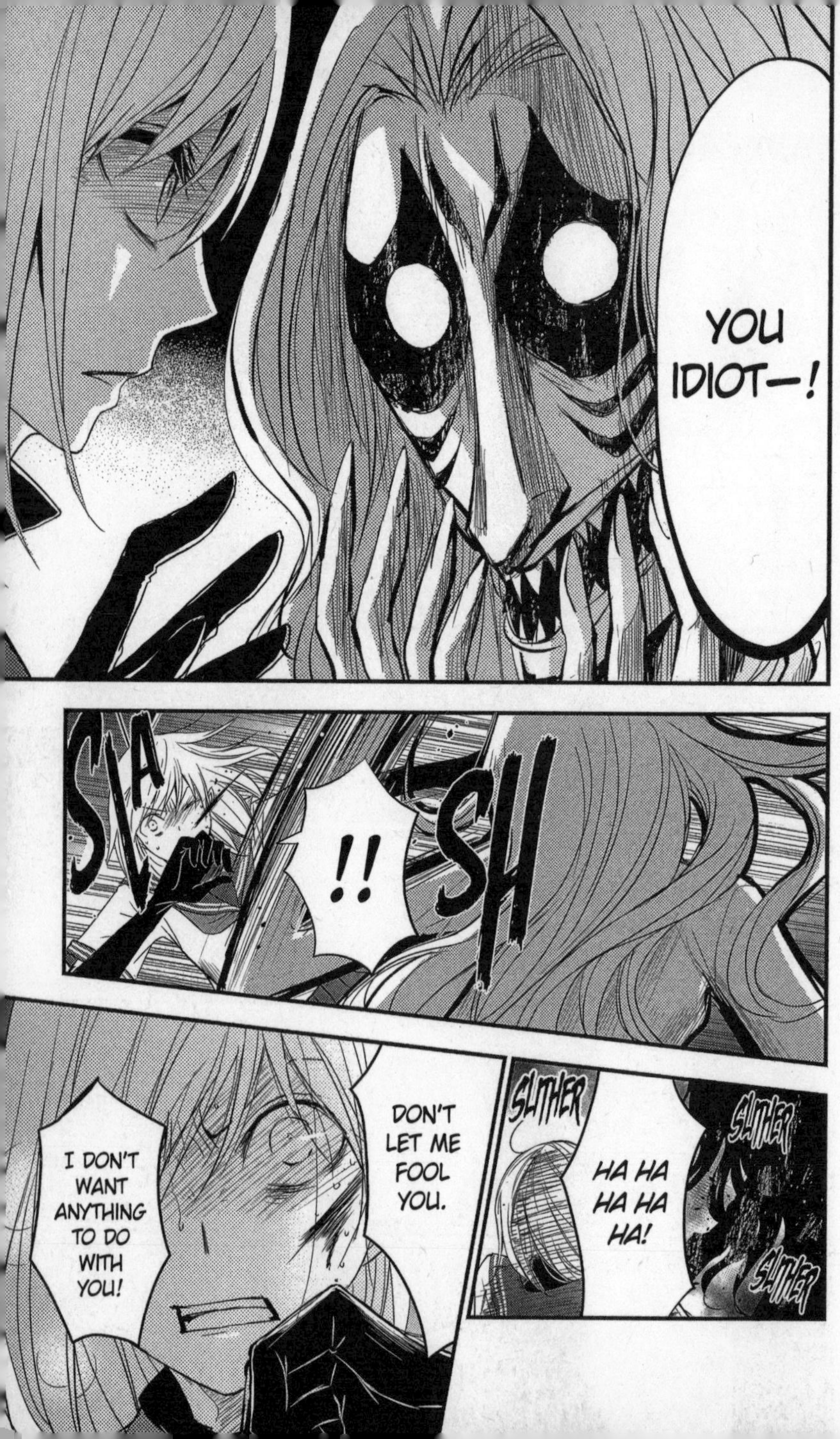
YOU IDIOT—!
SH
!!
SLA
SLITHER
SLITHER
HA HA HA HA HA!
SLITHER
DON'T LET ME FOOL YOU.
I DON'T WANT ANYTHING TO DO WITH YOU!

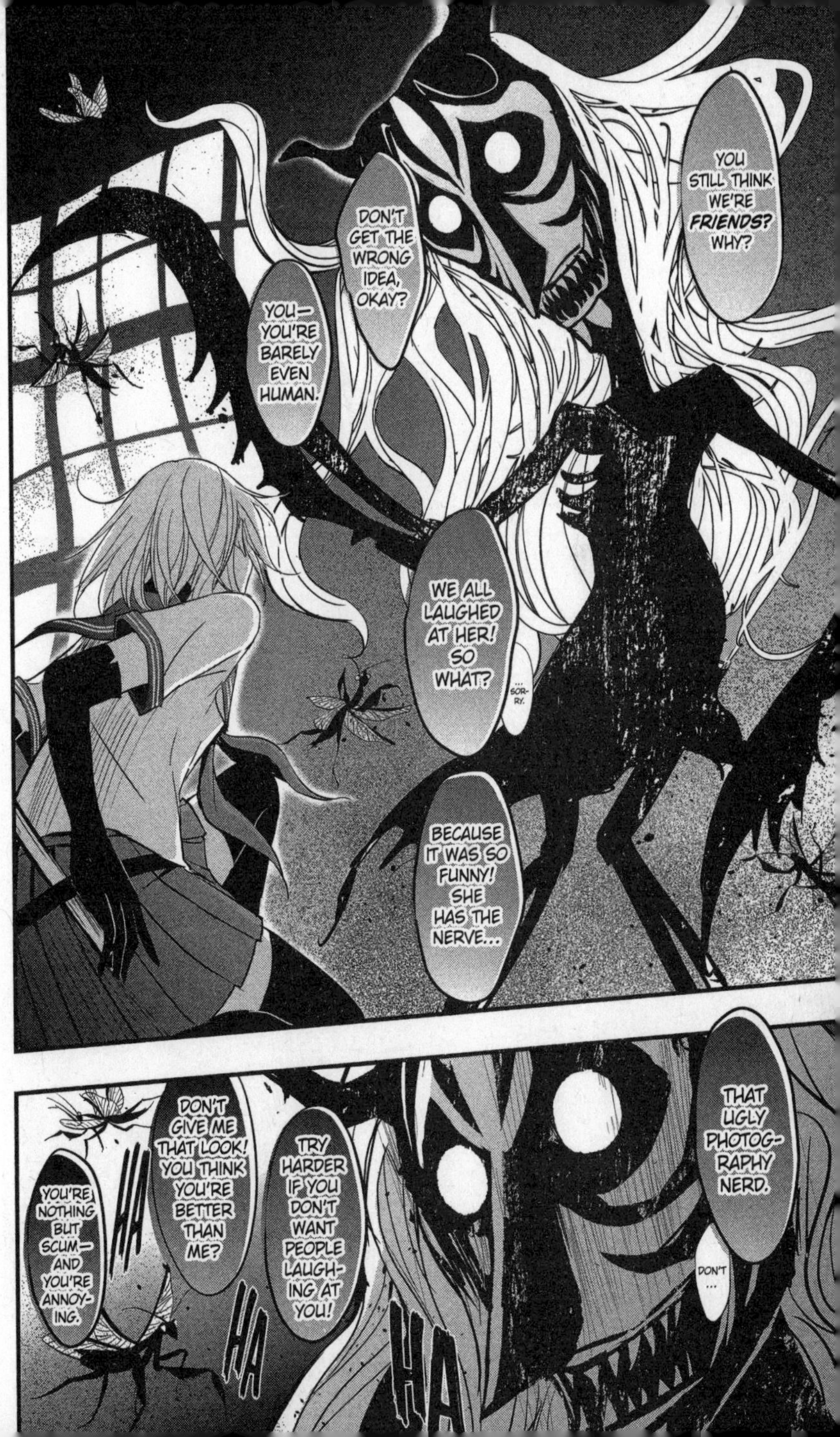
YOU STILL THINK WE'RE FRIENDS? WHY?
DON'T GET THE WRONG IDEA, OKAY?
YOU—YOU'RE BARELY EVEN HUMAN.
...SORRY.
WE ALL LAUGHED AT HER! SO WHAT?
BECAUSE IT WAS SO FUNNY! SHE HAS THE NERVE...
THAT UGLY PHOTOGRAPHY NERD.
DON'T...
HA
TRY HARDER IF YOU DON'T WANT PEOPLE LAUGHING AT YOU!
HA
DON'T GIVE ME THAT LOOK! YOU THINK YOU'RE BETTER THAN ME?
HA
YOU'RE NOTHING BUT SCUM—AND YOU'RE ANNOYING.

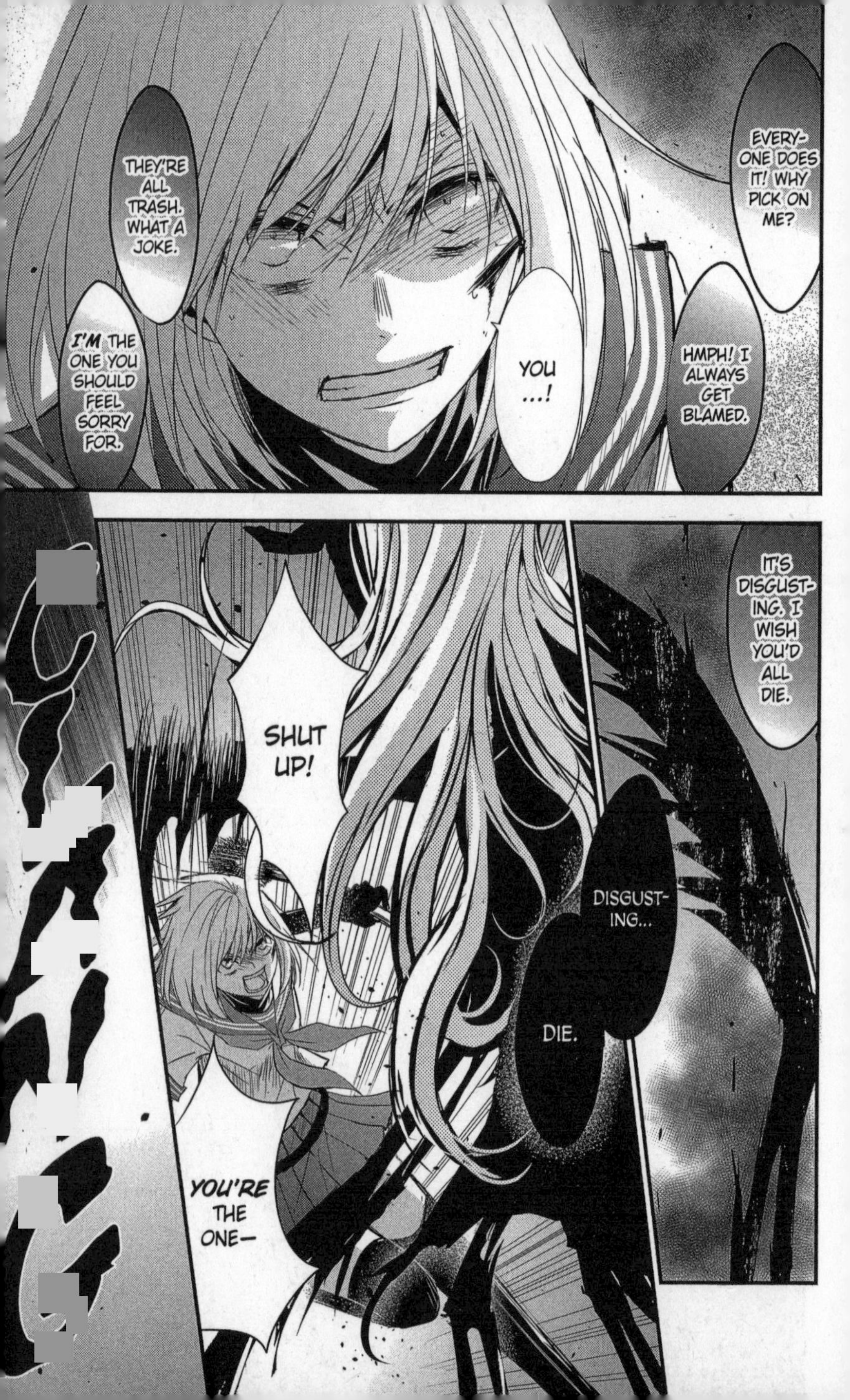
EVERY-ONE DOES IT! WHY PICK ON ME?
HMPH! I ALWAYS GET BLAMED.
YOU ...!
THEY'RE ALL TRASH. WHAT A JOKE.
I'M THE ONE YOU SHOULD FEEL SORRY FOR.
IT'S DISGUST-ING. I WISH YOU'D ALL DIE.
DISGUST-ING...
DIE.
SHUT UP!
YOU'RE THE ONE—

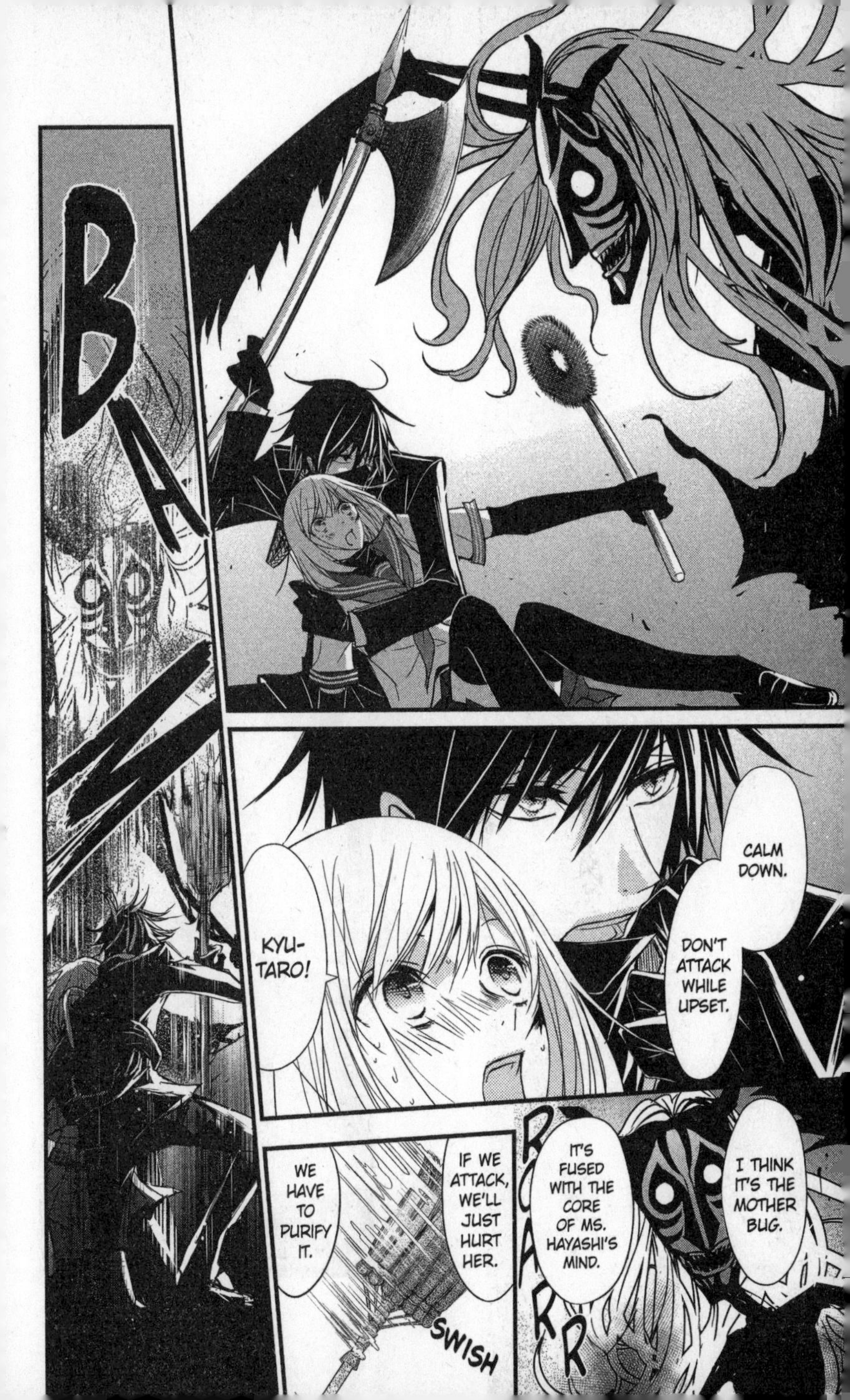
BAM
CALM DOWN.
DON'T ATTACK WHILE UPSET.
KYU-TARO!
I THINK IT'S THE MOTHER BUG.
ROARR
IT'S FUSED WITH THE CORE OF MS. HAYASHI'S MIND.
IF WE ATTACK, WE'LL JUST HURT HER.
WE HAVE TO PURIFY IT.
SWISH

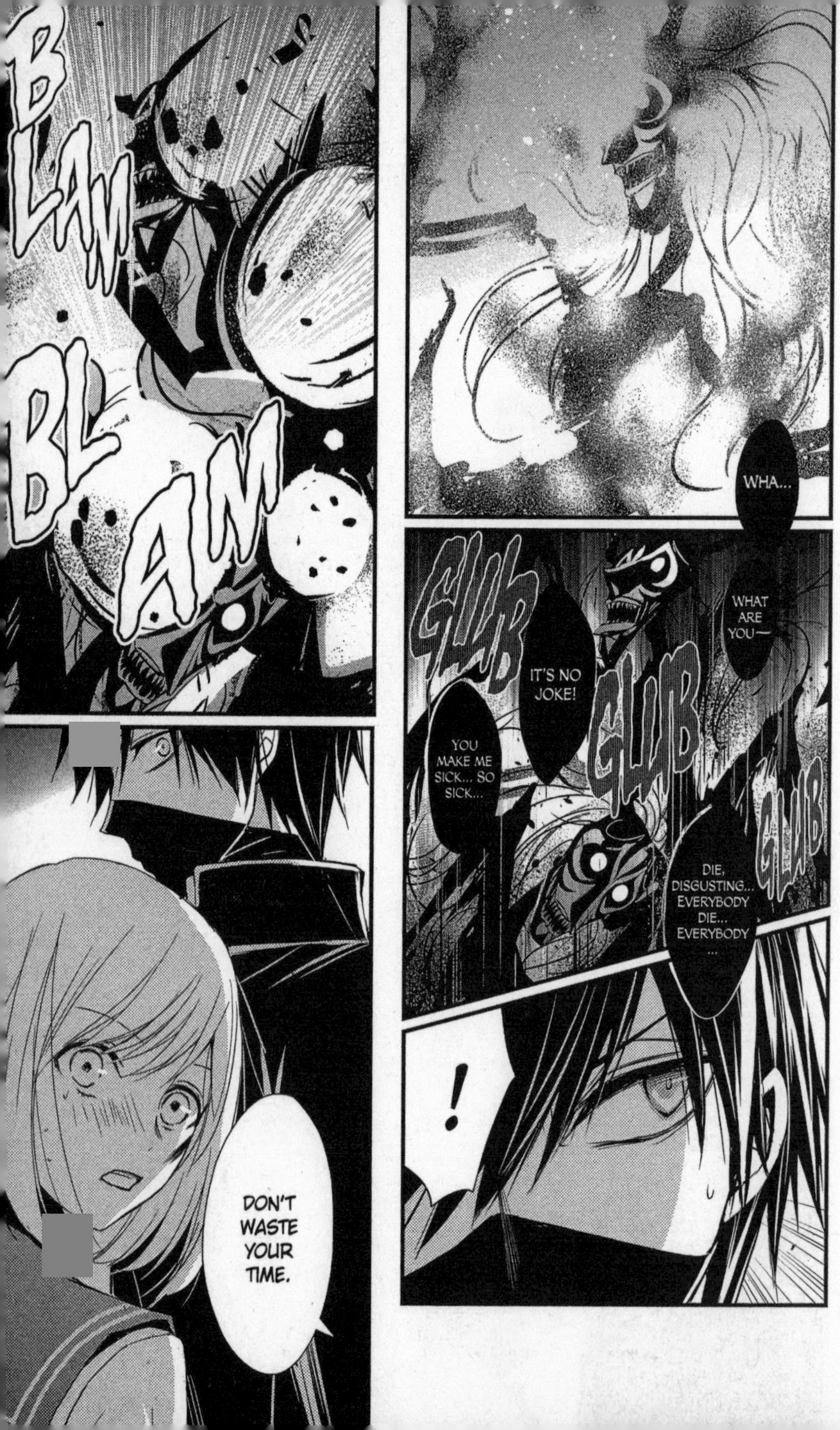
WHA...
WHAT ARE YOU—
GLUB
IT'S NO JOKE!
GLUB
YOU MAKE ME SICK... SO SICK...
GLUB
DIE, DISGUSTING... EVERYBODY DIE... EVERYBODY...
!
BLAM
BLAM
DON'T WASTE YOUR TIME.

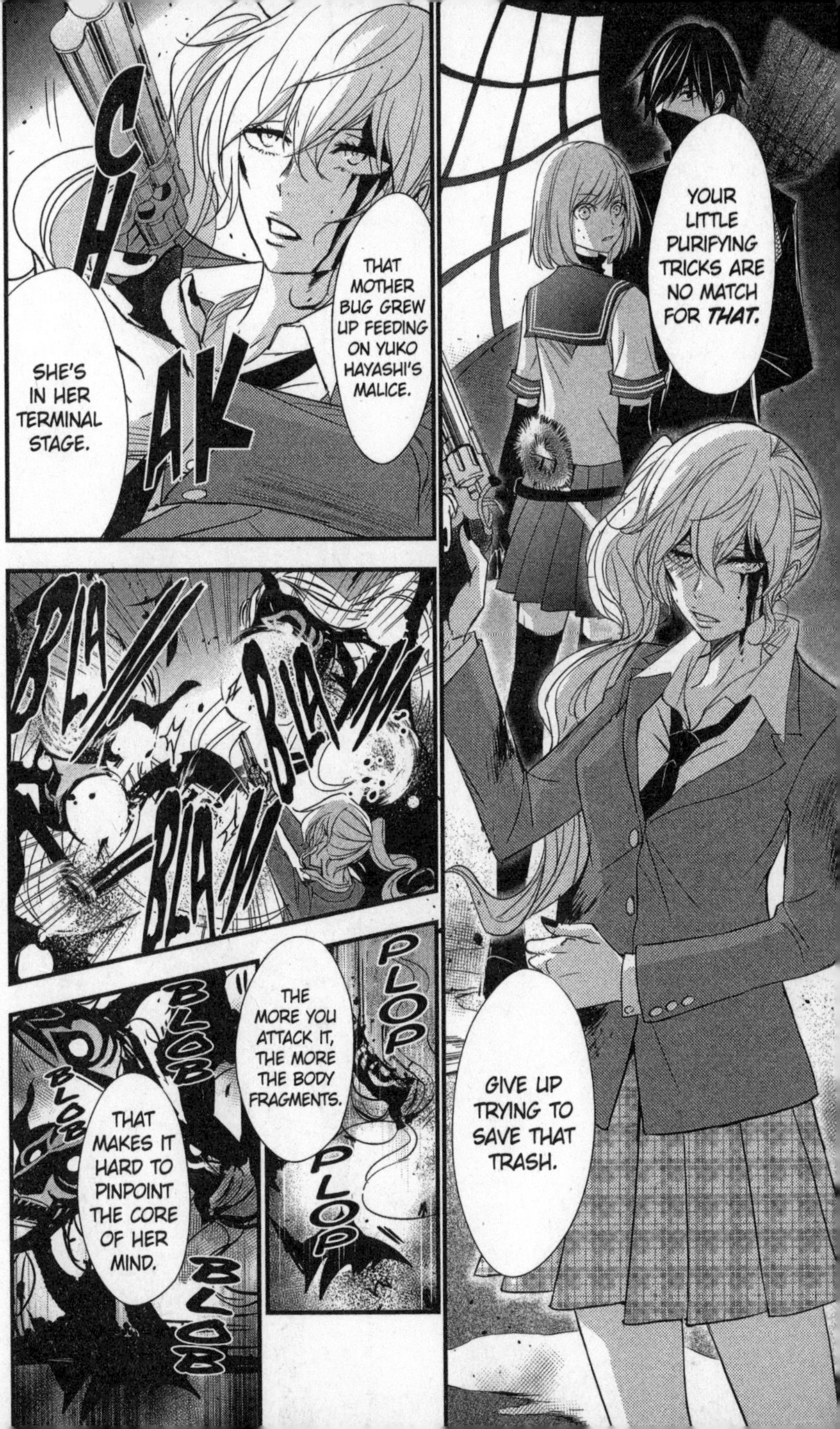
YOUR LITTLE PURIFYING TRICKS ARE NO MATCH FOR *THAT.*
GIVE UP TRYING TO SAVE THAT TRASH.
CHAK
THAT MOTHER BUG GREW UP FEEDING ON YUKO HAYASHI'S MALICE.
SHE'S IN HER TERMINAL STAGE.
BLAM
BLAM
BLAM
PLOP
THE MORE YOU ATTACK IT, THE MORE THE BODY FRAGMENTS.
PLOP
BLOB
BLOB
THAT MAKES IT HARD TO PINPOINT THE CORE OF HER MIND.
BLOB

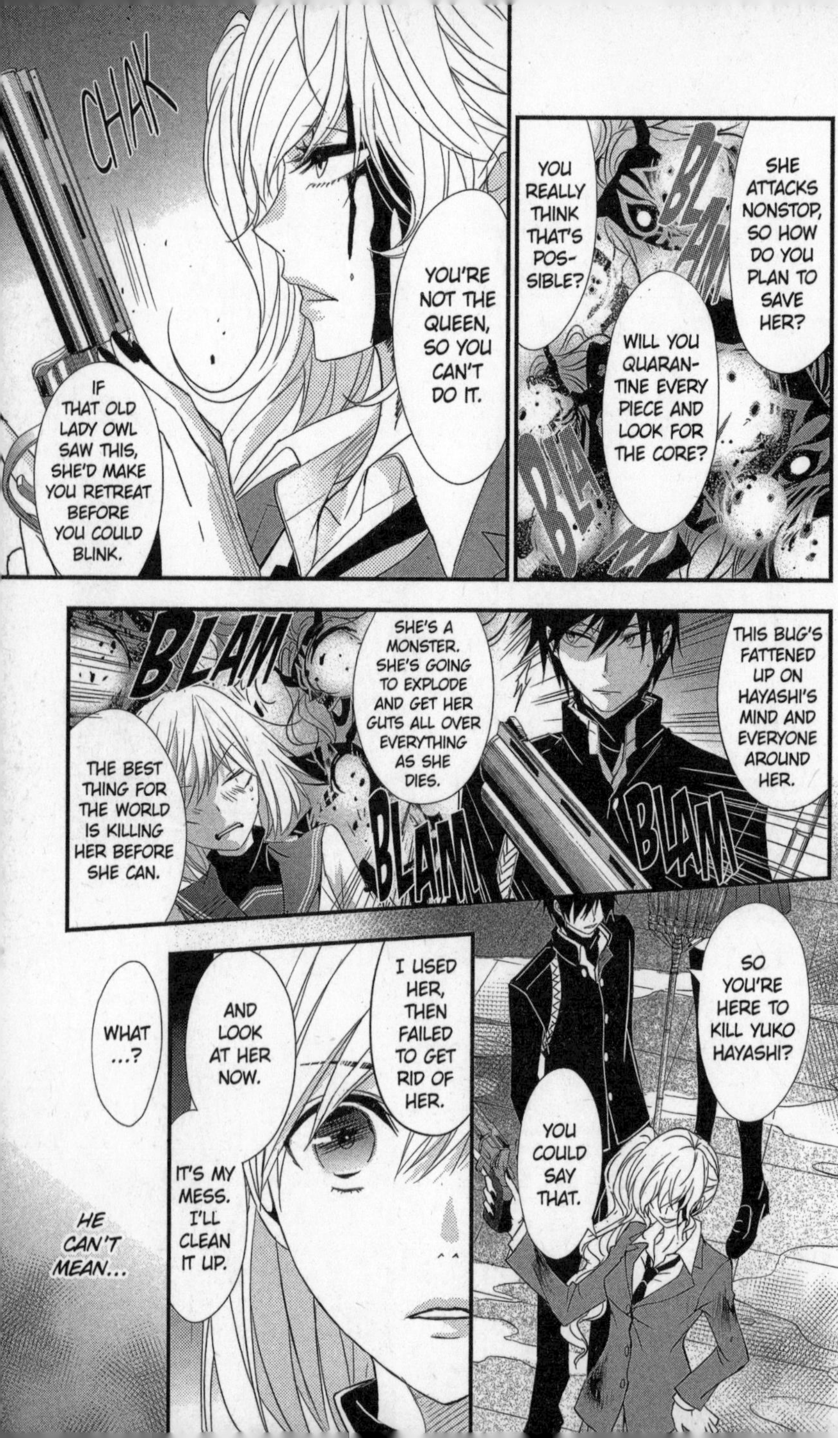
SHE ATTACKS NONSTOP, SO HOW DO YOU PLAN TO SAVE HER?
BLAM
YOU REALLY THINK THAT'S POS-SIBLE?
WILL YOU QUARAN-TINE EVERY PIECE AND LOOK FOR THE CORE?
BLAM
CHAK
YOU'RE NOT THE QUEEN, SO YOU CAN'T DO IT.
IF THAT OLD LADY OWL SAW THIS, SHE'D MAKE YOU RETREAT BEFORE YOU COULD BLINK.
THIS BUG'S FATTENED UP ON HAYASHI'S MIND AND EVERYONE AROUND HER.
BLAM
SHE'S A MONSTER. SHE'S GOING TO EXPLODE AND GET HER GUTS ALL OVER EVERYTHING AS SHE DIES.
BLAM
BLAM
THE BEST THING FOR THE WORLD IS KILLING HER BEFORE SHE CAN.
SO YOU'RE HERE TO KILL YUKO HAYASHI?
YOU COULD SAY THAT.
I USED HER, THEN FAILED TO GET RID OF HER.
AND LOOK AT HER NOW.
IT'S MY MESS. I'LL CLEAN IT UP.
WHAT ...?
HE CAN'T MEAN...

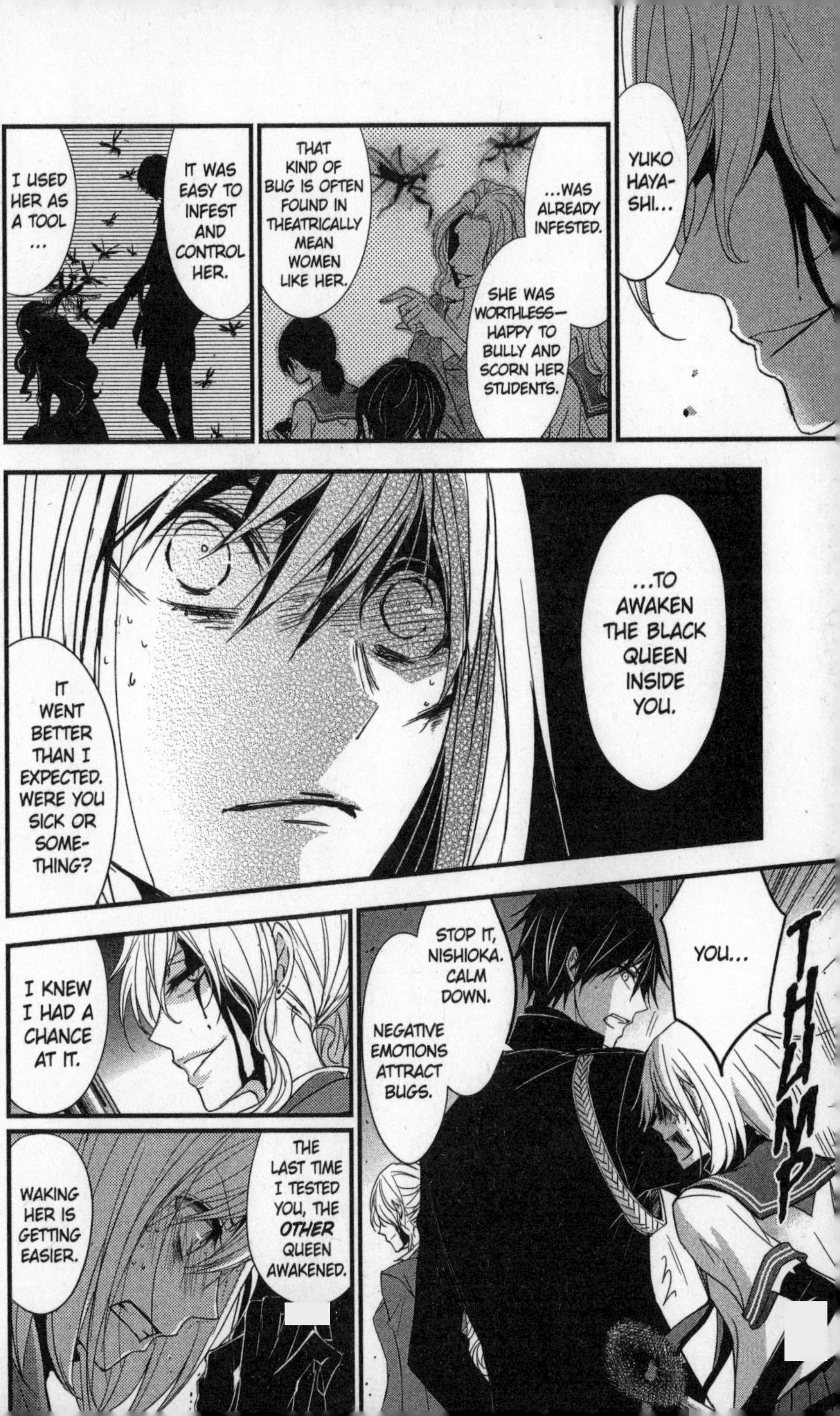
YUKO HAYA-SHI...
...WAS ALREADY INFESTED.
SHE WAS WORTHLESS—HAPPY TO BULLY AND SCORN HER STUDENTS.
THAT KIND OF BUG IS OFTEN FOUND IN THEATRICALLY MEAN WOMEN LIKE HER.
IT WAS EASY TO INFEST AND CONTROL HER.
I USED HER AS A TOOL ...
...TO AWAKEN THE BLACK QUEEN INSIDE YOU.
IT WENT BETTER THAN I EXPECTED. WERE YOU SICK OR SOME-THING?
YOU...
THUMP
STOP IT, NISHIOKA. CALM DOWN.
NEGATIVE EMOTIONS ATTRACT BUGS.
I KNEW I HAD A CHANCE AT IT.
THE LAST TIME I TESTED YOU, THE *OTHER* QUEEN AWAKENED.
WAKING HER IS GETTING EASIER.

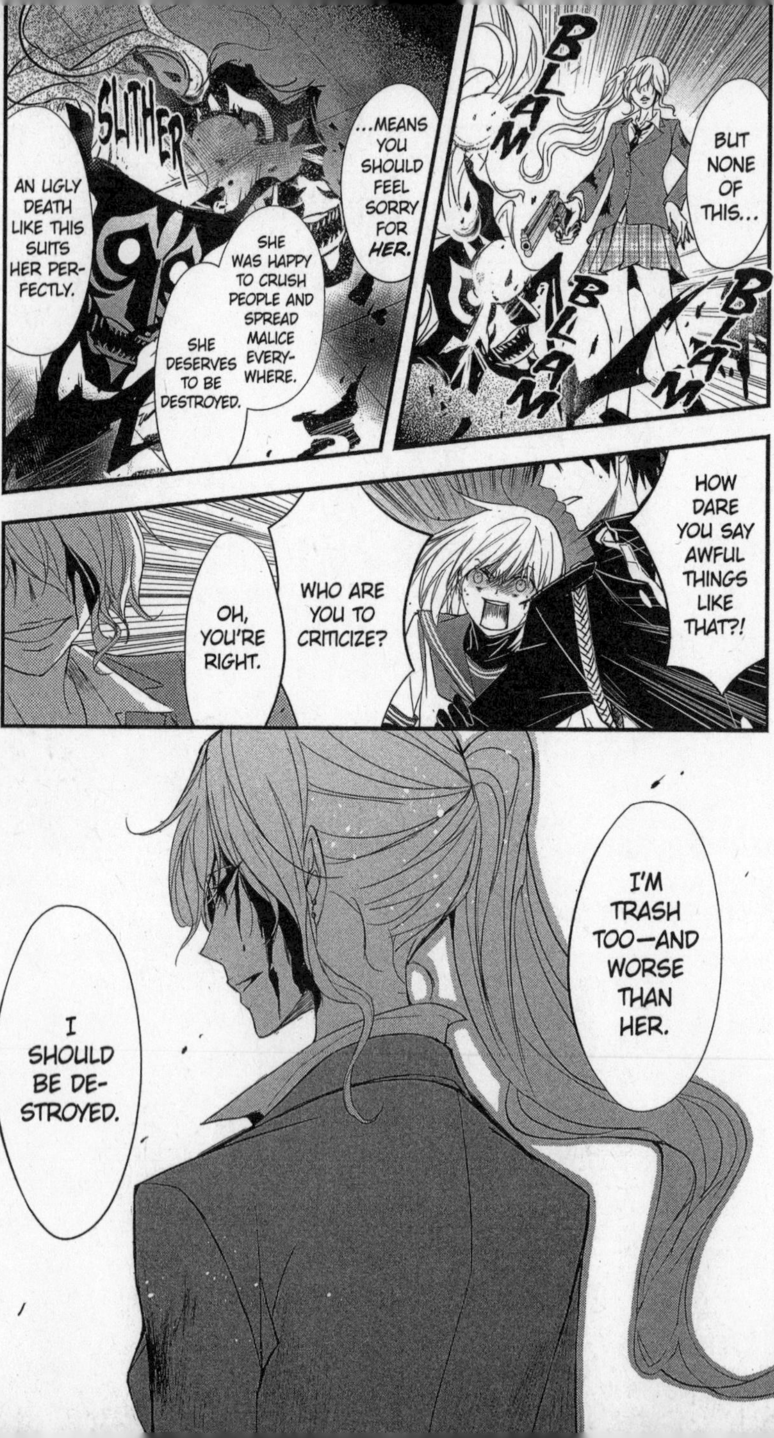
BUT NONE OF THIS...
BLAM
BLAM
BLAM
...MEANS YOU SHOULD FEEL SORRY FOR HER.
SHE WAS HAPPY TO CRUSH PEOPLE AND SPREAD MALICE EVERY-WHERE.
SHE DESERVES TO BE DESTROYED.
SLITHER
AN UGLY DEATH LIKE THIS SUITS HER PER-FECTLY.
HOW DARE YOU SAY AWFUL THINGS LIKE THAT?!
WHO ARE YOU TO CRITICIZE?
OH, YOU'RE RIGHT.
I'M TRASH TOO—AND WORSE THAN HER.
I SHOULD BE DE-STROYED.

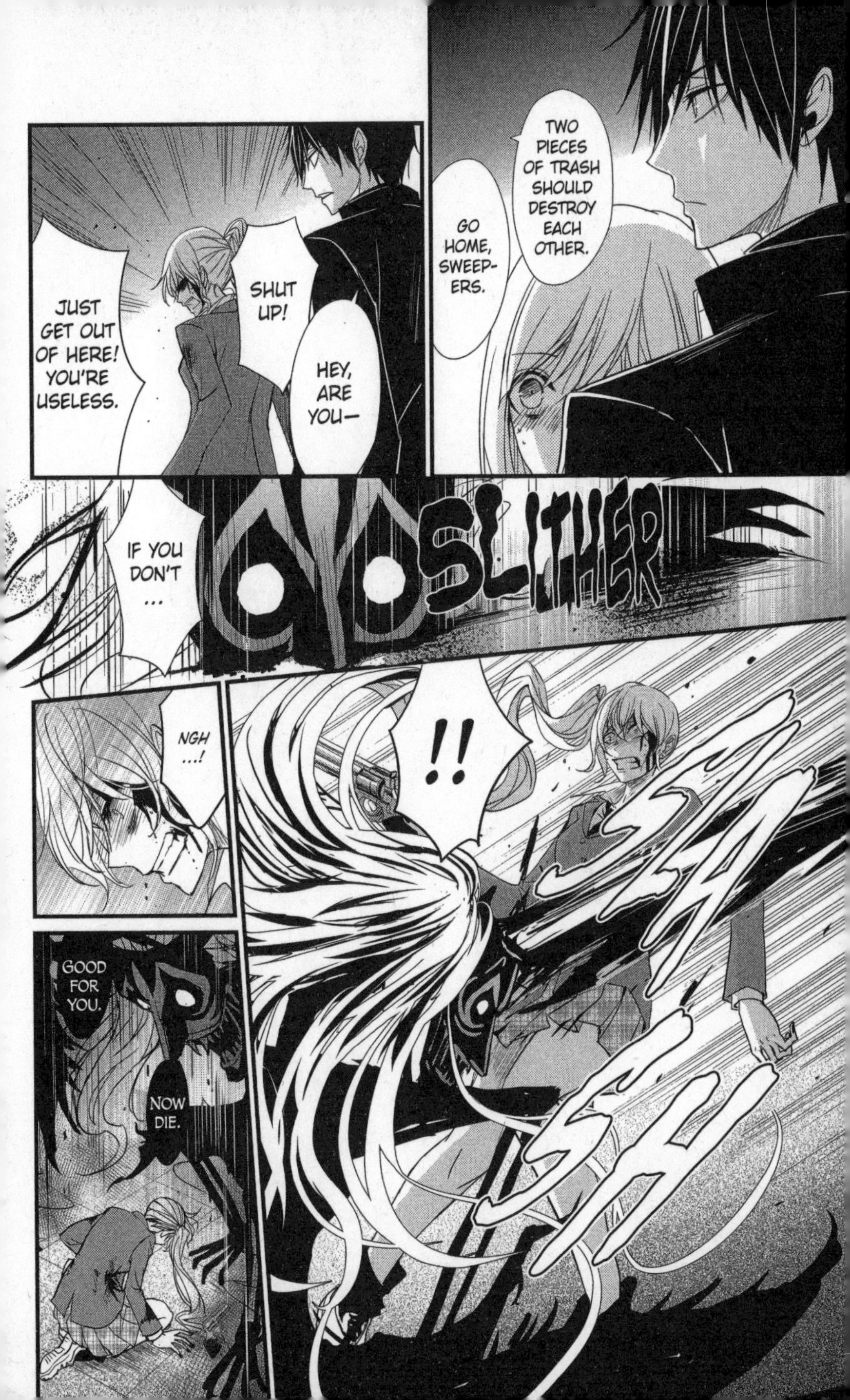
TWO PIECES OF TRASH SHOULD DESTROY EACH OTHER.
GO HOME, SWEEPERS.
HEY, ARE YOU—
SHUT UP!
JUST GET OUT OF HERE! YOU'RE USELESS.
SLITHER
IF YOU DON'T ...
!!
NGH ...!
GOOD FOR YOU.
NOW DIE.

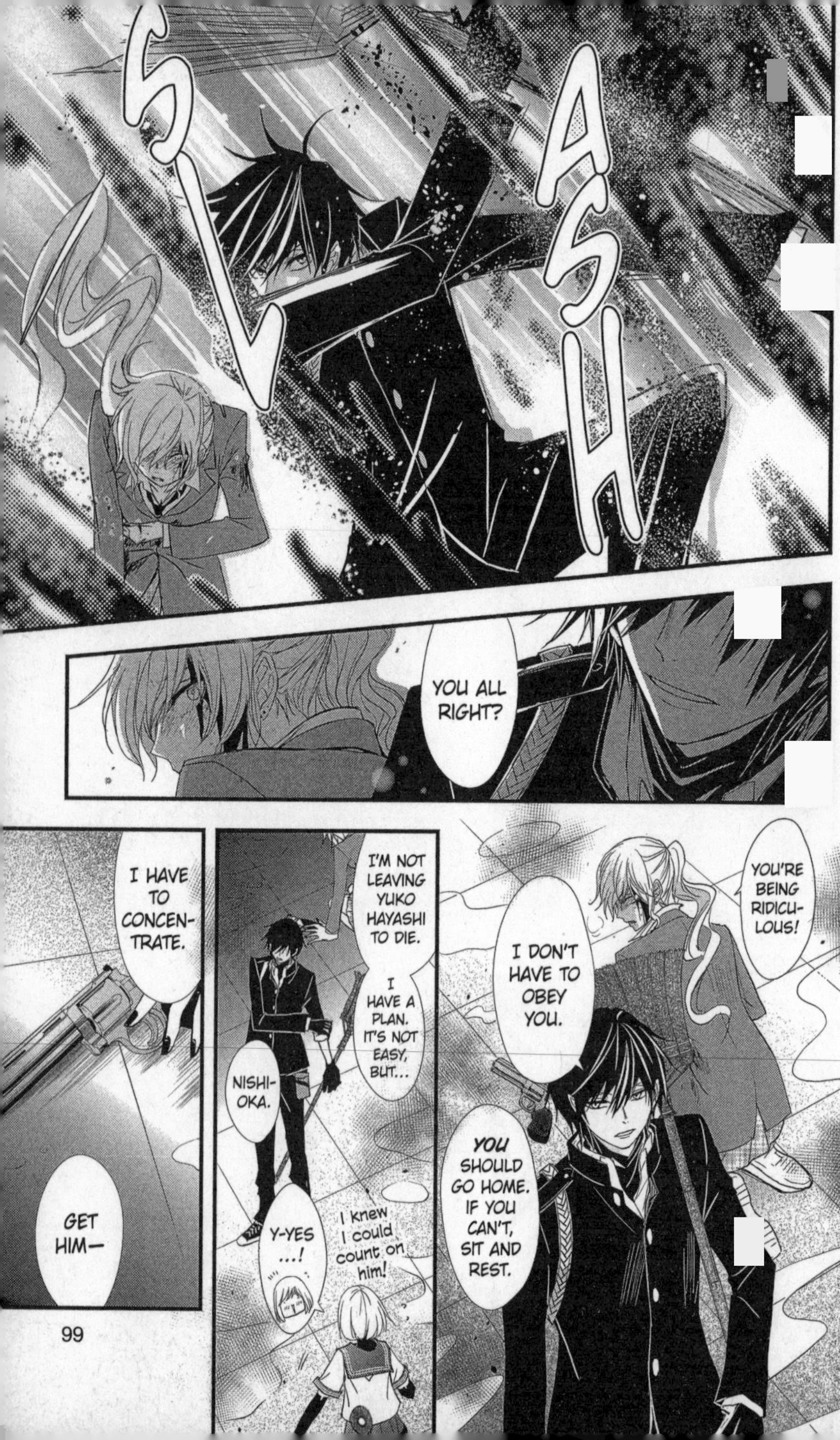
SLASH
YOU ALL RIGHT?
YOU'RE BEING RIDICULOUS!
I DON'T HAVE TO OBEY YOU.
YOU SHOULD GO HOME. IF YOU CAN'T, SIT AND REST.
I'M NOT LEAVING YUKO HAYASHI TO DIE.
I HAVE A PLAN. IT'S NOT EASY, BUT...
NISHIOKA.
Y-YES ...!
I knew I could count on him!
I HAVE TO CONCENTRATE.
GET HIM—

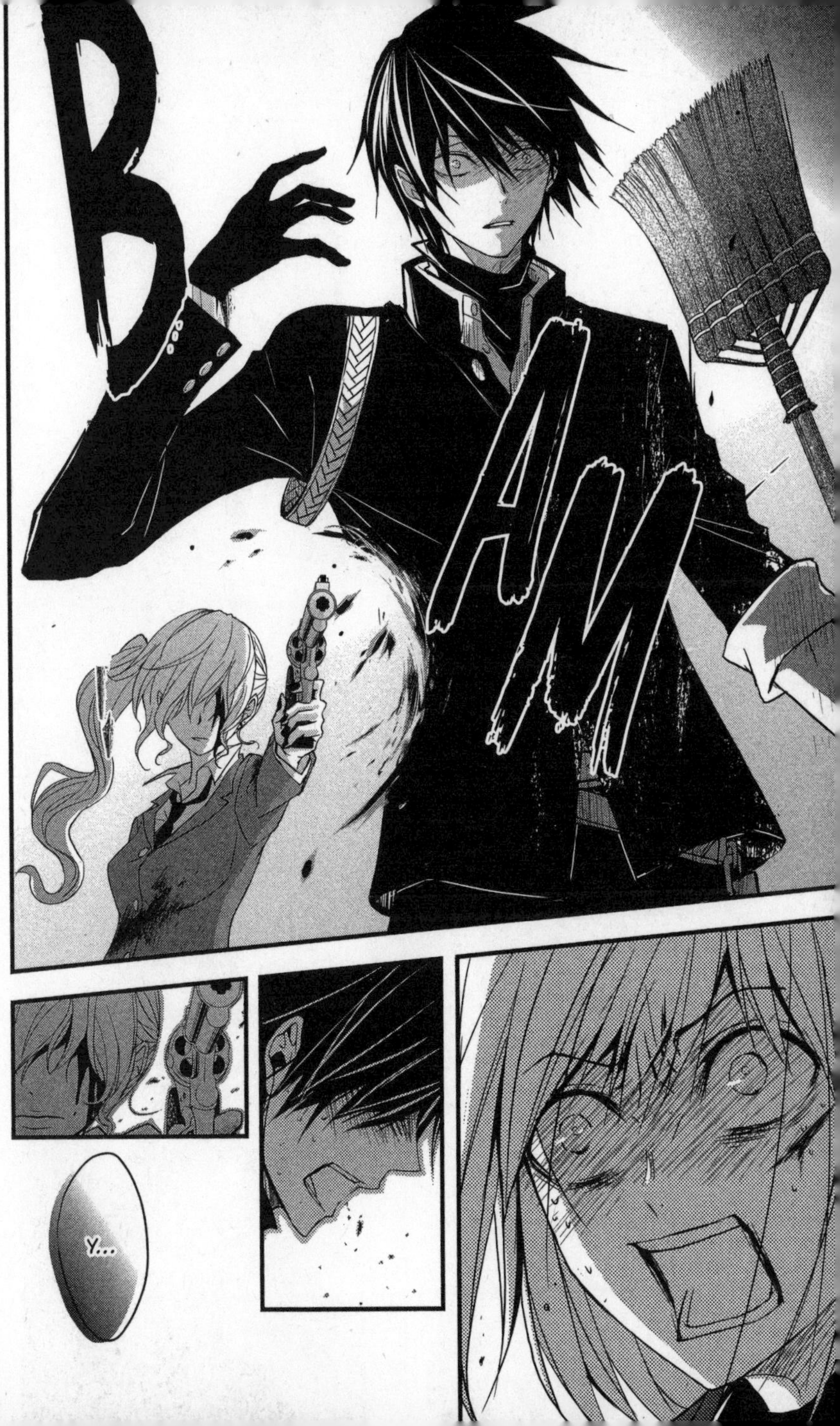
BAM
Y...

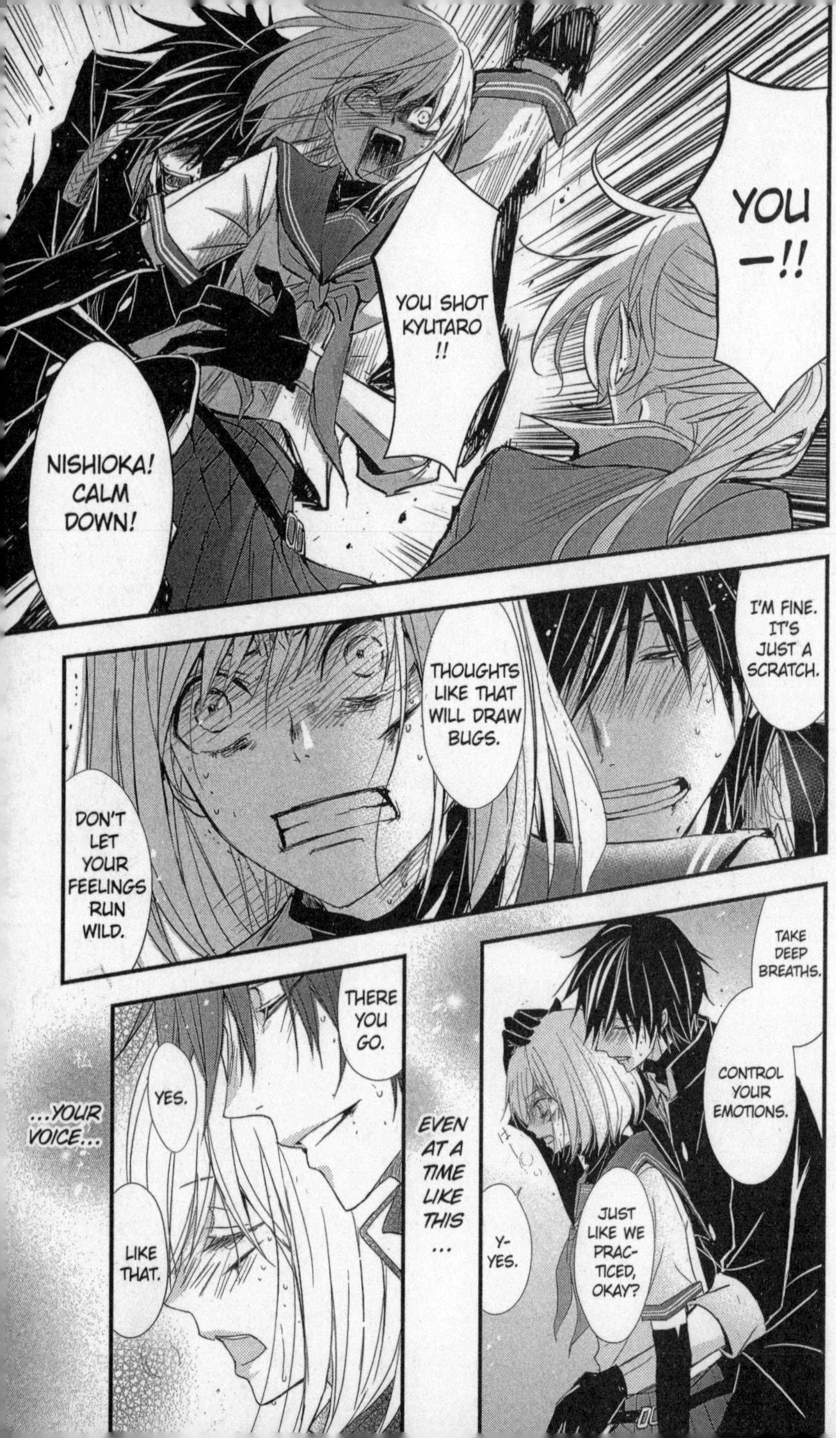
YOU—!!
YOU SHOT KYUTARO!!
NISHIOKA! CALM DOWN!
I'M FINE. IT'S JUST A SCRATCH.
THOUGHTS LIKE THAT WILL DRAW BUGS.
DON'T LET YOUR FEELINGS RUN WILD.
TAKE DEEP BREATHS.
CONTROL YOUR EMOTIONS.
JUST LIKE WE PRACTICED, OKAY?
Y-YES.
THERE YOU GO.
EVEN AT A TIME LIKE THIS...
YES.
...YOUR VOICE...
LIKE THAT.

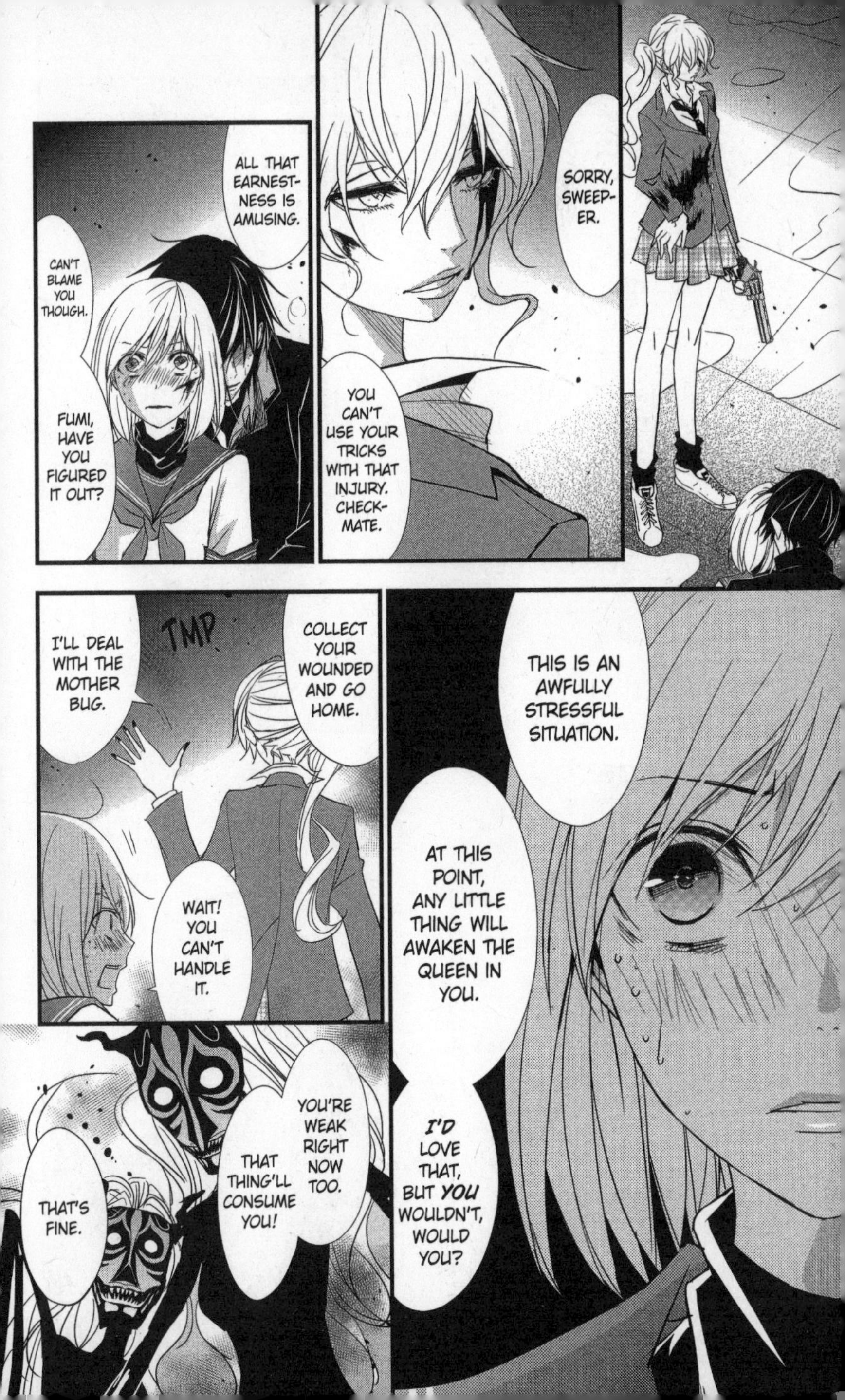
SORRY, SWEEPER.
YOU CAN'T USE YOUR TRICKS WITH THAT INJURY. CHECKMATE.
ALL THAT EARNESTNESS IS AMUSING.
CAN'T BLAME YOU THOUGH.
FUMI, HAVE YOU FIGURED IT OUT?
THIS IS AN AWFULLY STRESSFUL SITUATION.
AT THIS POINT, ANY LITTLE THING WILL AWAKEN THE QUEEN IN YOU.
I'D LOVE THAT, BUT *YOU* WOULDN'T, WOULD YOU?
COLLECT YOUR WOUNDED AND GO HOME.
TMP
I'LL DEAL WITH THE MOTHER BUG.
WAIT! YOU CAN'T HANDLE IT.
YOU'RE WEAK RIGHT NOW TOO.
THAT THING'LL CONSUME YOU!
THAT'S FINE.

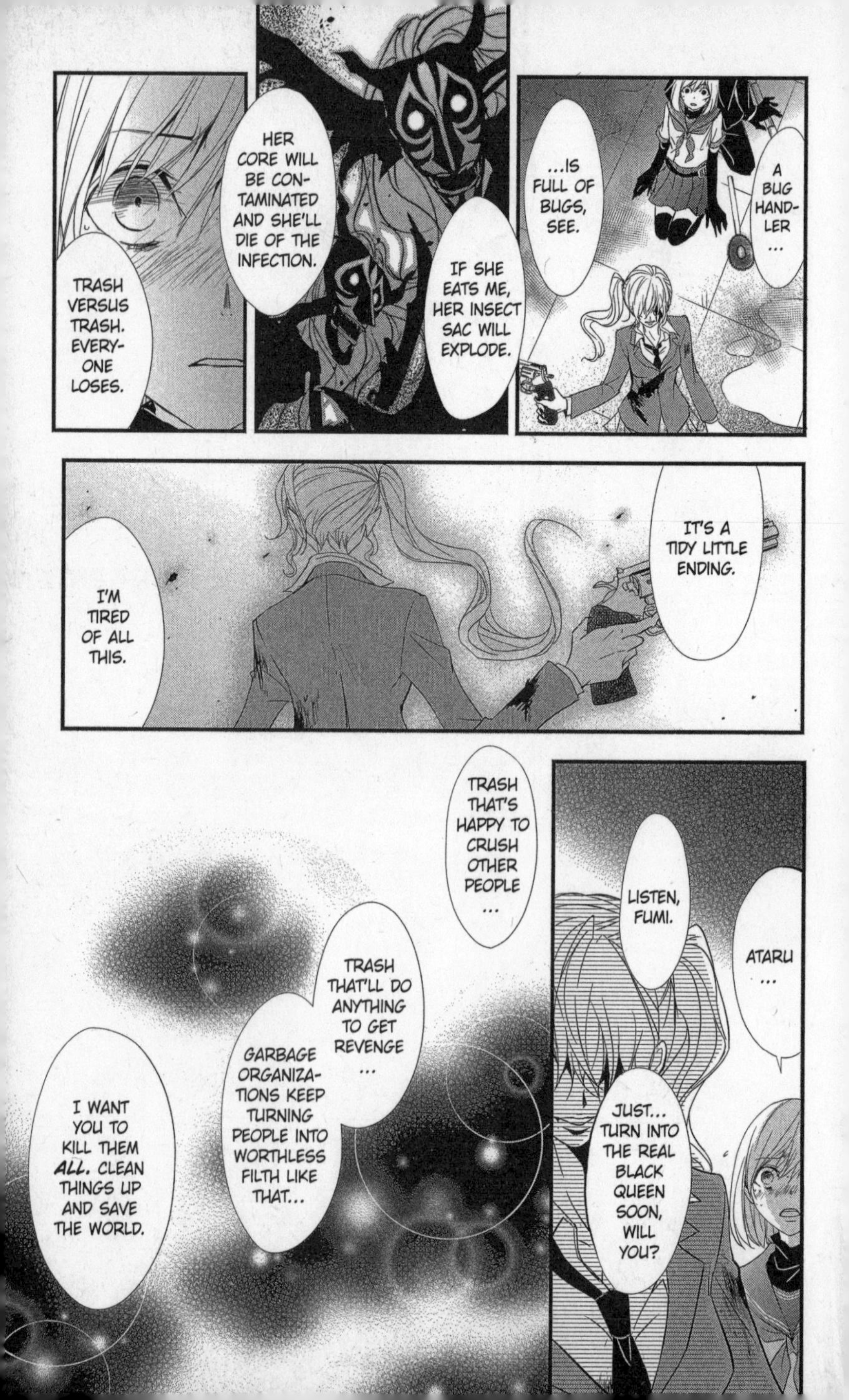
A BUG HANDLER...
...IS FULL OF BUGS, SEE.
IF SHE EATS ME, HER INSECT SAC WILL EXPLODE.
HER CORE WILL BE CONTAMINATED AND SHE'LL DIE OF THE INFECTION.
TRASH VERSUS TRASH. EVERYONE LOSES.
IT'S A TIDY LITTLE ENDING.
I'M TIRED OF ALL THIS.
ATARU...
LISTEN, FUMI.
JUST... TURN INTO THE REAL BLACK QUEEN SOON, WILL YOU?
TRASH THAT'S HAPPY TO CRUSH OTHER PEOPLE...
TRASH THAT'LL DO ANYTHING TO GET REVENGE...
GARBAGE ORGANIZATIONS KEEP TURNING PEOPLE INTO WORTHLESS FILTH LIKE THAT...
I WANT YOU TO KILL THEM ALL. CLEAN THINGS UP AND SAVE THE WORLD.

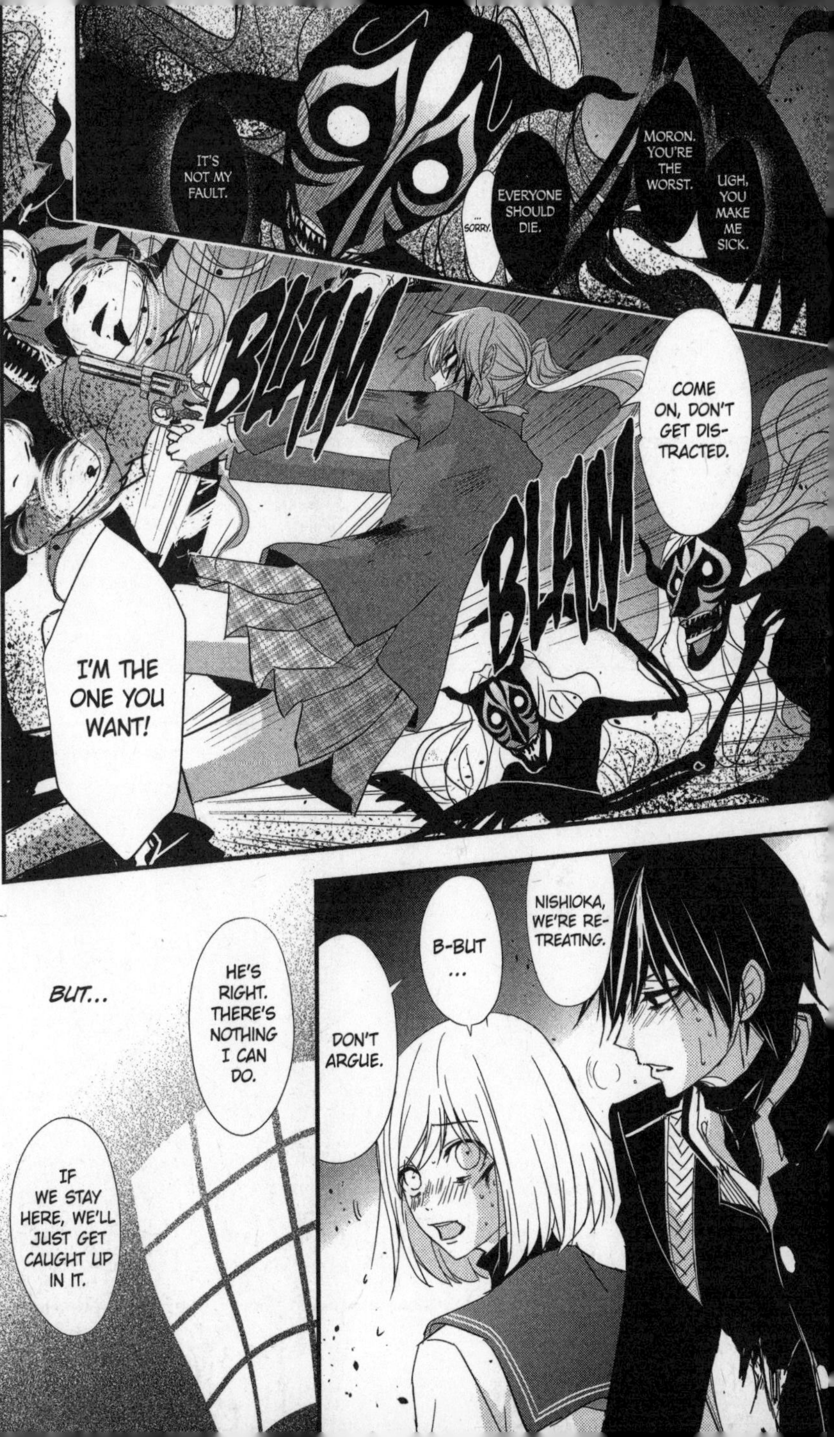
UGH, YOU MAKE ME SICK.
MORON. YOU'RE THE WORST.
EVERYONE SHOULD DIE.
...SORRY.
IT'S NOT MY FAULT.
COME ON, DON'T GET DIS-TRACTED.
BLAM
BLAM
I'M THE ONE YOU WANT!
NISHIOKA, WE'RE RE-TREATING.
B-BUT ...
DON'T ARGUE.
IF WE STAY HERE, WE'LL JUST GET CAUGHT UP IN IT.
HE'S RIGHT. THERE'S NOTHING I CAN DO.
BUT...

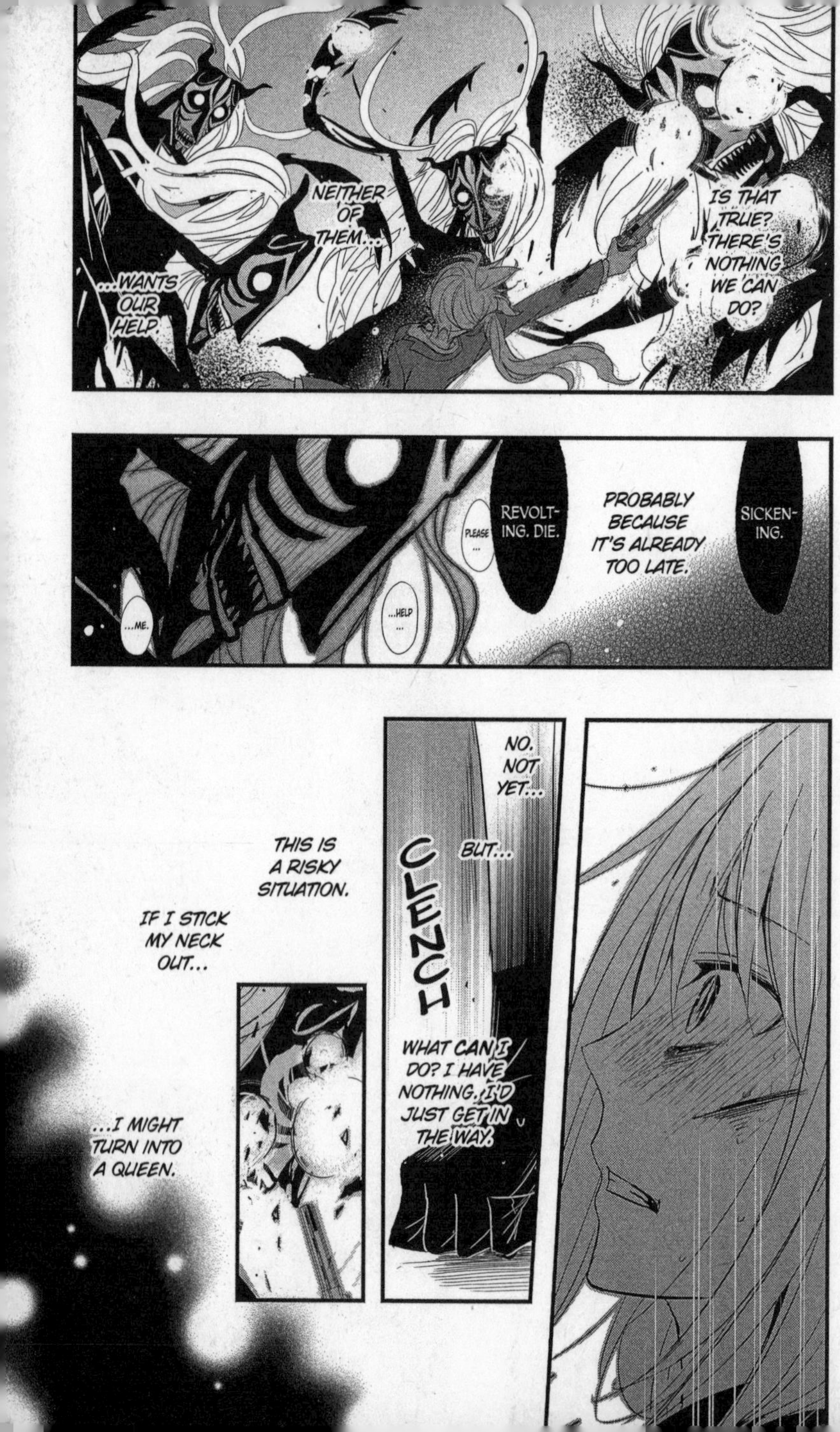
IS THAT TRUE? THERE'S NOTHING WE CAN DO?
NEITHER OF THEM...
...WANTS OUR HELP.
SICKEN-ING.
PROBABLY BECAUSE IT'S ALREADY TOO LATE.
REVOLT-ING. DIE.
PLEASE...
...HELP...
...ME.
NO. NOT YET...
BUT...
CLENCH
WHAT CAN I DO? I HAVE NOTHING. I'D JUST GET IN THE WAY.
THIS IS A RISKY SITUATION.
IF I STICK MY NECK OUT...
...I MIGHT TURN INTO A QUEEN.

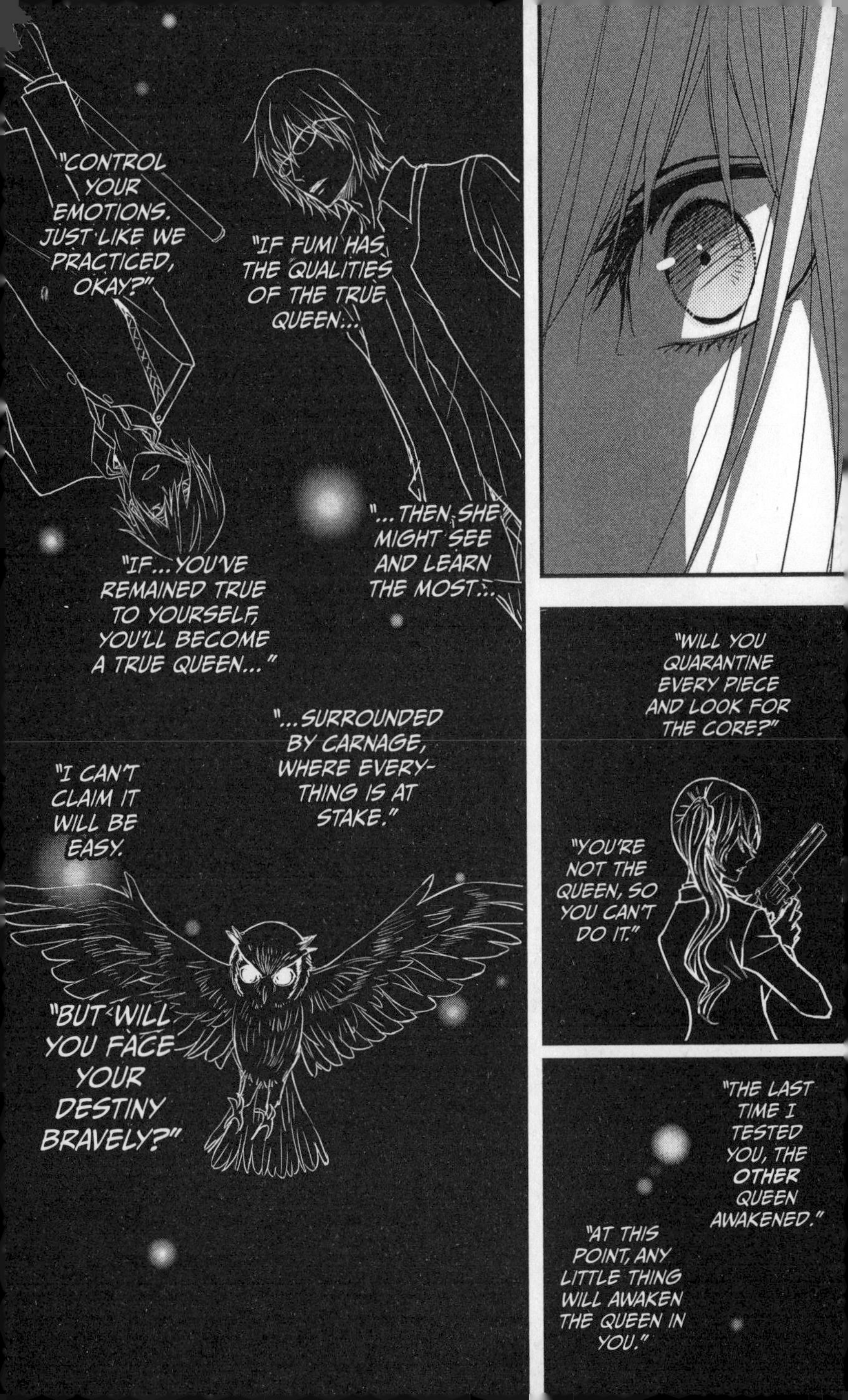
"WILL YOU QUARANTINE EVERY PIECE AND LOOK FOR THE CORE?"
"YOU'RE NOT THE QUEEN, SO YOU CAN'T DO IT."
"THE LAST TIME I TESTED YOU, THE **OTHER** QUEEN AWAKENED."
"AT THIS POINT, ANY LITTLE THING WILL AWAKEN THE QUEEN IN YOU."
"CONTROL YOUR EMOTIONS. JUST LIKE WE PRACTICED, OKAY?"
"IF FUMI HAS THE QUALITIES OF THE TRUE QUEEN...
"...THEN SHE MIGHT SEE AND LEARN THE MOST...
"IF... YOU'VE REMAINED TRUE TO YOURSELF, YOU'LL BECOME A TRUE QUEEN..."
"...SURROUNDED BY CARNAGE, WHERE EVERY-THING IS AT STAKE."
"I CAN'T CLAIM IT WILL BE EASY.
"BUT WILL YOU FACE YOUR DESTINY BRAVELY?"

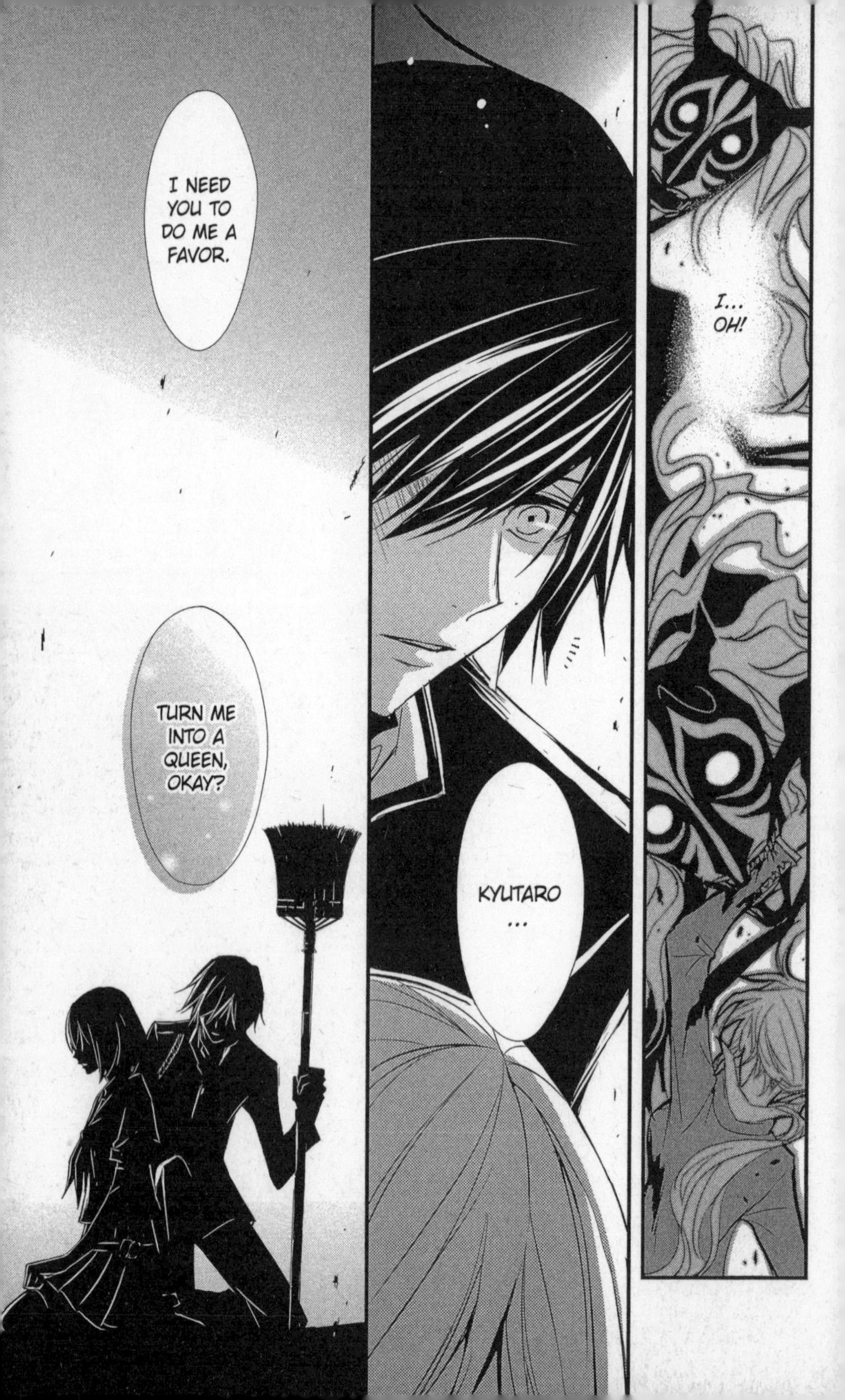
I... OH!
KYUTARO ...
I NEED YOU TO DO ME A FAVOR.
TURN ME INTO A QUEEN, OKAY?

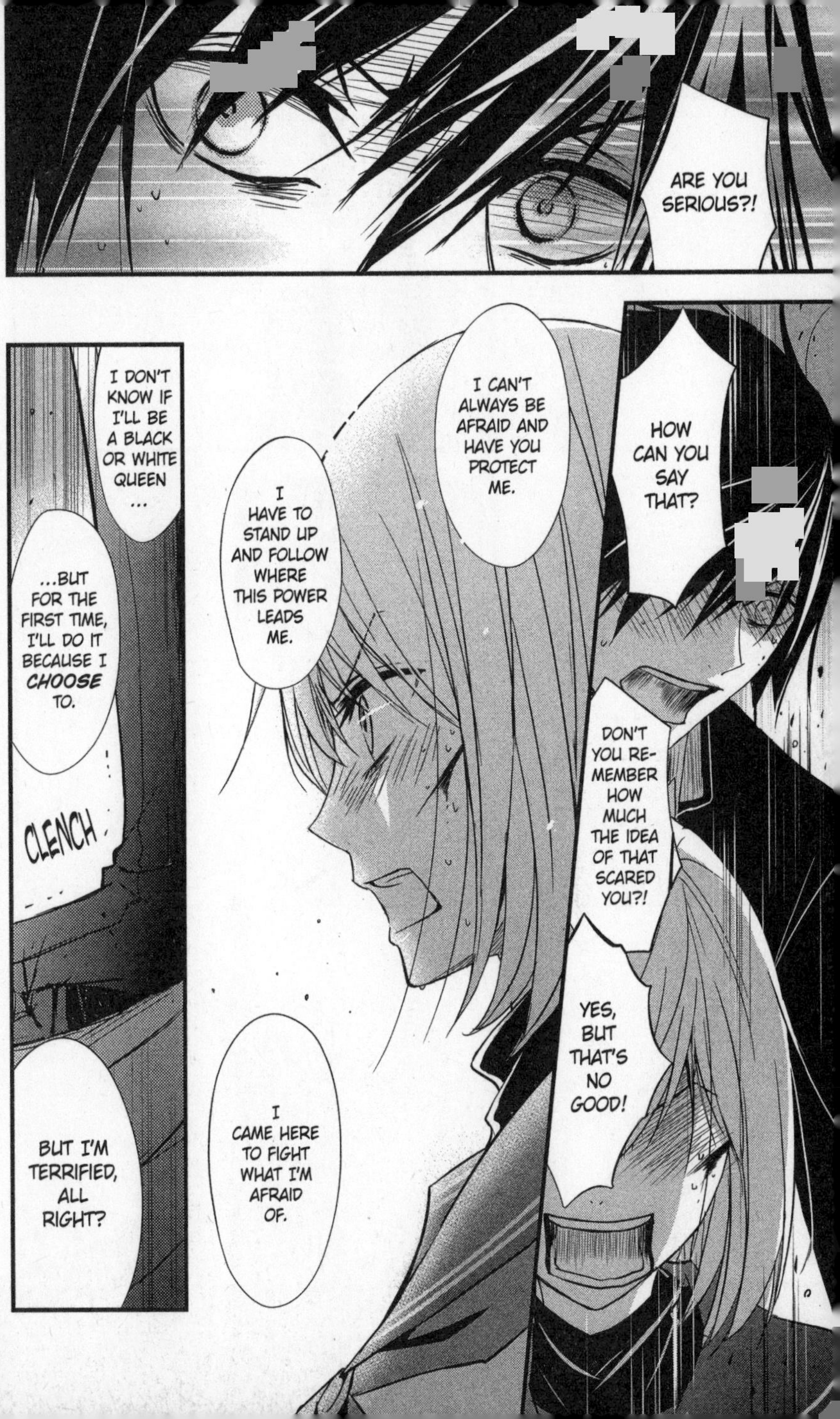
ARE YOU SERIOUS?!
HOW CAN YOU SAY THAT?
I CAN'T ALWAYS BE AFRAID AND HAVE YOU PROTECT ME.
I HAVE TO STAND UP AND FOLLOW WHERE THIS POWER LEADS ME.
DON'T YOU RE-MEMBER HOW MUCH THE IDEA OF THAT SCARED YOU?!
YES, BUT THAT'S NO GOOD!
I CAME HERE TO FIGHT WHAT I'M AFRAID OF.
I DON'T KNOW IF I'LL BE A BLACK OR WHITE QUEEN ...
...BUT FOR THE FIRST TIME, I'LL DO IT BECAUSE I *CHOOSE* TO.
CLENCH
BUT I'M TERRIFIED, ALL RIGHT?

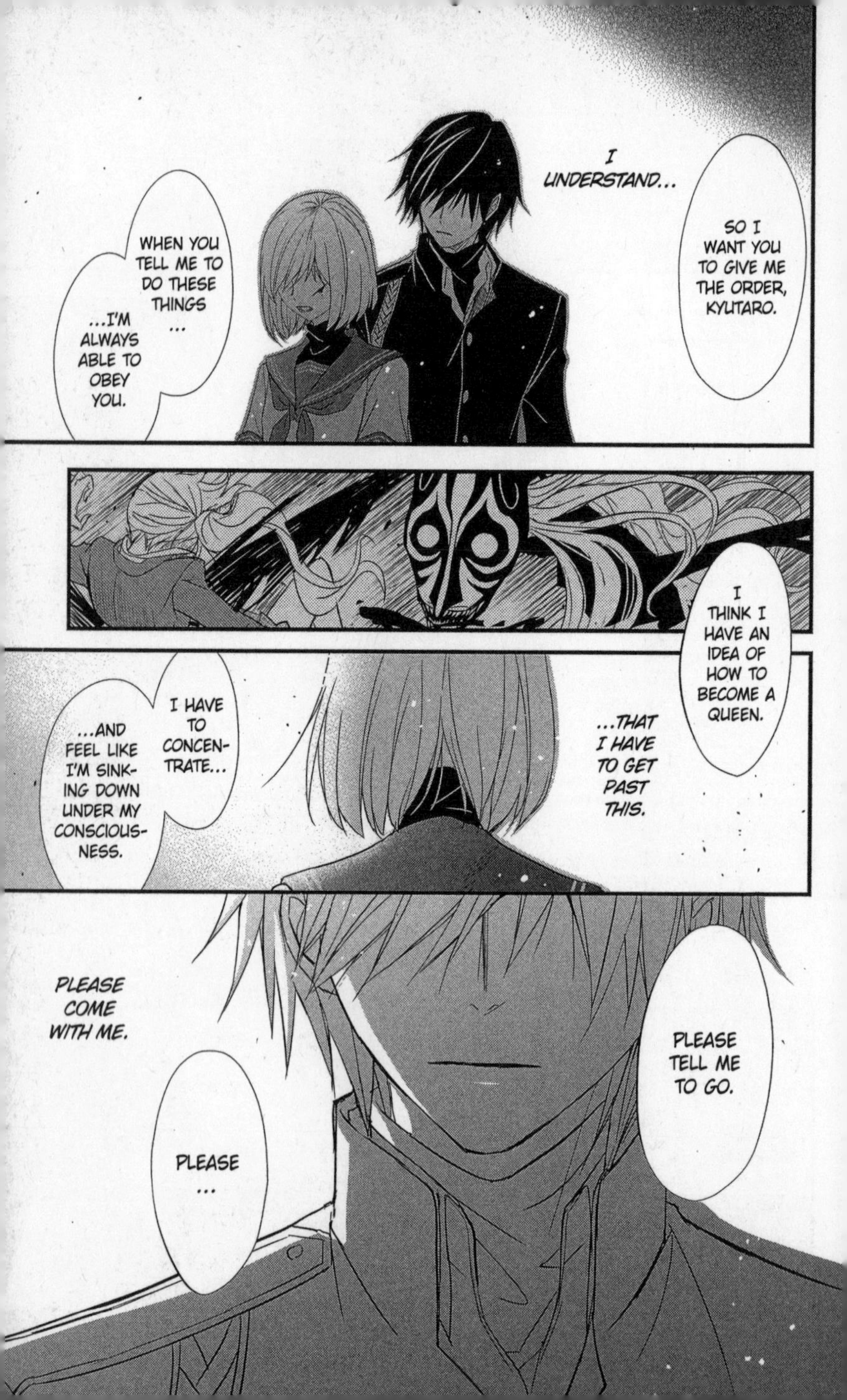
SO I WANT YOU TO GIVE ME THE ORDER, KYUTARO.
I UNDERSTAND...
WHEN YOU TELL ME TO DO THESE THINGS ...
...I'M ALWAYS ABLE TO OBEY YOU.
I THINK I HAVE AN IDEA OF HOW TO BECOME A QUEEN.
...THAT I HAVE TO GET PAST THIS.
I HAVE TO CONCENTRATE...
...AND FEEL LIKE I'M SINKING DOWN UNDER MY CONSCIOUSNESS.
PLEASE TELL ME TO GO.
PLEASE COME WITH ME.
PLEASE ...

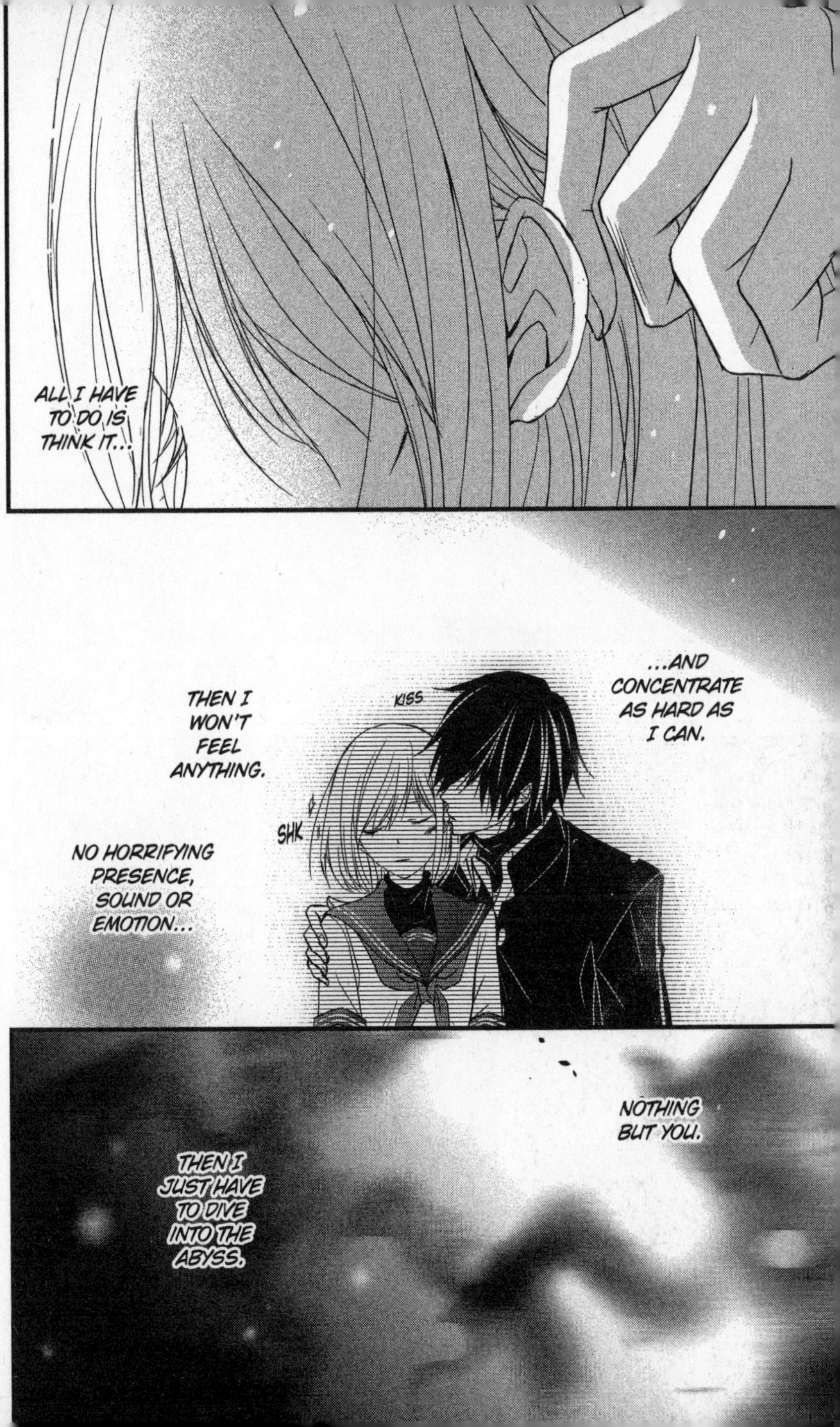
ALL I HAVE TO DO IS THINK IT...
...AND CONCENTRATE AS HARD AS I CAN.
KISS
THEN I WON'T FEEL ANYTHING.
SHK
NO HORRIFYING PRESENCE, SOUND OR EMOTION...
NOTHING BUT YOU.
THEN I JUST HAVE TO DIVE INTO THE ABYSS.

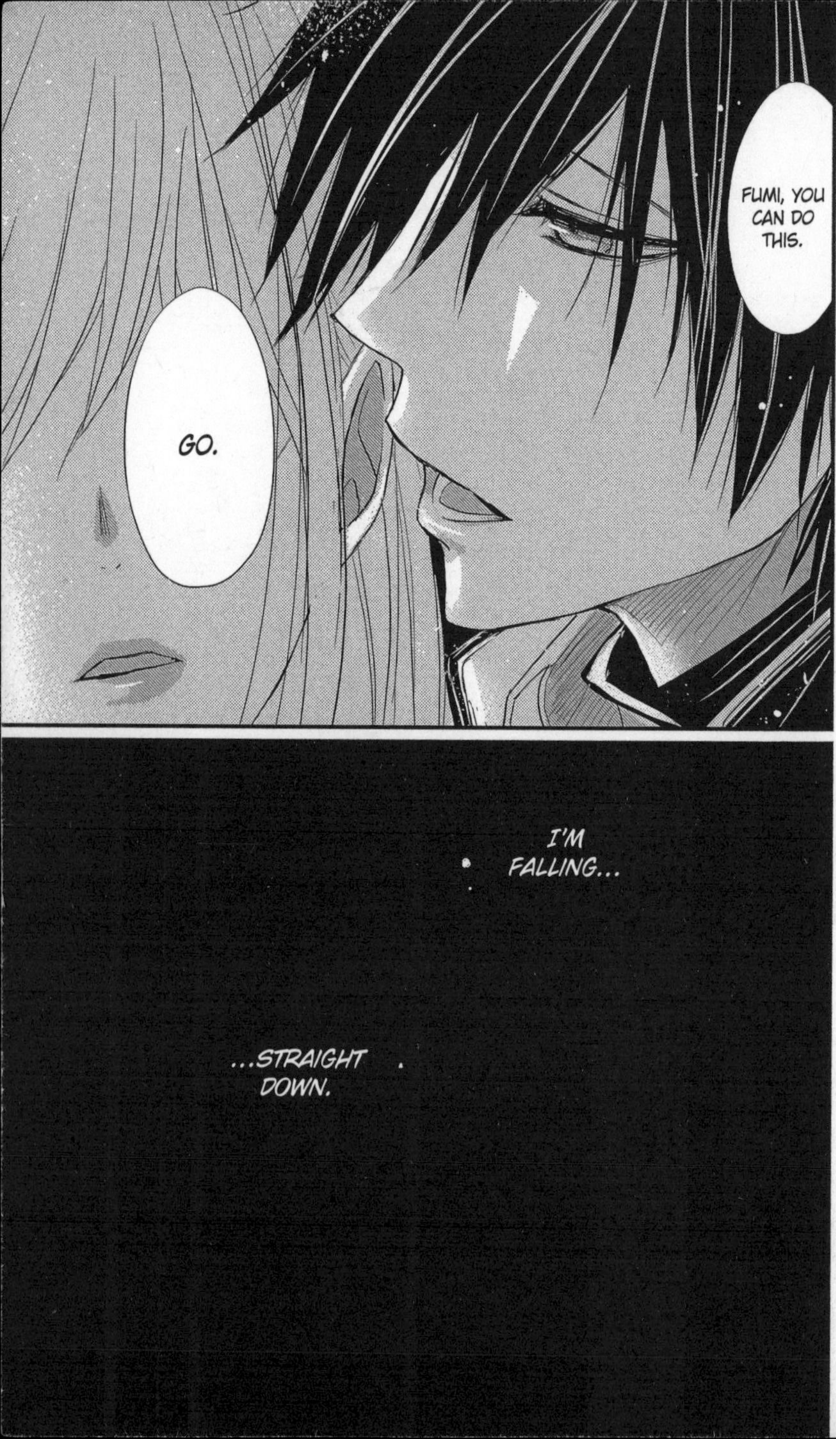
FUMI, YOU CAN DO THIS.
GO.
I'M FALLING...
...STRAIGHT DOWN.

MONTHLY *BETSUCOMI* SALE DATE NOTICE ON TWITTER

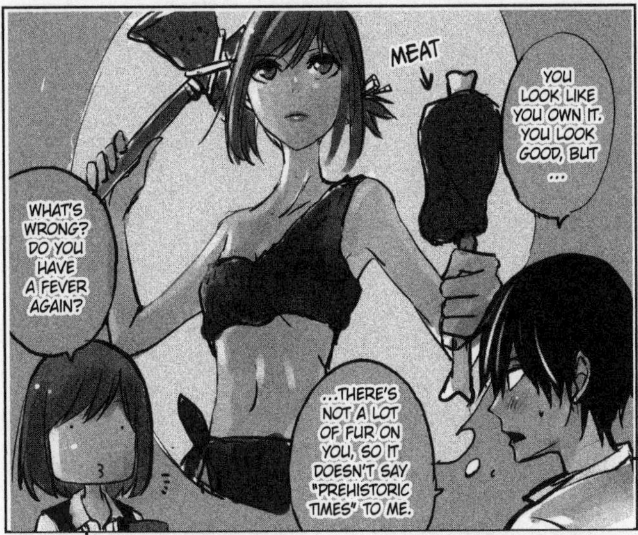
MEAT
YOU LOOK LIKE YOU OWN IT. YOU LOOK GOOD, BUT ...
...THERE'S NOT A LOT OF FUR ON YOU, SO IT DOESN'T SAY "PREHISTORIC TIMES" TO ME.
WHAT'S WRONG? DO YOU HAVE A FEVER AGAIN?

CHAPTER 10

WHAT'S UP IN *QUEEN'S QUALITY* THIS MONTH?
(1) ANOTHER ONE OF THE AUTHOR'S WISHES (SAKE!)
(2) YOUR HAIR GOT IN MY EYE AND I'M EVEN MORE TEARY... (' ; W ; ') *UNGH...*
(3) A WARM, GENTLE CONVERSATION
IN CHAPTER 10, KYUTARO'S SOMMELIER-ISH ABILITY AWAKENS!

I've been tweeting things like that every day. If you don't read it (and sometimes even if you do read it), it can be hard to understand. I post these illustrations in color on Twitter. I sometimes even post brand-new illustrations or notices, or just everyday mutterings. Please check it out from time to time! @motomikyosuke

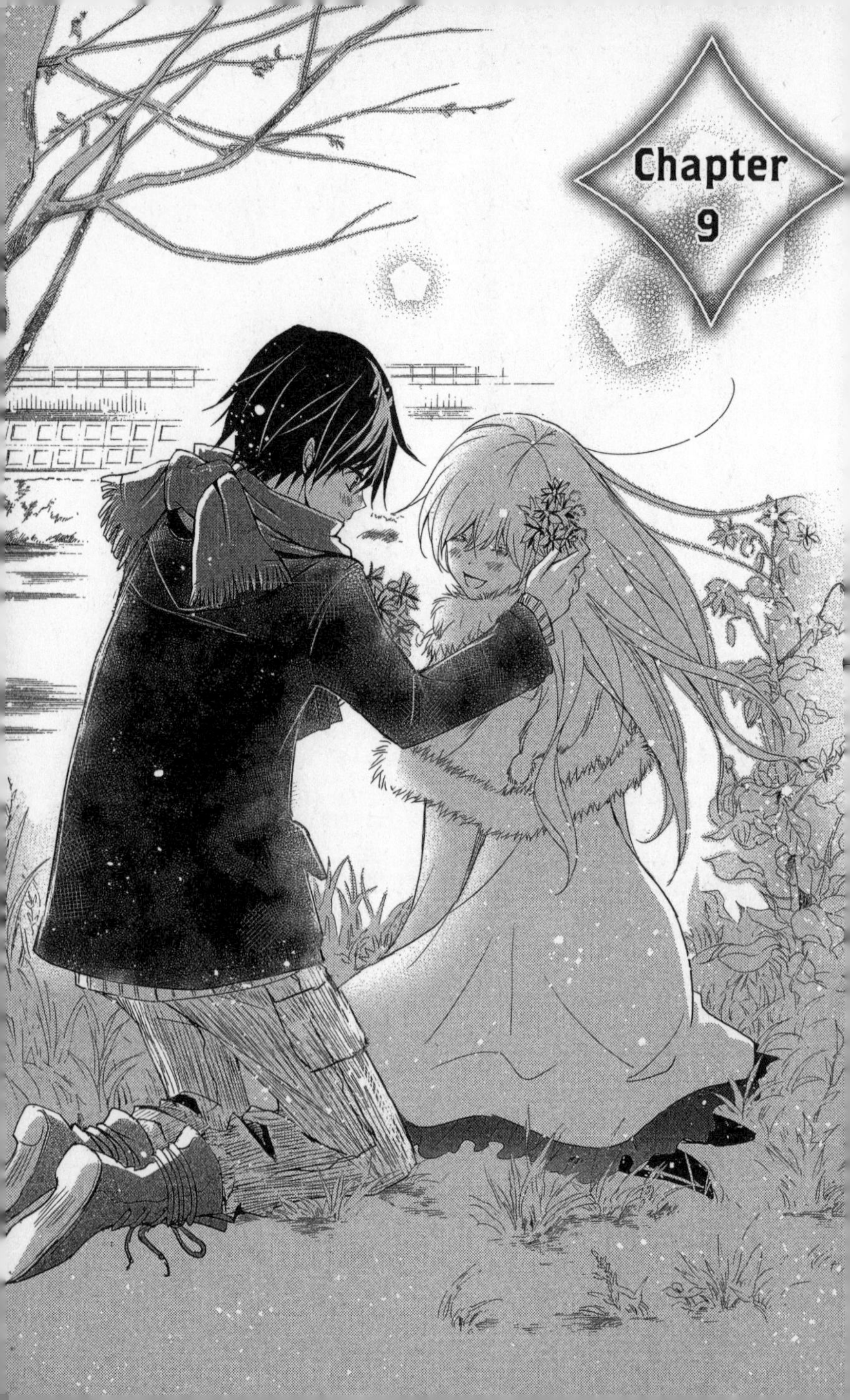
Chapter
9

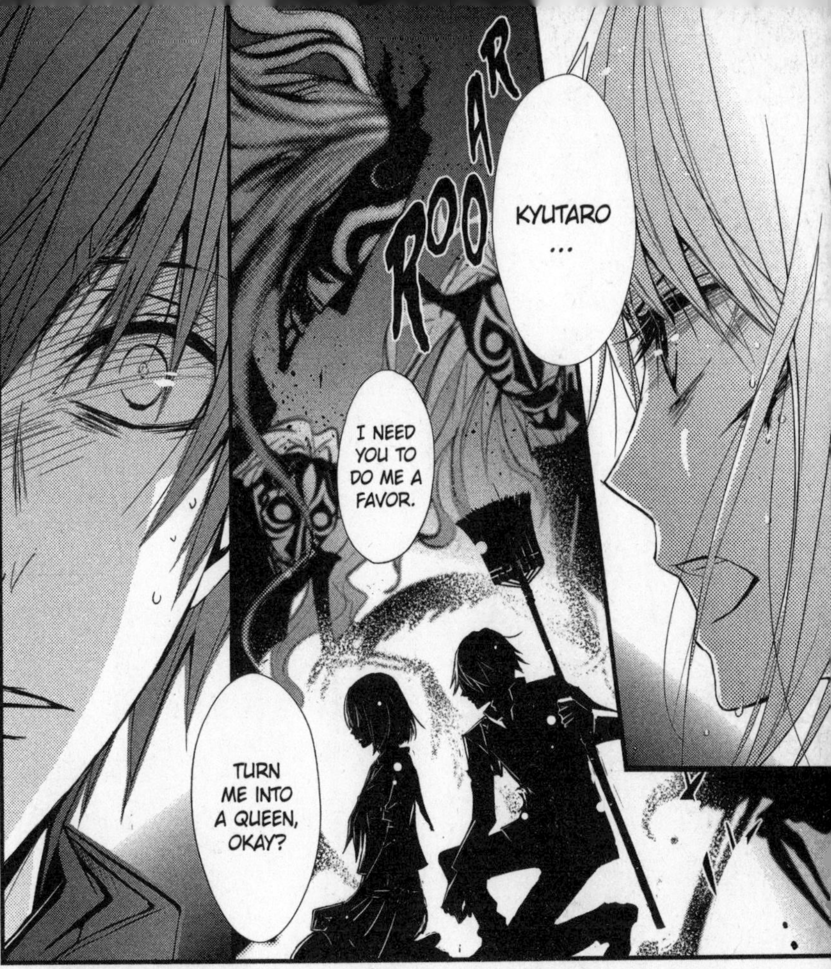
KYUTARO ...
ROOAR
I NEED YOU TO DO ME A FAVOR.
TURN ME INTO A QUEEN, OKAY?

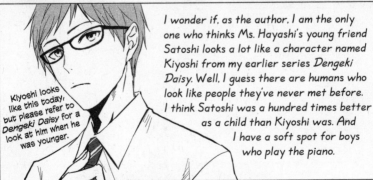

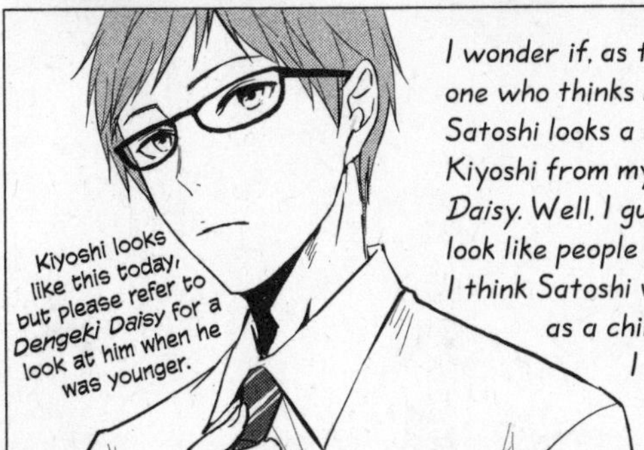
Kiyoshi looks like this today, but please refer to *Dengeki Daisy* for a look at him when he was younger.

I wonder if, as the author, I am the only one who thinks Ms. Hayashi's young friend Satoshi looks a lot like a character named Kiyoshi from my earlier series *Dengeki Daisy*. Well, I guess there are humans who look like people they've never met before. I think Satoshi was a hundred times better as a child than Kiyoshi was. And I have a soft spot for boys who play the piano.

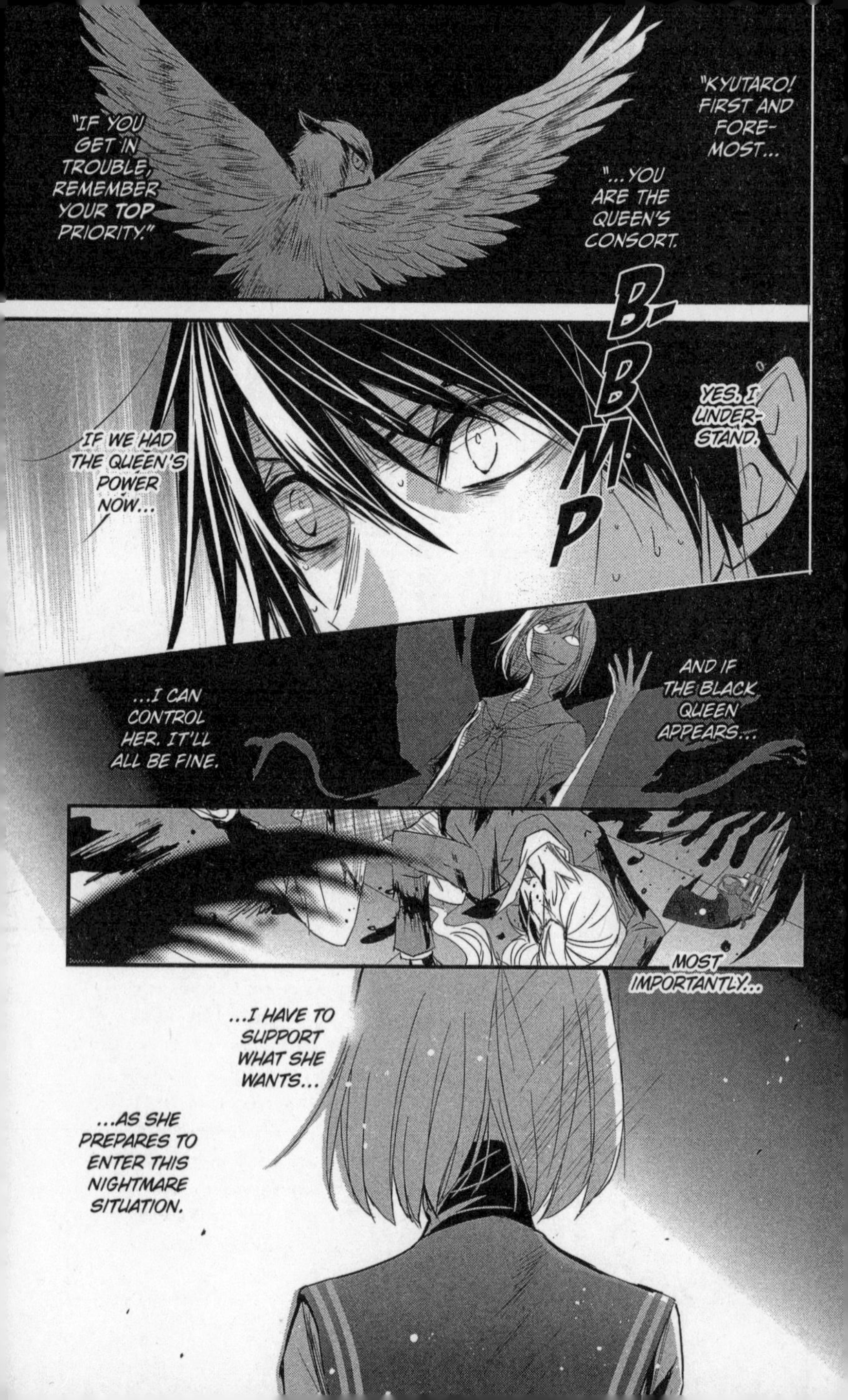
"KYUTARO! FIRST AND FORE-MOST...
"...YOU ARE THE QUEEN'S CONSORT.
"IF YOU GET IN TROUBLE, REMEMBER YOUR TOP PRIORITY."
B-BMP
YES. I UNDER-STAND.
IF WE HAD THE QUEEN'S POWER NOW...
AND IF THE BLACK QUEEN APPEARS...
...I CAN CONTROL HER. IT'LL ALL BE FINE.
MOST IMPORTANTLY...
...I HAVE TO SUPPORT WHAT SHE WANTS...
...AS SHE PREPARES TO ENTER THIS NIGHTMARE SITUATION.

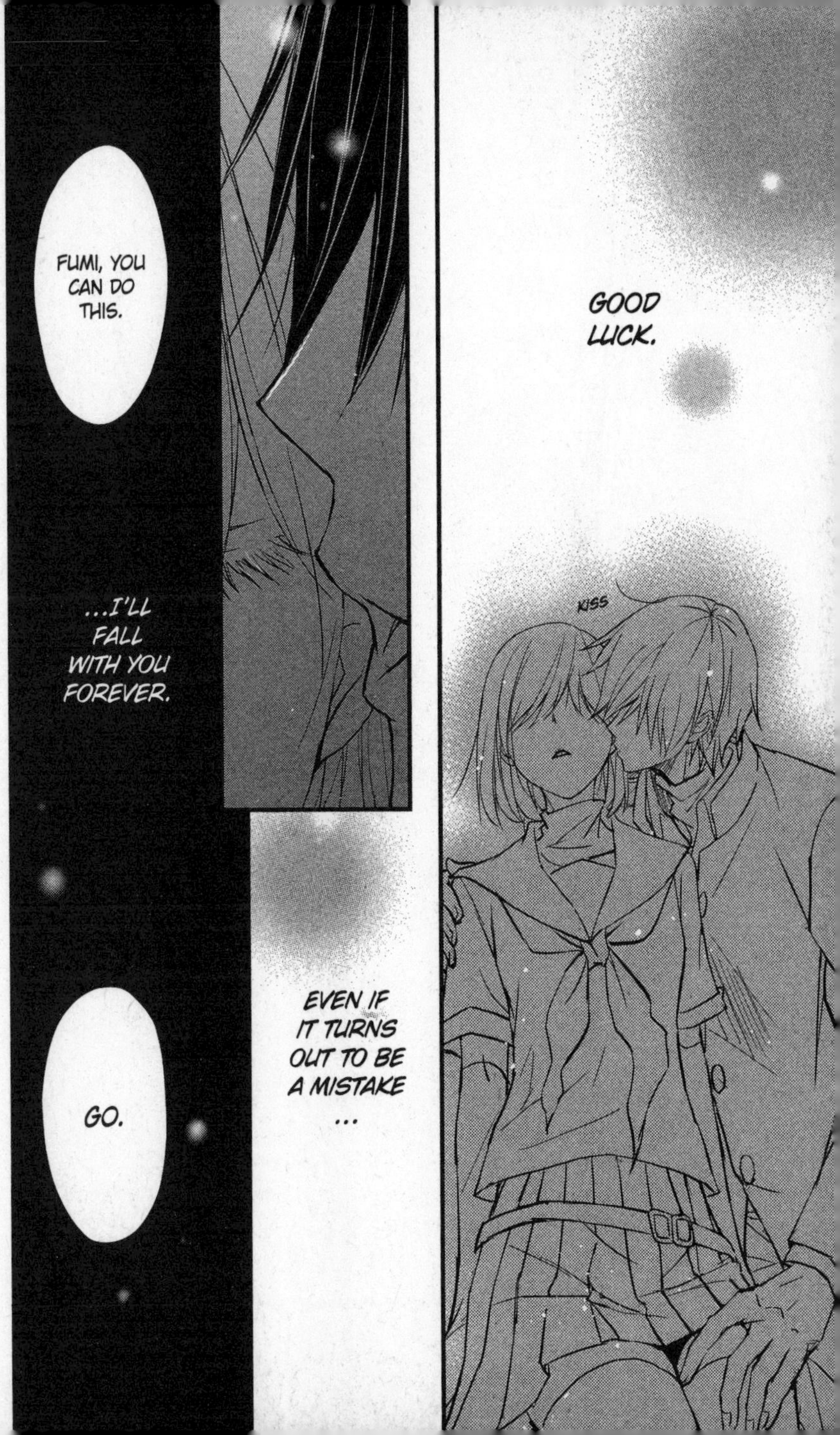
GOOD LUCK.
KISS
EVEN IF IT TURNS OUT TO BE A MISTAKE...
FUMI, YOU CAN DO THIS.
...I'LL FALL WITH YOU FOREVER.
GO.

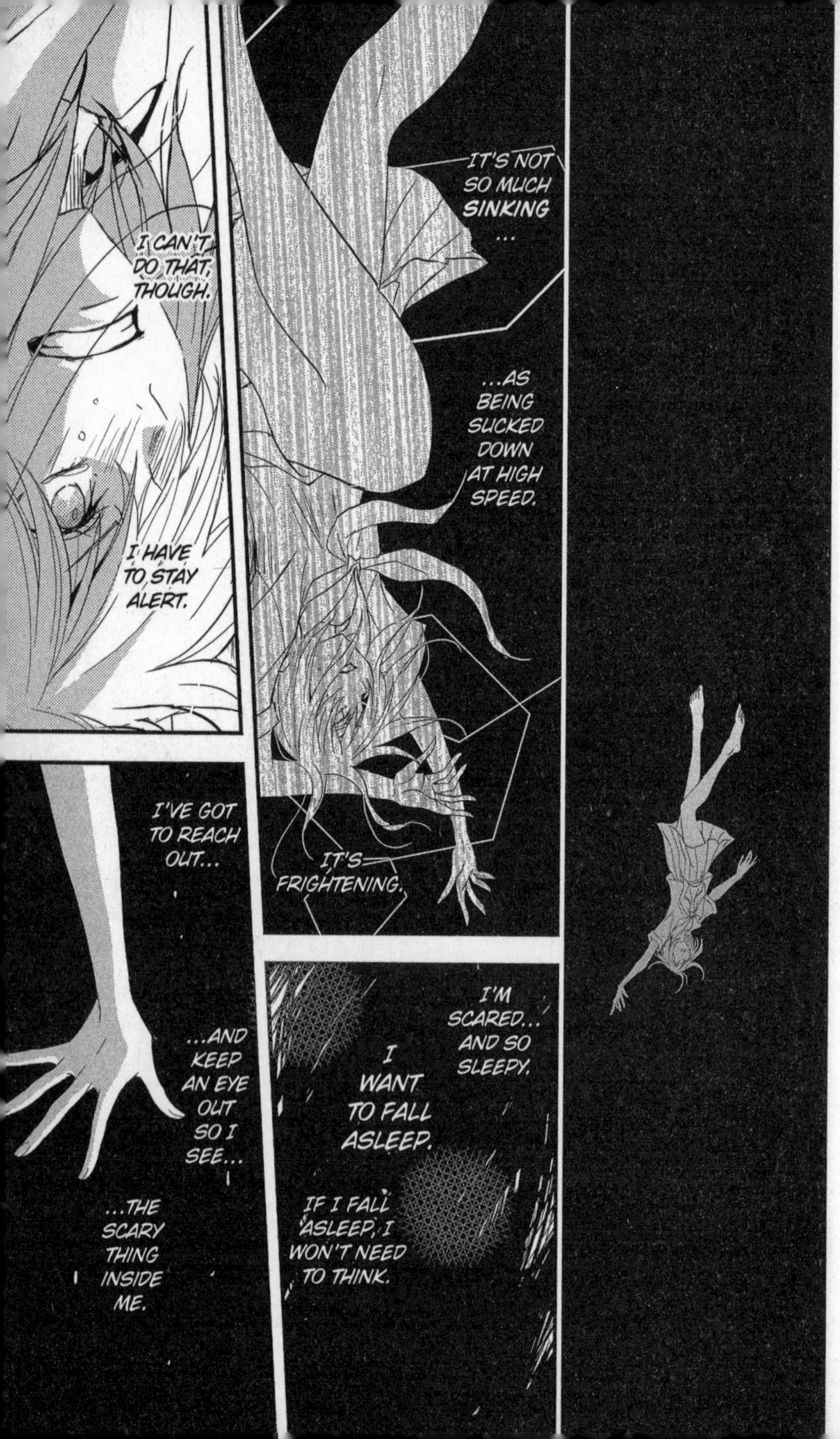
IT'S NOT SO MUCH SINKING...
...AS BEING SUCKED DOWN AT HIGH SPEED.
IT'S FRIGHTENING.
I CAN'T DO THAT, THOUGH.
I HAVE TO STAY ALERT.
I'M SCARED... AND SO SLEEPY.
I WANT TO FALL ASLEEP.
IF I FALL ASLEEP, I WON'T NEED TO THINK.
I'VE GOT TO REACH OUT...
...AND KEEP AN EYE OUT SO I SEE...
...THE SCARY THING INSIDE ME.

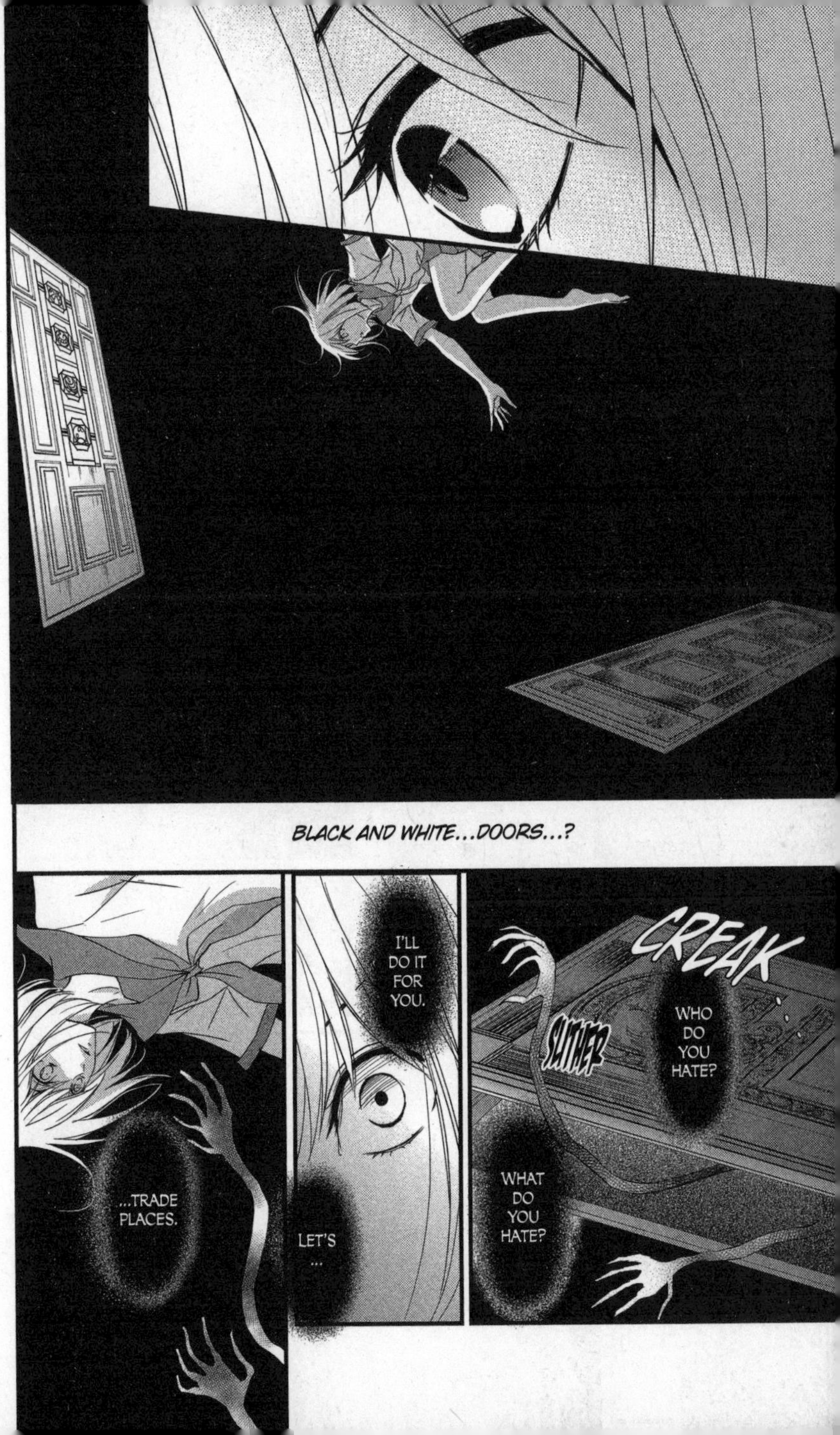
BLACK AND WHITE...DOORS...?
CREAK
WHO DO YOU HATE?
SLITHER
WHAT DO YOU HATE?
I'LL DO IT FOR YOU.
LET'S...
...TRADE PLACES.

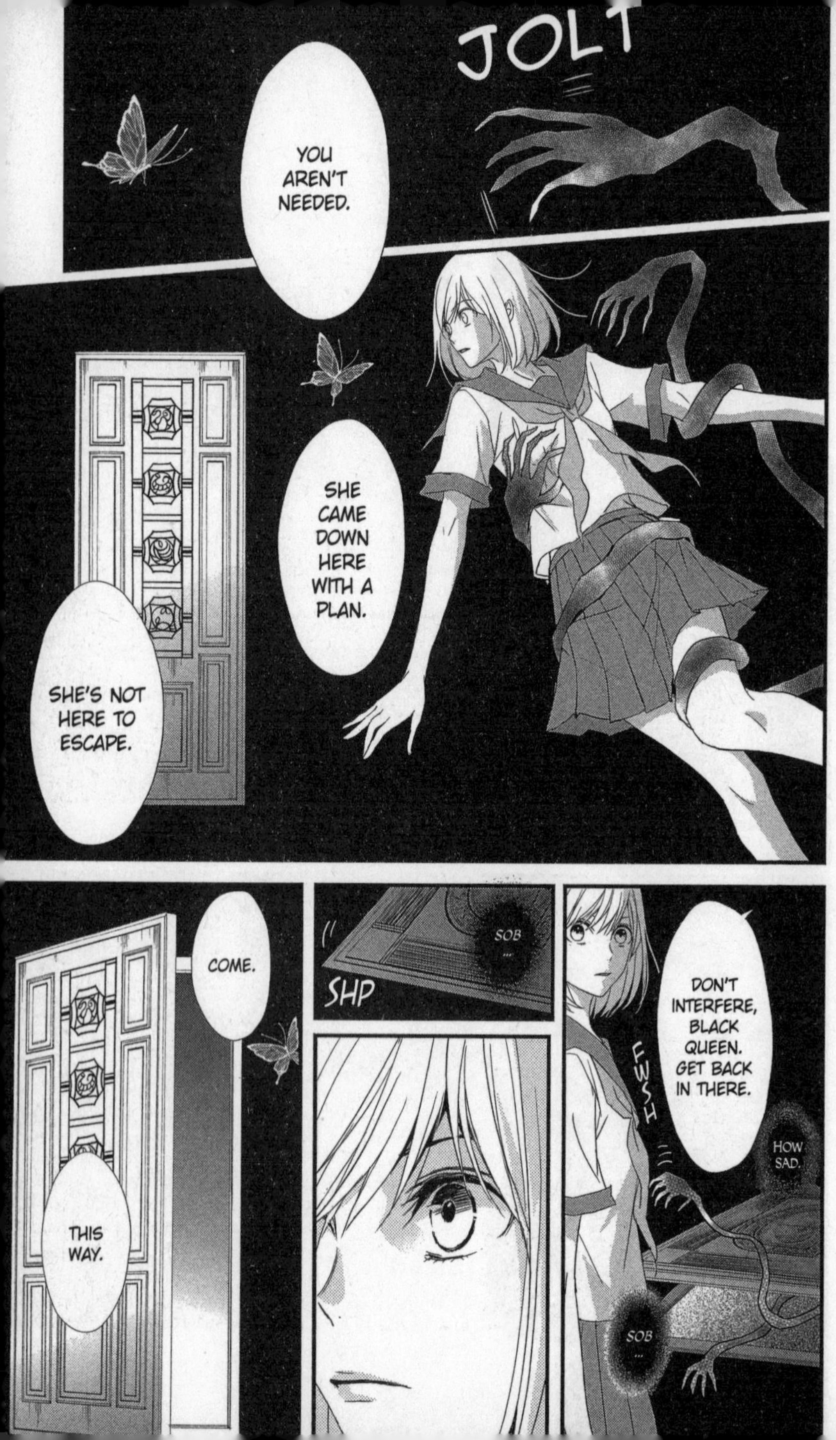
JOLT
YOU AREN'T NEEDED.
SHE CAME DOWN HERE WITH A PLAN.
SHE'S NOT HERE TO ESCAPE.
DON'T INTERFERE, BLACK QUEEN. GET BACK IN THERE.
FWSH
HOW SAD.
SOB...
SOB...
SHP
COME.
THIS WAY.

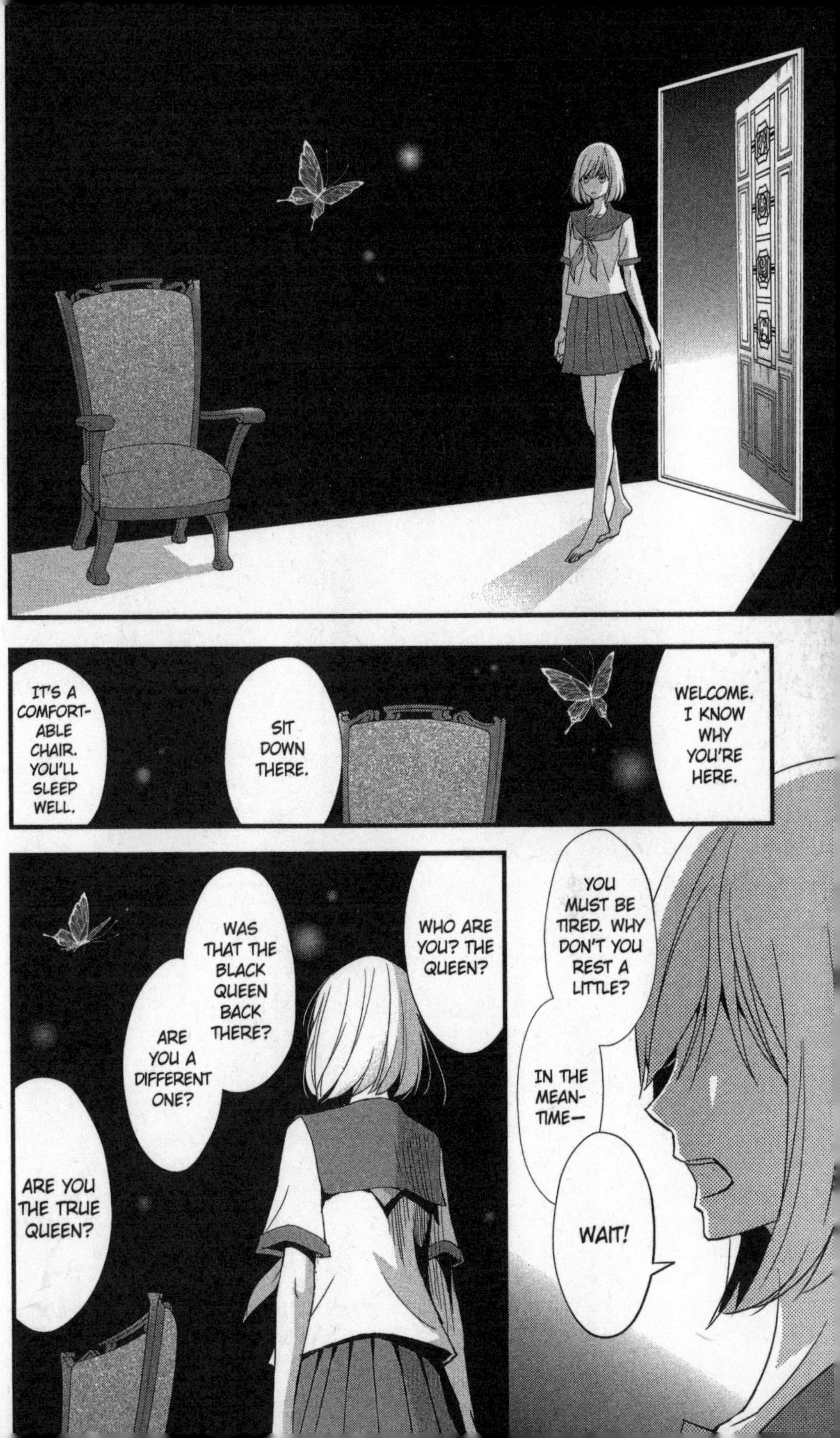
WELCOME. I KNOW WHY YOU'RE HERE.
SIT DOWN THERE.
IT'S A COMFORTABLE CHAIR. YOU'LL SLEEP WELL.
YOU MUST BE TIRED. WHY DON'T YOU REST A LITTLE?
IN THE MEANTIME—
WAIT!
WHO ARE YOU? THE QUEEN?
WAS THAT THE BLACK QUEEN BACK THERE?
ARE YOU A DIFFERENT ONE?
ARE YOU THE TRUE QUEEN?

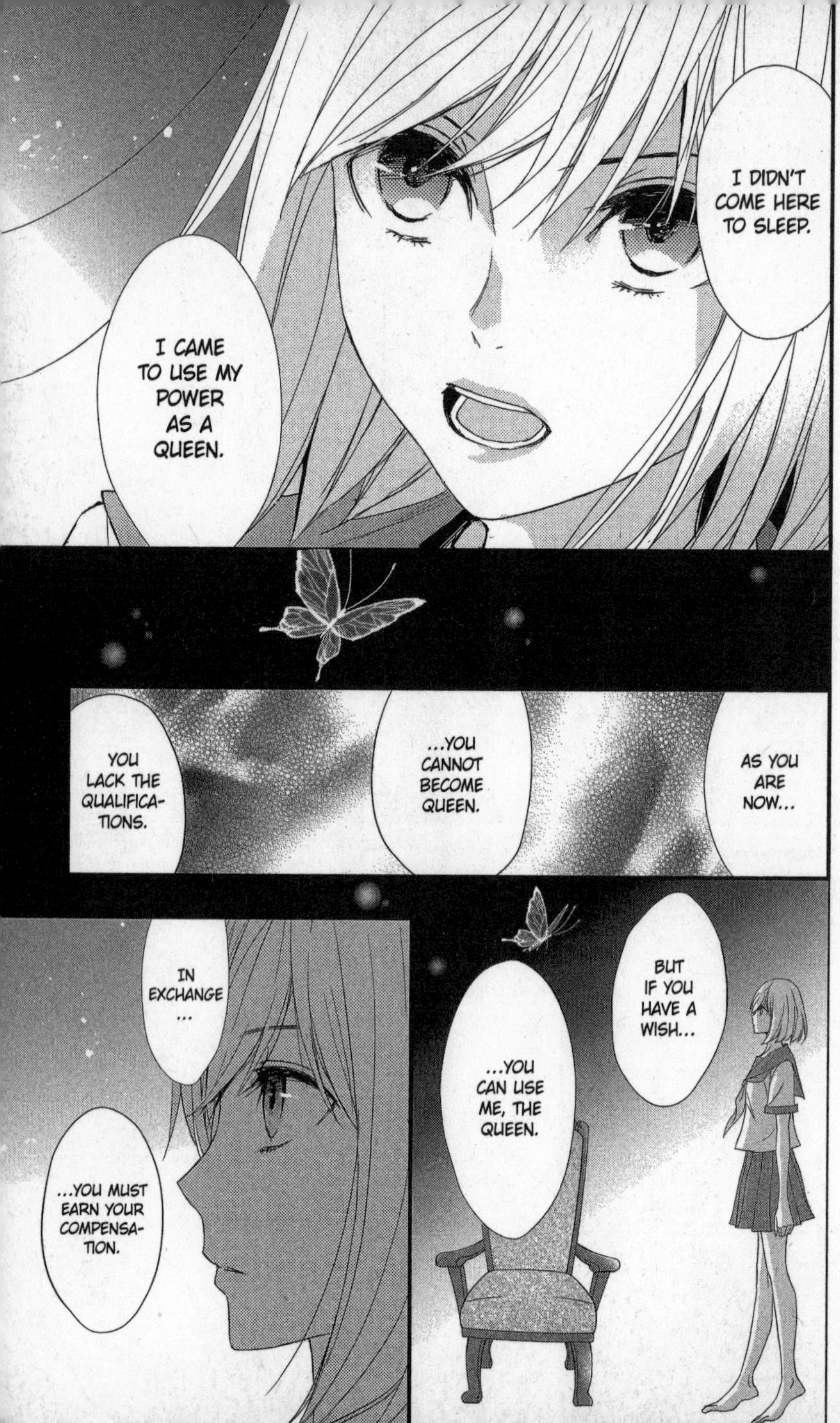
I DIDN'T COME HERE TO SLEEP.
I CAME TO USE MY POWER AS A QUEEN.
AS YOU ARE NOW...
...YOU CANNOT BECOME QUEEN.
YOU LACK THE QUALIFICA-TIONS.
BUT IF YOU HAVE A WISH...
...YOU CAN USE ME, THE QUEEN.
IN EXCHANGE...
...YOU MUST EARN YOUR COMPENSA-TION.

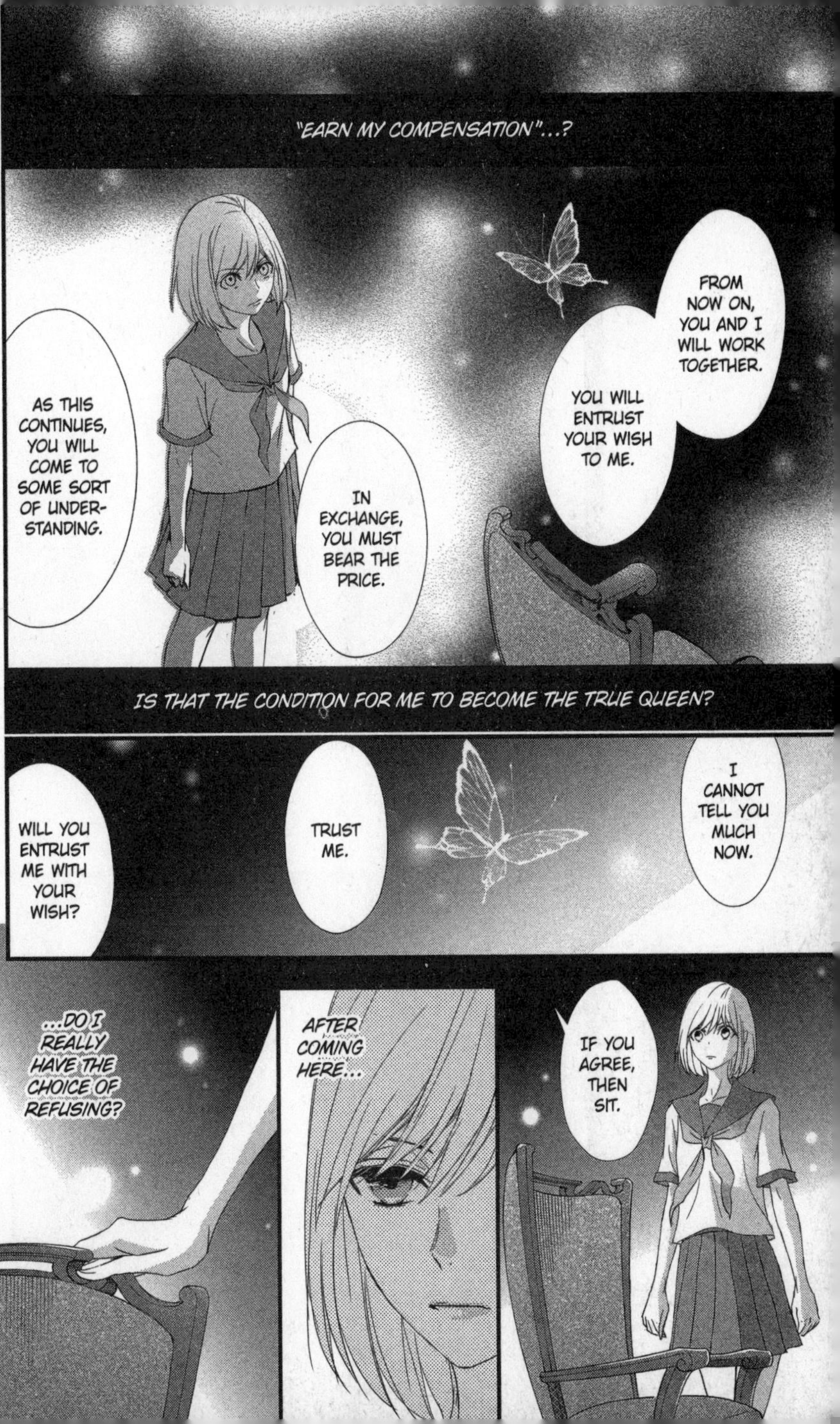
"EARN MY COMPENSATION"...?
FROM NOW ON, YOU AND I WILL WORK TOGETHER.
YOU WILL ENTRUST YOUR WISH TO ME.
IN EXCHANGE, YOU MUST BEAR THE PRICE.
AS THIS CONTINUES, YOU WILL COME TO SOME SORT OF UNDER-STANDING.
IS THAT THE CONDITION FOR ME TO BECOME THE TRUE QUEEN?
I CANNOT TELL YOU MUCH NOW.
TRUST ME.
WILL YOU ENTRUST ME WITH YOUR WISH?
IF YOU AGREE, THEN SIT.
AFTER COMING HERE...
...DO I REALLY HAVE THE CHOICE OF REFUSING?

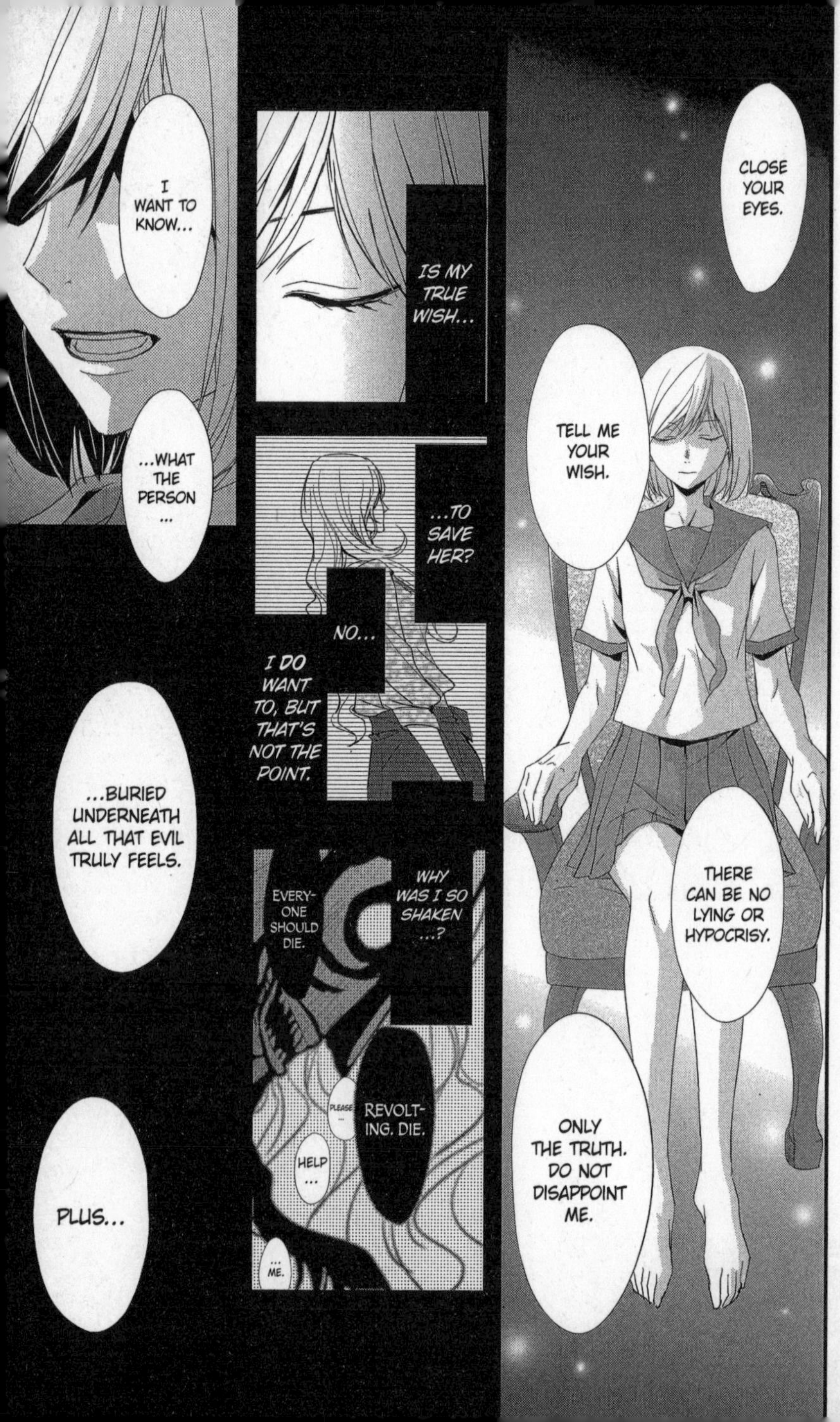
CLOSE YOUR EYES.
TELL ME YOUR WISH.
THERE CAN BE NO LYING OR HYPOCRISY.
ONLY THE TRUTH. DO NOT DISAPPOINT ME.
IS MY TRUE WISH...
...TO SAVE HER?
NO...
I DO WANT TO, BUT THAT'S NOT THE POINT.
WHY WAS I SO SHAKEN ...?
EVERY-ONE SHOULD DIE.
REVOLT-ING. DIE.
PLEASE ...
HELP ...
... ME.
I WANT TO KNOW...
...WHAT THE PERSON ...
...BURIED UNDERNEATH ALL THAT EVIL TRULY FEELS.
PLUS...

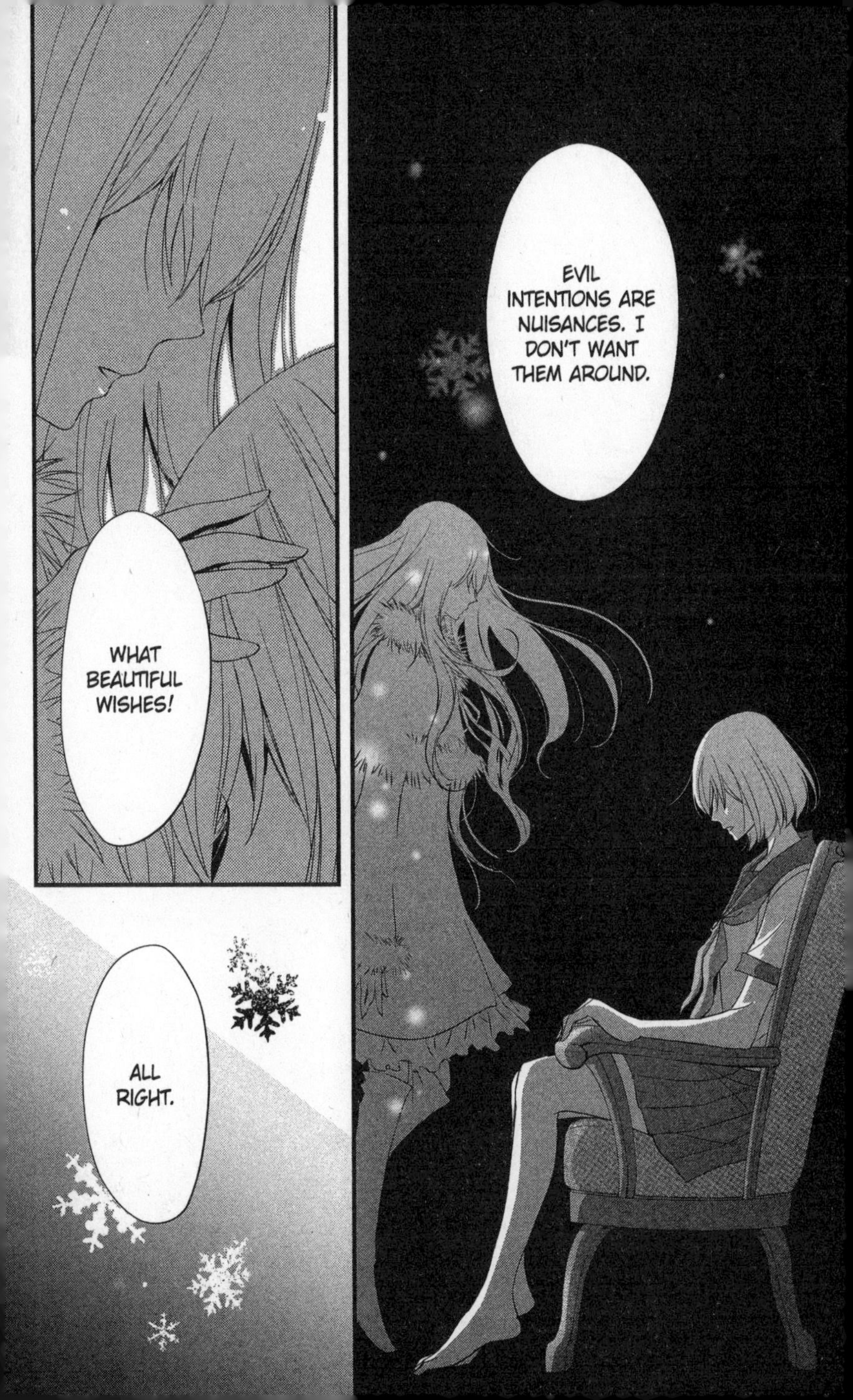
EVIL INTENTIONS ARE NUISANCES. I DON'T WANT THEM AROUND.
WHAT BEAUTIFUL WISHES!
ALL RIGHT.

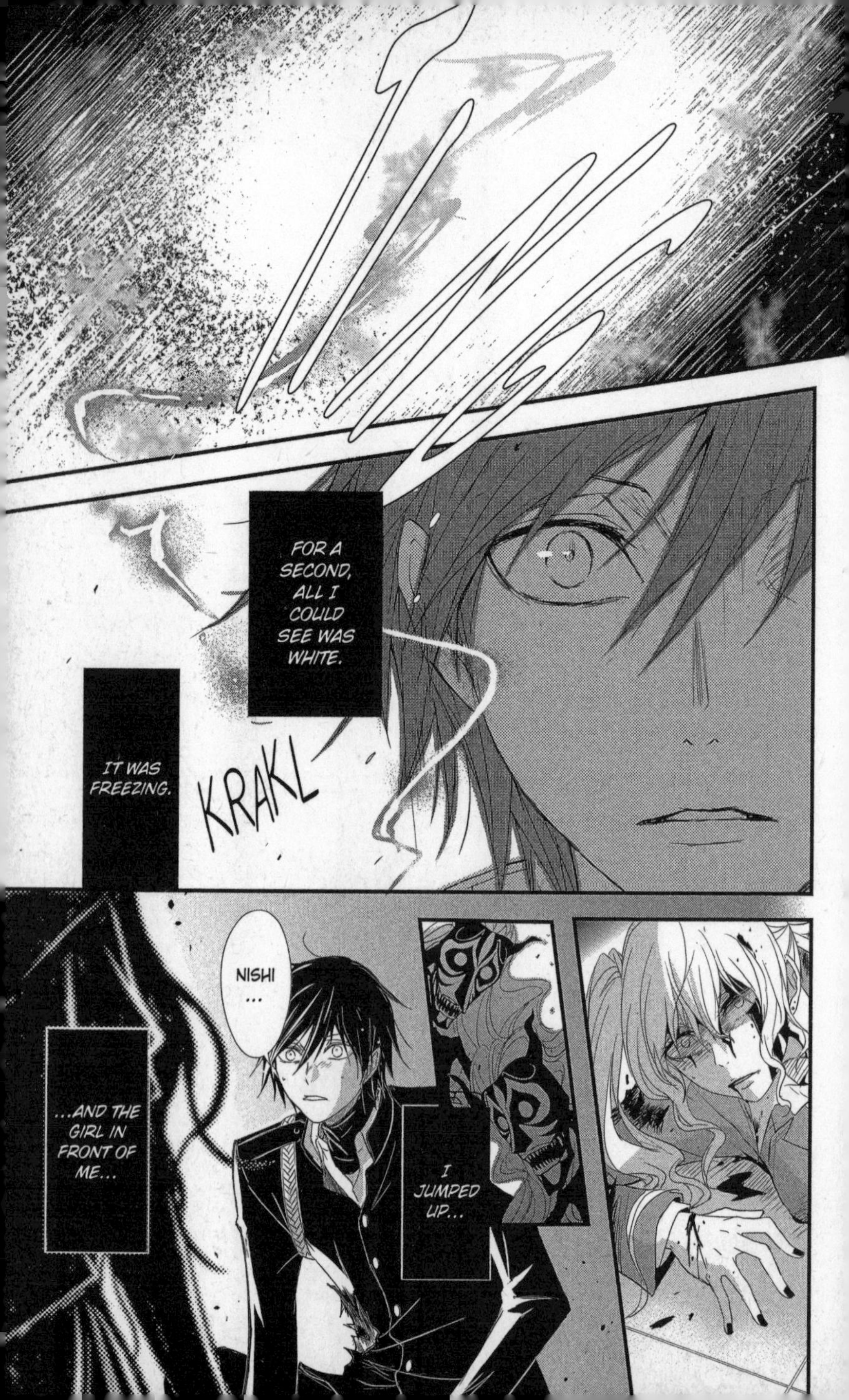
FOR A SECOND, ALL I COULD SEE WAS WHITE.
KRAKL
IT WAS FREEZING.
I JUMPED UP...
NISHI ...
...AND THE GIRL IN FRONT OF ME...

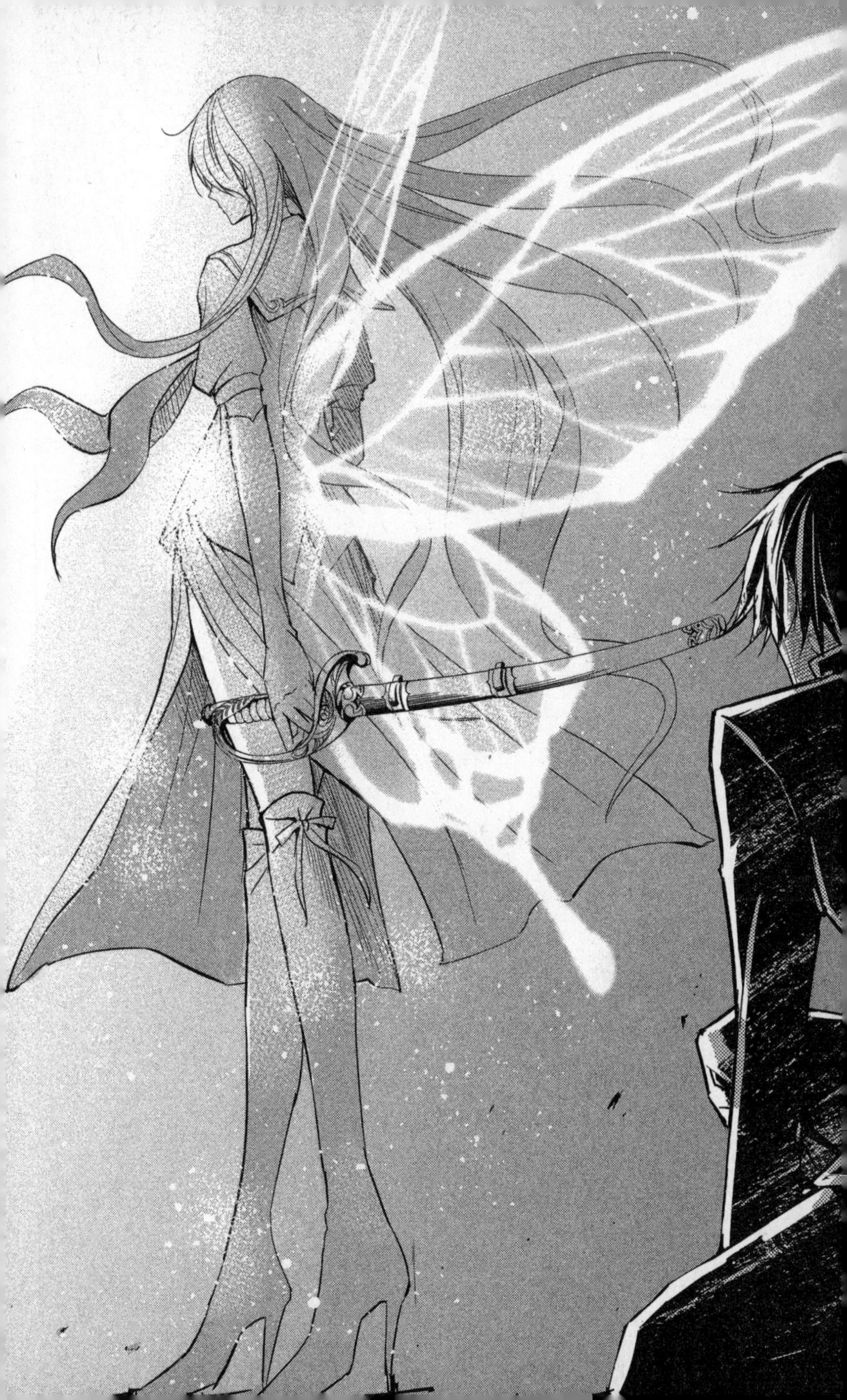

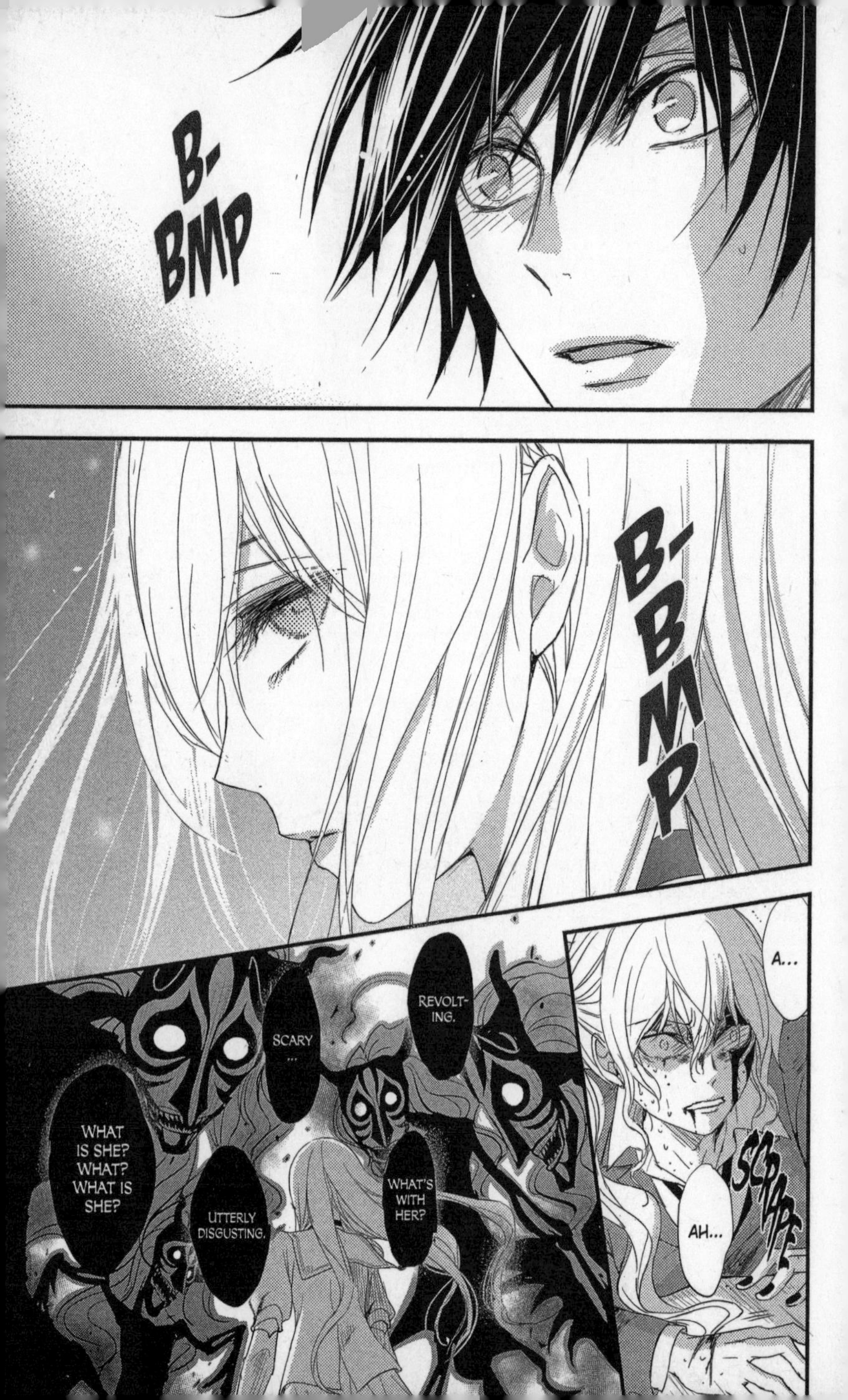
B-BMP
B-BMP
A...
AH...
SCRAPE
REVOLTING.
SCARY...
WHAT'S WITH HER?
UTTERLY DISGUSTING.
WHAT IS SHE? WHAT? WHAT IS SHE?

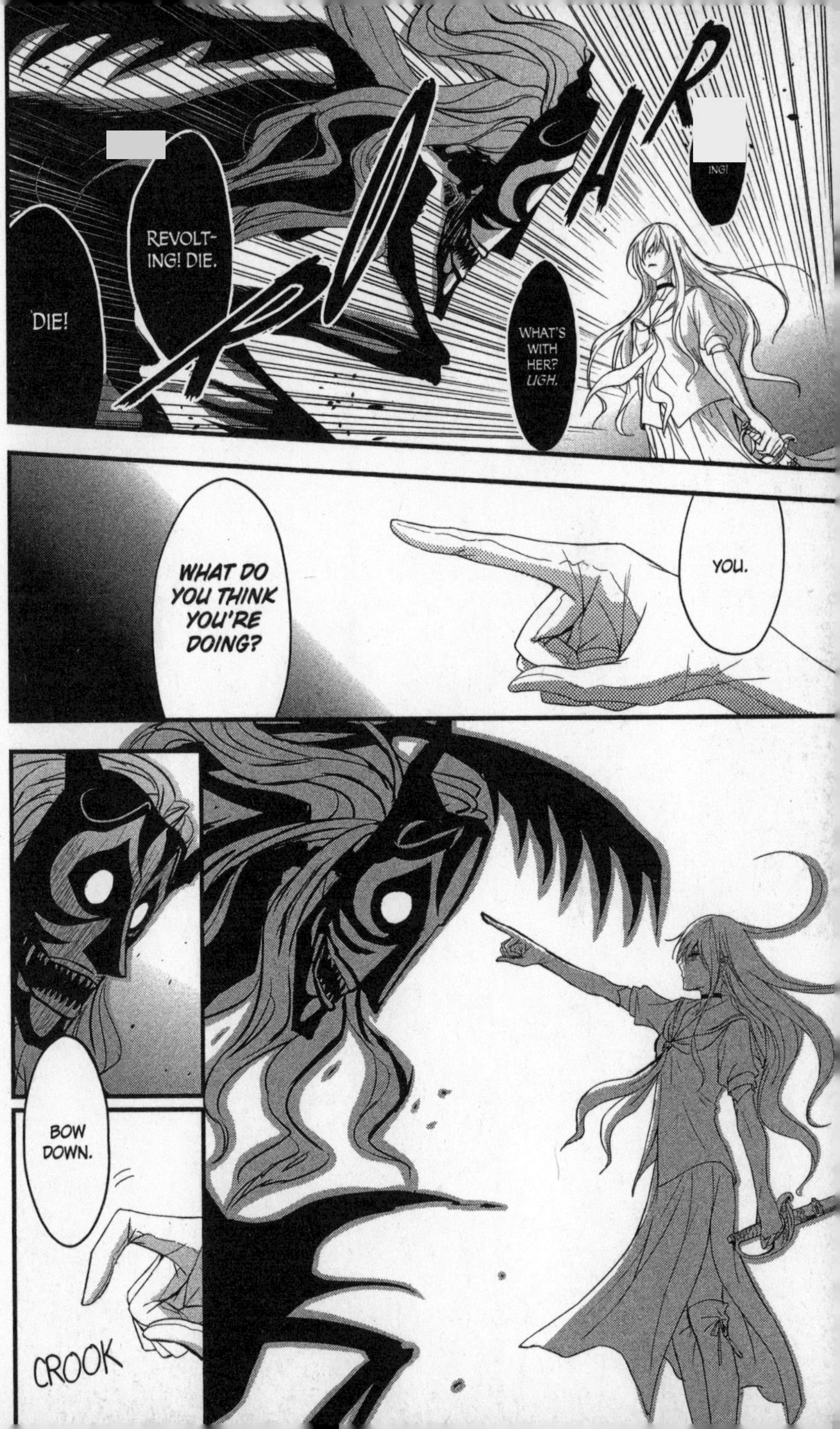
ING!
WHAT'S WITH HER? *UGH.*
REVOLT-ING! DIE.
DIE!
YOU.
WHAT DO YOU THINK YOU'RE DOING?
BOW DOWN.
CROOK

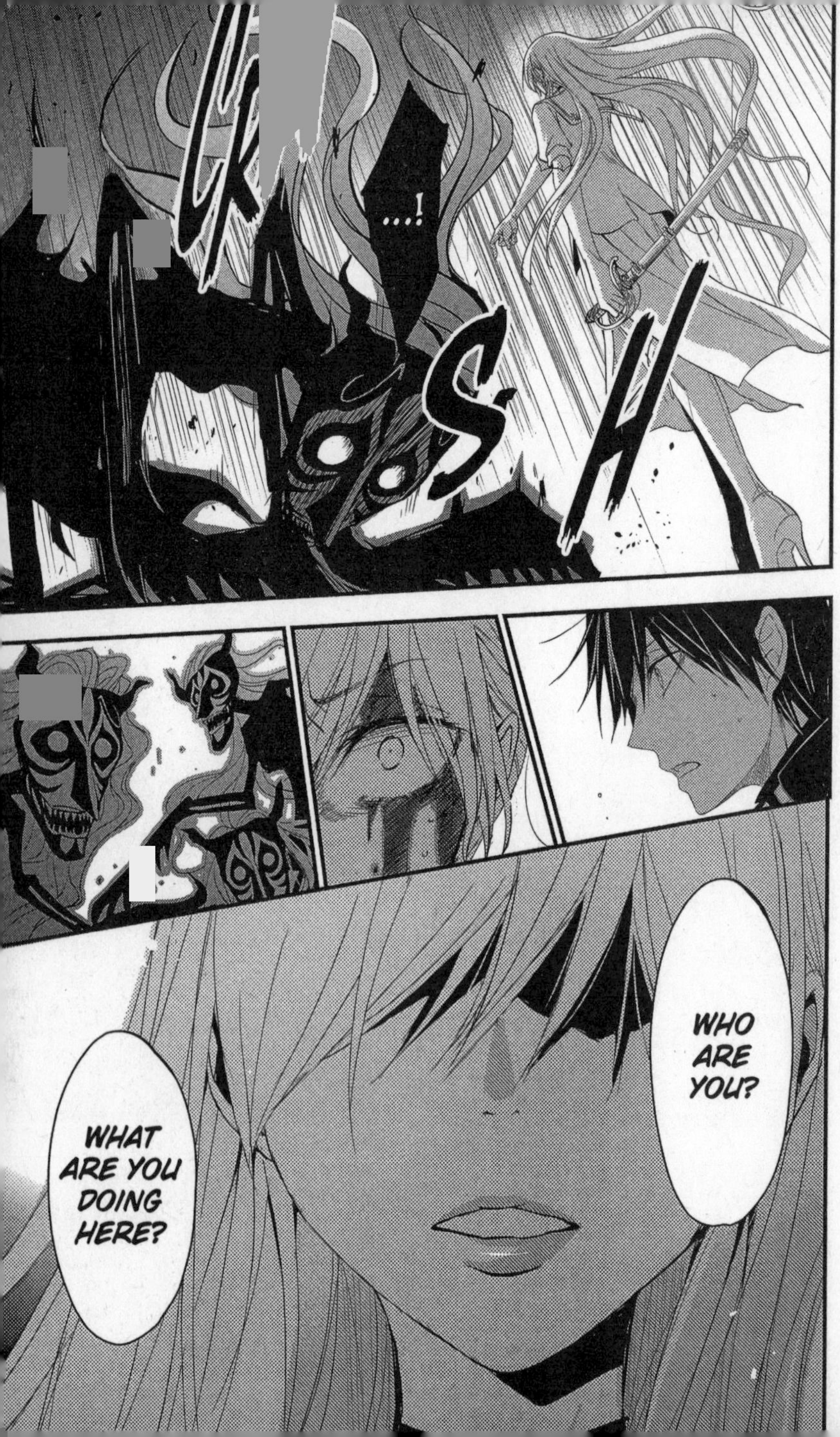
...!
WHO ARE YOU?
WHAT ARE YOU DOING HERE?

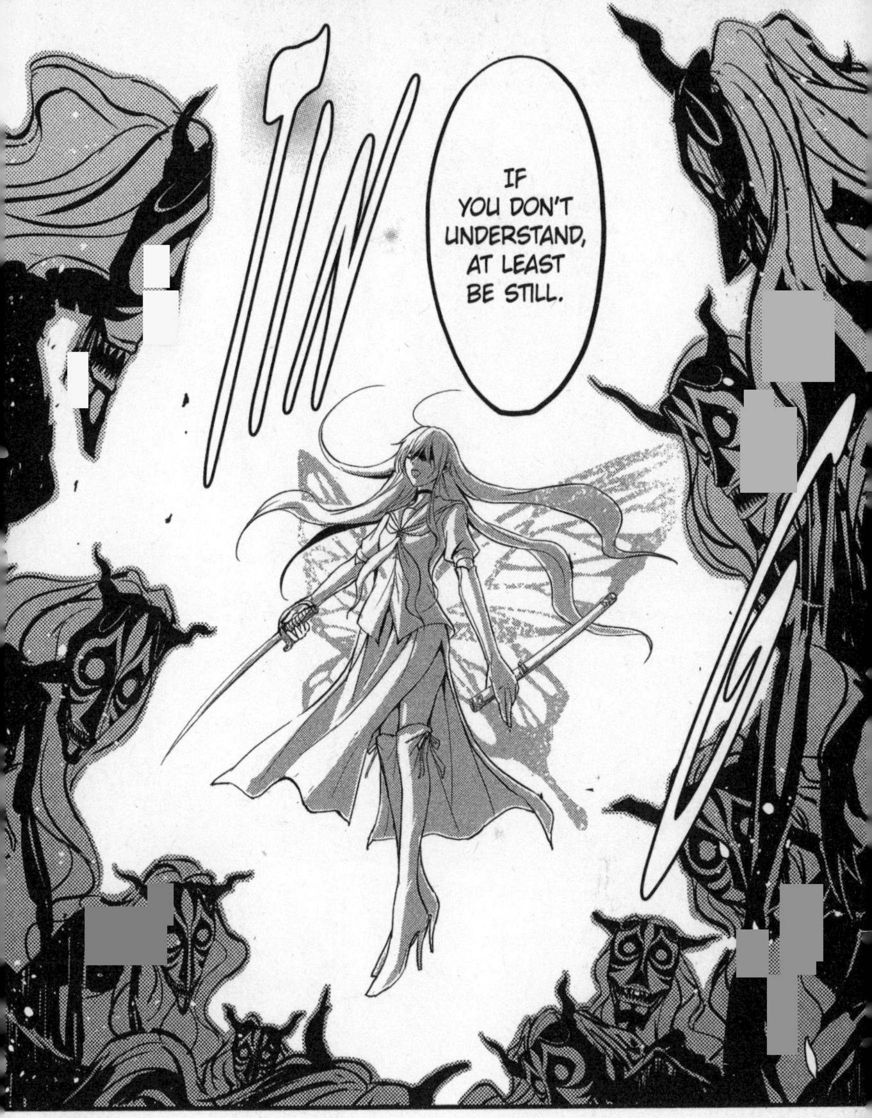
IF YOU DON'T UNDERSTAND, AT LEAST BE STILL.

WITH RIDICULOUS EASE...

...SHE CONQUERED THE PLACE, MIND AND SOUL.

THE QUEEN'S POWER DEMANDED SUBMISSION.

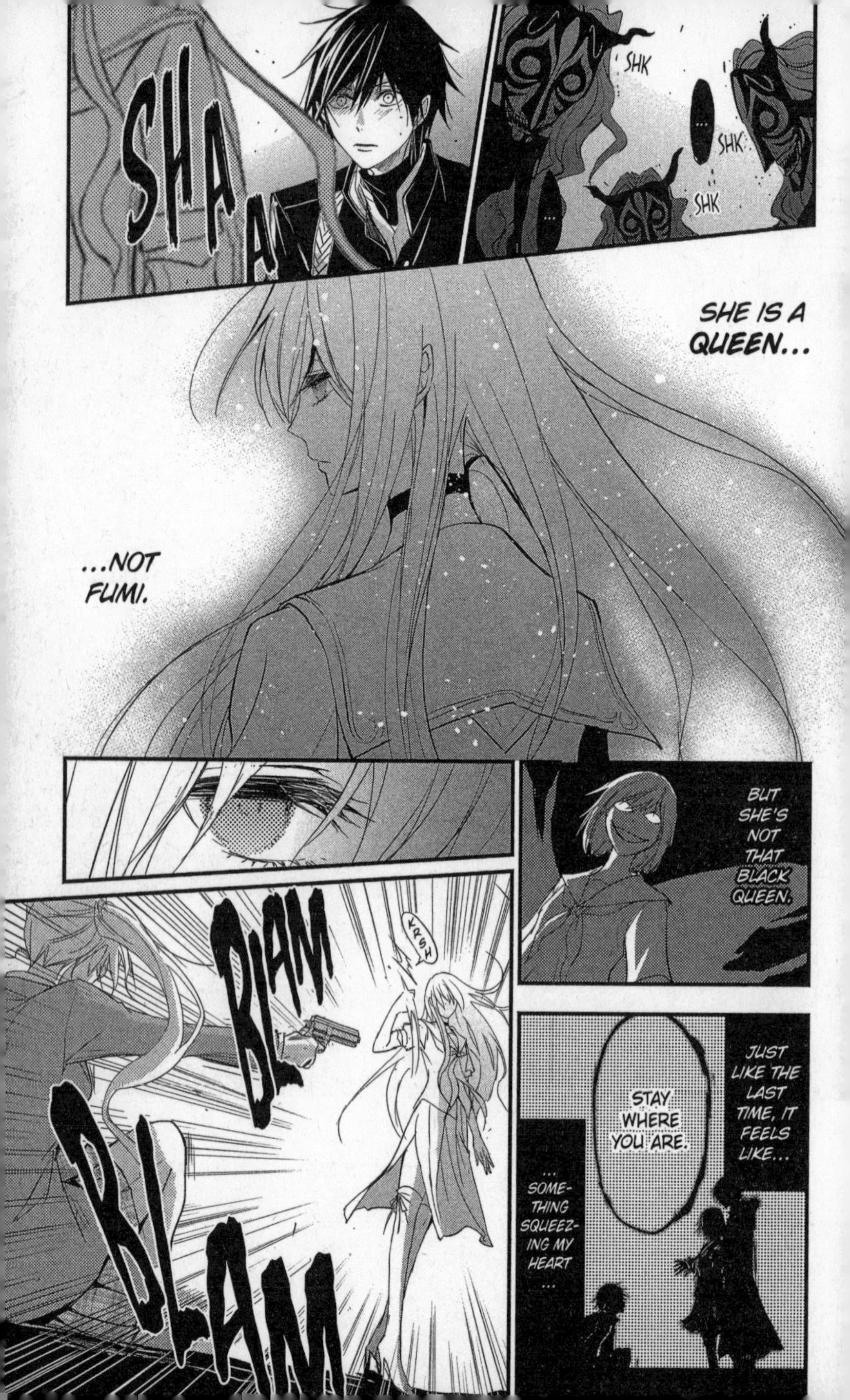
SHK
...
SHK
SHK
...
SHA
A
SHE IS A QUEEN...
...NOT FUMI.
BUT SHE'S NOT THAT BLACK QUEEN.
JUST LIKE THE LAST TIME, IT FEELS LIKE...
STAY WHERE YOU ARE.
...SOME-THING SQUEEZ-ING MY HEART...
KRSH
BLAM
BLAM

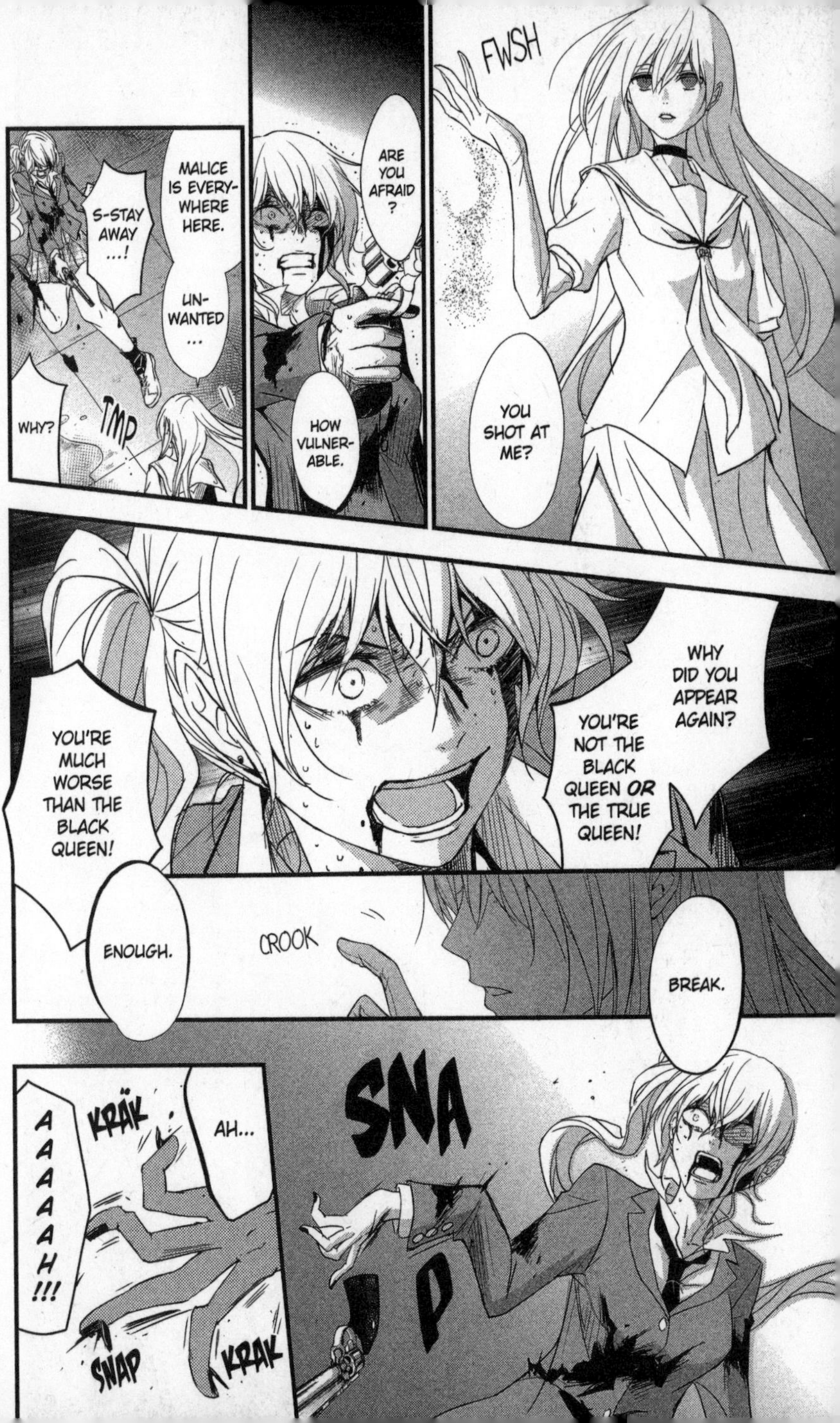
FWSH
YOU SHOT AT ME?
ARE YOU AFRAID?
HOW VULNERABLE.
MALICE IS EVERYWHERE HERE.
UN-WANTED...
S-STAY AWAY...!
TMP
WHY?
WHY DID YOU APPEAR AGAIN?
YOU'RE NOT THE BLACK QUEEN *OR* THE TRUE QUEEN!
YOU'RE MUCH WORSE THAN THE BLACK QUEEN!
BREAK.
CROOK
ENOUGH.
SNAP
AH...
KRÄK
AAAAAAAH!!!
KRAK
SNAP

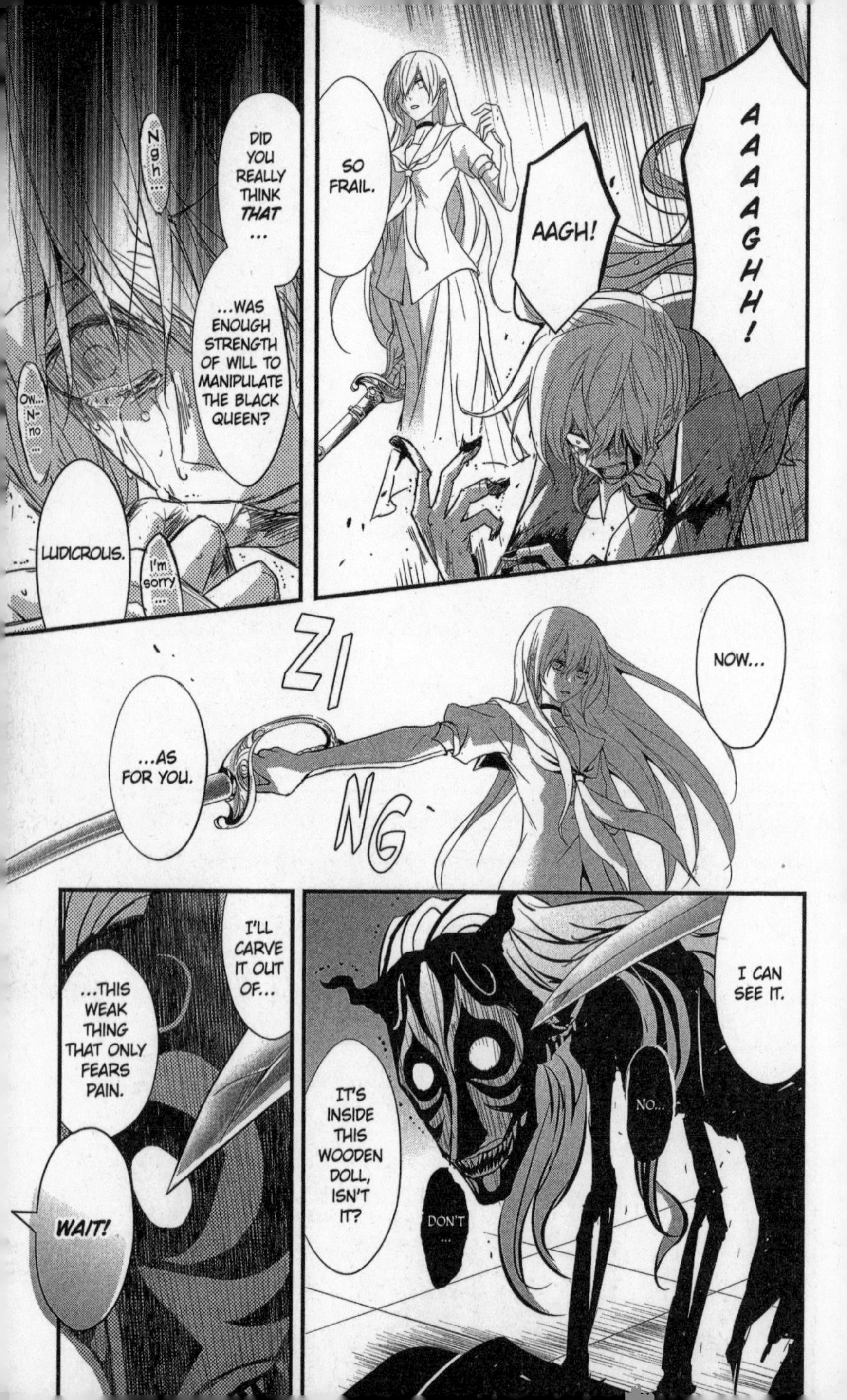
AAAAGHH!
AAGH!
SO FRAIL.
DID YOU REALLY THINK THAT...
Ngh...
...WAS ENOUGH STRENGTH OF WILL TO MANIPULATE THE BLACK QUEEN?
Ow... N-no...
I'm sorry...
LUDICROUS.
NOW...
ZING
...AS FOR YOU.
I CAN SEE IT.
NO...
IT'S INSIDE THIS WOODEN DOLL, ISN'T IT?
DON'T...
I'LL CARVE IT OUT OF...
...THIS WEAK THING THAT ONLY FEARS PAIN.
WAIT!

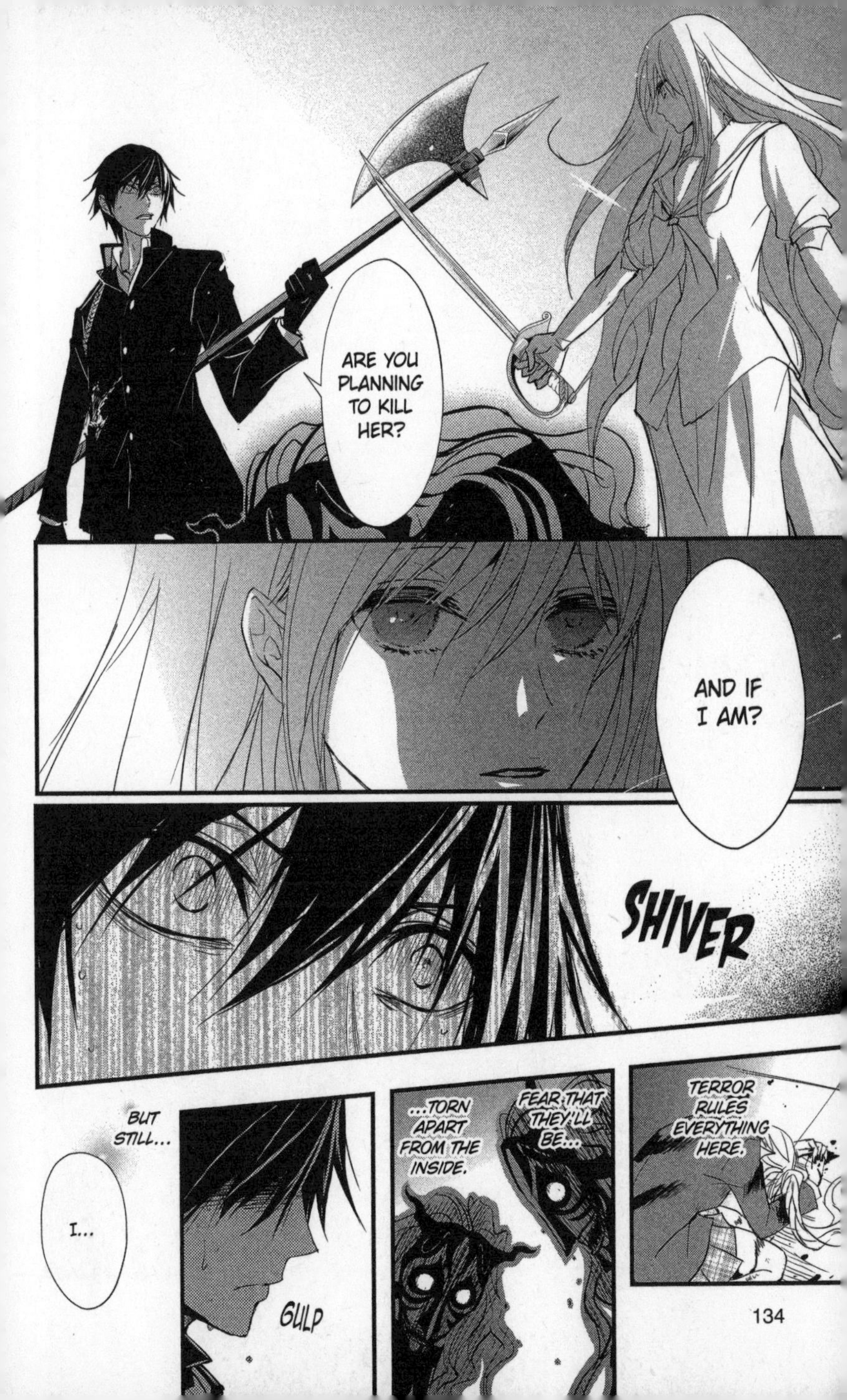
ARE YOU PLANNING TO KILL HER?
AND IF I AM?
SHIVER
TERROR RULES EVERYTHING HERE.
FEAR THAT THEY'LL BE...
...TORN APART FROM THE INSIDE.
BUT STILL...
I...
GULP

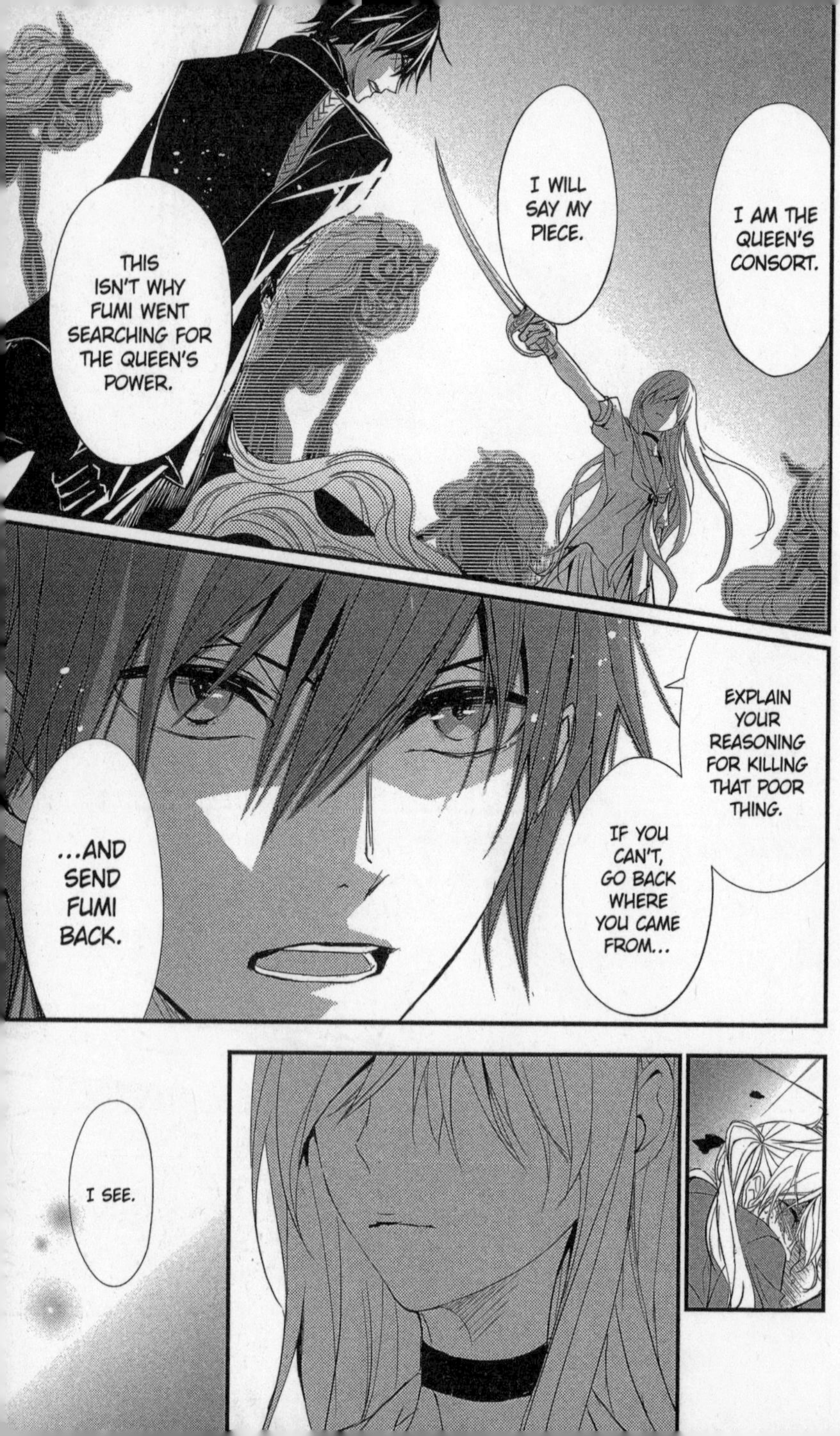
I AM THE QUEEN'S CONSORT.
I WILL SAY MY PIECE.
THIS ISN'T WHY FUMI WENT SEARCHING FOR THE QUEEN'S POWER.
EXPLAIN YOUR REASONING FOR KILLING THAT POOR THING.
IF YOU CAN'T, GO BACK WHERE YOU CAME FROM...
...AND SEND FUMI BACK.
I SEE.

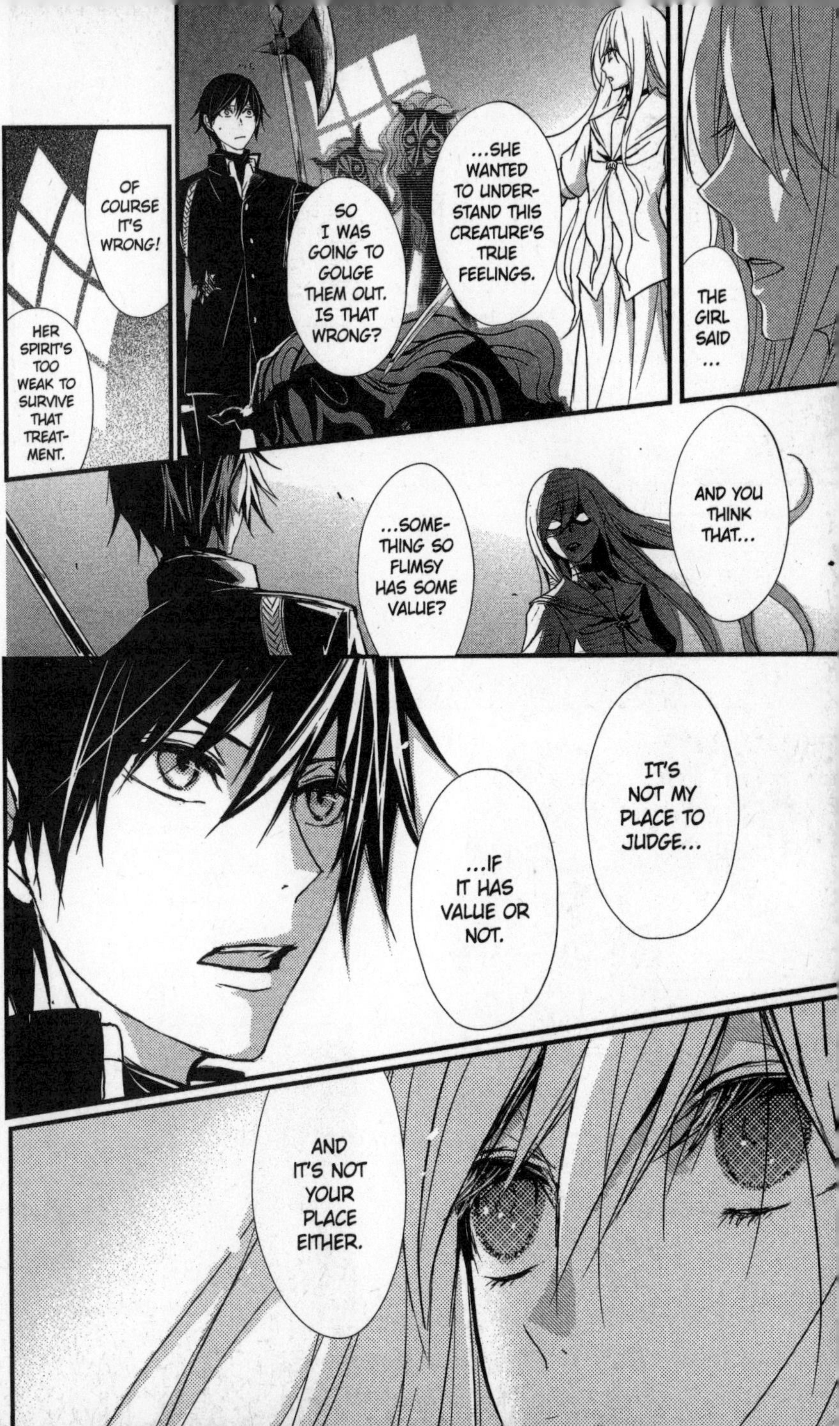
THE GIRL SAID...
...SHE WANTED TO UNDERSTAND THIS CREATURE'S TRUE FEELINGS.
SO I WAS GOING TO GOUGE THEM OUT. IS THAT WRONG?
OF COURSE IT'S WRONG!
HER SPIRIT'S TOO WEAK TO SURVIVE THAT TREATMENT.
AND YOU THINK THAT...
...SOMETHING SO FLIMSY HAS SOME VALUE?
IT'S NOT MY PLACE TO JUDGE...
...IF IT HAS VALUE OR NOT.
AND IT'S NOT YOUR PLACE EITHER.

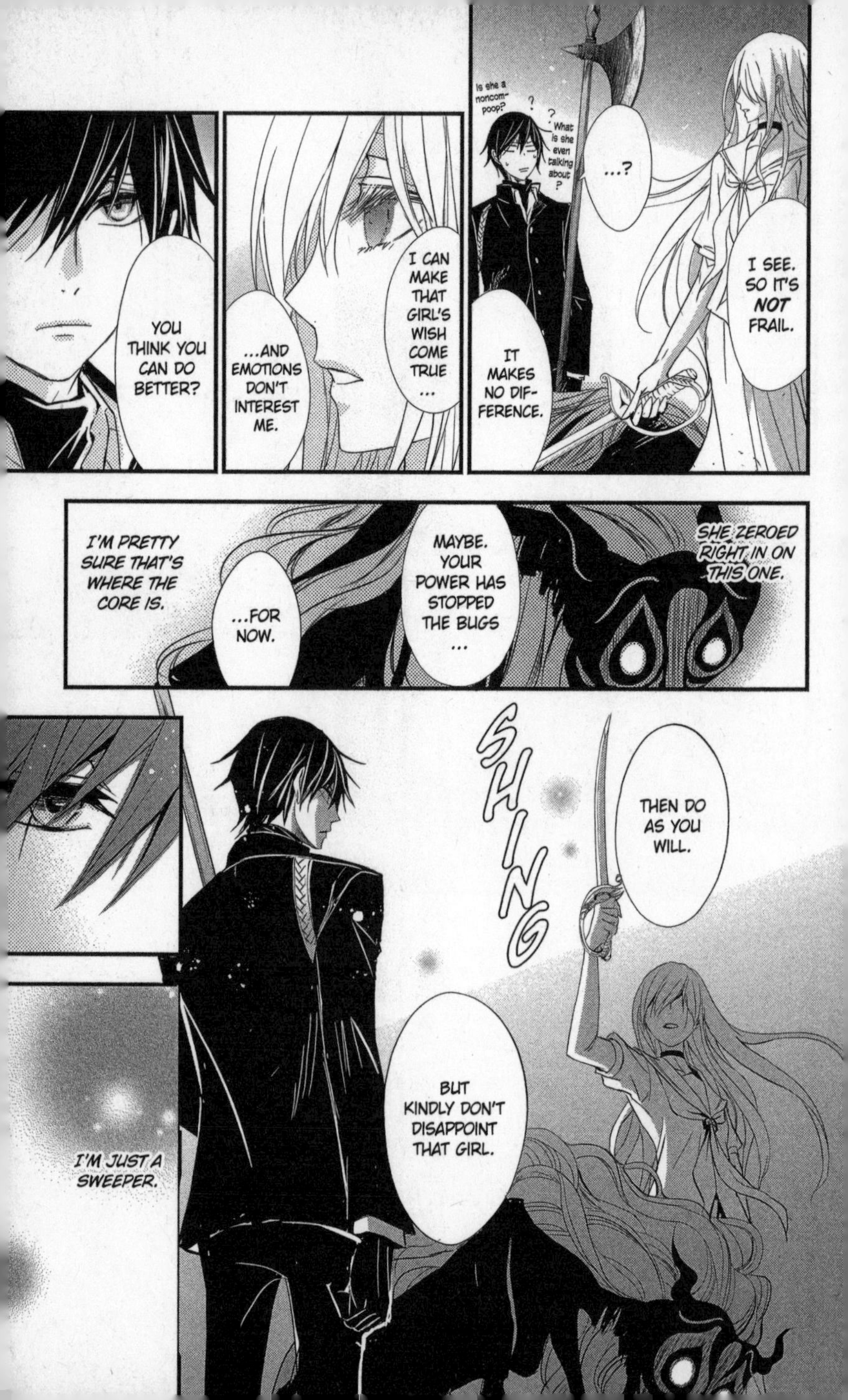
...?
What is she even talking about?
Is she a noncom-poop?
I SEE. SO IT'S *NOT* FRAIL.
IT MAKES NO DIF-FERENCE.
I CAN MAKE THAT GIRL'S WISH COME TRUE...
...AND EMOTIONS DON'T INTEREST ME.
YOU THINK YOU CAN DO BETTER?
SHE ZEROED RIGHT IN ON THIS ONE.
MAYBE. YOUR POWER HAS STOPPED THE BUGS...
...FOR NOW.
I'M PRETTY SURE THAT'S WHERE THE CORE IS.
THEN DO AS YOU WILL.
SHING
BUT KINDLY DON'T DISAPPOINT THAT GIRL.
I'M JUST A SWEEPER.

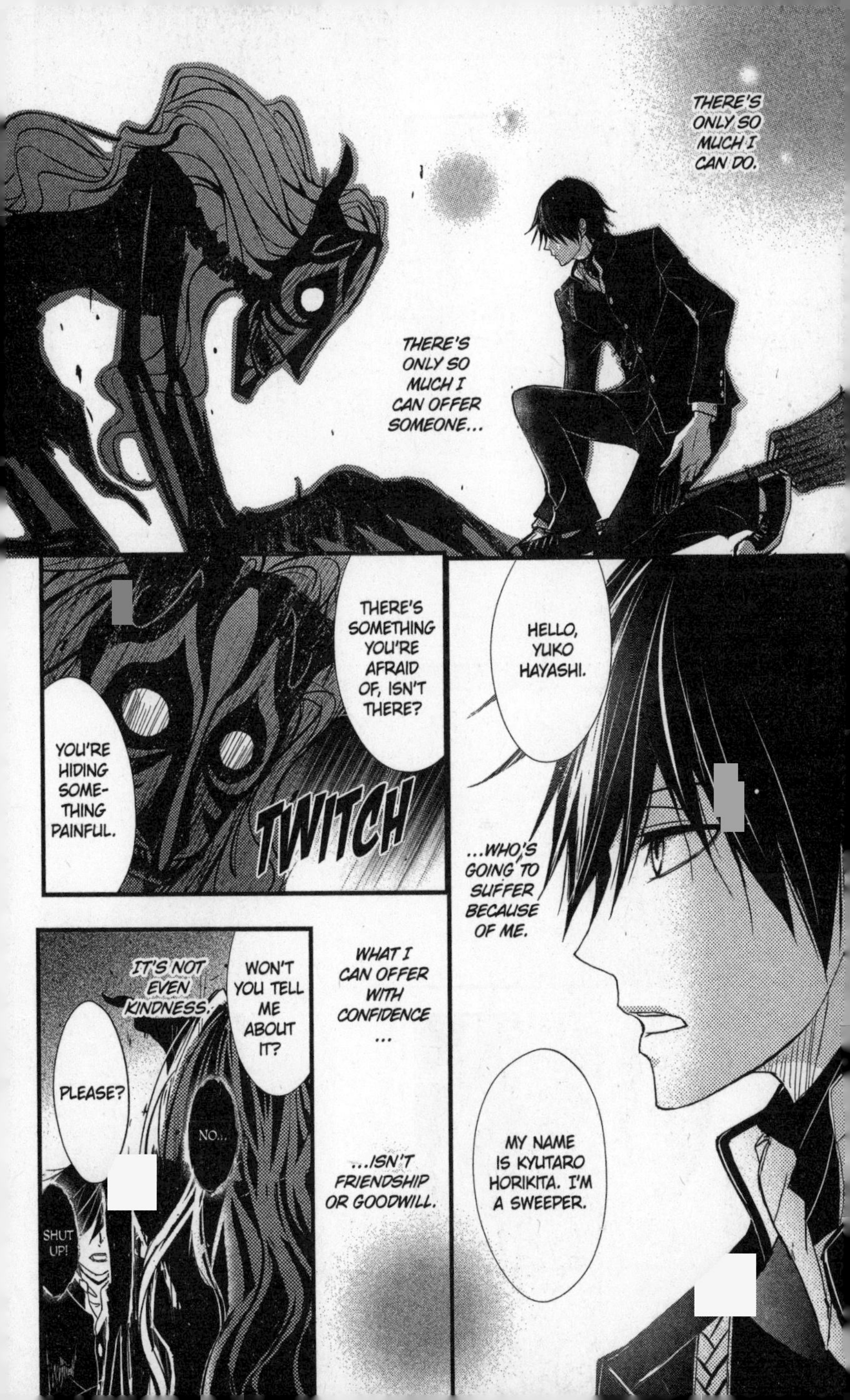
THERE'S ONLY SO MUCH I CAN DO.
THERE'S ONLY SO MUCH I CAN OFFER SOMEONE...
HELLO, YUKO HAYASHI.
...WHO'S GOING TO SUFFER BECAUSE OF ME.
MY NAME IS KYUTARO HORIKITA. I'M A SWEEPER.
THERE'S SOMETHING YOU'RE AFRAID OF, ISN'T THERE?
YOU'RE HIDING SOME-THING PAINFUL.
TWITCH
WHAT I CAN OFFER WITH CONFIDENCE...
...ISN'T FRIENDSHIP OR GOODWILL.
WON'T YOU TELL ME ABOUT IT?
IT'S NOT EVEN KINDNESS.
PLEASE?
NO...
SHUT UP!

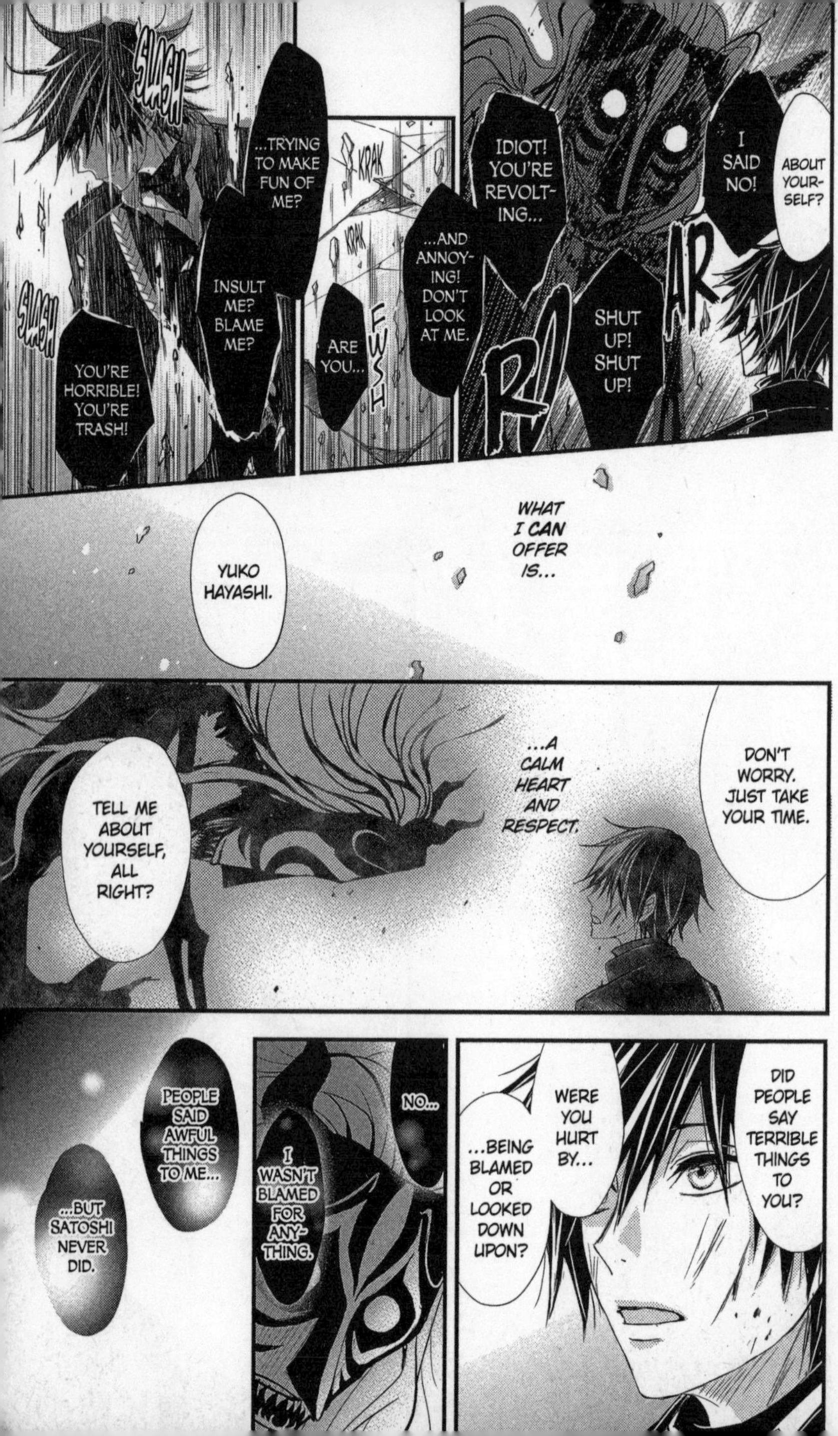
ABOUT YOURSELF?
I SAID NO!
IDIOT! YOU'RE REVOLTING...
SHUT UP! SHUT UP!
KRAK
...AND ANNOYING! DON'T LOOK AT ME.
KRAK
FWSH
ARE YOU...
SLASH
...TRYING TO MAKE FUN OF ME?
INSULT ME? BLAME ME?
YOU'RE HORRIBLE! YOU'RE TRASH!
SLASH
WHAT I CAN OFFER IS...
YUKO HAYASHI.
DON'T WORRY. JUST TAKE YOUR TIME.
...A CALM HEART AND RESPECT.
TELL ME ABOUT YOURSELF, ALL RIGHT?
DID PEOPLE SAY TERRIBLE THINGS TO YOU?
WERE YOU HURT BY...
...BEING BLAMED OR LOOKED DOWN UPON?
NO...
I WASN'T BLAMED FOR ANYTHING.
PEOPLE SAID AWFUL THINGS TO ME...
...BUT SATOSHI NEVER DID.

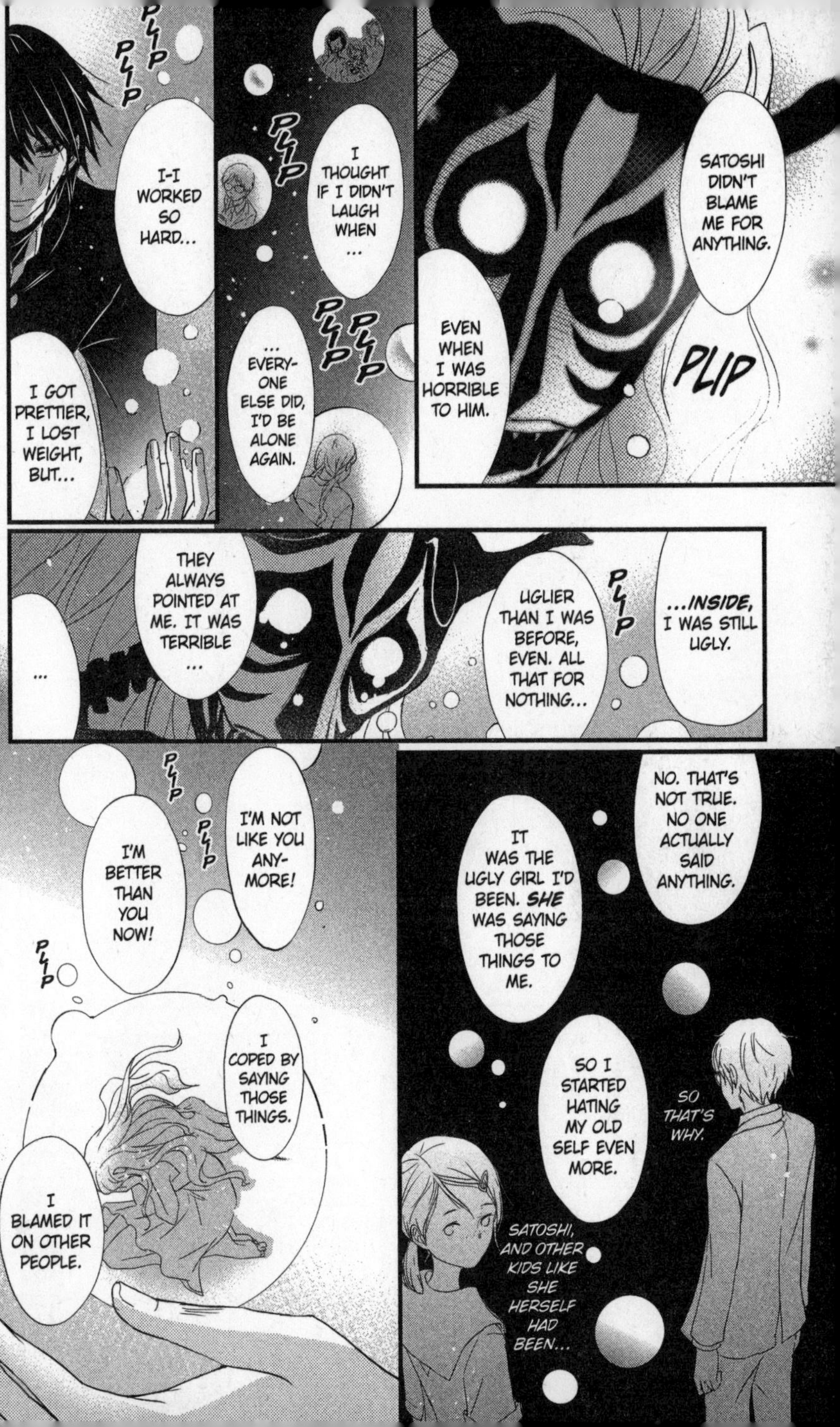
SATOSHI DIDN'T BLAME ME FOR ANYTHING.
PLIP
EVEN WHEN I WAS HORRIBLE TO HIM.
PLIP
I THOUGHT IF I DIDN'T LAUGH WHEN ...
PLIP PLIP
... EVERY-ONE ELSE DID, I'D BE ALONE AGAIN.
PLIP PLIP
I-I WORKED SO HARD...
I GOT PRETTIER, I LOST WEIGHT, BUT...
...*INSIDE,* I WAS STILL UGLY.
PLIP
UGLIER THAN I WAS BEFORE, EVEN. ALL THAT FOR NOTHING...
THEY ALWAYS POINTED AT ME. IT WAS TERRIBLE ...
...
NO. THAT'S NOT TRUE. NO ONE ACTUALLY SAID ANYTHING.
IT WAS THE UGLY GIRL I'D BEEN. *SHE* WAS SAYING THOSE THINGS TO ME.
SO I STARTED HATING MY OLD SELF EVEN MORE.
SO THAT'S WHY.
SATOSHI, AND OTHER KIDS LIKE SHE HERSELF HAD BEEN...
PLIP
I'M NOT LIKE YOU ANY-MORE!
PLIP
I'M BETTER THAN YOU NOW!
PLIP
I COPED BY SAYING THOSE THINGS.
I BLAMED IT ON OTHER PEOPLE.

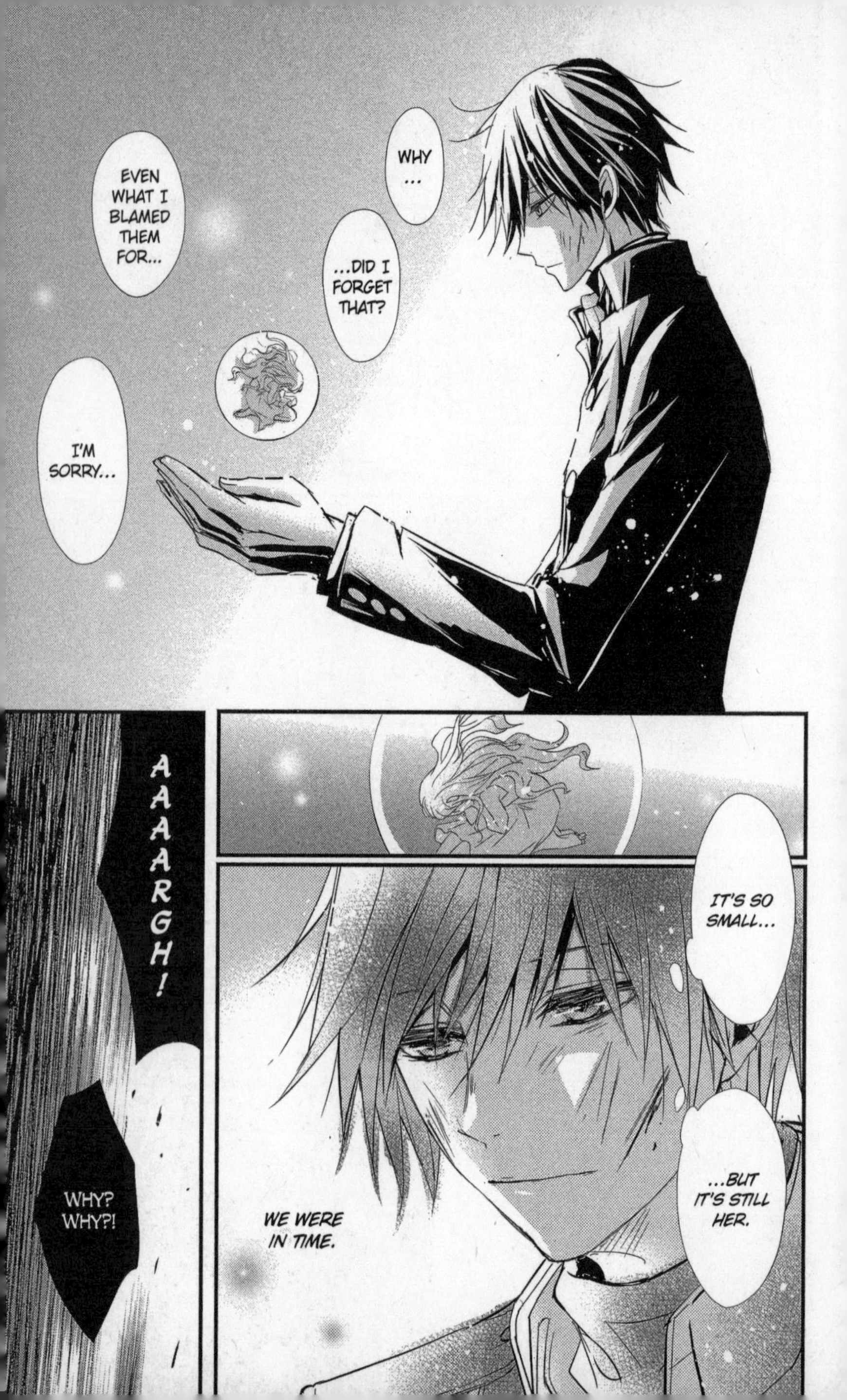
WHY ...
...DID I FORGET THAT?
EVEN WHAT I BLAMED THEM FOR...
I'M SORRY...
IT'S SO SMALL...
...BUT IT'S STILL HER.
WE WERE IN TIME.
AAAAARGH!
WHY? WHY?!

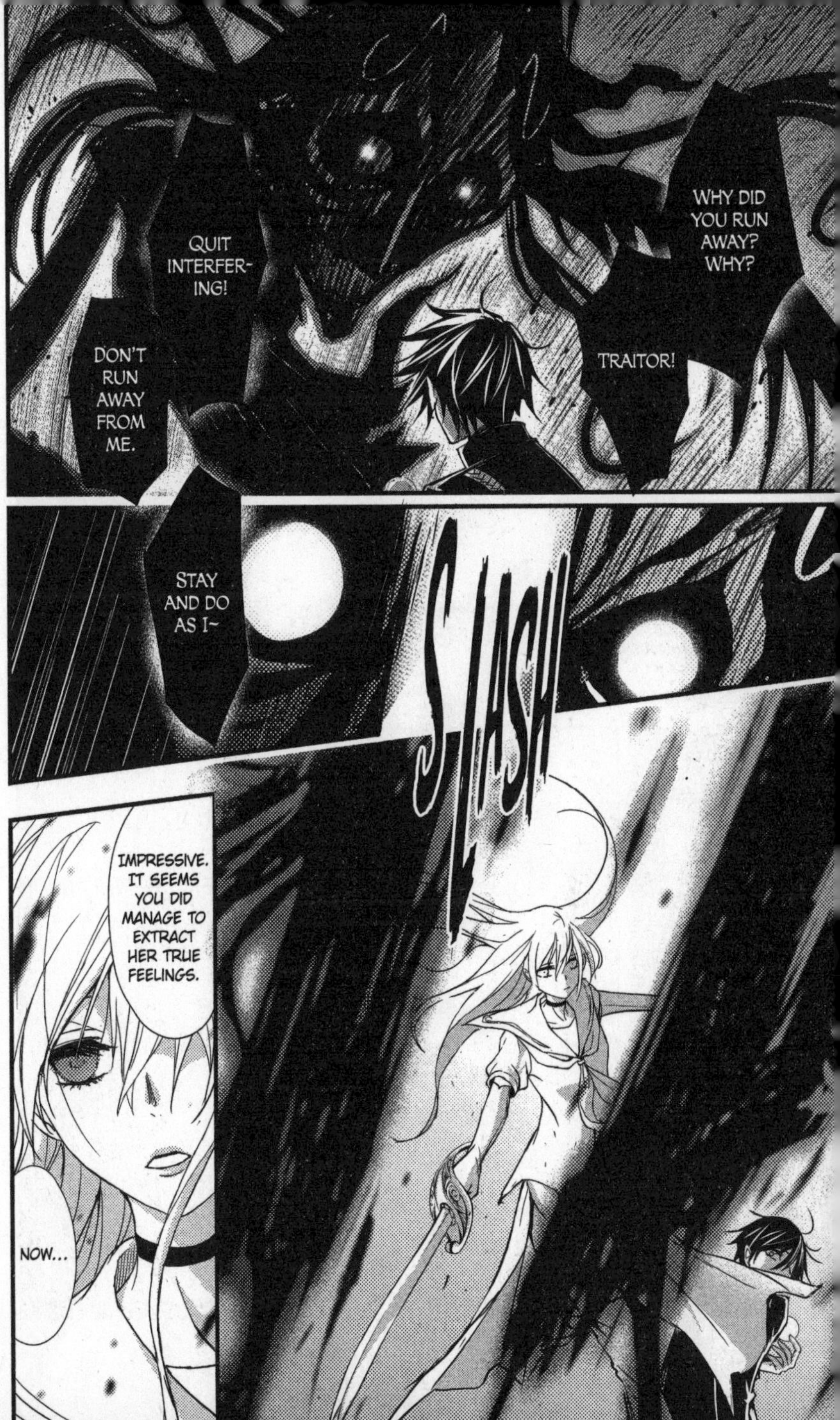
WHY DID YOU RUN AWAY? WHY?
QUIT INTERFER-ING!
TRAITOR!
DON'T RUN AWAY FROM ME.
STAY AND DO AS I~
SLASH
IMPRESSIVE. IT SEEMS YOU DID MANAGE TO EXTRACT HER TRUE FEELINGS.
NOW...

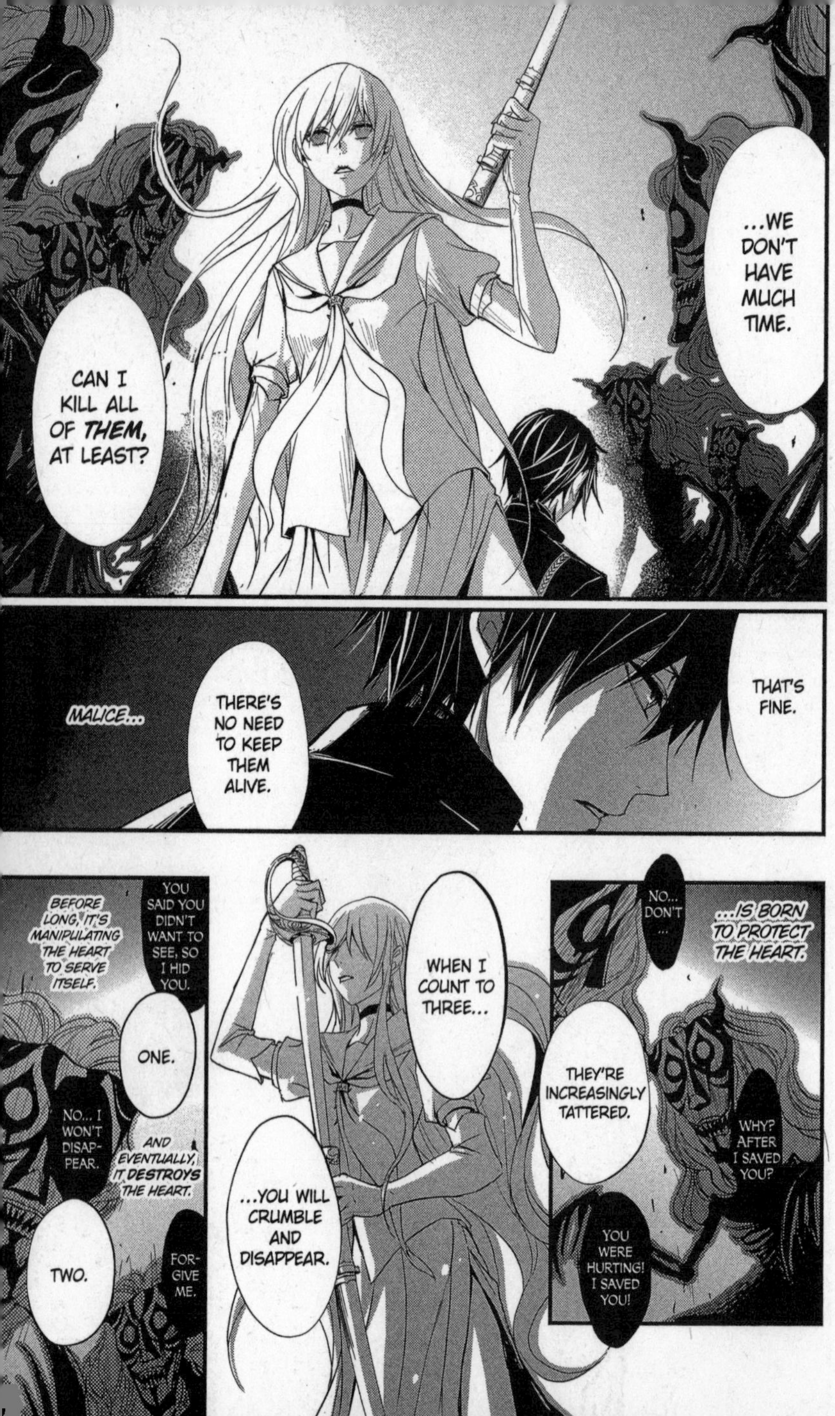
...WE DON'T HAVE MUCH TIME.
CAN I KILL ALL OF *THEM*, AT LEAST?
THAT'S FINE.
THERE'S NO NEED TO KEEP THEM ALIVE.
MALICE...
...IS BORN TO PROTECT THE HEART.
NO... DON'T ...
THEY'RE INCREASINGLY TATTERED.
WHY? AFTER I SAVED YOU?
YOU WERE HURTING! I SAVED YOU!
WHEN I COUNT TO THREE...
...YOU WILL CRUMBLE AND DISAPPEAR.
YOU SAID YOU DIDN'T WANT TO SEE, SO I HID YOU.
BEFORE LONG, IT'S MANIPULATING THE HEART TO SERVE ITSELF.
ONE.
NO... I WON'T DISAP-PEAR.
AND EVENTUALLY, IT DESTROYS THE HEART.
FORGIVE ME.
TWO.

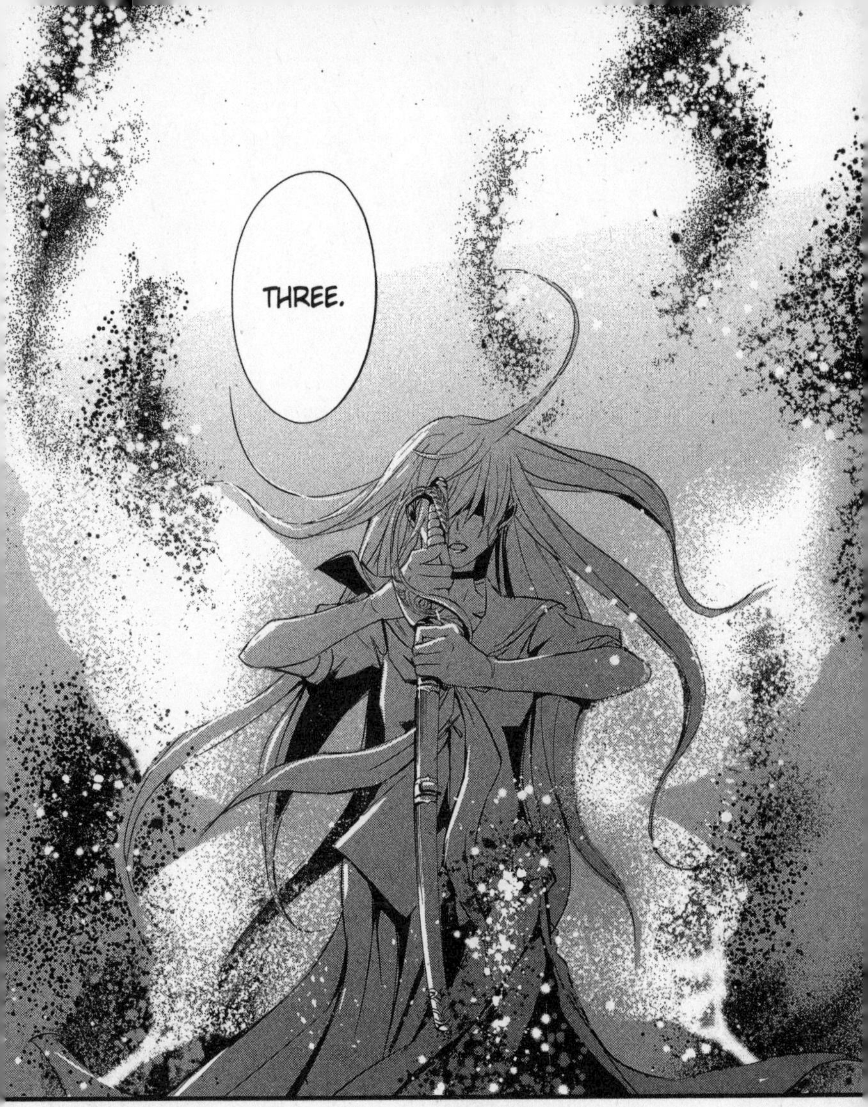
THREE.

THE FOOLISH HUSKS OF EMOTIONS THAT HAVE FORGOTTEN...

...THE REASON FOR THEIR BIRTH, AND THEIR PURPOSE...

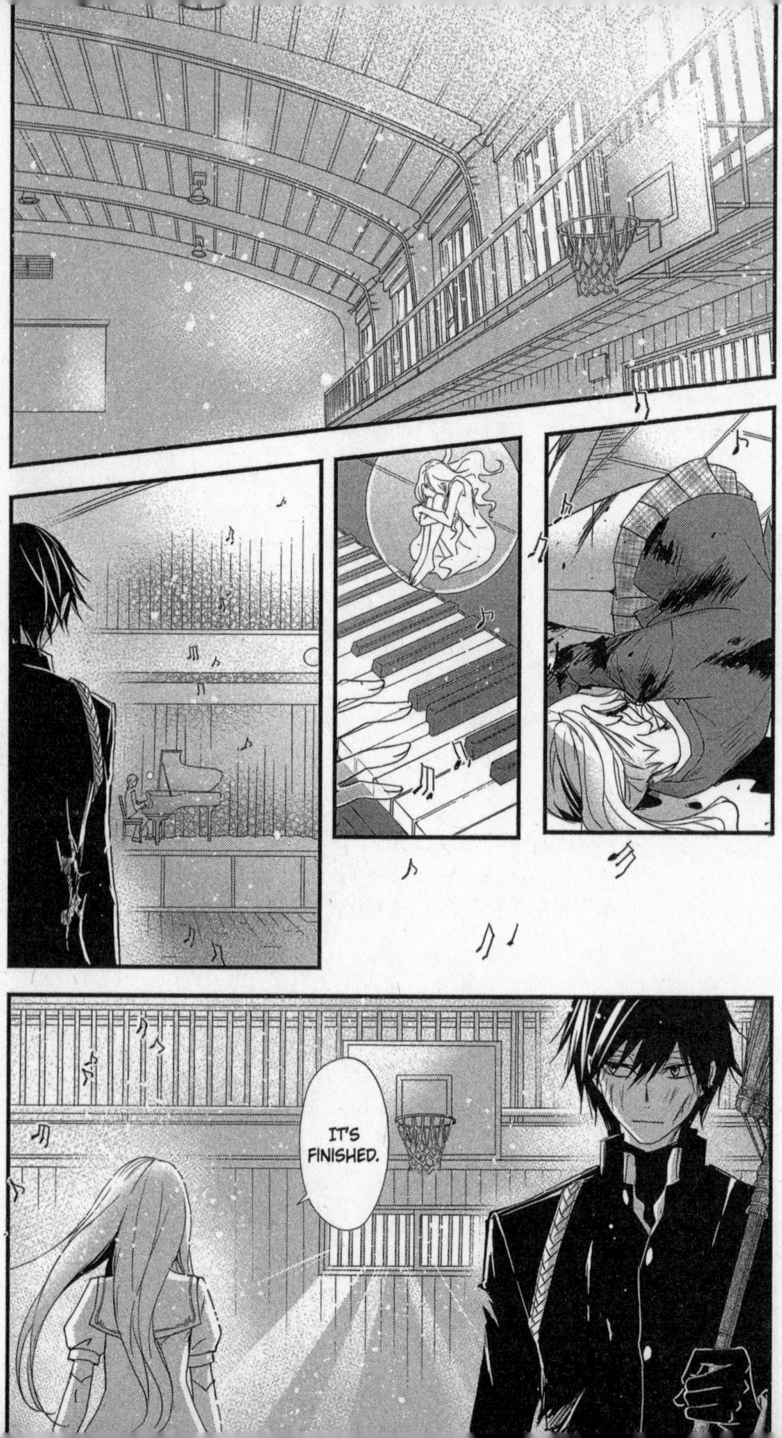
IT'S FINISHED.

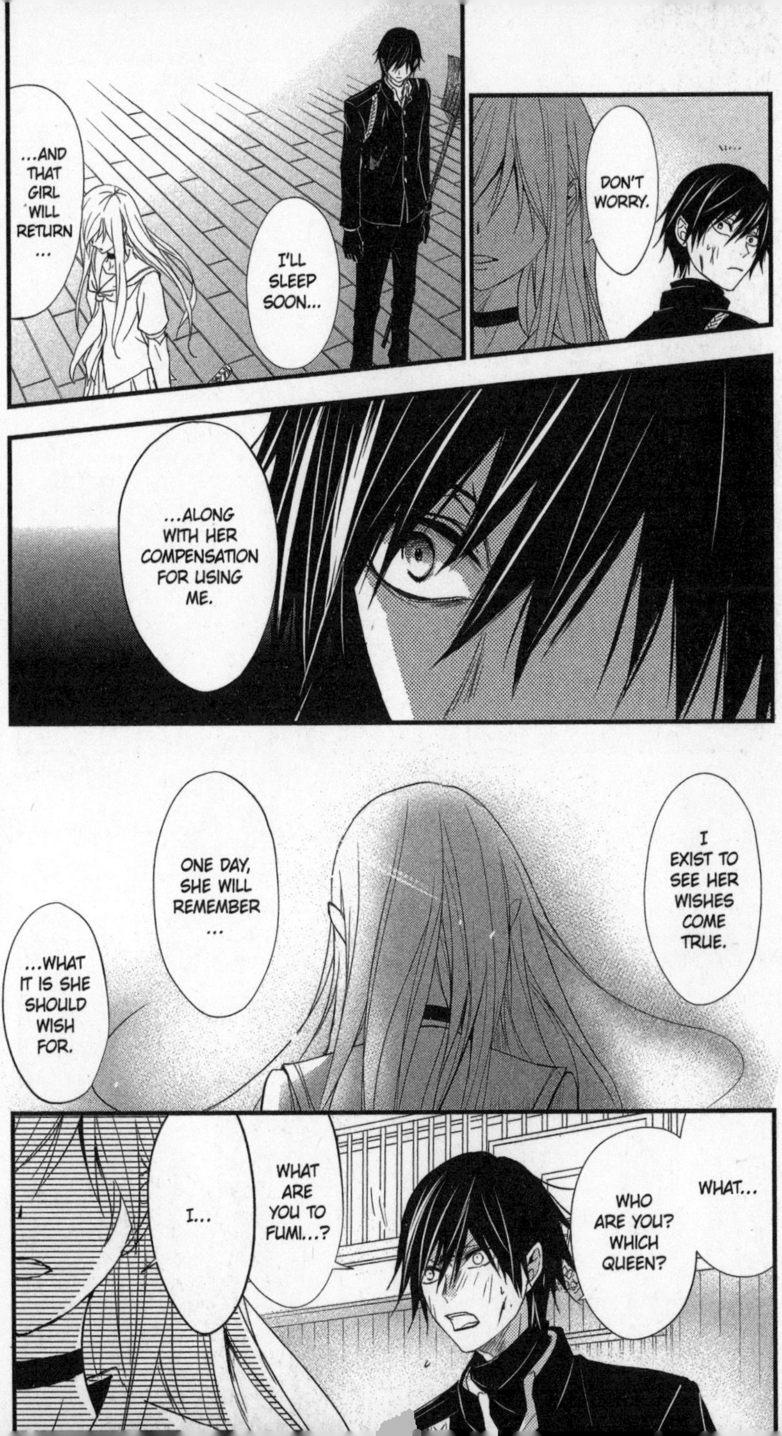
...
DON'T WORRY.
I'LL SLEEP SOON...
...AND THAT GIRL WILL RETURN ...
...ALONG WITH HER COMPENSATION FOR USING ME.
I EXIST TO SEE HER WISHES COME TRUE.
ONE DAY, SHE WILL REMEMBER ...
...WHAT IT IS SHE SHOULD WISH FOR.
WHAT...
WHO ARE YOU? WHICH QUEEN?
WHAT ARE YOU TO FUMI...?
I...

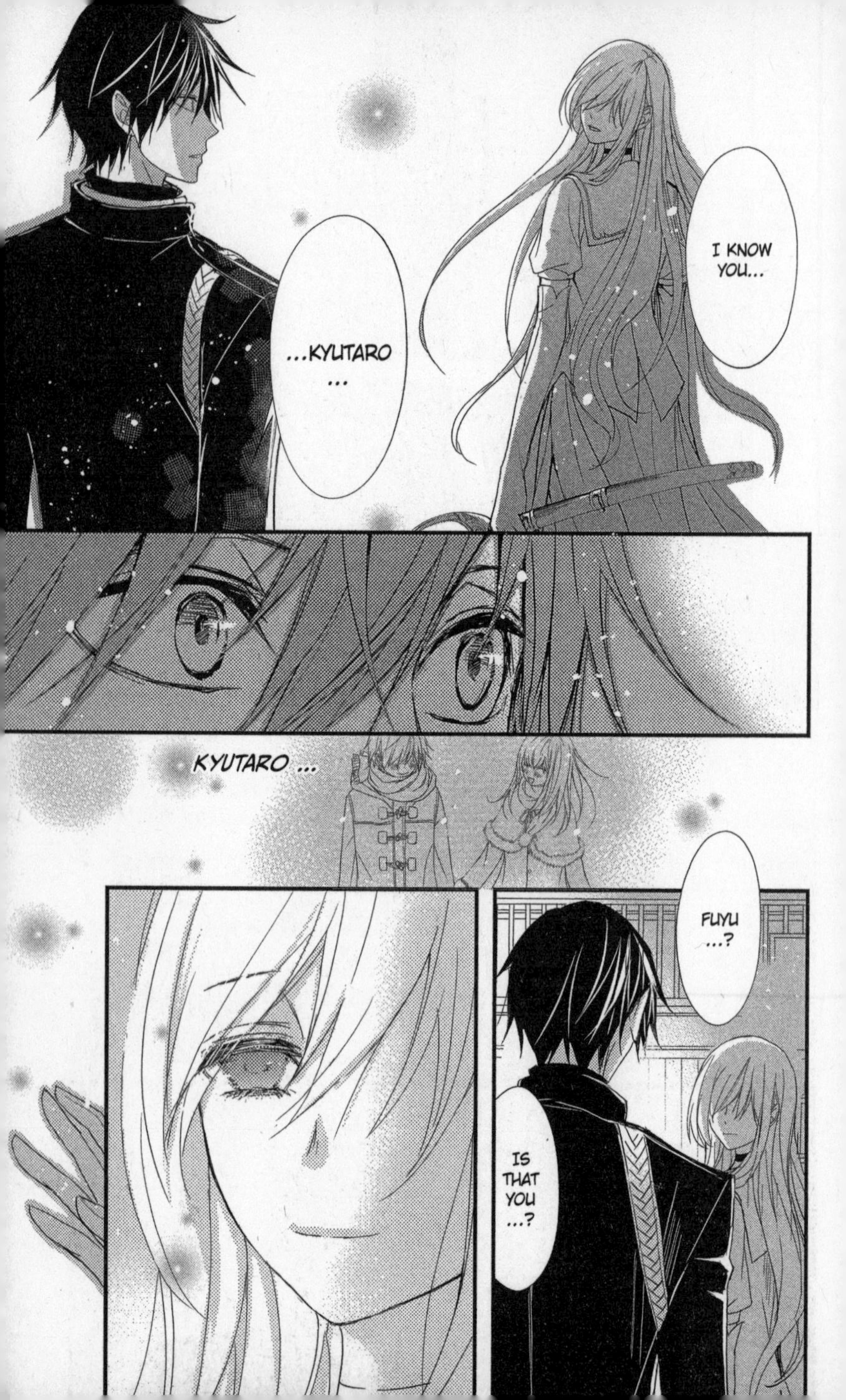
I KNOW YOU...
...KYUTARO ...
KYUTARO ...
FUYU ...?
IS THAT YOU ...?

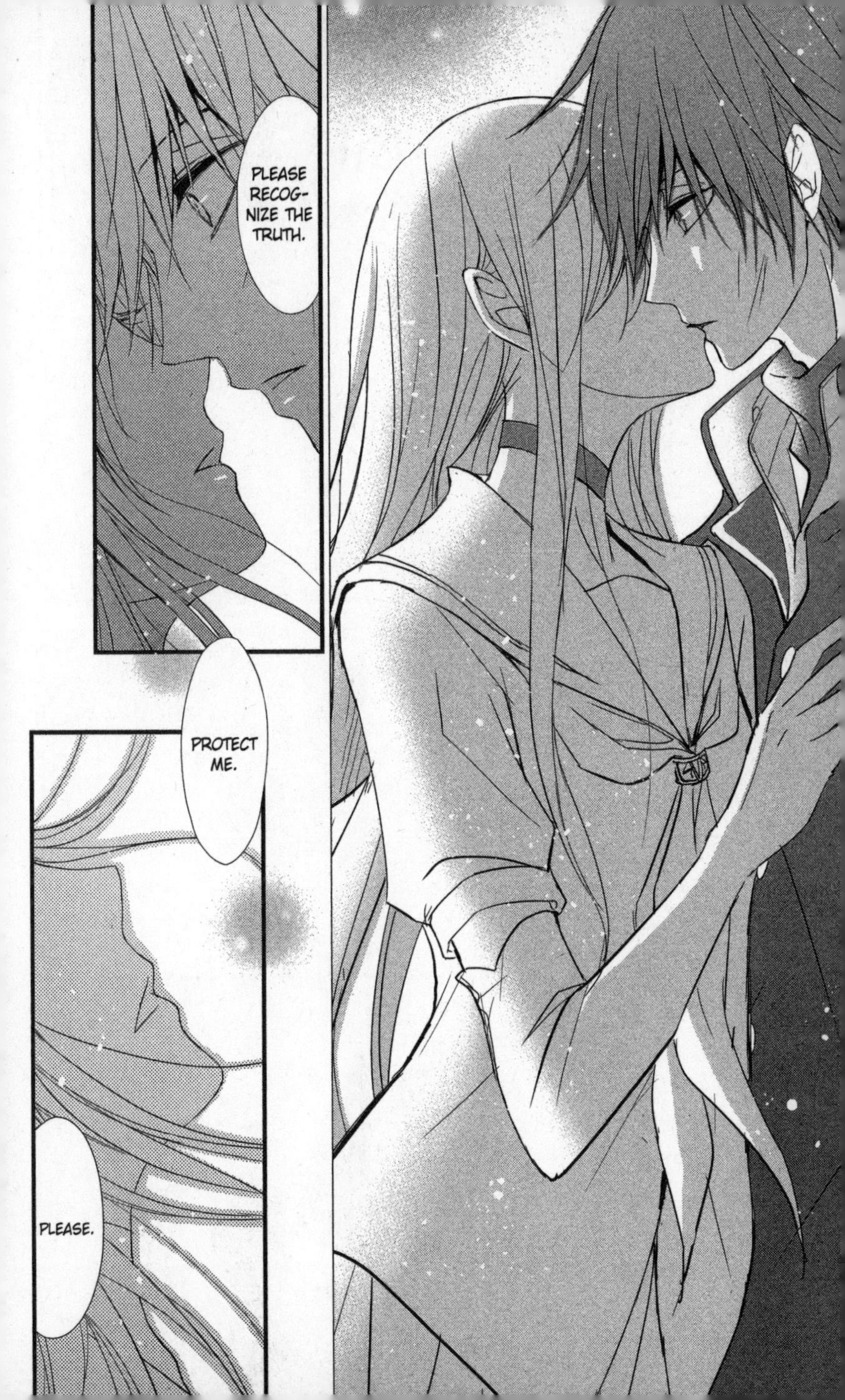
PLEASE RECOG-NIZE THE TRUTH.
PROTECT ME.
PLEASE.

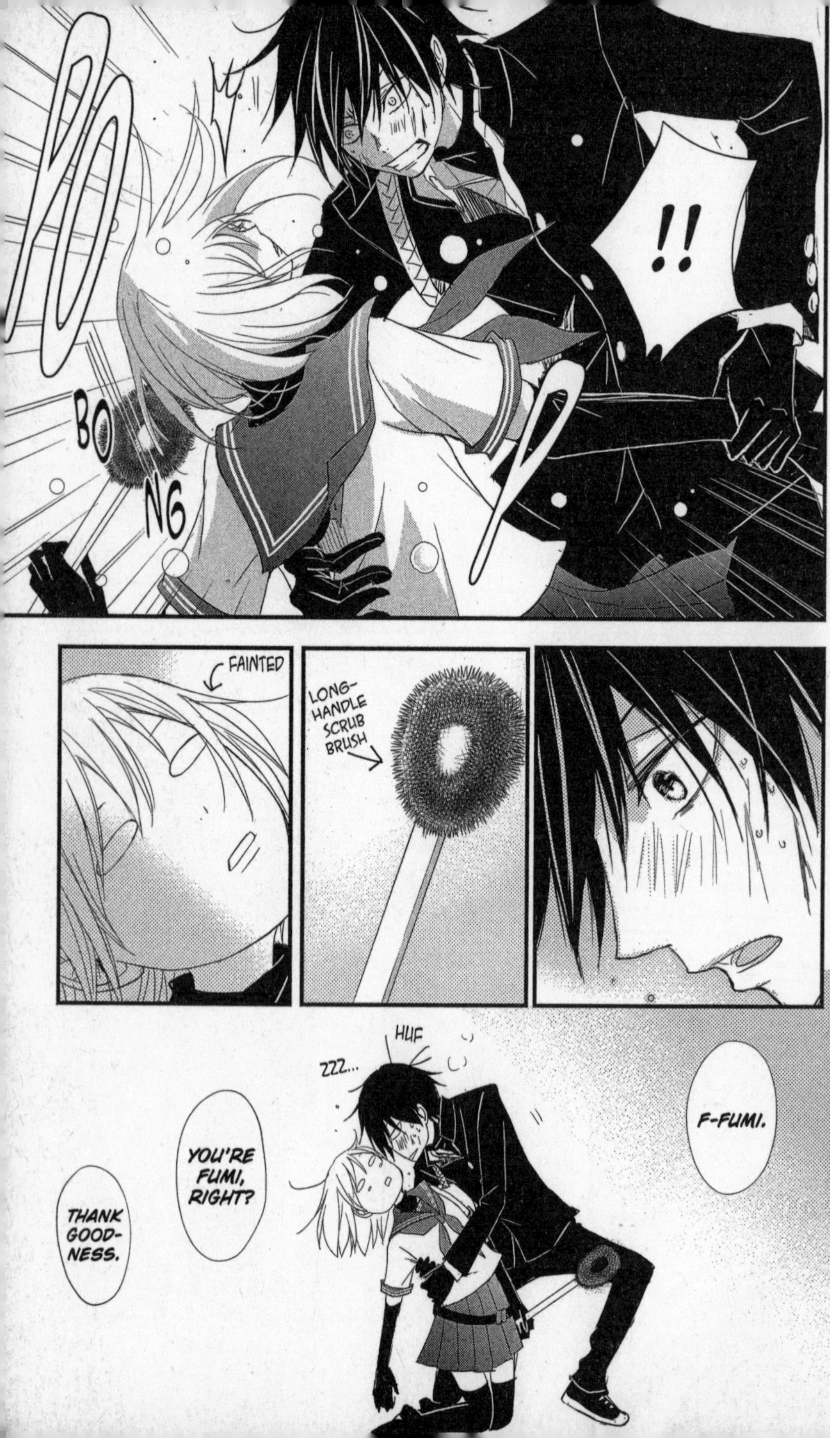
!!
BONG
LONG-HANDLE SCRUB BRUSH
FAINTED
F-FUMI.
HUF
ZZZ...
YOU'RE FUMI, RIGHT?
THANK GOODNESS.

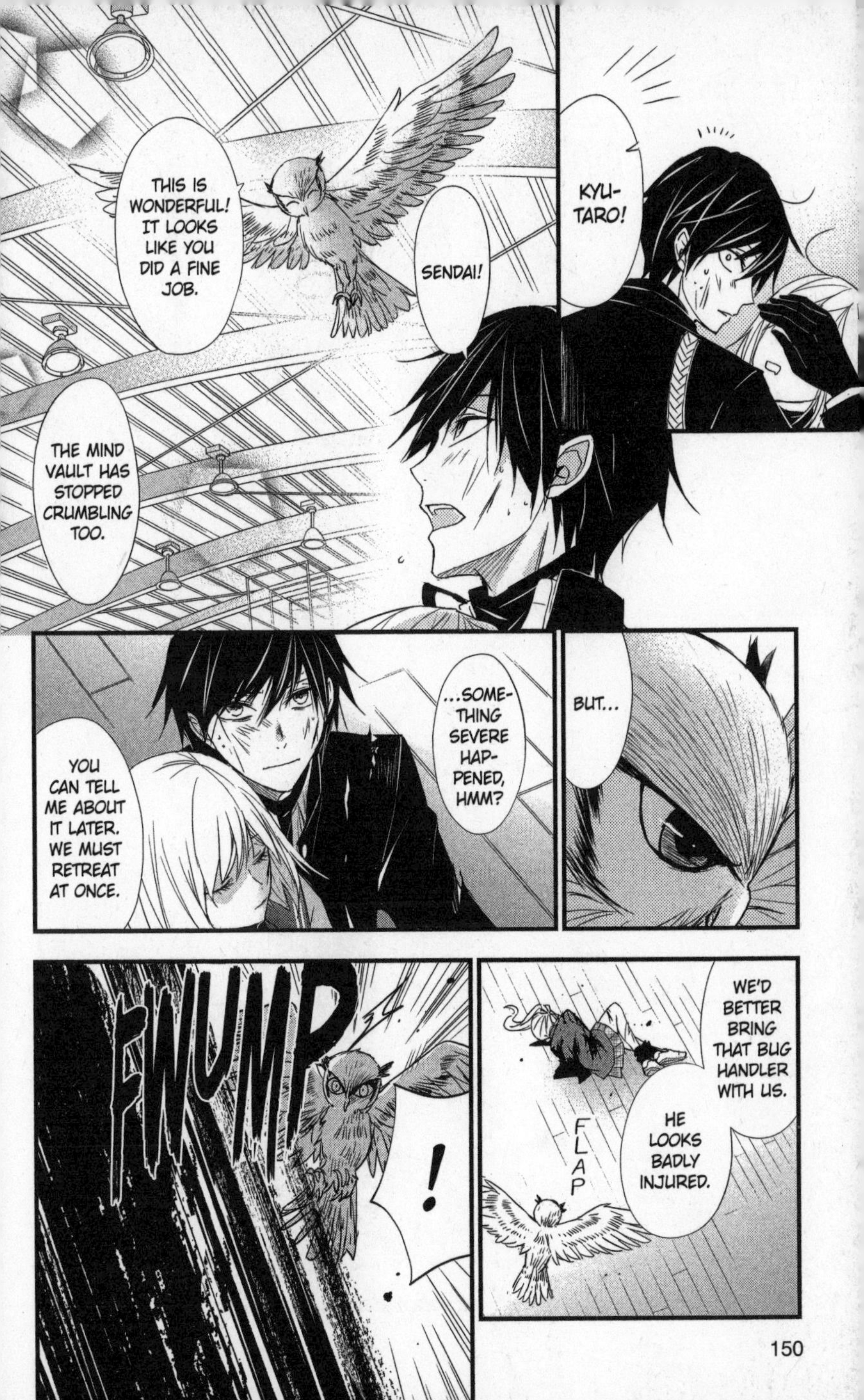
KYU-TARO!
SENDAI!
THIS IS WONDERFUL! IT LOOKS LIKE YOU DID A FINE JOB.
THE MIND VAULT HAS STOPPED CRUMBLING TOO.
BUT...
...SOME-THING SEVERE HAP-PENED, HMM?
YOU CAN TELL ME ABOUT IT LATER. WE MUST RETREAT AT ONCE.
WE'D BETTER BRING THAT BUG HANDLER WITH US.
HE LOOKS BADLY INJURED.
FLAP
FWUMP
!

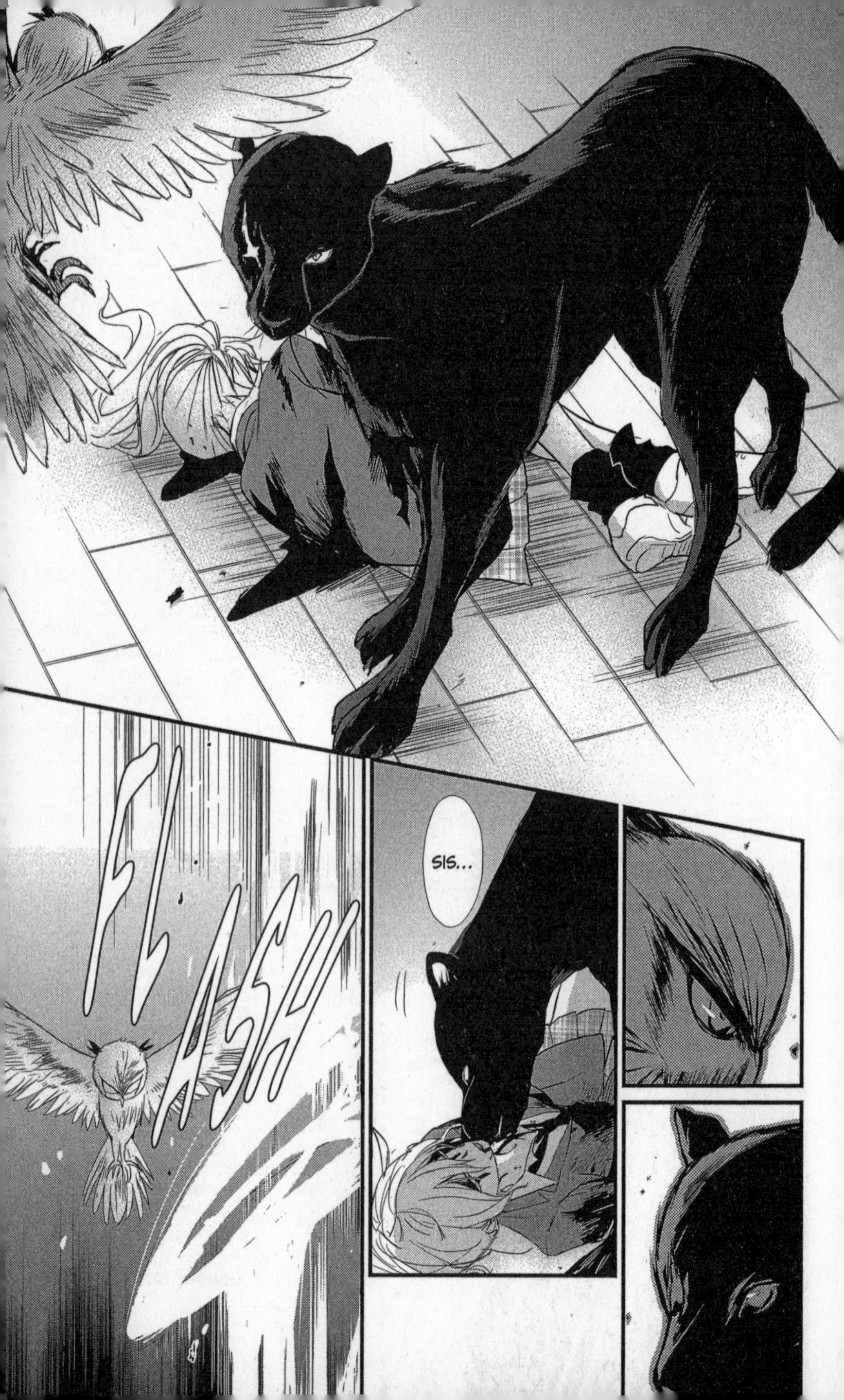
SIS...
FLASH

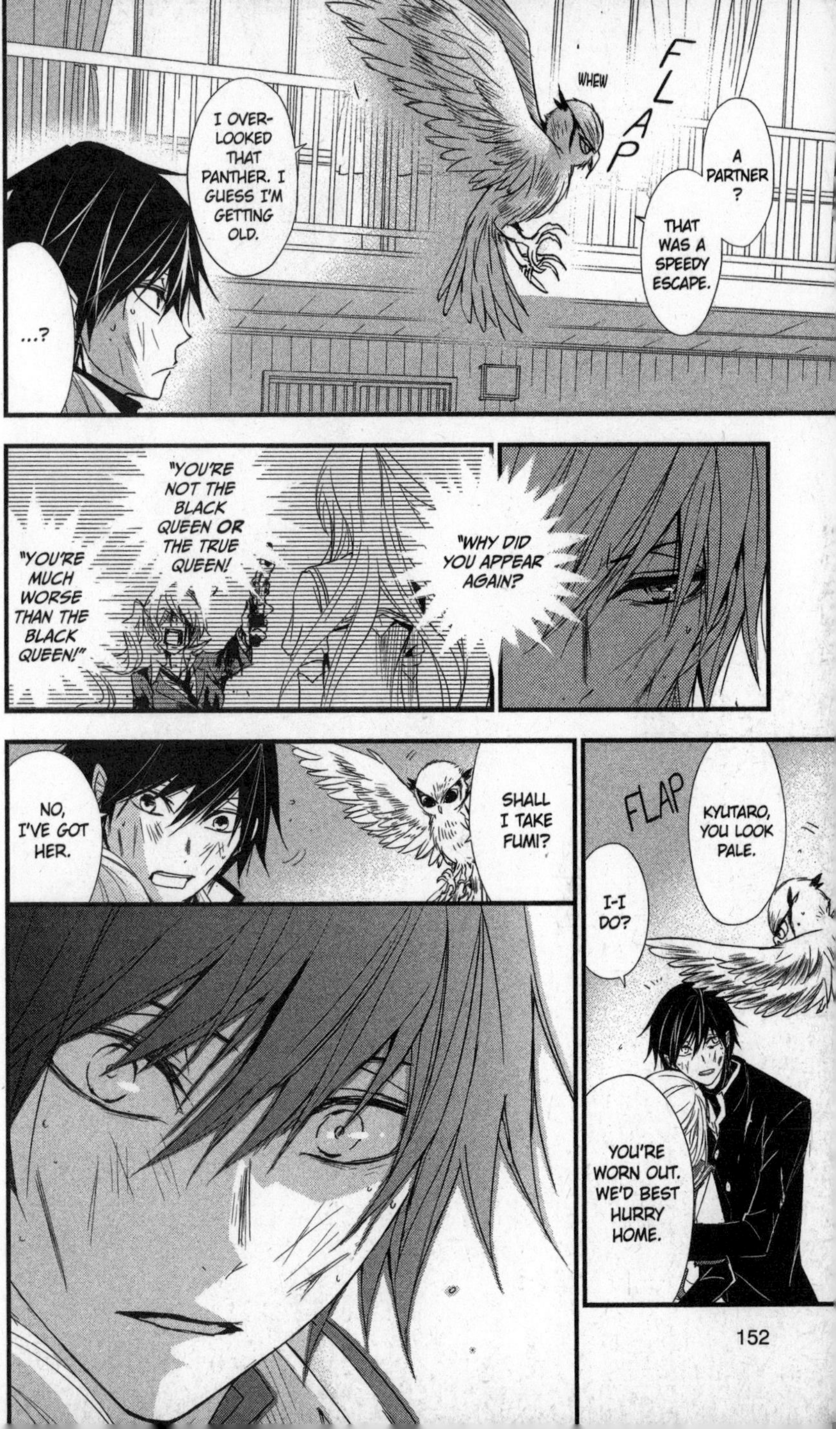
FLAP
A PARTNER?
THAT WAS A SPEEDY ESCAPE.
WHEW
I OVERLOOKED THAT PANTHER. I GUESS I'M GETTING OLD.
...?
"WHY DID YOU APPEAR AGAIN?
"YOU'RE NOT THE BLACK QUEEN OR THE TRUE QUEEN!
"YOU'RE MUCH WORSE THAN THE BLACK QUEEN!"
FLAP
KYUTARO, YOU LOOK PALE.
I-I DO?
YOU'RE WORN OUT. WE'D BEST HURRY HOME.
SHALL I TAKE FUMI?
NO, I'VE GOT HER.

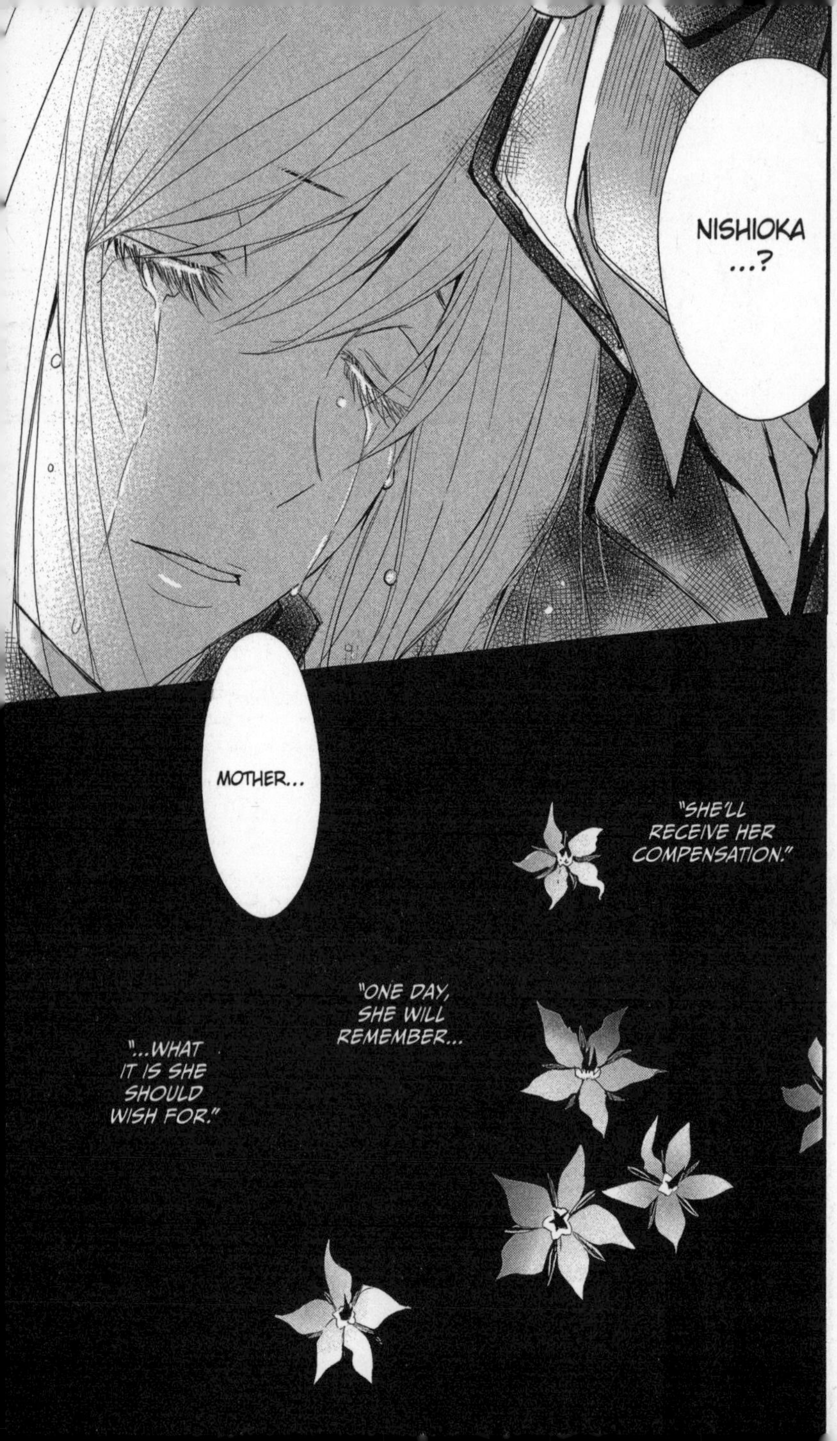
NISHIOKA ...?
MOTHER...
"SHE'LL RECEIVE HER COMPENSATION."
"ONE DAY, SHE WILL REMEMBER...
"...WHAT IT IS SHE SHOULD WISH FOR."

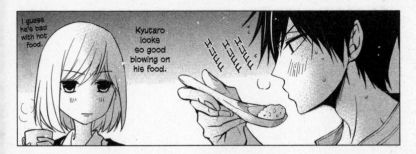

HFFF
HFFF
HFFF
Kyutaro looks so good blowing on his food.
I guess he's bad with hot food.

Hi. Once again, the afterword has wound up here. Thank you very much for reading *Queen's Quality* volume 2!

It's only the second volume, but there's a fair bit of violence going on. If you count the three volumes in the *QQ Sweeper* series, though, this is the fifth volume, so I guess it's not that early for bloodshed. If any of you haven't read the previous series, I do urge you to catch up.

Well, I hope to see you all in volume 3!

Kyousuke Motomi

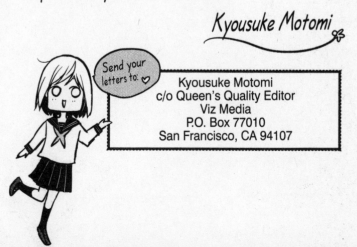

Send your letters to: ♡

Kyousuke Motomi
c/o Queen's Quality Editor
Viz Media
P.O. Box 77010
San Francisco, CA 94107

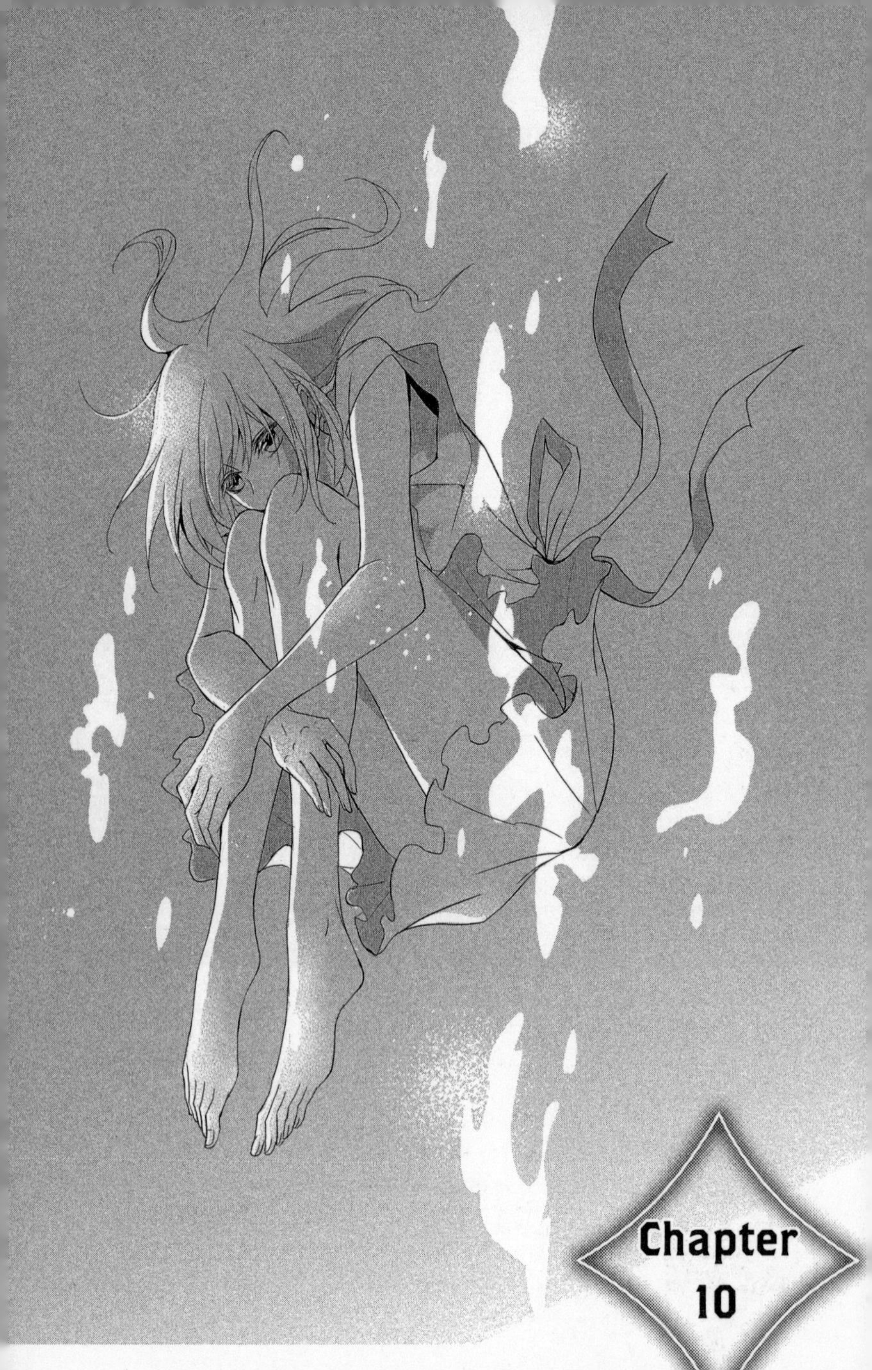

Chapter 10

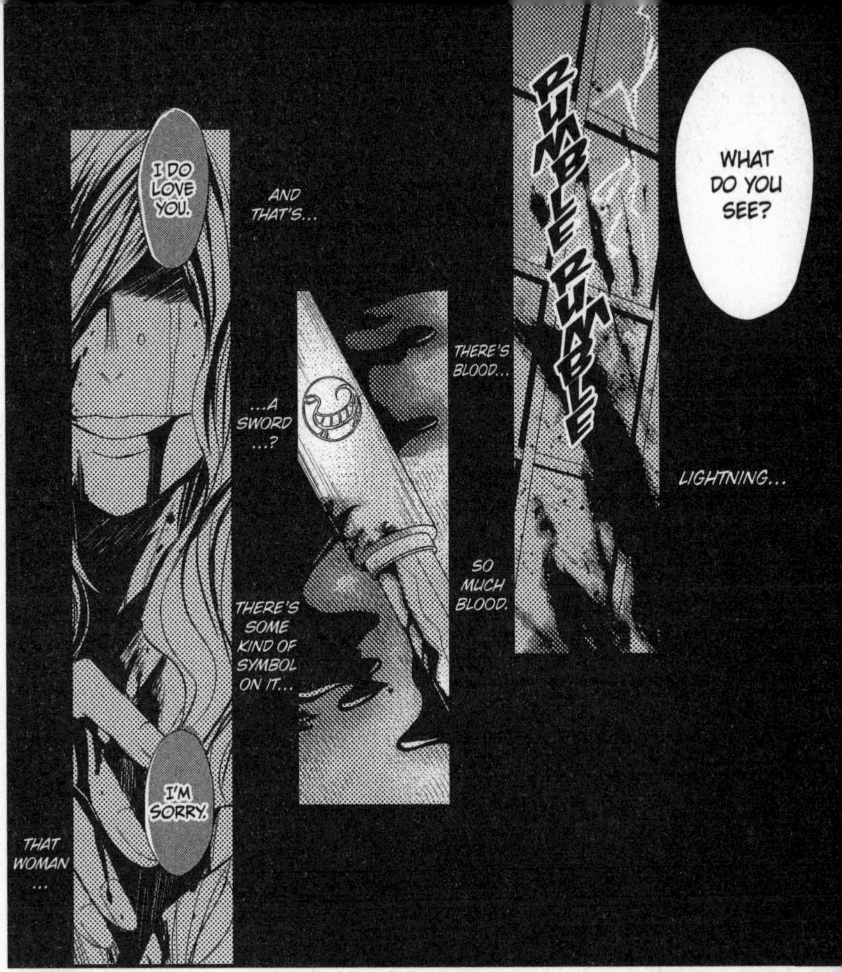
WHAT DO YOU SEE?
LIGHTNING...
RUMBLE RUMBLE
THERE'S BLOOD...
SO MUCH BLOOD.
...A SWORD ...?
THERE'S SOME KIND OF SYMBOL ON IT...
AND THAT'S...
I DO LOVE YOU.
I'M SORRY.
THAT WOMAN ...

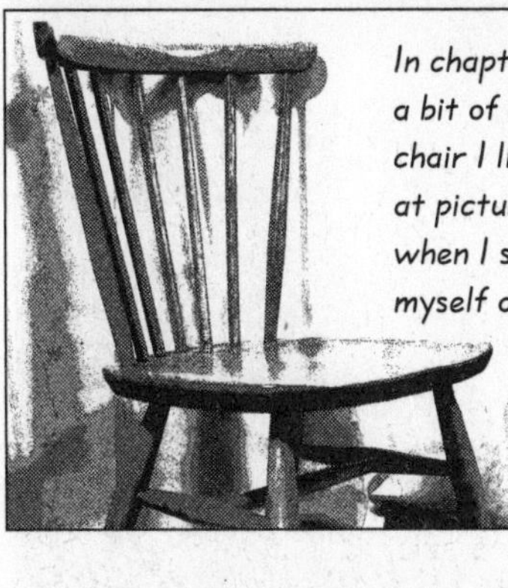

In chapter 9, there's a comfortable chair. It has a bit of an antique look—exactly the kind of chair I like. For the most part, I just sit and grin at pictures in catalogs and on the internet, but when I started work on *Queen's Quality*, I told myself a million times that I needed something for reference for my work. So I finally bought myself a used Ercol chair! It's for reference, but I treasure it.

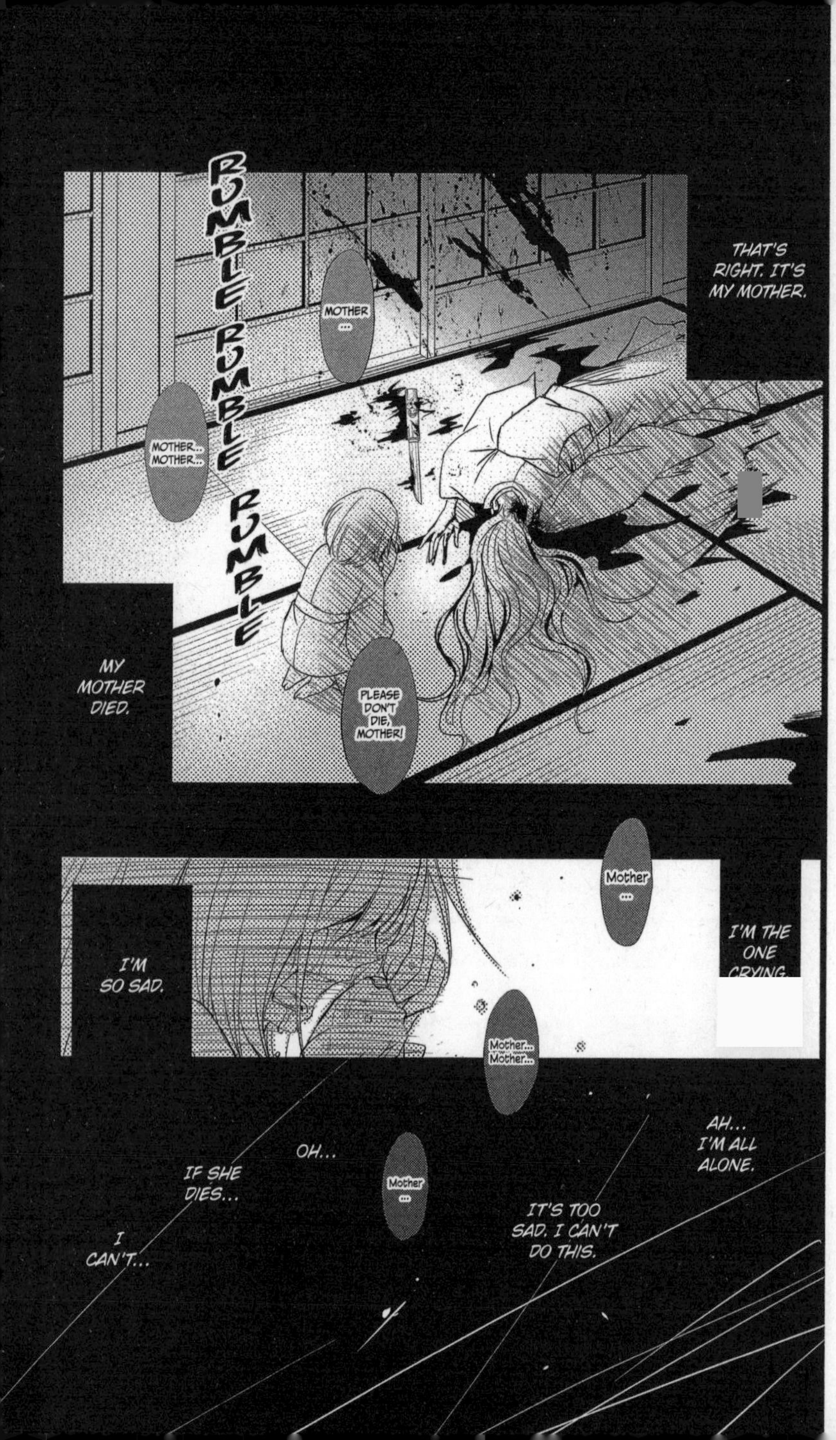
THAT'S RIGHT. IT'S MY MOTHER.
MOTHER...
MOTHER... MOTHER...
RUMBLE RUMBLE
RUMBLE
PLEASE DON'T DIE, MOTHER!
MY MOTHER DIED.
Mother...
I'M THE ONE CRYING.
Mother... Mother...
I'M SO SAD.
AH... I'M ALL ALONE.
IT'S TOO SAD. I CAN'T DO THIS.
Mother...
OH...
IF SHE DIES...
I CAN'T...

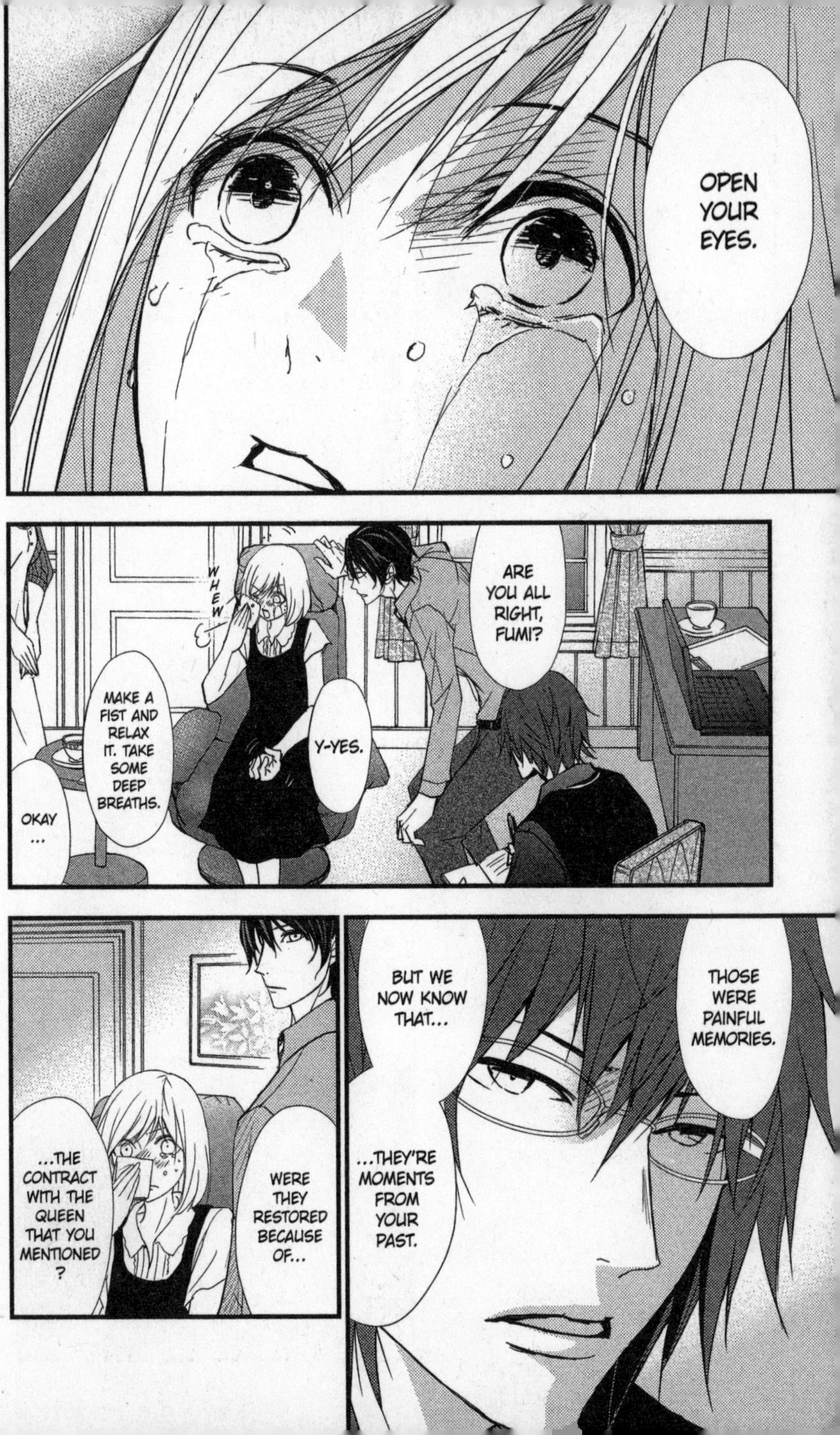
OPEN YOUR EYES.
ARE YOU ALL RIGHT, FUMI?
WHEW
Y-YES.
MAKE A FIST AND RELAX IT. TAKE SOME DEEP BREATHS.
OKAY ...
THOSE WERE PAINFUL MEMORIES.
BUT WE NOW KNOW THAT...
...THEY'RE MOMENTS FROM YOUR PAST.
WERE THEY RESTORED BECAUSE OF...
...THE CONTRACT WITH THE QUEEN THAT YOU MENTIONED?

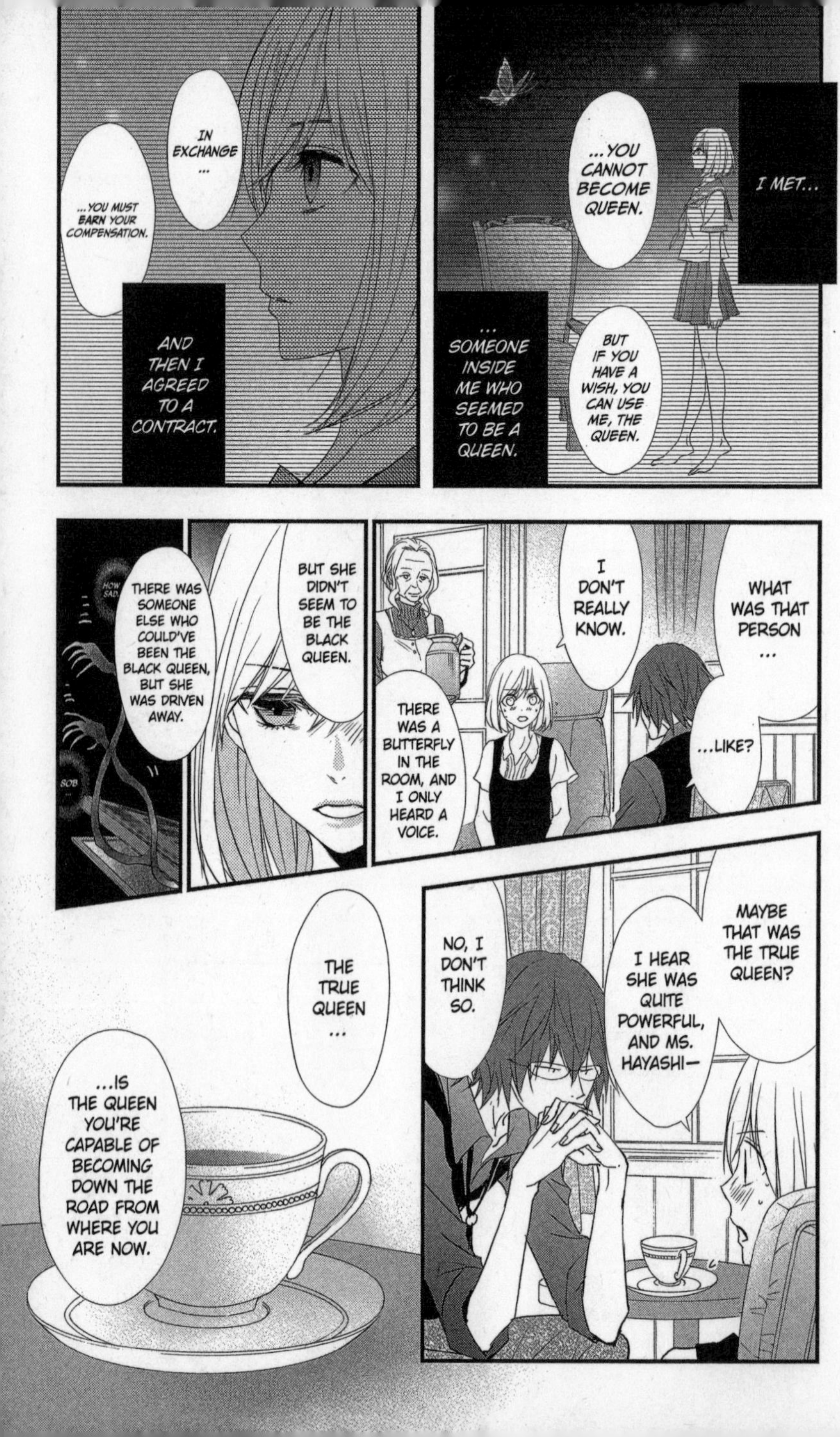
I MET...
...YOU CANNOT BECOME QUEEN.
BUT IF YOU HAVE A WISH, YOU CAN USE ME, THE QUEEN.
...SOMEONE INSIDE ME WHO SEEMED TO BE A QUEEN.
IN EXCHANGE...
...YOU MUST EARN YOUR COMPENSATION.
AND THEN I AGREED TO A CONTRACT.
WHAT WAS THAT PERSON...
...LIKE?
I DON'T REALLY KNOW.
THERE WAS A BUTTERFLY IN THE ROOM, AND I ONLY HEARD A VOICE.
BUT SHE DIDN'T SEEM TO BE THE BLACK QUEEN.
THERE WAS SOMEONE ELSE WHO COULD'VE BEEN THE BLACK QUEEN, BUT SHE WAS DRIVEN AWAY.
HOW SAD.
SOB...
MAYBE THAT WAS THE TRUE QUEEN?
I HEAR SHE WAS QUITE POWERFUL, AND MS. HAYASHI—
NO, I DON'T THINK SO.
THE TRUE QUEEN...
...IS THE QUEEN YOU'RE CAPABLE OF BECOMING DOWN THE ROAD FROM WHERE YOU ARE NOW.

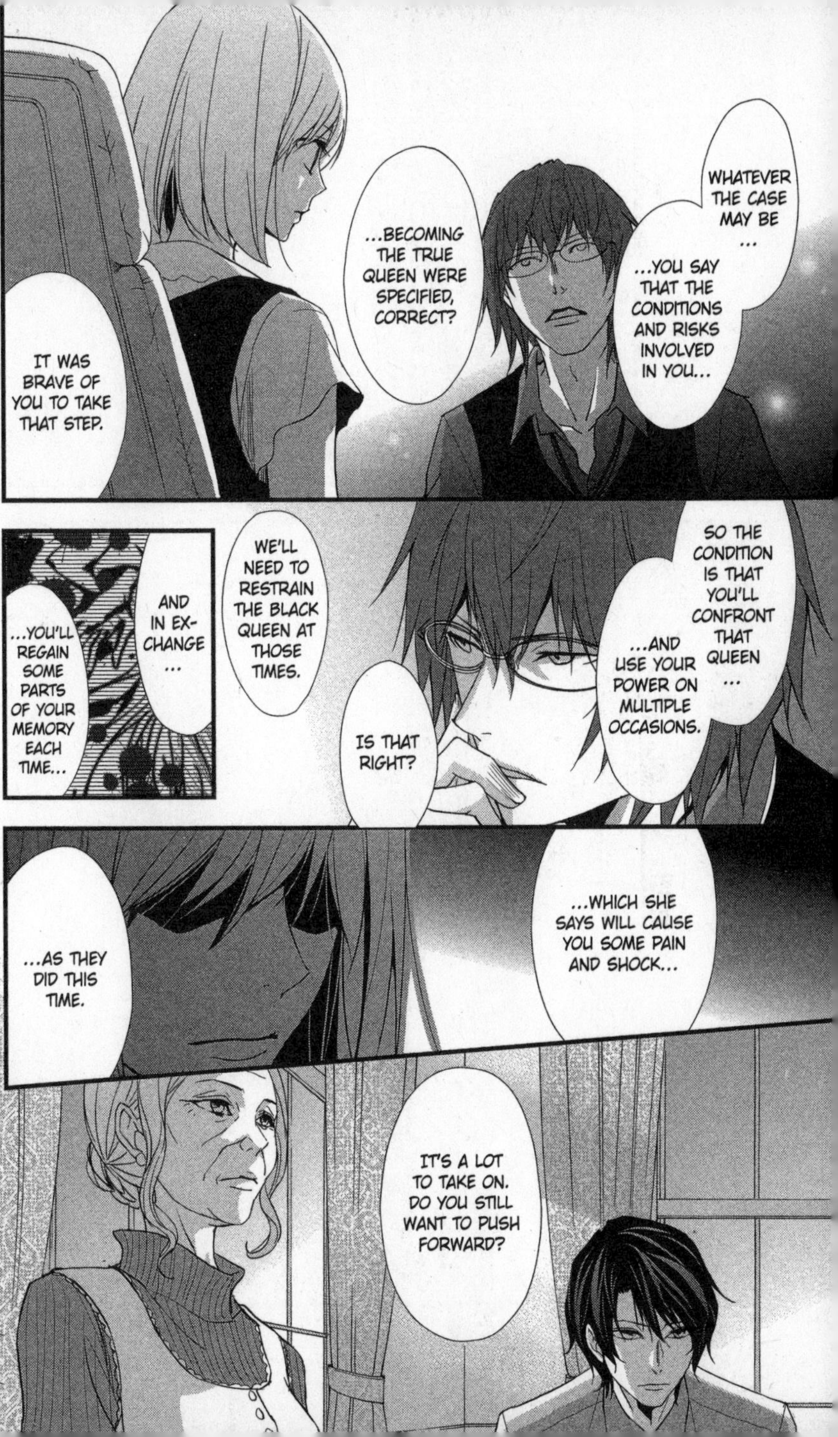
WHATEVER THE CASE MAY BE ...
...YOU SAY THAT THE CONDITIONS AND RISKS INVOLVED IN YOU...
...BECOMING THE TRUE QUEEN WERE SPECIFIED, CORRECT?
IT WAS BRAVE OF YOU TO TAKE THAT STEP.
SO THE CONDITION IS THAT YOU'LL CONFRONT THAT QUEEN ...
...AND USE YOUR POWER ON MULTIPLE OCCASIONS.
WE'LL NEED TO RESTRAIN THE BLACK QUEEN AT THOSE TIMES.
IS THAT RIGHT?
AND IN EX-CHANGE ...
...YOU'LL REGAIN SOME PARTS OF YOUR MEMORY EACH TIME...
...WHICH SHE SAYS WILL CAUSE YOU SOME PAIN AND SHOCK...
...AS THEY DID THIS TIME.
IT'S A LOT TO TAKE ON. DO YOU STILL WANT TO PUSH FORWARD?

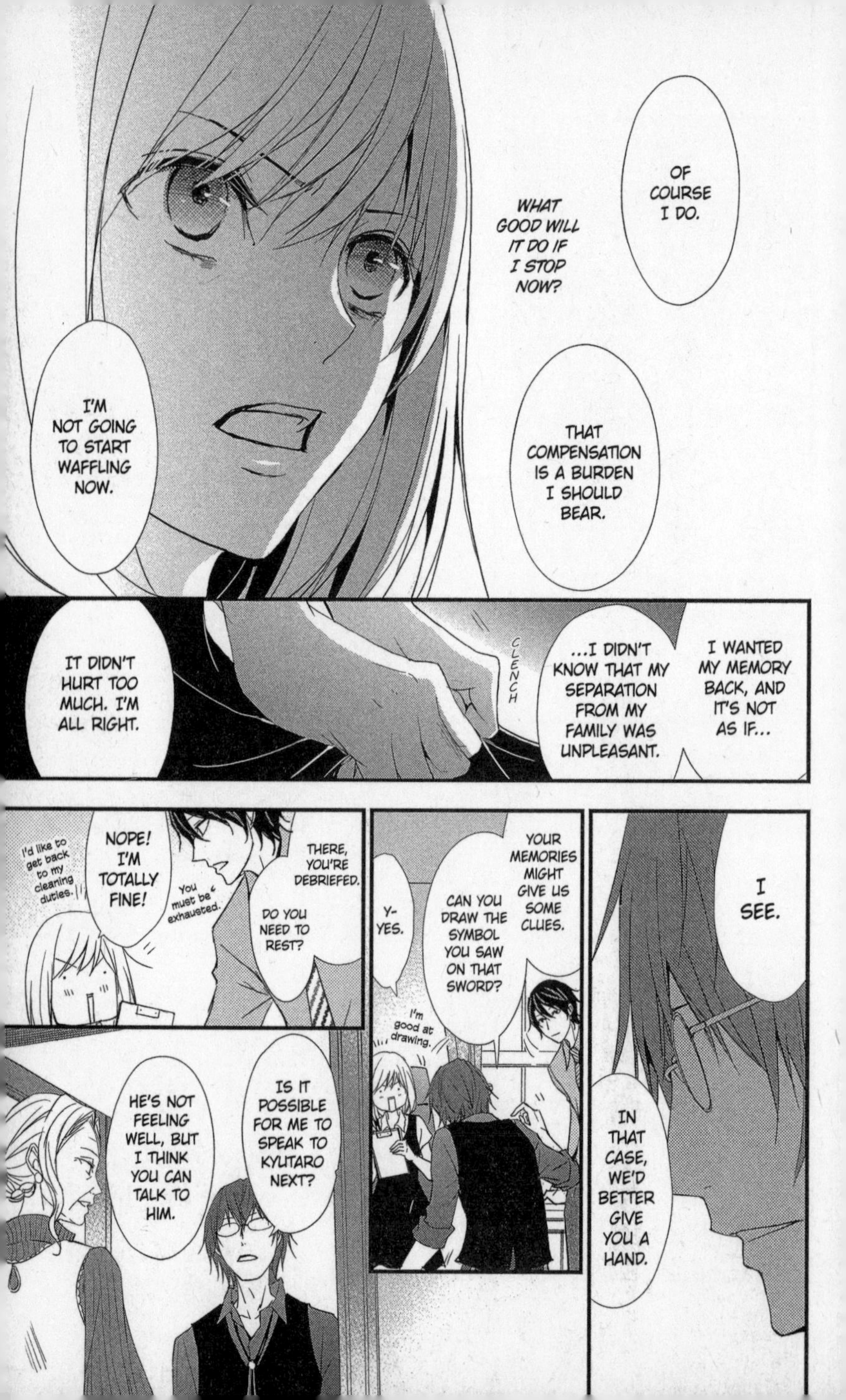
OF COURSE I DO.
WHAT GOOD WILL IT DO IF I STOP NOW?
THAT COMPENSATION IS A BURDEN I SHOULD BEAR.
I'M NOT GOING TO START WAFFLING NOW.
I WANTED MY MEMORY BACK, AND IT'S NOT AS IF...
...I DIDN'T KNOW THAT MY SEPARATION FROM MY FAMILY WAS UNPLEASANT.
CLENCH
IT DIDN'T HURT TOO MUCH. I'M ALL RIGHT.
I SEE.
IN THAT CASE, WE'D BETTER GIVE YOU A HAND.
YOUR MEMORIES MIGHT GIVE US SOME CLUES.
CAN YOU DRAW THE SYMBOL YOU SAW ON THAT SWORD?
Y-YES.
I'm good at drawing.
THERE, YOU'RE DEBRIEFED.
DO YOU NEED TO REST?
You must be exhausted.
NOPE! I'M TOTALLY FINE!
I'd like to get back to my cleaning duties.
IS IT POSSIBLE FOR ME TO SPEAK TO KYUTARO NEXT?
HE'S NOT FEELING WELL, BUT I THINK YOU CAN TALK TO HIM.

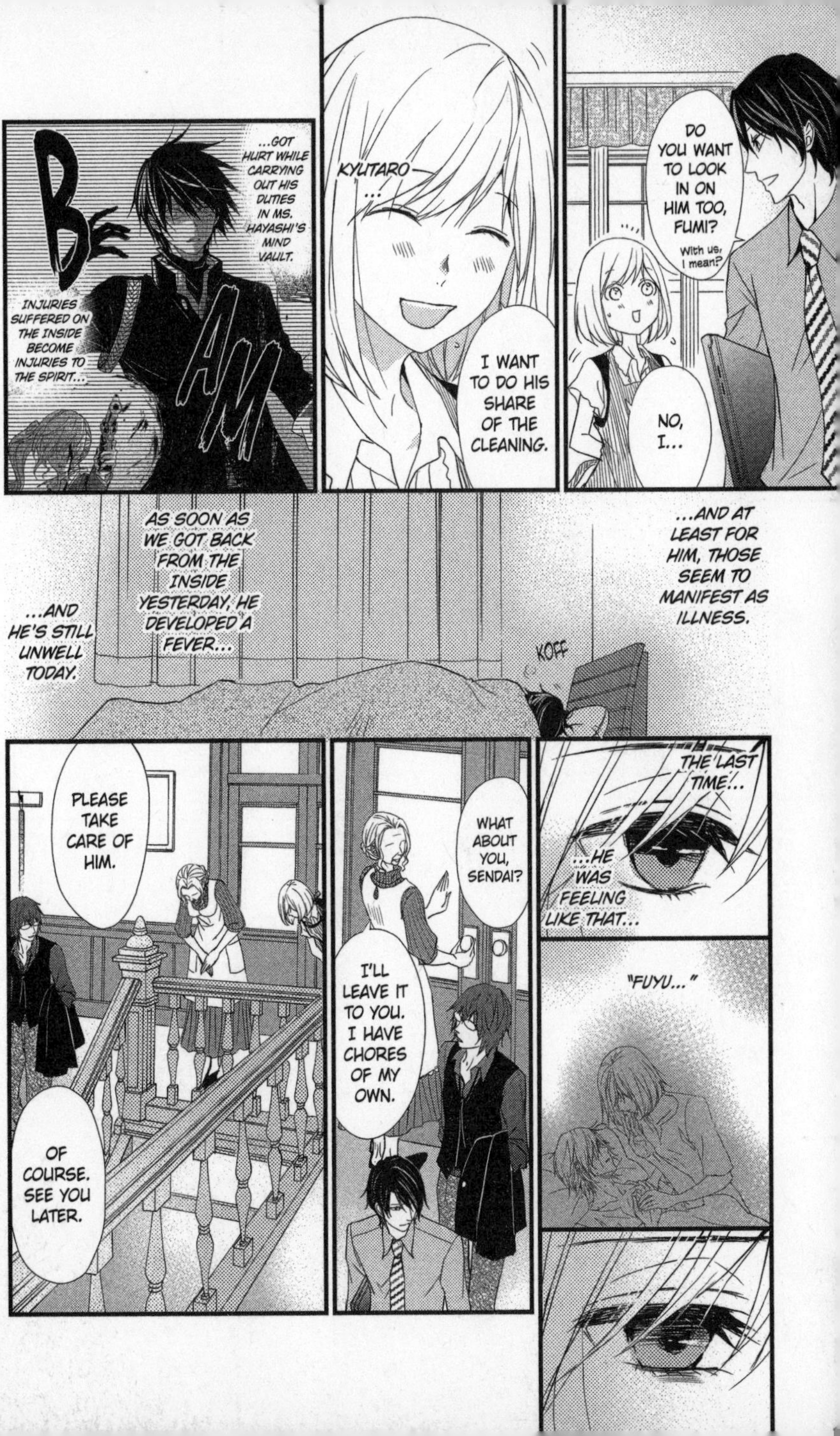
DO YOU WANT TO LOOK IN ON HIM TOO, FUMI?
With us, I mean?
...
NO, I...
KYUTARO...
I WANT TO DO HIS SHARE OF THE CLEANING.
...GOT HURT WHILE CARRYING OUT HIS DUTIES IN MS. HAYASHI'S MIND VAULT.
BAM
INJURIES SUFFERED ON THE INSIDE BECOME INJURIES TO THE SPIRIT...
...AND AT LEAST FOR HIM, THOSE SEEM TO MANIFEST AS ILLNESS.
KOFF
AS SOON AS WE GOT BACK FROM THE INSIDE YESTERDAY, HE DEVELOPED A FEVER...
...AND HE'S STILL UNWELL TODAY.
THE LAST TIME...
...HE WAS FEELING LIKE THAT...
"FUYU..."
WHAT ABOUT YOU, SENDAI?
I'LL LEAVE IT TO YOU. I HAVE CHORES OF MY OWN.
PLEASE TAKE CARE OF HIM.
OF COURSE. SEE YOU LATER.

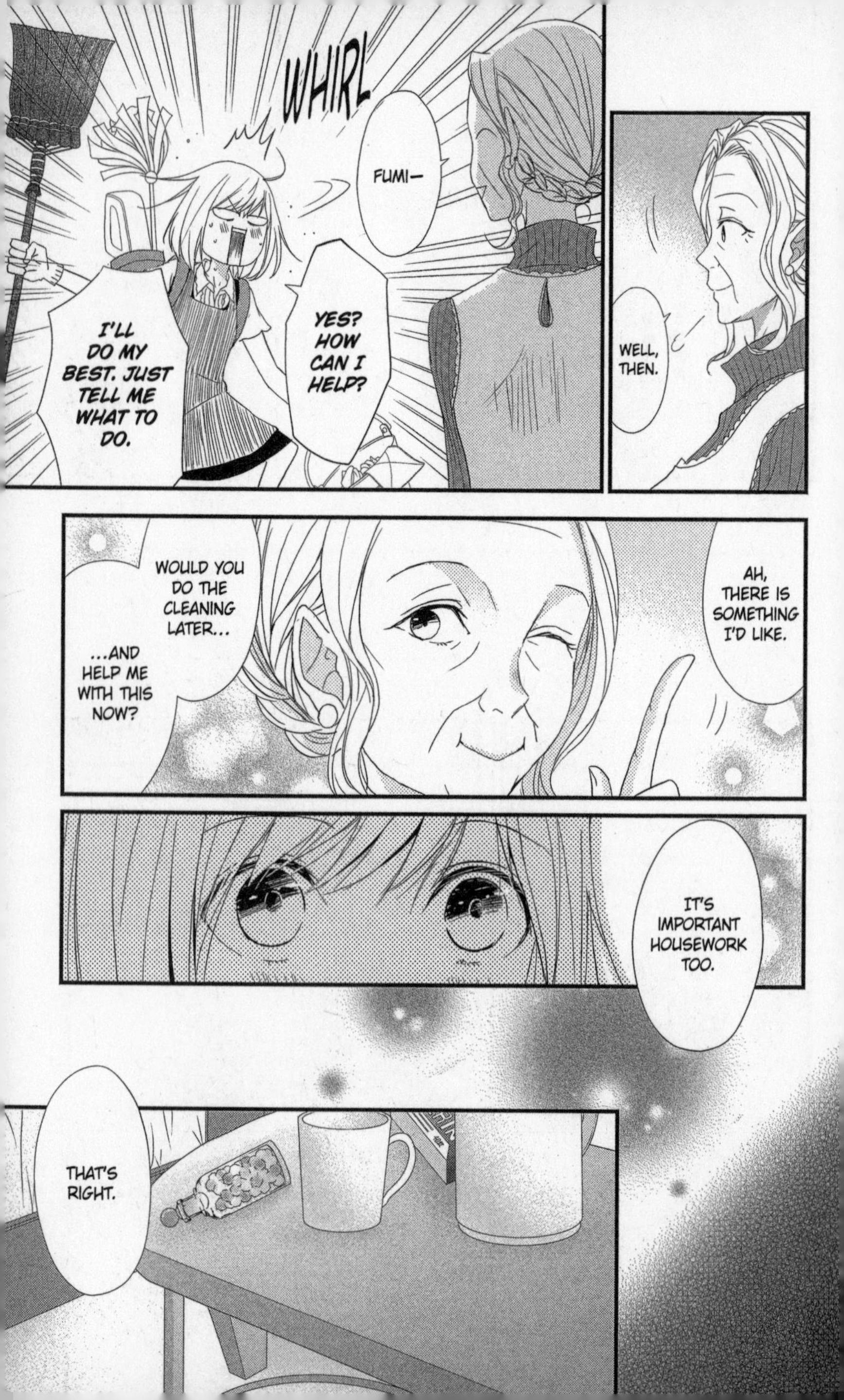
WELL, THEN.
FUMI—
WHIRL
YES? HOW CAN I HELP?
I'LL DO MY BEST. JUST TELL ME WHAT TO DO.
AH, THERE IS SOMETHING I'D LIKE.
WOULD YOU DO THE CLEANING LATER...
...AND HELP ME WITH THIS NOW?
IT'S IMPORTANT HOUSEWORK TOO.
THAT'S RIGHT.

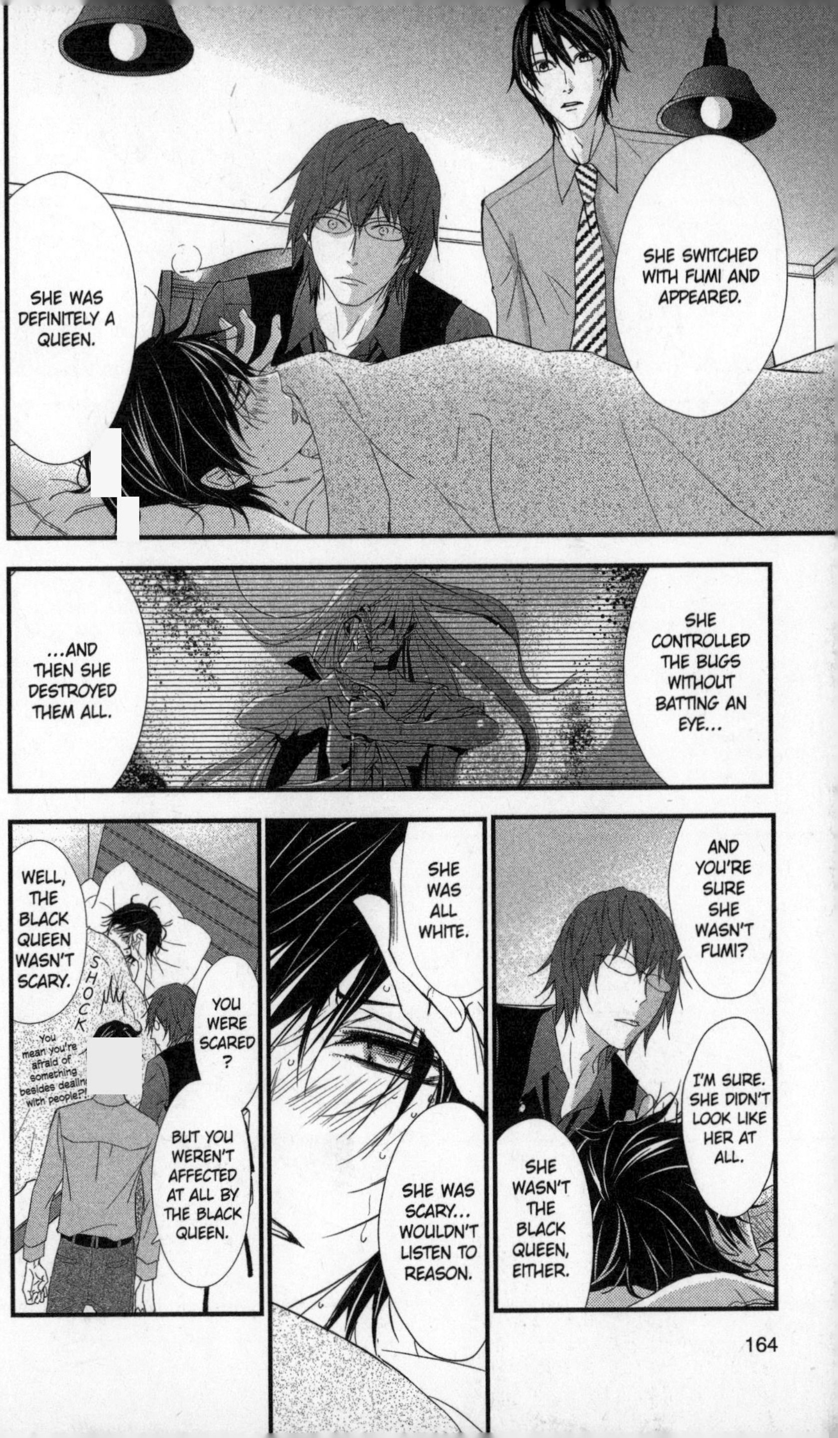
SHE SWITCHED WITH FUMI AND APPEARED.
SHE WAS DEFINITELY A QUEEN.
SHE CONTROLLED THE BUGS WITHOUT BATTING AN EYE...
...AND THEN SHE DESTROYED THEM ALL.
AND YOU'RE SURE SHE WASN'T FUMI?
I'M SURE. SHE DIDN'T LOOK LIKE HER AT ALL.
SHE WASN'T THE BLACK QUEEN, EITHER.
SHE WAS ALL WHITE.
SHE WAS SCARY... WOULDN'T LISTEN TO REASON.
YOU WERE SCARED?
BUT YOU WEREN'T AFFECTED AT ALL BY THE BLACK QUEEN.
WELL, THE BLACK QUEEN WASN'T SCARY.
SHOCK
You mean you're afraid of something besides dealin with people?!

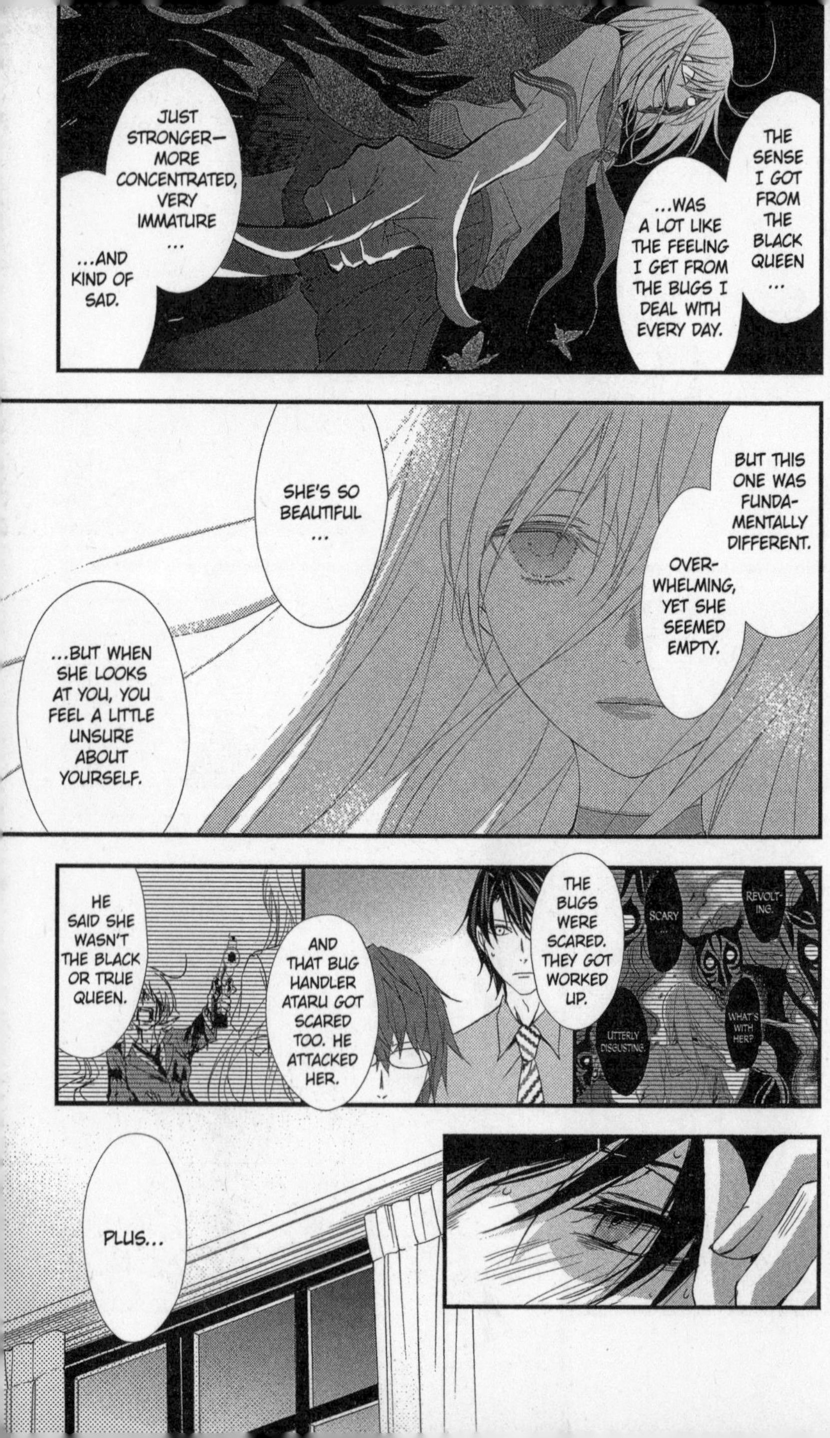
THE SENSE I GOT FROM THE BLACK QUEEN...
...WAS A LOT LIKE THE FEELING I GET FROM THE BUGS I DEAL WITH EVERY DAY.
JUST STRONGER—MORE CONCENTRATED, VERY IMMATURE...
...AND KIND OF SAD.
BUT THIS ONE WAS FUNDAMENTALLY DIFFERENT.
OVERWHELMING, YET SHE SEEMED EMPTY.
SHE'S SO BEAUTIFUL...
...BUT WHEN SHE LOOKS AT YOU, YOU FEEL A LITTLE UNSURE ABOUT YOURSELF.
REVOLTING.
SCARY...
WHAT'S WITH HER?
UTTERLY DISGUSTING.
THE BUGS WERE SCARED. THEY GOT WORKED UP.
AND THAT BUG HANDLER ATARU GOT SCARED TOO. HE ATTACKED HER.
HE SAID SHE WASN'T THE BLACK OR TRUE QUEEN.
PLUS...

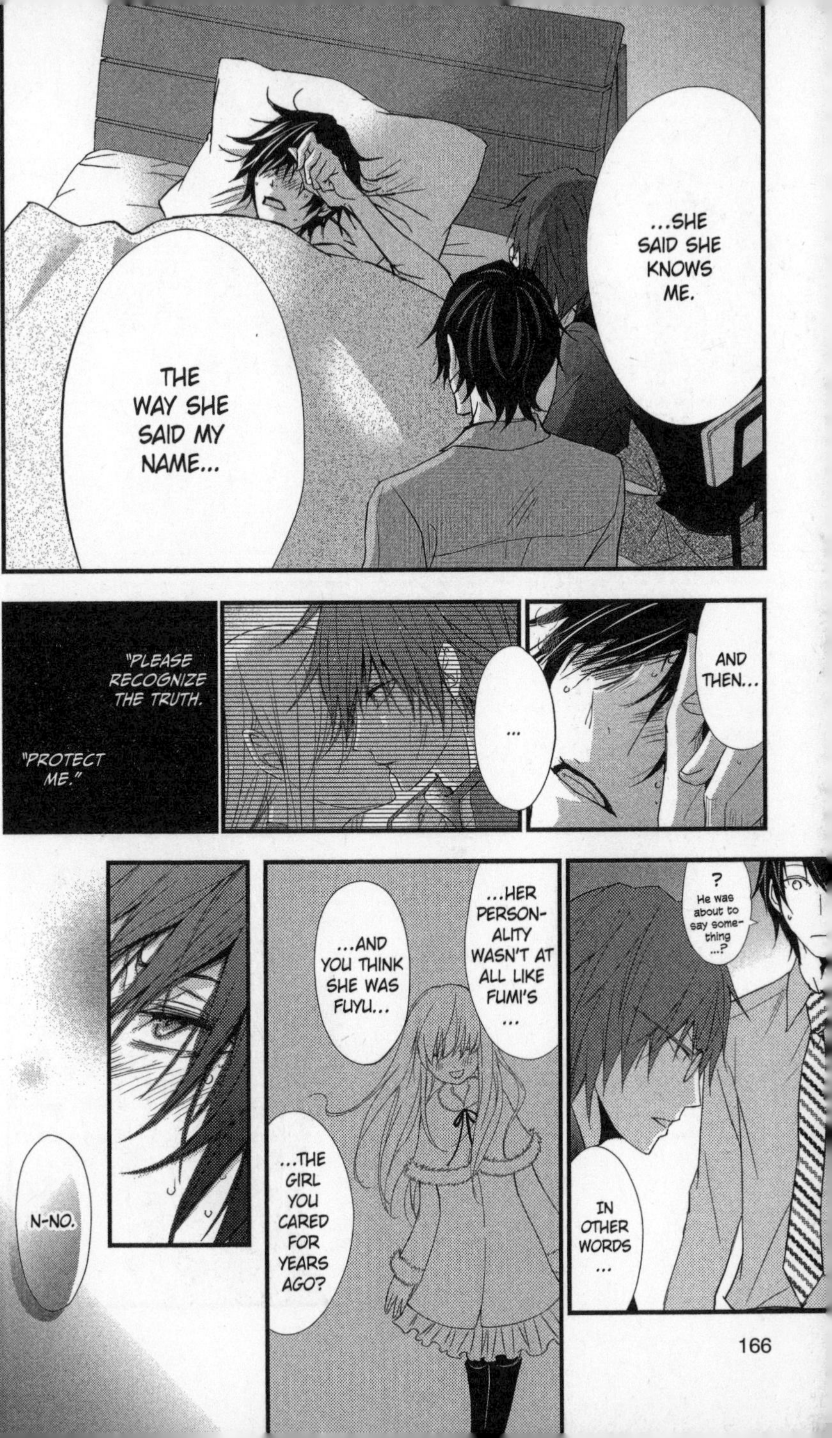
...SHE SAID SHE KNOWS ME.
THE WAY SHE SAID MY NAME...
AND THEN...
...
"PLEASE RECOGNIZE THE TRUTH.
"PROTECT ME."
? He was about to say something ...?
IN OTHER WORDS ...
...HER PERSONALITY WASN'T AT ALL LIKE FUMI'S ...
...AND YOU THINK SHE WAS FUYU...
...THE GIRL YOU CARED FOR YEARS AGO?
N-NO.

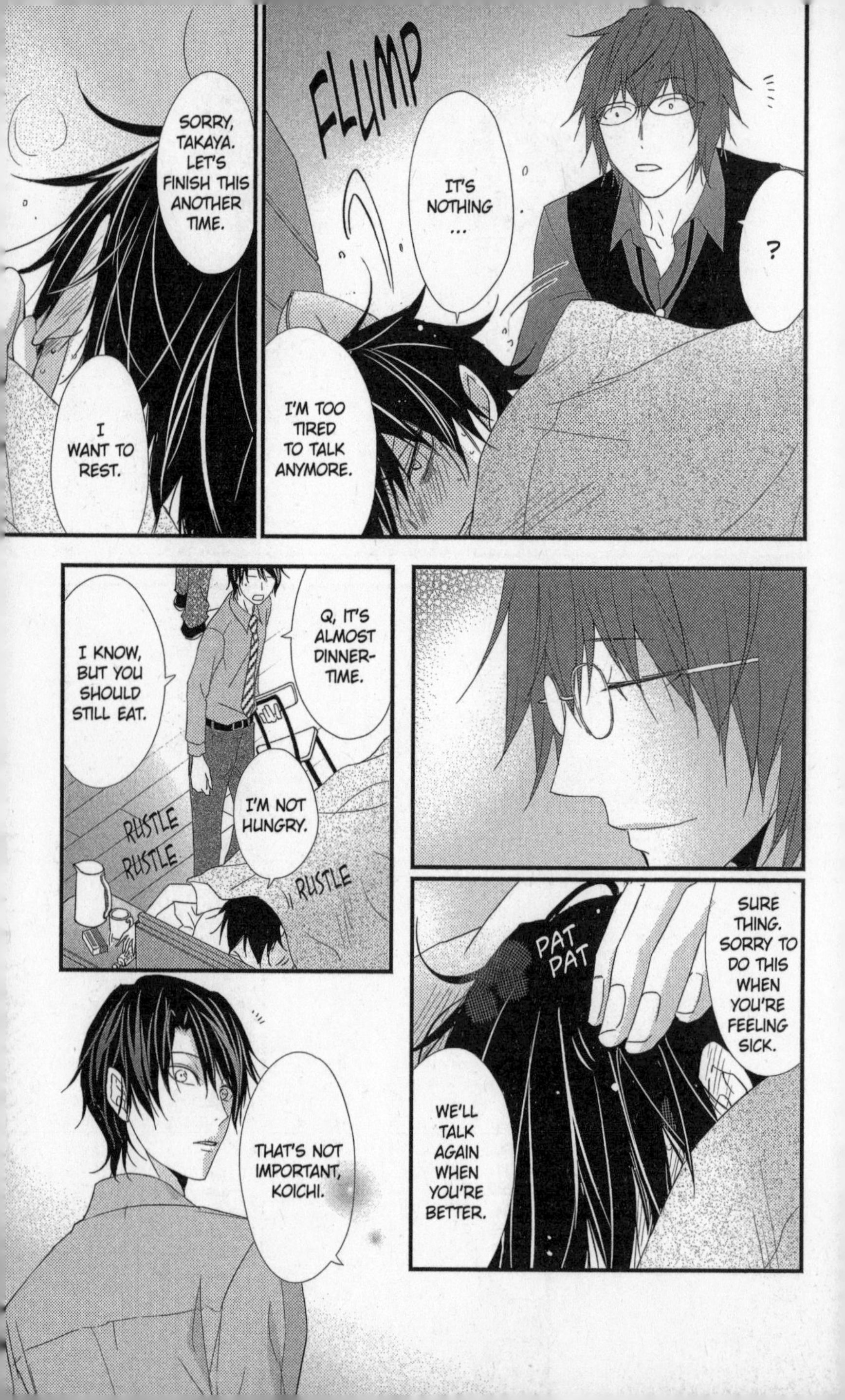
?
FLUMP
IT'S NOTHING ...
I'M TOO TIRED TO TALK ANYMORE.
SORRY, TAKAYA. LET'S FINISH THIS ANOTHER TIME.
I WANT TO REST.
PAT PAT
SURE THING. SORRY TO DO THIS WHEN YOU'RE FEELING SICK.
WE'LL TALK AGAIN WHEN YOU'RE BETTER.
Q, IT'S ALMOST DINNER-TIME.
I KNOW, BUT YOU SHOULD STILL EAT.
I'M NOT HUNGRY.
RUSTLE RUSTLE
RUSTLE
THAT'S NOT IMPORTANT, KOICHI.

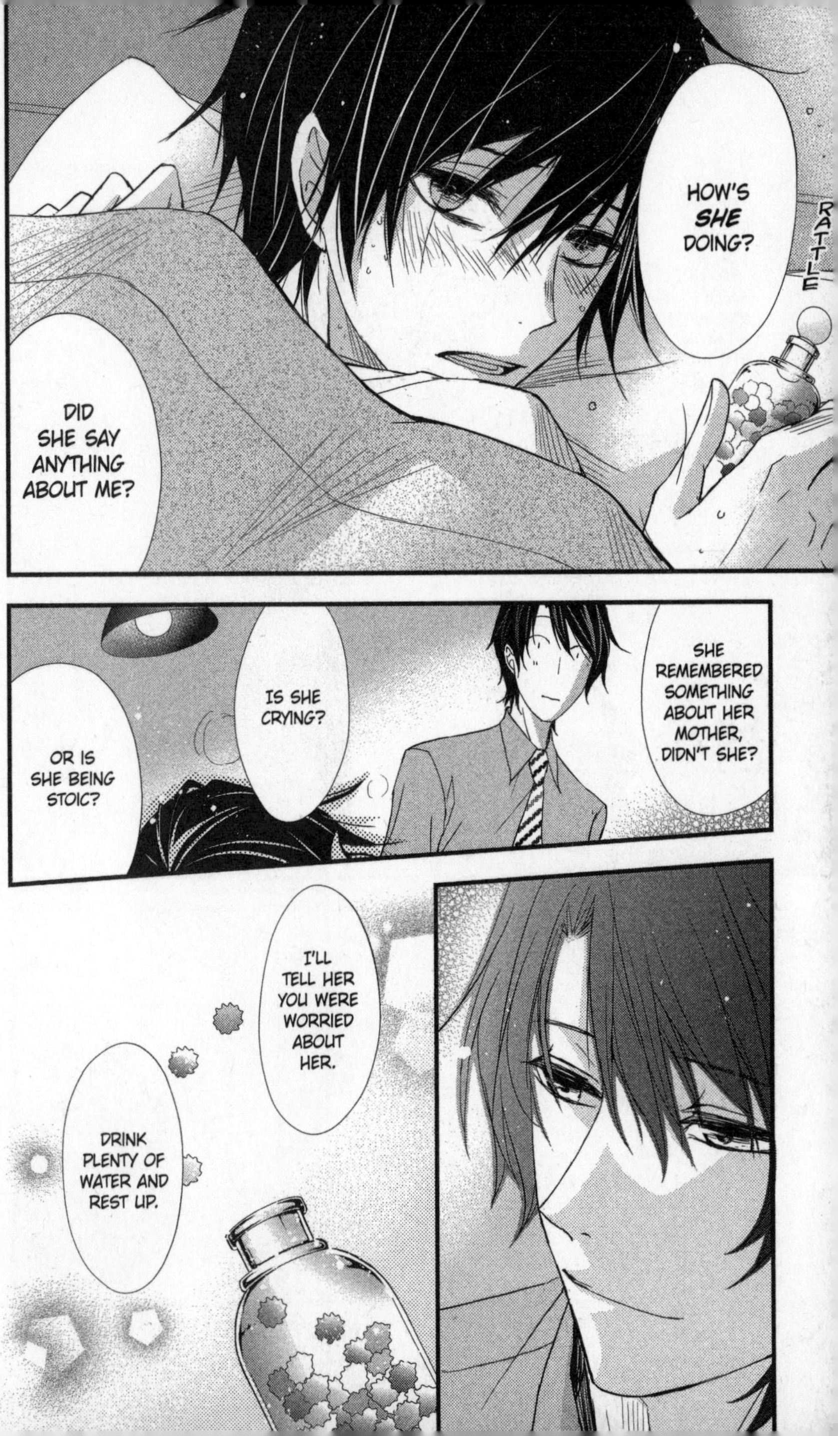
HOW'S SHE DOING?
RATTLE
DID SHE SAY ANYTHING ABOUT ME?
SHE REMEMBERED SOMETHING ABOUT HER MOTHER, DIDN'T SHE?
IS SHE CRYING?
OR IS SHE BEING STOIC?
I'LL TELL HER YOU WERE WORRIED ABOUT HER.
DRINK PLENTY OF WATER AND REST UP.

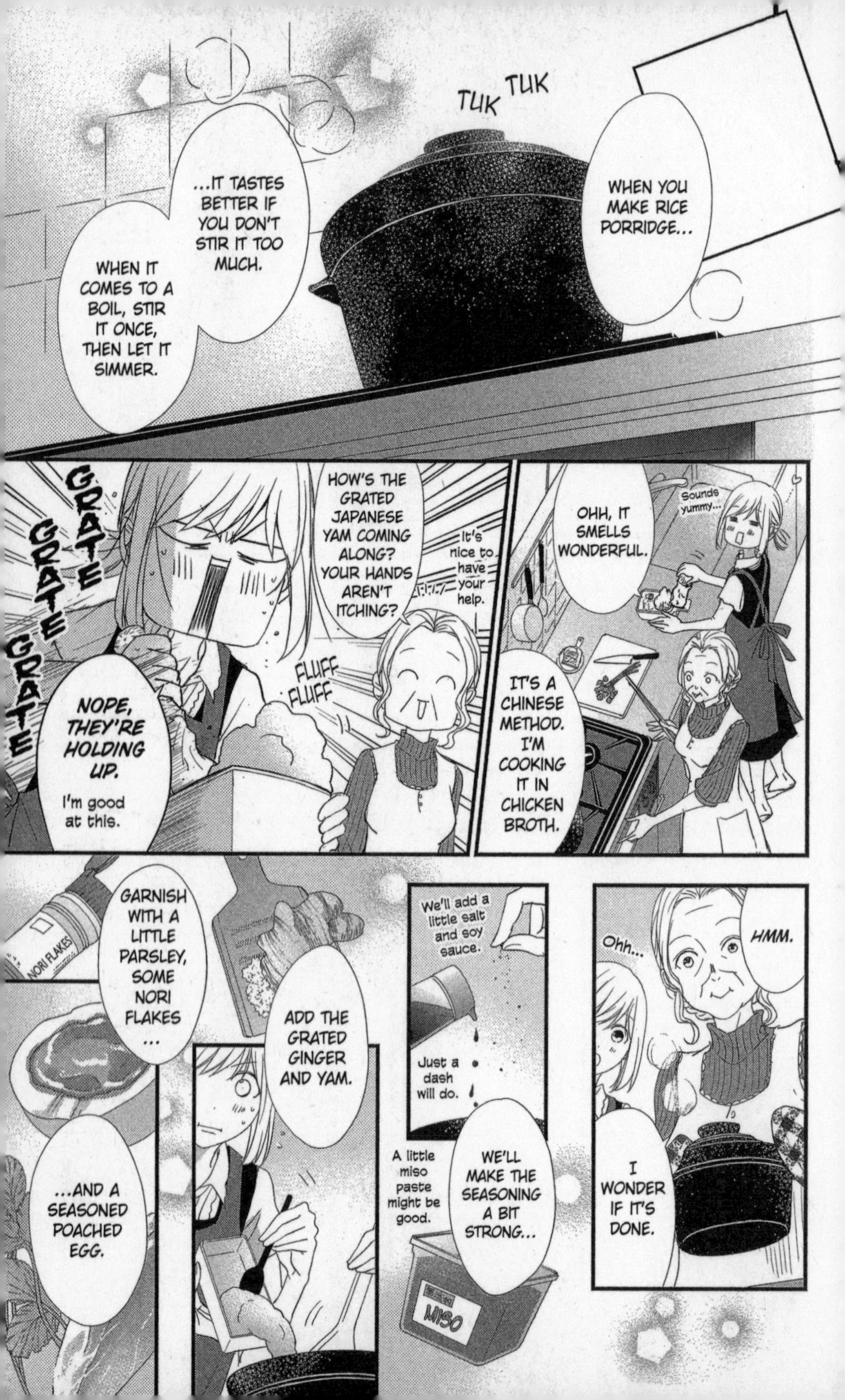
TUK TUK
WHEN YOU MAKE RICE PORRIDGE...
...IT TASTES BETTER IF YOU DON'T STIR IT TOO MUCH.
WHEN IT COMES TO A BOIL, STIR IT ONCE, THEN LET IT SIMMER.
Sounds yummy...
OHH, IT SMELLS WONDERFUL.
IT'S A CHINESE METHOD. I'M COOKING IT IN CHICKEN BROTH.
HOW'S THE GRATED JAPANESE YAM COMING ALONG? YOUR HANDS AREN'T ITCHING?
It's nice to have your help.
FLUFF FLUFF
GRATE GRATE GRATE GRATE
NOPE, THEY'RE HOLDING UP.
I'm good at this.
HMM.
Ohh...
I WONDER IF IT'S DONE.
We'll add a little salt and soy sauce.
Just a dash will do.
WE'LL MAKE THE SEASONING A BIT STRONG...
A little miso paste might be good.
MISO
ADD THE GRATED GINGER AND YAM.
GARNISH WITH A LITTLE PARSLEY, SOME NORI FLAKES ...
NORI FLAKES
...AND A SEASONED POACHED EGG.

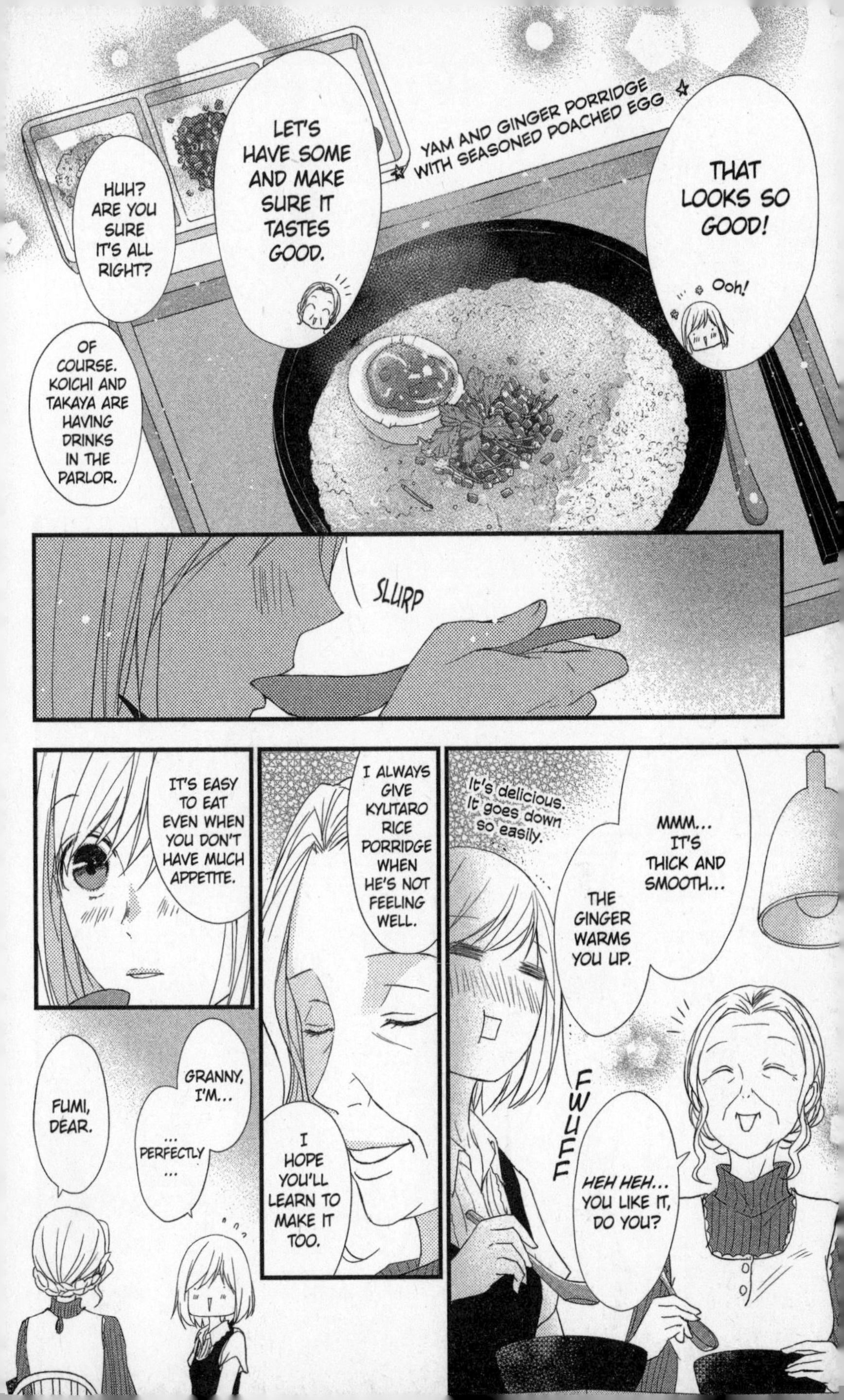
THAT LOOKS SO GOOD!
Ooh!
YAM AND GINGER PORRIDGE WITH SEASONED POACHED EGG
LET'S HAVE SOME AND MAKE SURE IT TASTES GOOD.
HUH? ARE YOU SURE IT'S ALL RIGHT?
OF COURSE. KOICHI AND TAKAYA ARE HAVING DRINKS IN THE PARLOR.
SLURP
MMM... IT'S THICK AND SMOOTH...
THE GINGER WARMS YOU UP.
It's delicious. It goes down so easily.
FWUFF
HEH HEH... YOU LIKE IT, DO YOU?
I ALWAYS GIVE KYUTARO RICE PORRIDGE WHEN HE'S NOT FEELING WELL.
I HOPE YOU'LL LEARN TO MAKE IT TOO.
IT'S EASY TO EAT EVEN WHEN YOU DON'T HAVE MUCH APPETITE.
GRANNY, I'M...
... PERFECTLY ...
FUMI, DEAR.

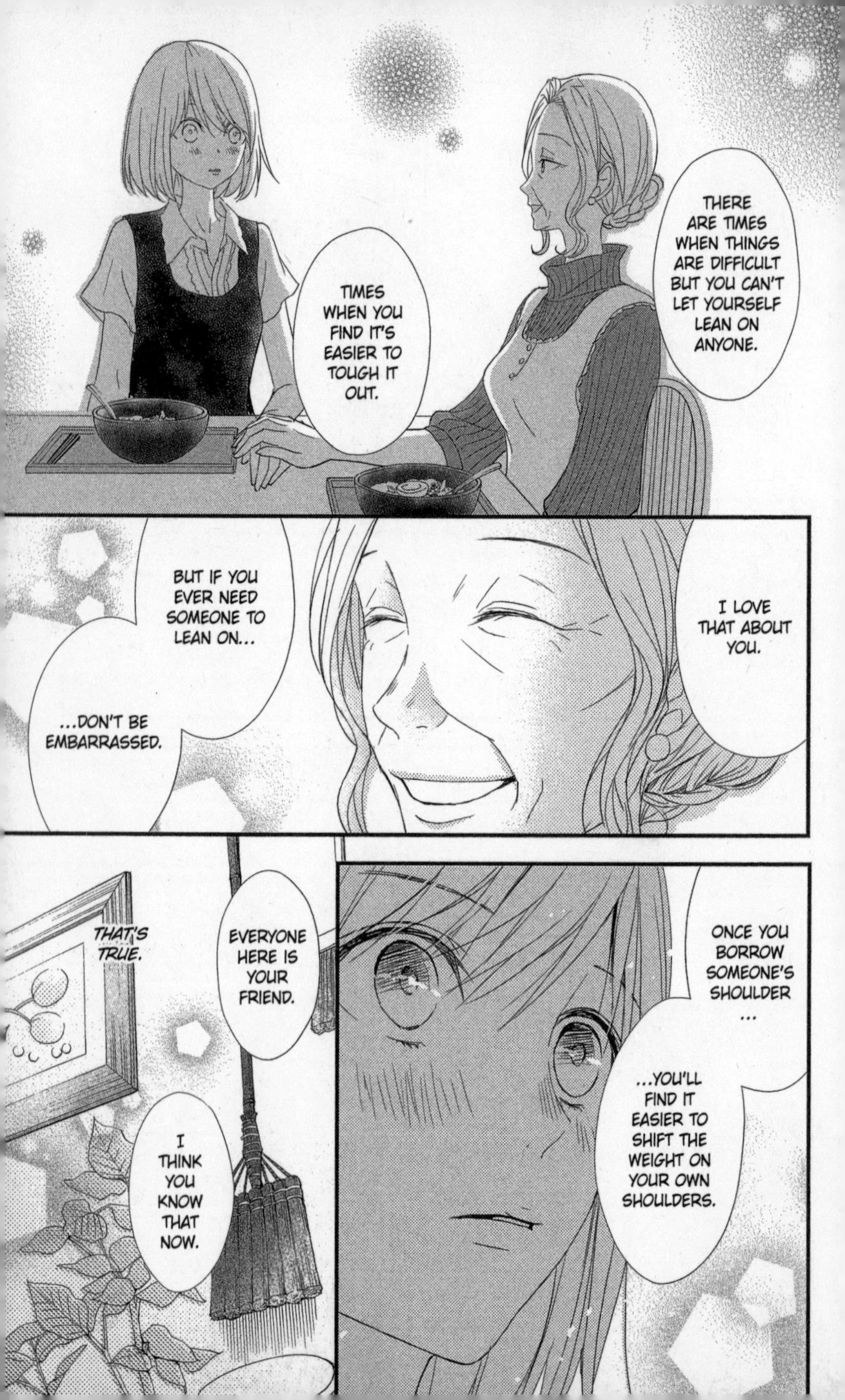
THERE ARE TIMES WHEN THINGS ARE DIFFICULT BUT YOU CAN'T LET YOURSELF LEAN ON ANYONE.
TIMES WHEN YOU FIND IT'S EASIER TO TOUGH IT OUT.
I LOVE THAT ABOUT YOU.
BUT IF YOU EVER NEED SOMEONE TO LEAN ON...
...DON'T BE EMBARRASSED.
ONCE YOU BORROW SOMEONE'S SHOULDER ...
...YOU'LL FIND IT EASIER TO SHIFT THE WEIGHT ON YOUR OWN SHOULDERS.
EVERYONE HERE IS YOUR FRIEND.
THAT'S TRUE.
I THINK YOU KNOW THAT NOW.

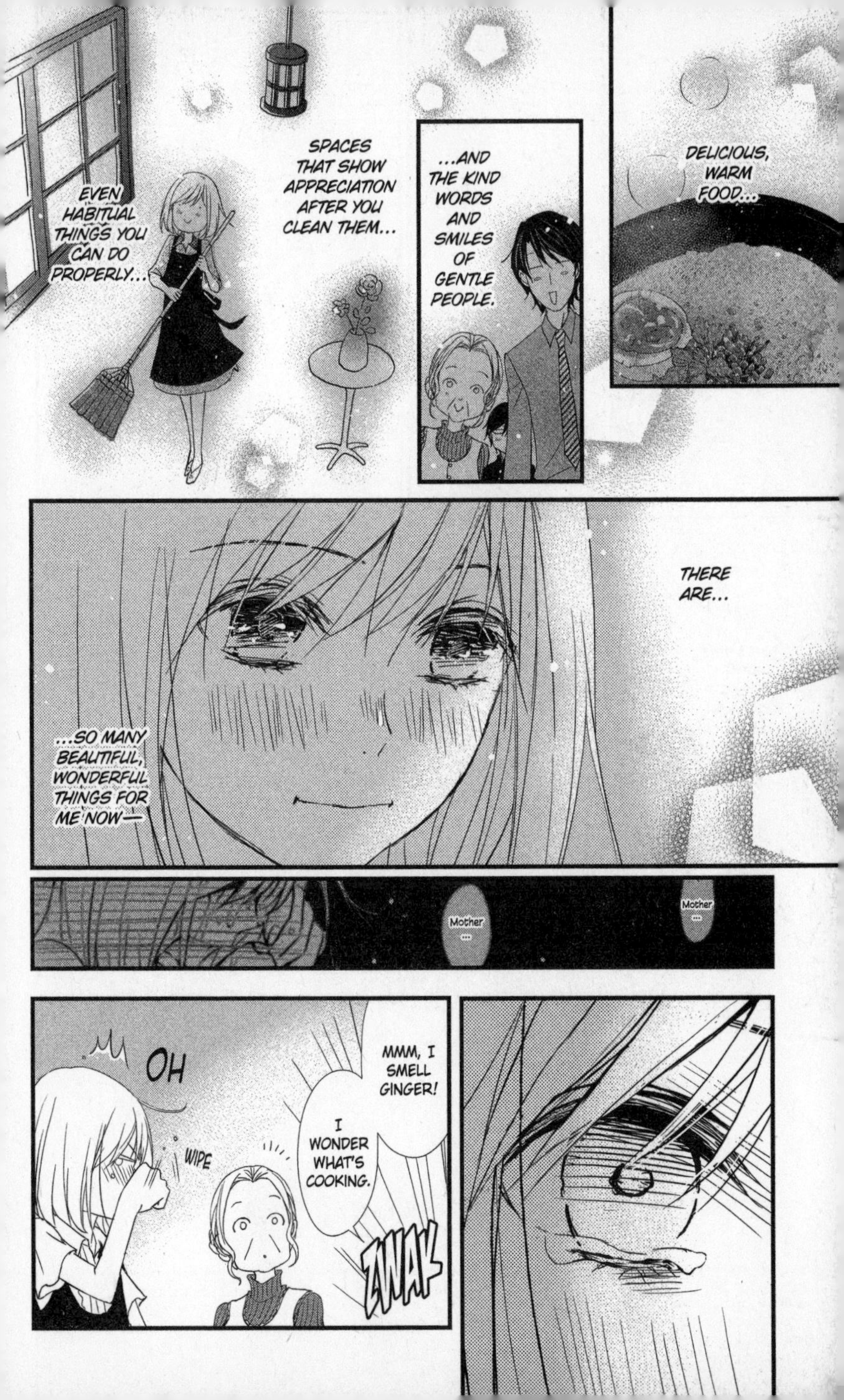
DELICIOUS, WARM FOOD...
...AND THE KIND WORDS AND SMILES OF GENTLE PEOPLE.
SPACES THAT SHOW APPRECIATION AFTER YOU CLEAN THEM...
EVEN HABITUAL THINGS YOU CAN DO PROPERLY...
THERE ARE...
...SO MANY BEAUTIFUL, WONDERFUL THINGS FOR ME NOW—
Mother...
Mother...
MMM, I SMELL GINGER!
I WONDER WHAT'S COOKING.
ZWAK
OH
WIPE

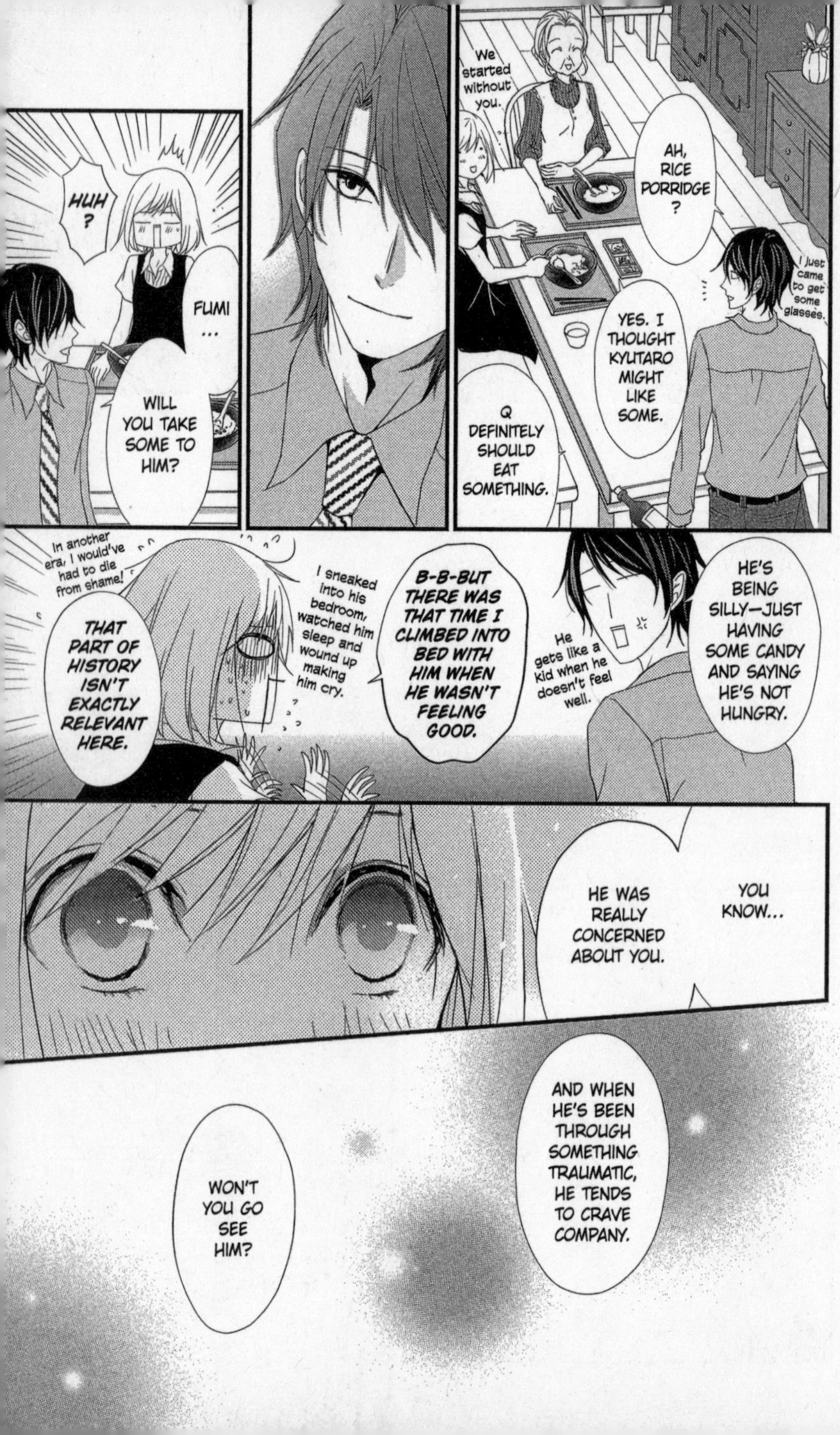

We started without you.
AH, RICE PORRIDGE?
I just came to get some glasses.
YES. I THOUGHT KYUTARO MIGHT LIKE SOME.
Q DEFINITELY SHOULD EAT SOMETHING.
FUMI...
WILL YOU TAKE SOME TO HIM?
HUH?
HE'S BEING SILLY—JUST HAVING SOME CANDY AND SAYING HE'S NOT HUNGRY.
He gets like a kid when he doesn't feel well.
B-B-BUT THERE WAS THAT TIME I CLIMBED INTO BED WITH HIM WHEN HE WASN'T FEELING GOOD.
I sneaked into his bedroom, watched him sleep and wound up making him cry.
In another era, I would've had to die from shame!
THAT PART OF HISTORY ISN'T EXACTLY RELEVANT HERE.
YOU KNOW...
HE WAS REALLY CONCERNED ABOUT YOU.
AND WHEN HE'S BEEN THROUGH SOMETHING TRAUMATIC, HE TENDS TO CRAVE COMPANY.
WON'T YOU GO SEE HIM?

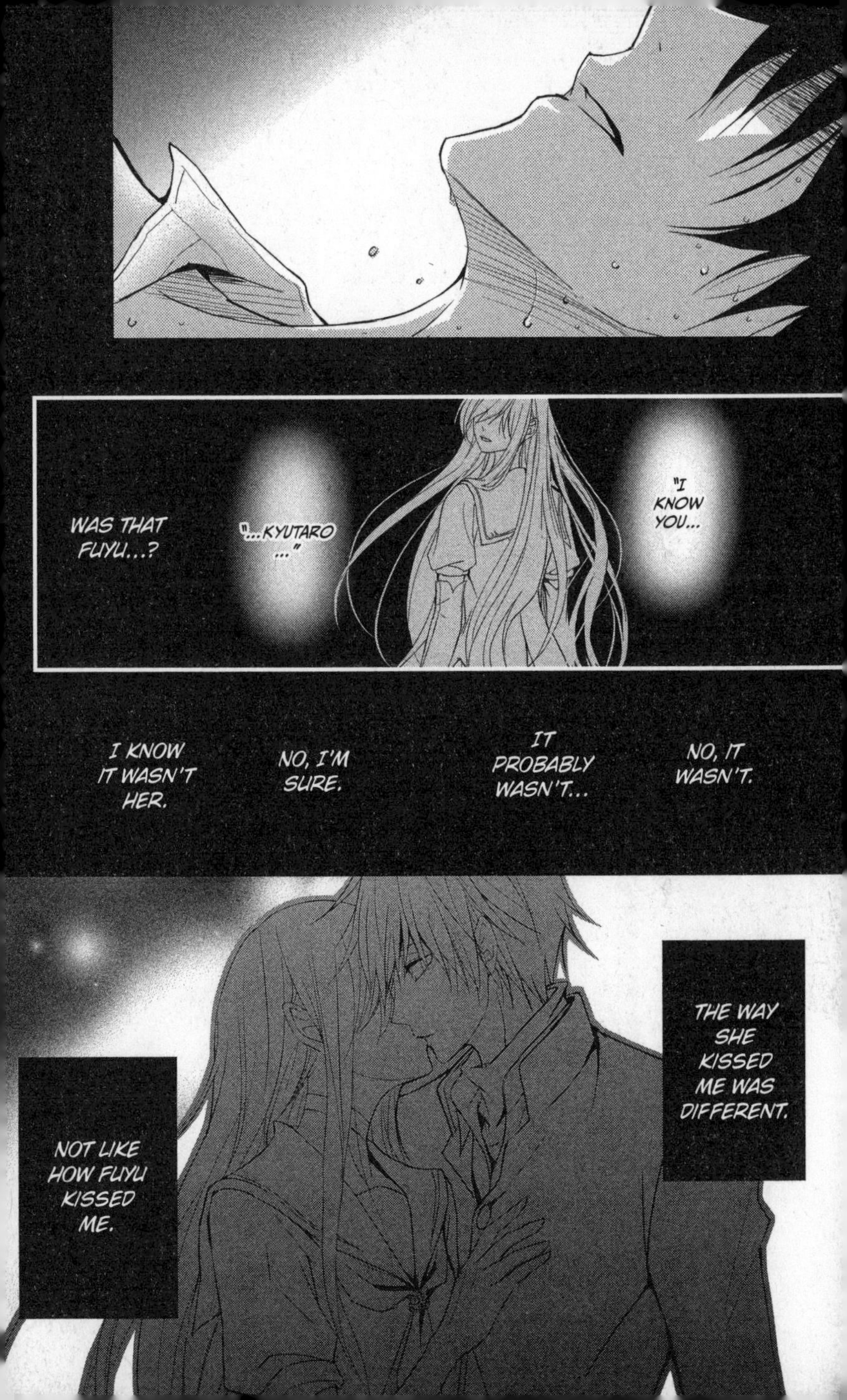
"I KNOW YOU...
"...KYUTARO..."
WAS THAT FUYU...?
NO, IT WASN'T.
IT PROBABLY WASN'T...
NO, I'M SURE.
I KNOW IT WASN'T HER.
THE WAY SHE KISSED ME WAS DIFFERENT.
NOT LIKE HOW FUYU KISSED ME.

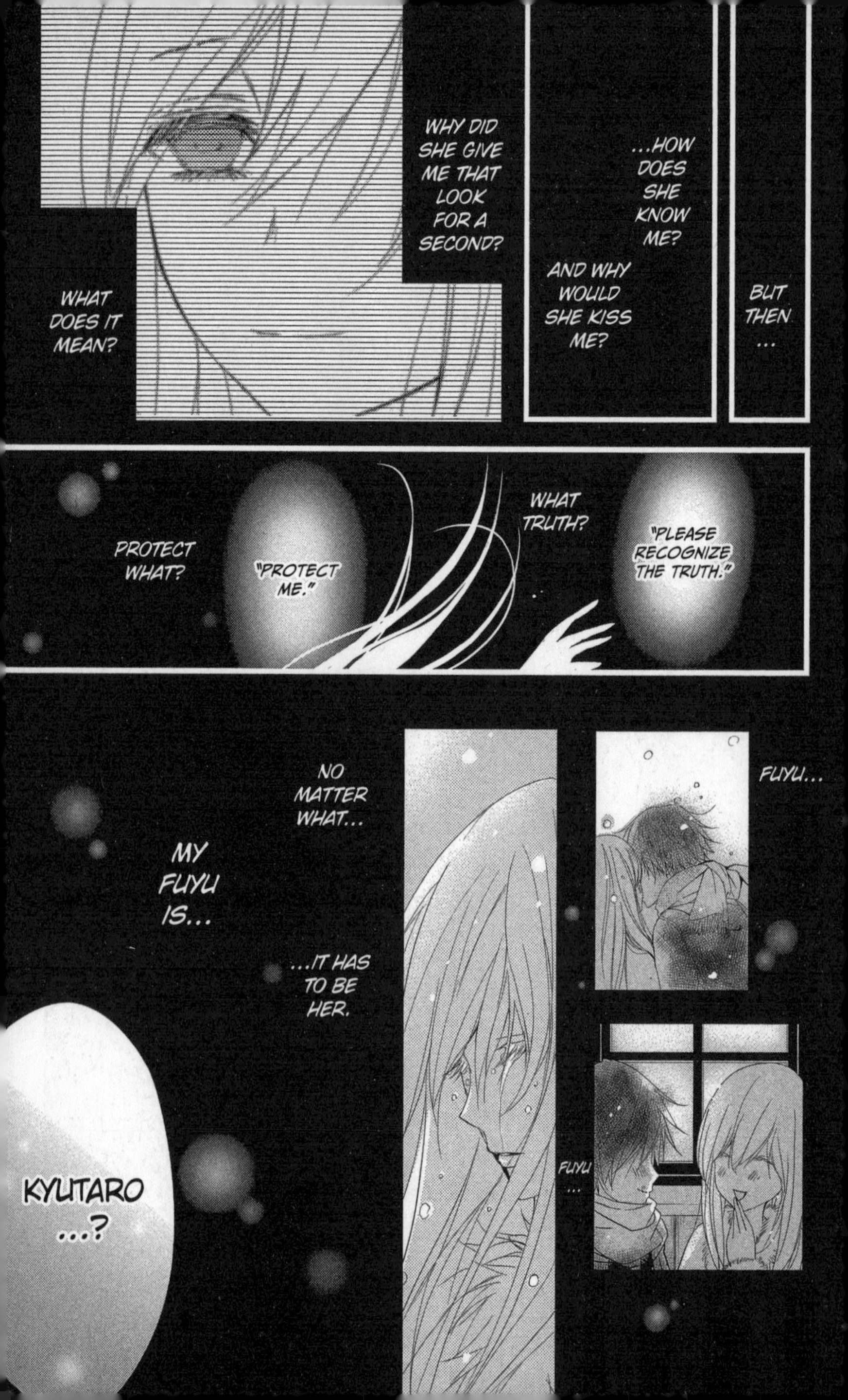
BUT THEN...
...HOW DOES SHE KNOW ME?
AND WHY WOULD SHE KISS ME?
WHY DID SHE GIVE ME THAT LOOK FOR A SECOND?
WHAT DOES IT MEAN?
"PLEASE RECOGNIZE THE TRUTH."
WHAT TRUTH?
"PROTECT ME."
PROTECT WHAT?
FUYU...
FUYU...
NO MATTER WHAT...
MY FUYU IS...
...IT HAS TO BE HER.
KYUTARO...?

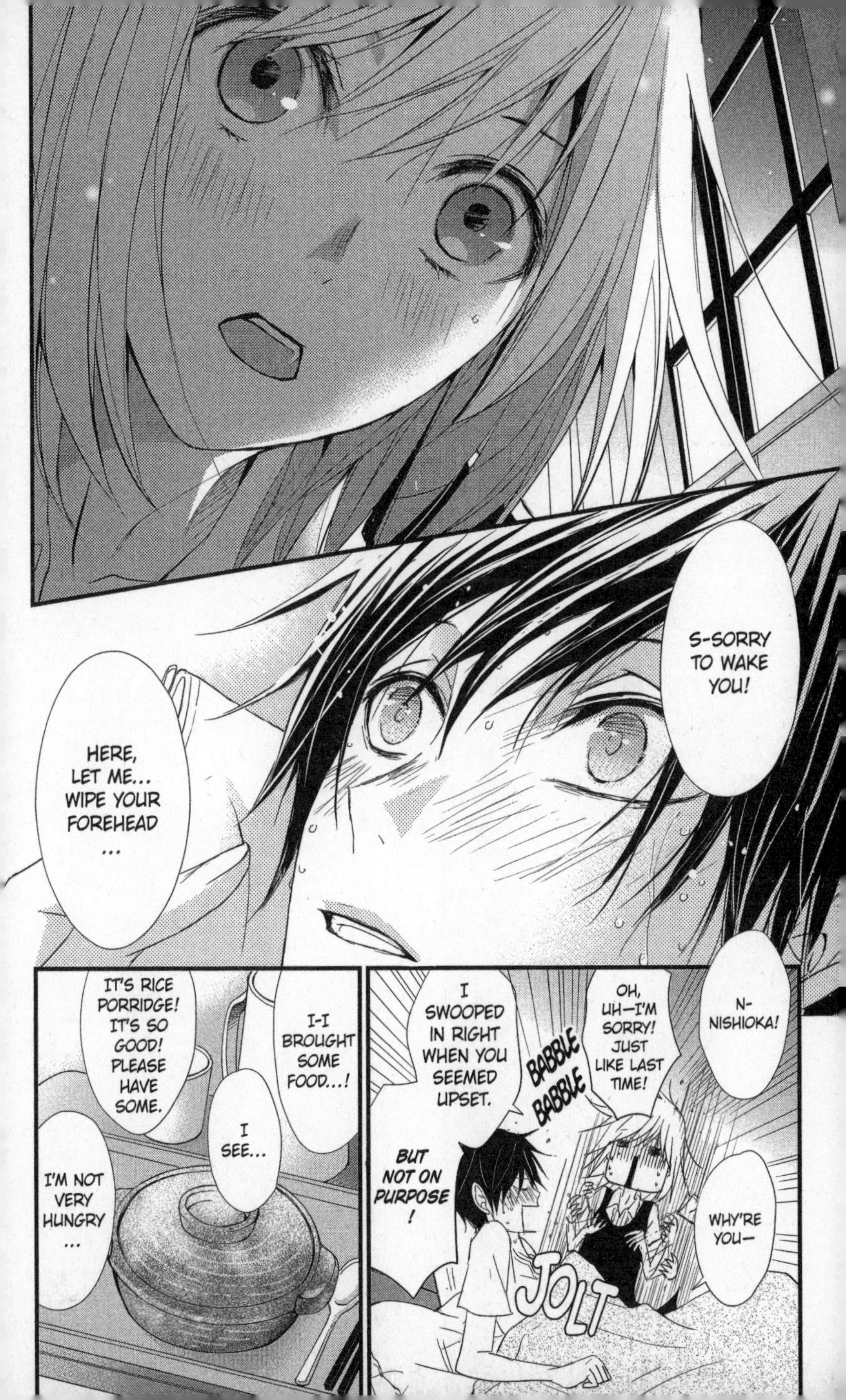
S-SORRY TO WAKE YOU!
HERE, LET ME... WIPE YOUR FOREHEAD ...
N-NISHIOKA!
WHY'RE YOU—
OH, UH—I'M SORRY! JUST LIKE LAST TIME!
BABBLE BABBLE
I SWOOPED IN RIGHT WHEN YOU SEEMED UPSET.
BUT NOT ON PURPOSE!
JOLT
I-I BROUGHT SOME FOOD...!
IT'S RICE PORRIDGE! IT'S SO GOOD! PLEASE HAVE SOME.
I SEE...
I'M NOT VERY HUNGRY ...

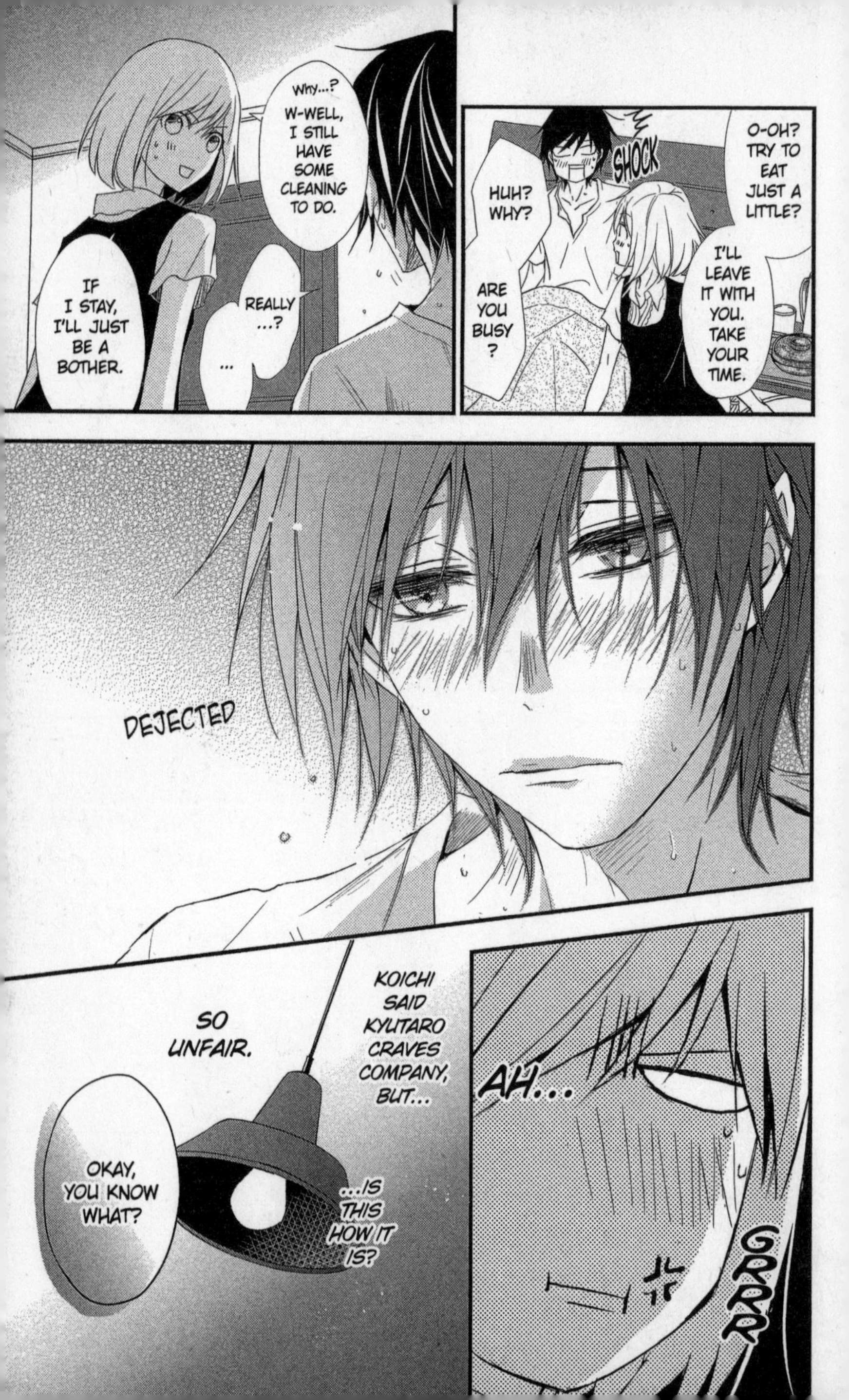
O-OH? TRY TO EAT JUST A LITTLE?
SHOCK
HUH? WHY?
I'LL LEAVE IT WITH YOU. TAKE YOUR TIME.
ARE YOU BUSY?
Why...? W-WELL, I STILL HAVE SOME CLEANING TO DO.
REALLY ...?
...
IF I STAY, I'LL JUST BE A BOTHER.
DEJECTED
AH...
GRRR
KOICHI SAID KYUTARO CRAVES COMPANY, BUT...
...IS THIS HOW IT IS?
SO UNFAIR.
OKAY, YOU KNOW WHAT?

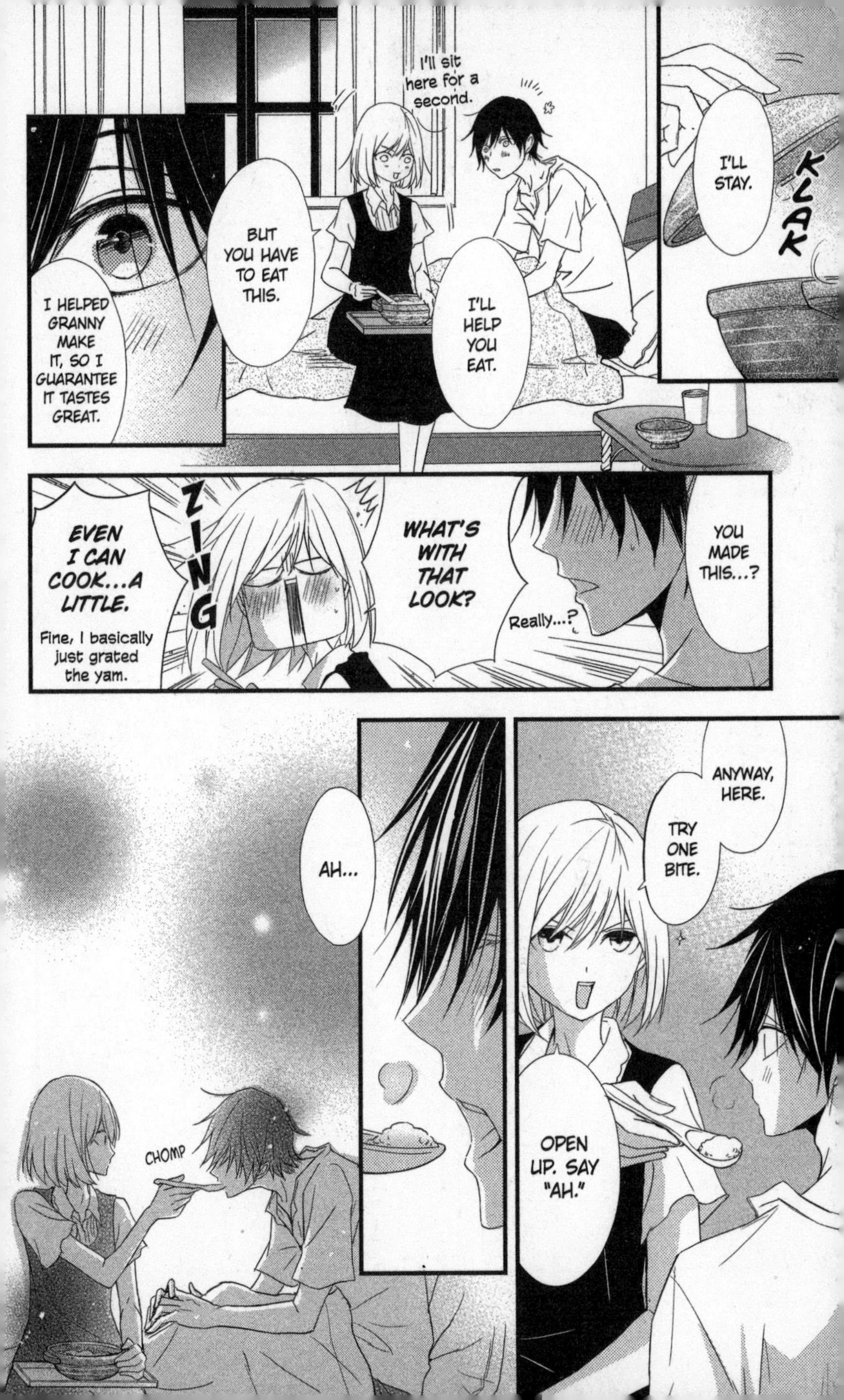

I'LL STAY.
KLAK
I'll sit here for a second.
I'LL HELP YOU EAT.
BUT YOU HAVE TO EAT THIS.
I HELPED GRANNY MAKE IT, SO I GUARANTEE IT TASTES GREAT.
YOU MADE THIS...?
Really...?
WHAT'S WITH THAT LOOK?
ZING
EVEN I CAN COOK...A LITTLE.
Fine, I basically just grated the yam.
ANYWAY, HERE.
TRY ONE BITE.
OPEN UP. SAY "AH."
AH...
CHOMP

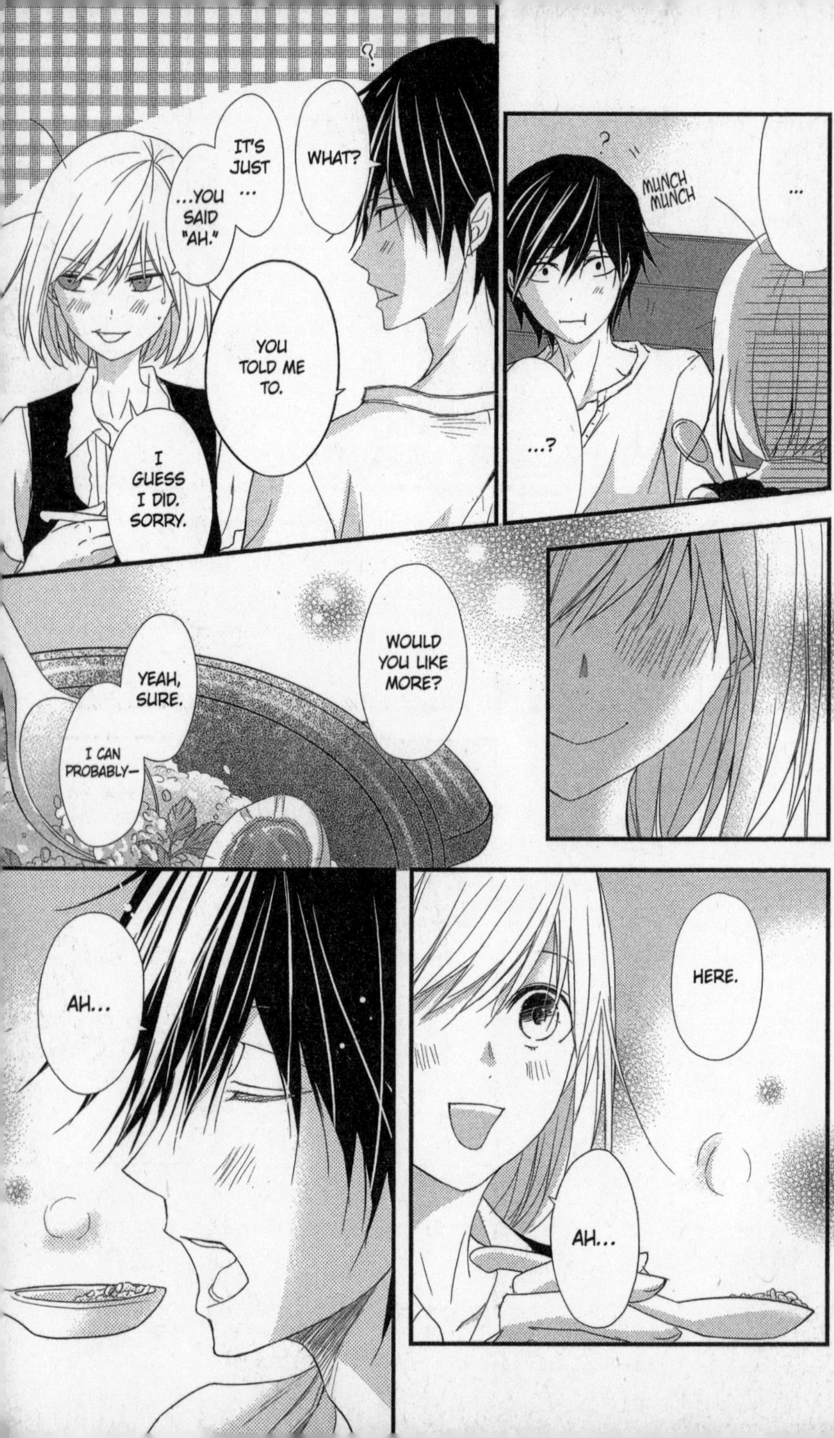
?
MUNCH MUNCH
...
...?
?
WHAT?
IT'S JUST ...
...YOU SAID "AH."
YOU TOLD ME TO.
I GUESS I DID. SORRY.
WOULD YOU LIKE MORE?
YEAH, SURE.
I CAN PROBABLY—
HERE.
AH...
AH...

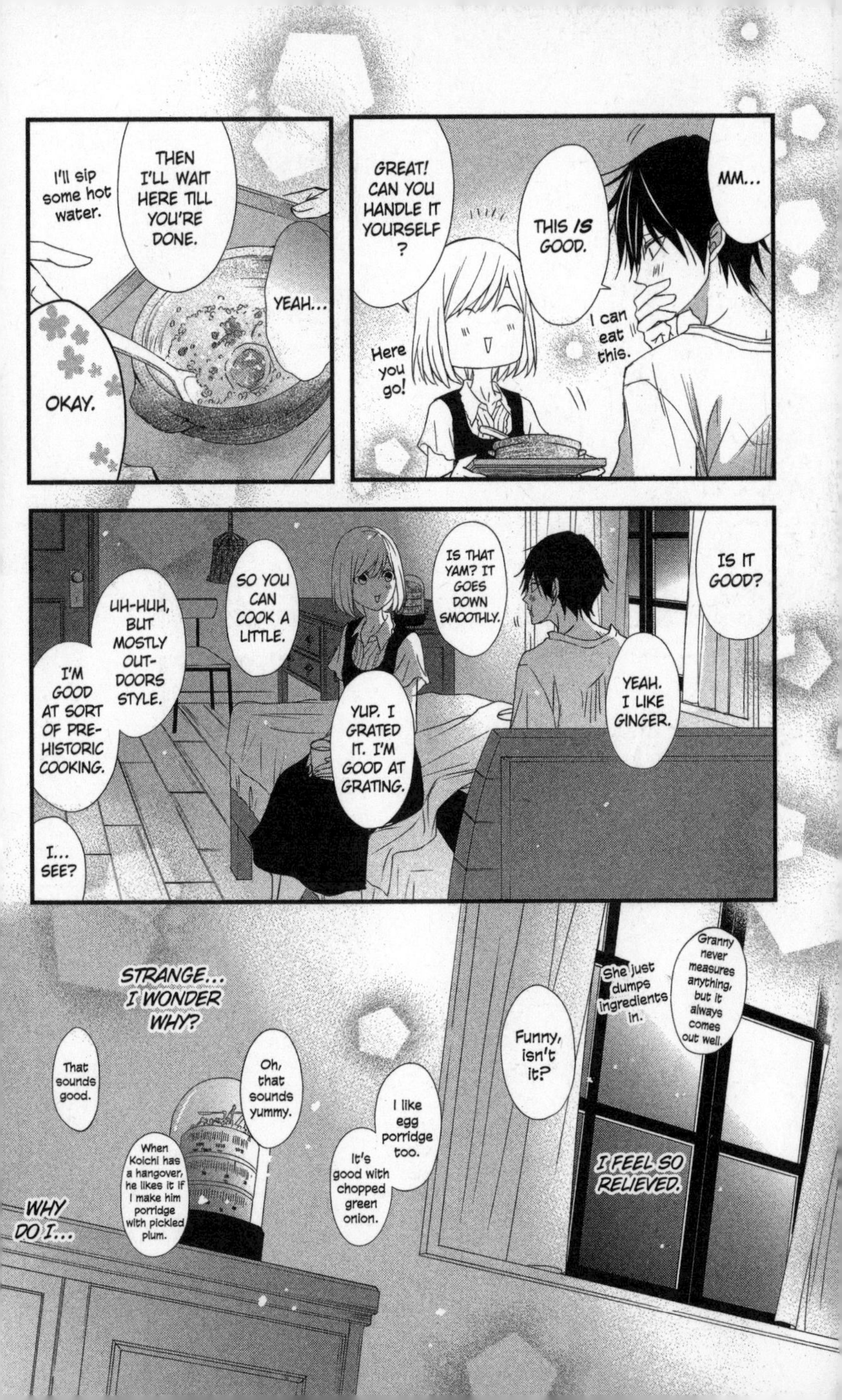
MM...
THIS *IS* GOOD.
I can eat this.
GREAT! CAN YOU HANDLE IT YOURSELF?
Here you go!
YEAH...
THEN I'LL WAIT HERE TILL YOU'RE DONE.
I'll sip some hot water.
OKAY.
IS IT GOOD?
IS THAT YAM? IT GOES DOWN SMOOTHLY.
YEAH. I LIKE GINGER.
YUP. I GRATED IT. I'M GOOD AT GRATING.
SO YOU CAN COOK A LITTLE.
UH-HUH, BUT MOSTLY OUT-DOORS STYLE.
I'M GOOD AT SORT OF PRE-HISTORIC COOKING.
I... SEE?
Granny never measures anything, but it always comes out well.
She just dumps ingredients in.
Funny, isn't it?
I FEEL SO RELIEVED.
I like egg porridge too.
It's good with chopped green onion.
Oh, that sounds yummy.
When Koichi has a hangover, he likes it if I make him porridge with pickled plum.
That sounds good.
STRANGE... I WONDER WHY?
WHY DO I...

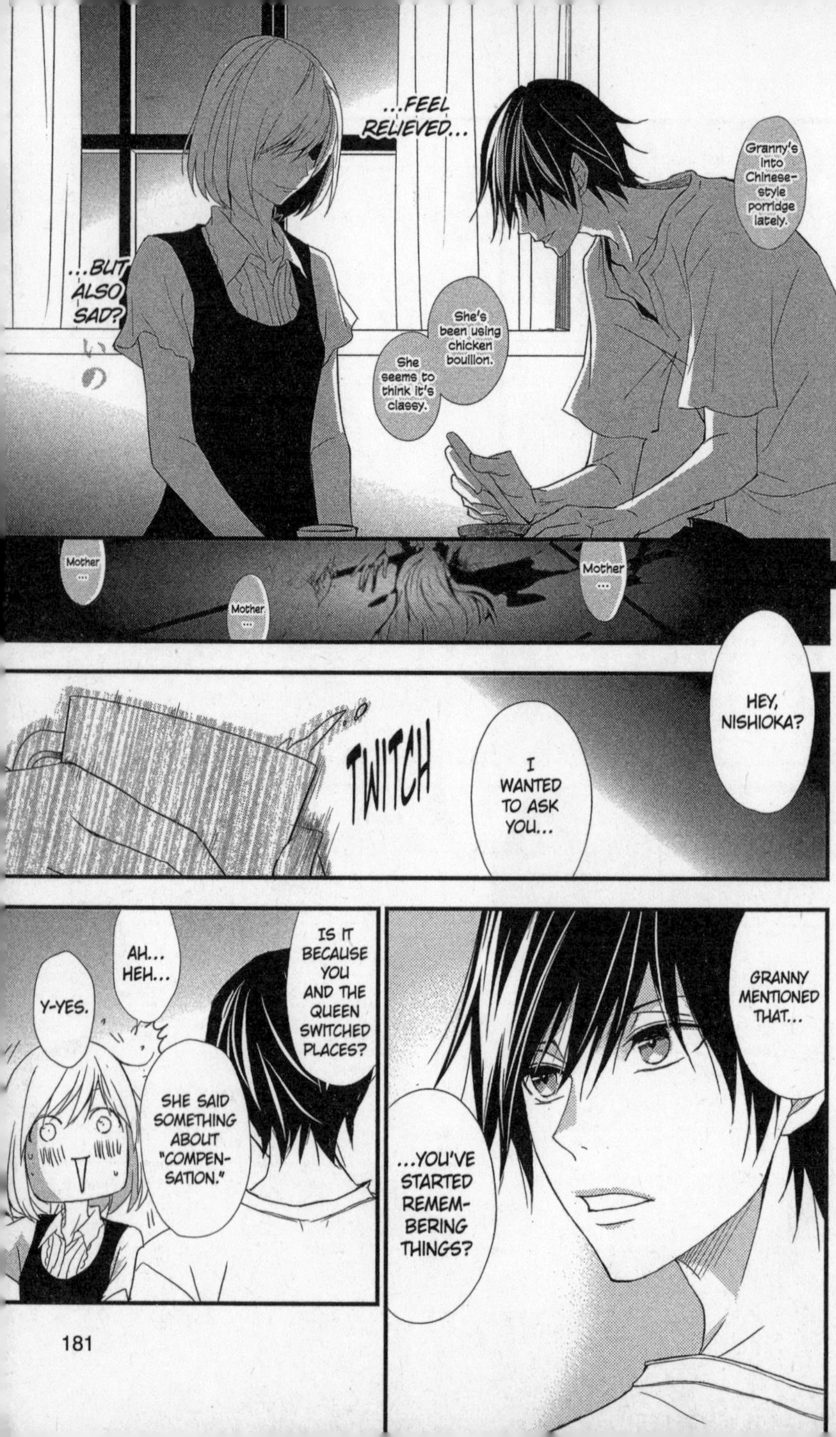
Granny's into Chinese-style porridge lately.
...FEEL RELIEVED...
She's been using chicken bouillon.
She seems to think it's classy.
...BUT ALSO SAD?
Mother...
Mother...
Mother...
HEY, NISHIOKA?
I WANTED TO ASK YOU...
TWITCH
GRANNY MENTIONED THAT...
...YOU'VE STARTED REMEMBERING THINGS?
IS IT BECAUSE YOU AND THE QUEEN SWITCHED PLACES?
AH... HEH...
SHE SAID SOMETHING ABOUT "COMPENSATION."
Y-YES.

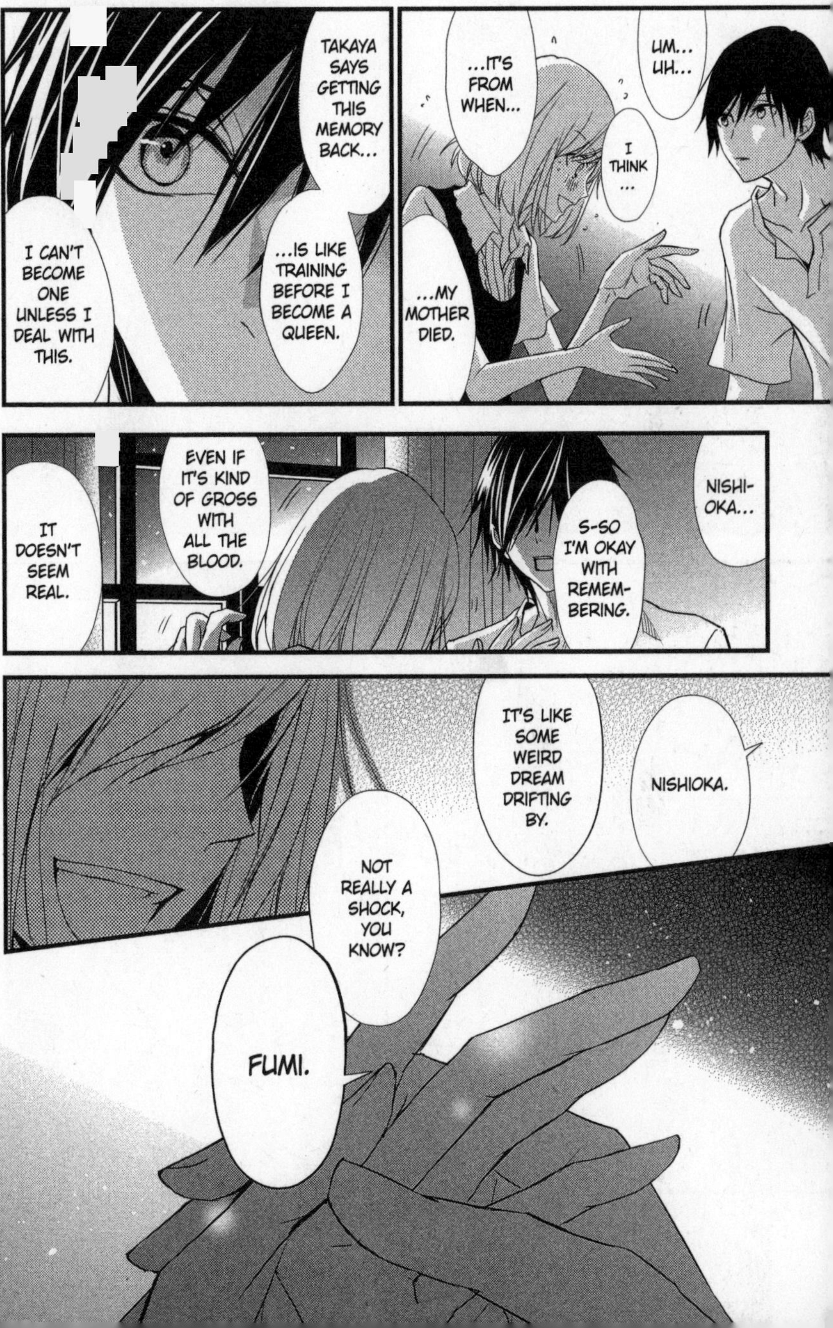
UM... UH...
...IT'S FROM WHEN...
I THINK...
...MY MOTHER DIED.
TAKAYA SAYS GETTING THIS MEMORY BACK...
...IS LIKE TRAINING BEFORE I BECOME A QUEEN.
I CAN'T BECOME ONE UNLESS I DEAL WITH THIS.
NISHI-OKA...
S-SO I'M OKAY WITH REMEMBERING.
EVEN IF IT'S KIND OF GROSS WITH ALL THE BLOOD.
IT DOESN'T SEEM REAL.
NISHIOKA.
IT'S LIKE SOME WEIRD DREAM DRIFTING BY.
NOT REALLY A SHOCK, YOU KNOW?
FUMI.

WHA... WHAT...?

I'M SORRY, I...

TUG

GRP

NO, DON'T LEAVE.

HUH?

KYUTARO...

LET GO...

OH...

PLEASE DON'T LEAVE.

OH...

HA HA...

PLIP

PLIP

PLIP

WHUMP

CREAK

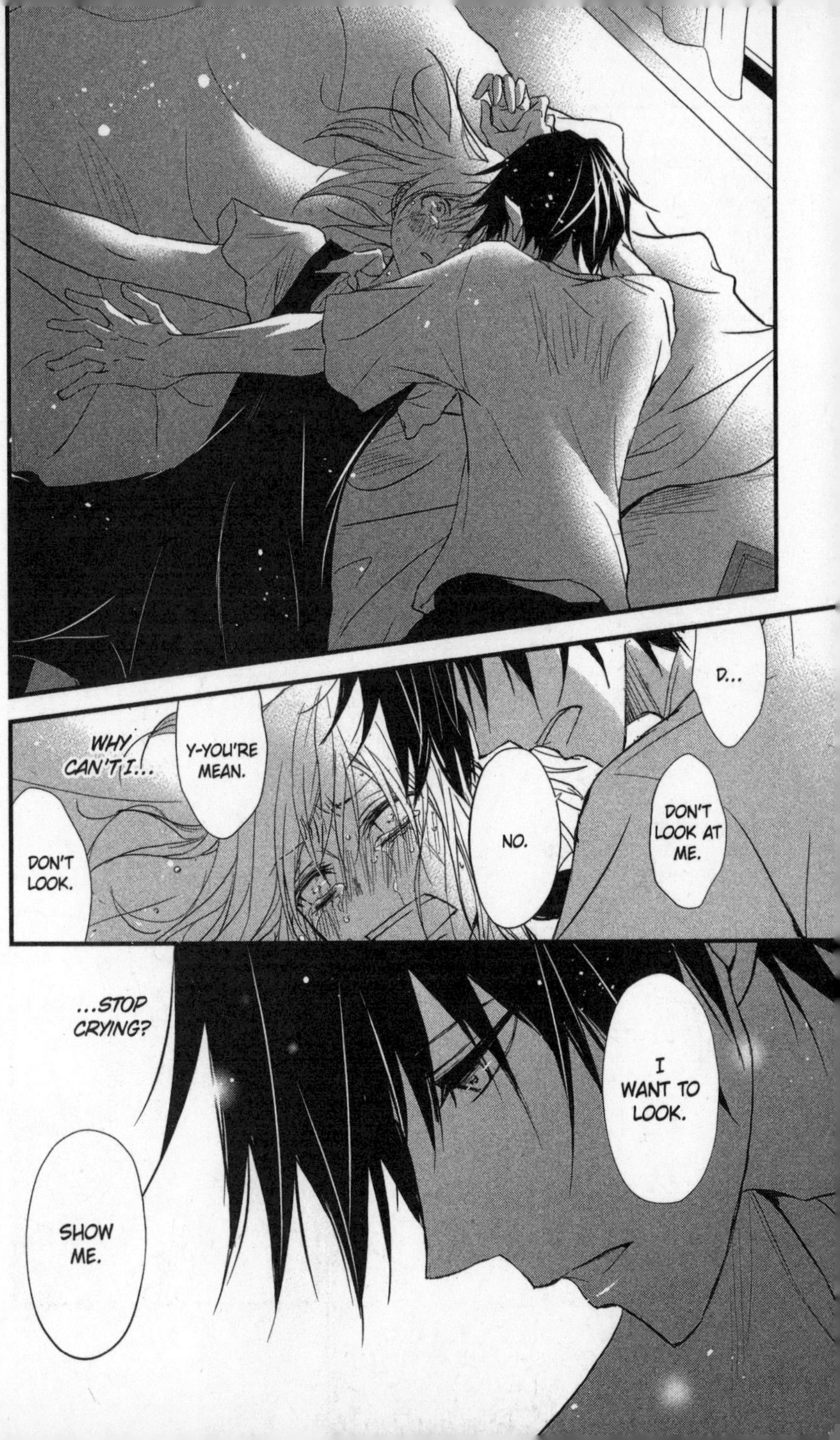
D...
DON'T LOOK AT ME.
NO.
Y-YOU'RE MEAN.
WHY CAN'T I...
DON'T LOOK.
I WANT TO LOOK.
...STOP CRYING?
SHOW ME.

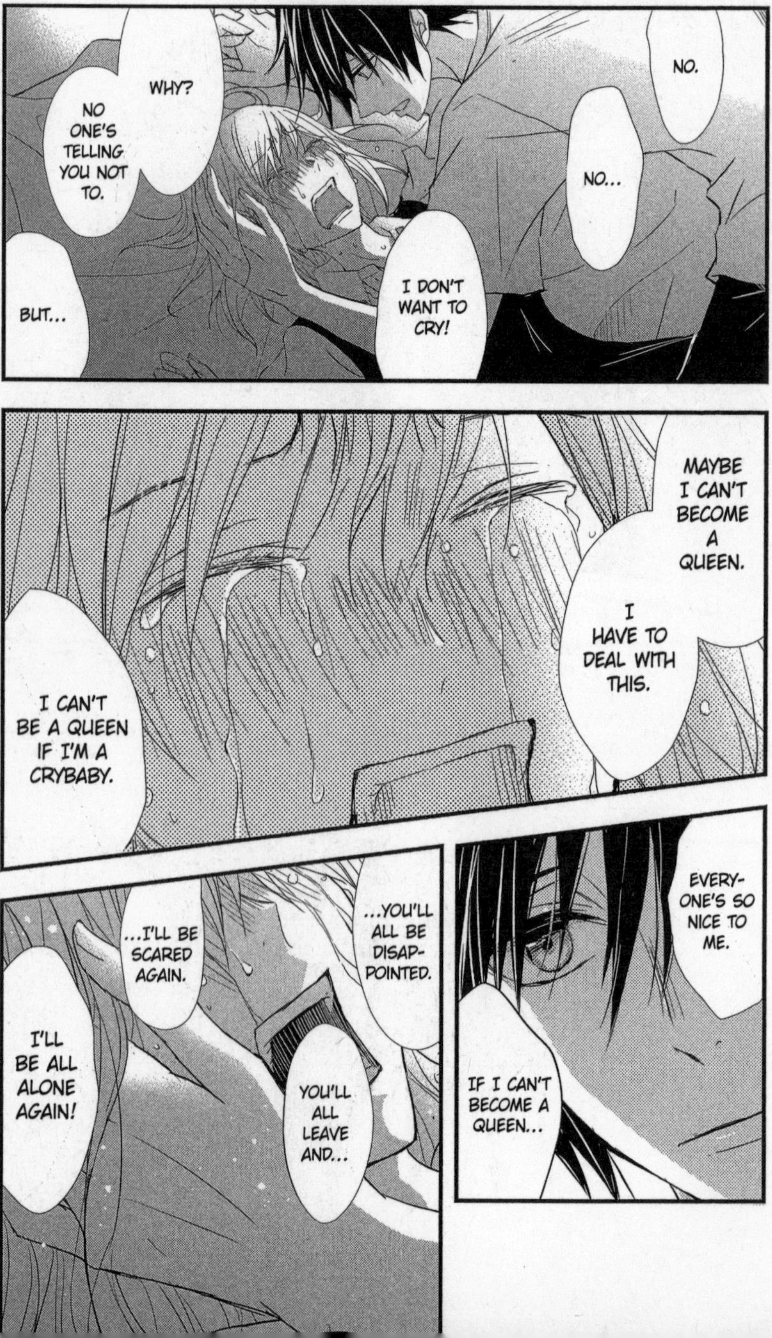
NO.
NO...
I DON'T WANT TO CRY!
WHY?
NO ONE'S TELLING YOU NOT TO.
BUT...
MAYBE I CAN'T BECOME A QUEEN.
I HAVE TO DEAL WITH THIS.
I CAN'T BE A QUEEN IF I'M A CRYBABY.
EVERYONE'S SO NICE TO ME.
IF I CAN'T BECOME A QUEEN...
...YOU'LL ALL BE DISAPPOINTED.
...I'LL BE SCARED AGAIN.
YOU'LL ALL LEAVE AND...
I'LL BE ALL ALONE AGAIN!

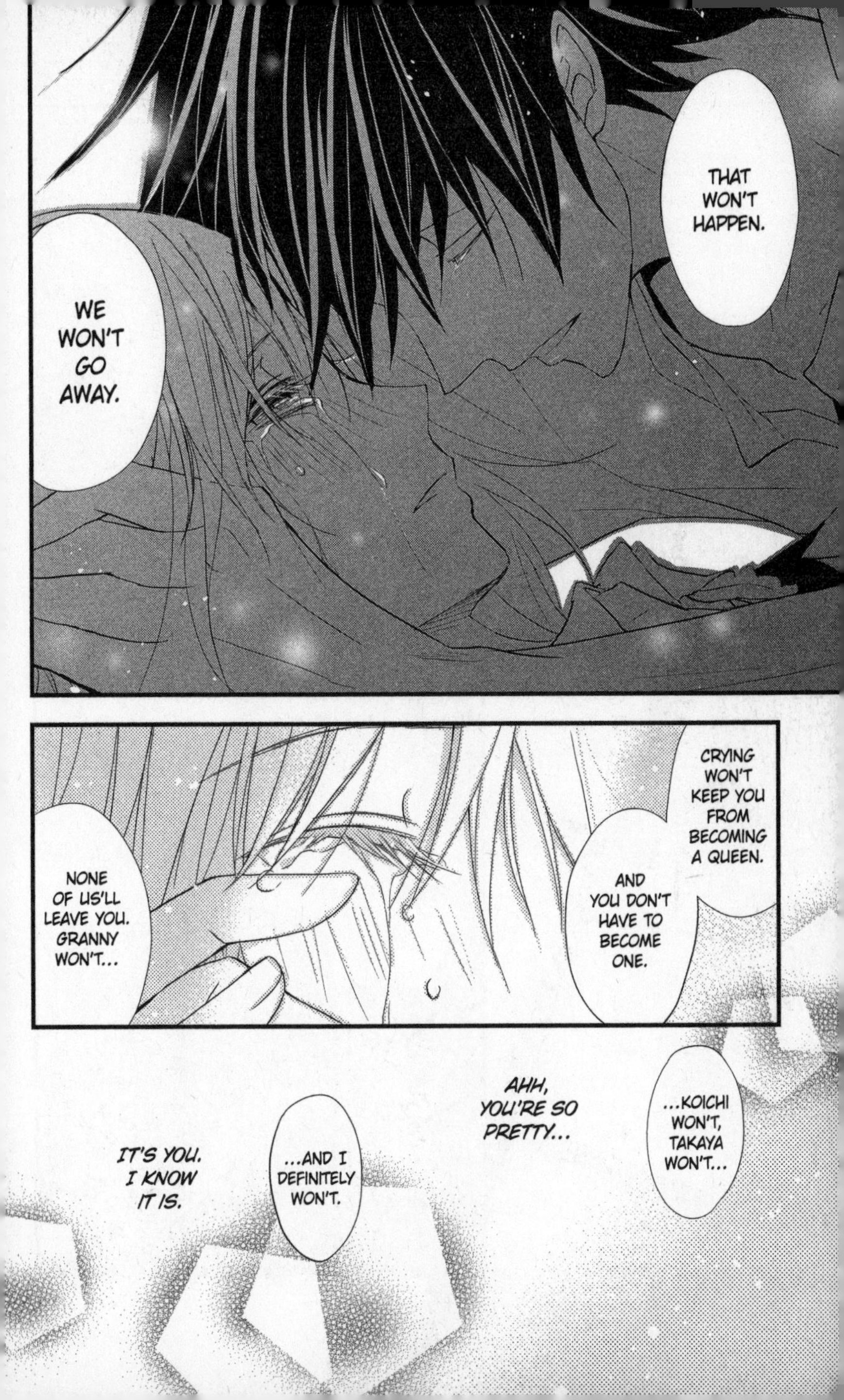
THAT WON'T HAPPEN.
WE WON'T GO AWAY.
CRYING WON'T KEEP YOU FROM BECOMING A QUEEN.
AND YOU DON'T HAVE TO BECOME ONE.
NONE OF US'LL LEAVE YOU. GRANNY WON'T...
...KOICHI WON'T, TAKAYA WON'T...
AHH, YOU'RE SO PRETTY...
...AND I DEFINITELY WON'T.
IT'S YOU. I KNOW IT IS.

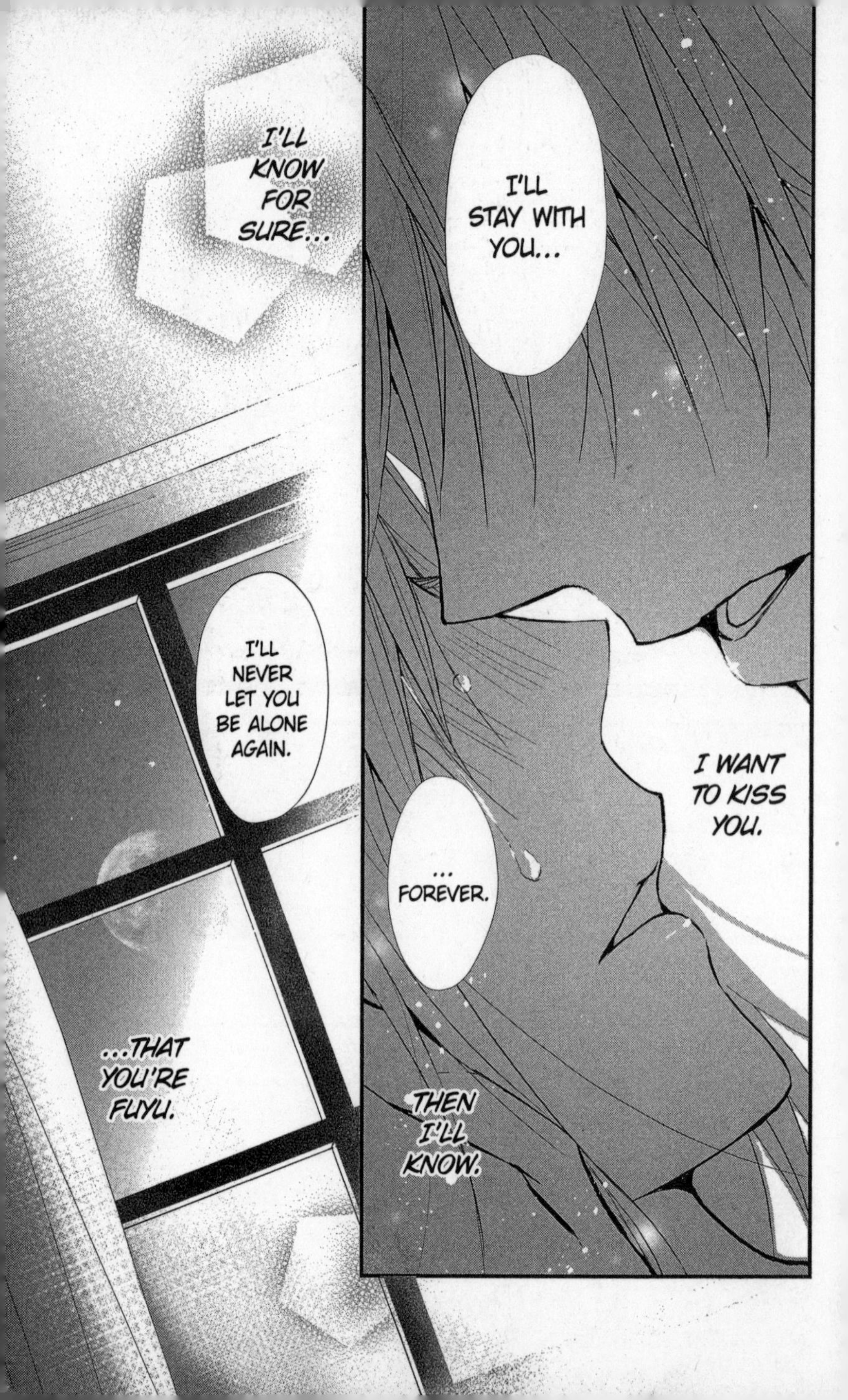
I'LL STAY WITH YOU...
...FOREVER.
I WANT TO KISS YOU.
THEN I'LL KNOW.
I'LL KNOW FOR SURE...
I'LL NEVER LET YOU BE ALONE AGAIN.
...THAT YOU'RE FUYU.

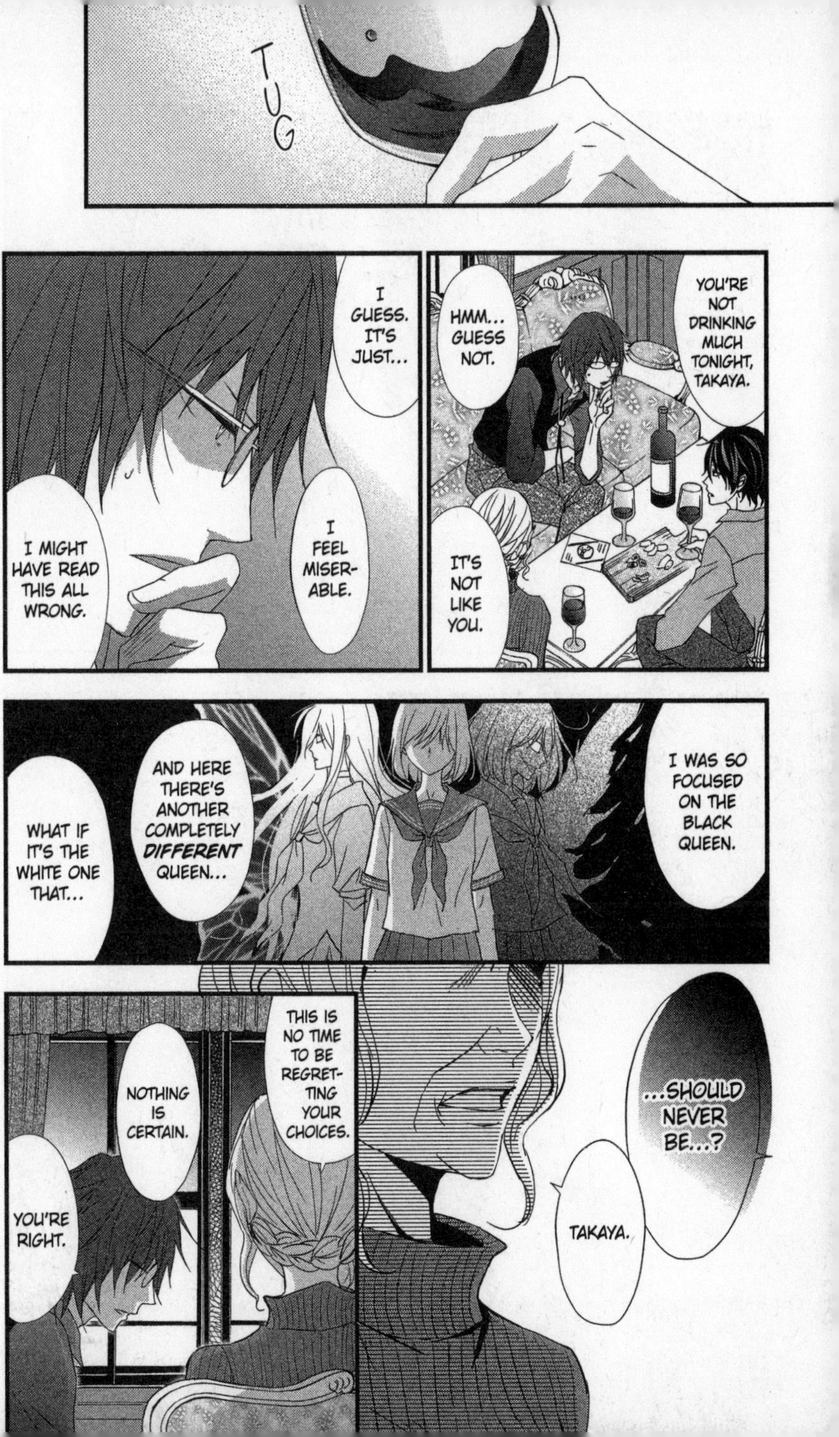
TUG
YOU'RE NOT DRINKING MUCH TONIGHT, TAKAYA.
HMM... GUESS NOT.
IT'S NOT LIKE YOU.
I GUESS. IT'S JUST...
I FEEL MISER-ABLE.
I MIGHT HAVE READ THIS ALL WRONG.
I WAS SO FOCUSED ON THE BLACK QUEEN.
AND HERE THERE'S ANOTHER COMPLETELY *DIFFERENT* QUEEN...
WHAT IF IT'S THE WHITE ONE THAT...
...SHOULD NEVER BE...?
TAKAYA.
THIS IS NO TIME TO BE REGRET-TING YOUR CHOICES.
NOTHING IS CERTAIN.
YOU'RE RIGHT.

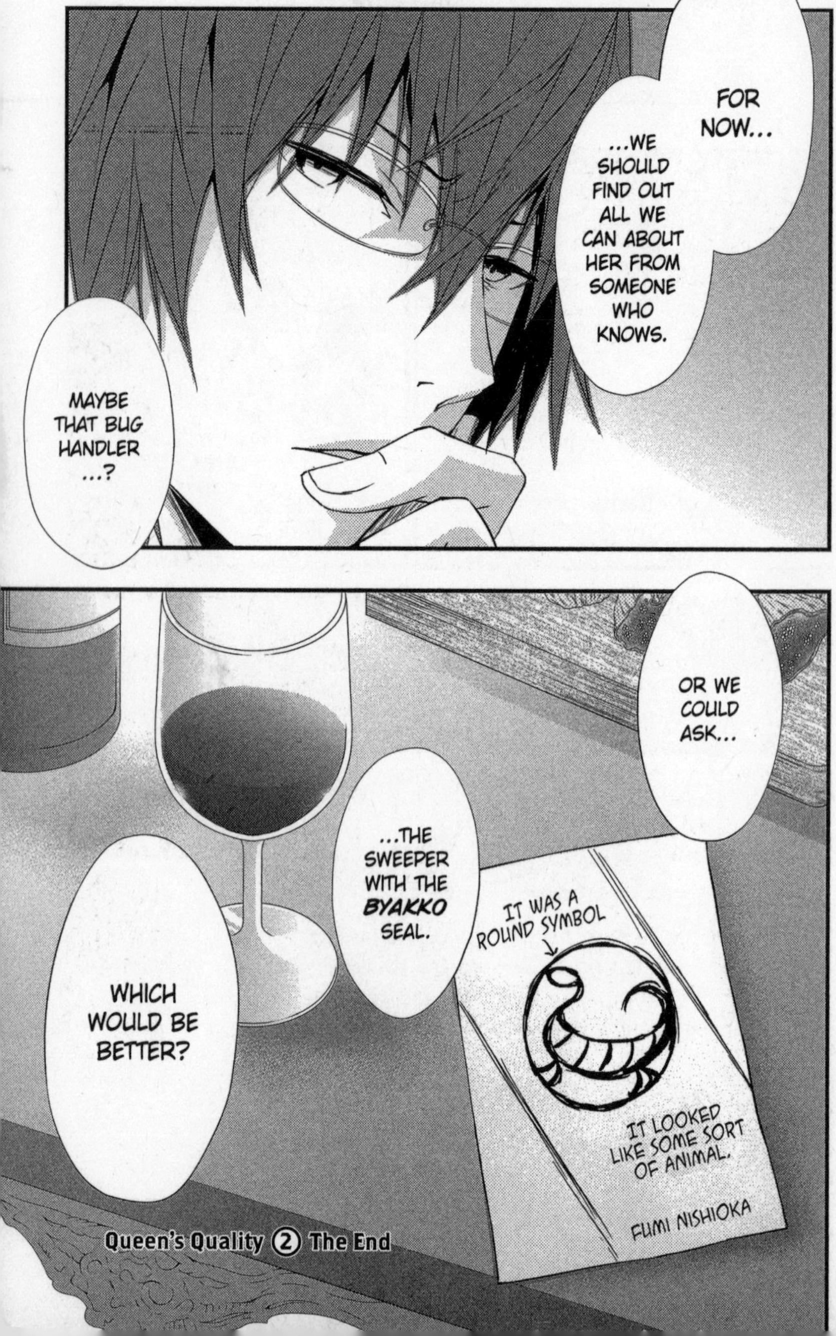
FOR NOW...
...WE SHOULD FIND OUT ALL WE CAN ABOUT HER FROM SOMEONE WHO KNOWS.
MAYBE THAT BUG HANDLER ...?
OR WE COULD ASK...
...THE SWEEPER WITH THE *BYAKKO* SEAL.
IT WAS A ROUND SYMBOL
IT LOOKED LIKE SOME SORT OF ANIMAL.
FUMI NISHIOKA
WHICH WOULD BE BETTER?
Queen's Quality 2 The End

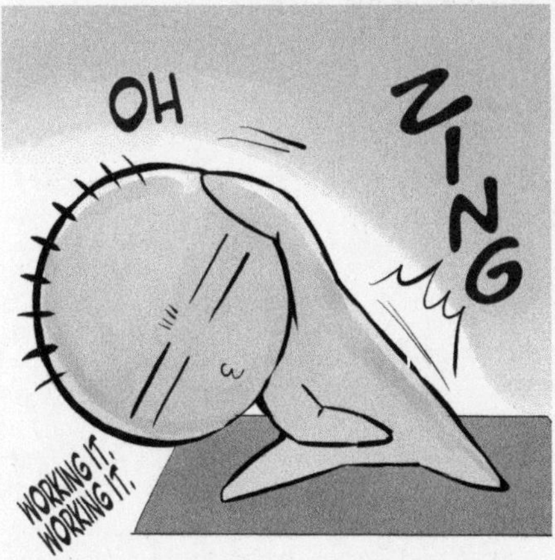
OH
ZING
WORKING IT, WORKING IT,

I always do stretches. They hurt just right for my masochistic heart. Using a shot like this to represent myself probably looks a bit dodgy. Maybe I should stop rendering myself in the nude...

—Kyousuke Motomi

Author Bio

Born on August 1, Kyousuke Motomi debuted in *Deluxe Betsucomi* with *Hetakuso Kyupiddo* (No Good Cupid) in 2002. She is the creator of *Dengeki Daisy*, *Beast Master* and *QQ Sweeper*, all available in North America from VIZ Media. Motomi enjoys sleeping, tea ceremonies and reading Haruki Murakami.